The School Library Manager

The School Library Manager

Leading through Change

Seventh Edition

Blanche Woolls, Joyce Kasman Valenza, and April M. Dawkins

Preface by Sharon Coatney

Library and Information Science Text Series

BLOOMSBURY LIBRARIES UNLIMITED
NEW YORK · LONDON · OXFORD · NEW DELHI · SYDNEY

Online resources to accompany this book are available at
https://bloomsbury.pub/school-library-manager-7e.
If you experience any problems, please contact Bloomsbury at:
onlineresources@bloomsbury.com

BLOOMSBURY LIBRARIES UNLIMITED
Bloomsbury Publishing Inc
1385 Broadway, New York, NY 10018, USA
50 Bedford Square, London, WC1B 3DP, UK
29 Earlsfort Terrace, Dublin 2, Ireland

BLOOMSBURY, BLOOMSBURY LIBRARIES UNLIMITED and the Diana logo
are trademarks of Bloomsbury Publishing Plc

First published in the United States of America 2024

Library of Congress Cataloging in Publication Control Number: 2022049118

ISBN: HB: 978-1-4408-7999-9
PB: 978-1-4408-7929-6
ePDF: 978-1-4408-7930-2
eBook: 979-8-216-17235-2

Series: Library and Information Science Text Series

Typeset by Westchester Publishing Services, LLC
Printed and bound in the United States of America

To find out more about our authors and books visit www.bloomsbury.com and sign
up for our newsletters.

Contents

Preface

A Life in School Librarianship: Managing Choices, Mentors, Changes, Growing, and Leadership

After a long and successful career in a great profession, I can say without any caveat that long ago I made the perfect choice for my life's work and I have never had reason to rethink that decision. Perhaps my journey will help others understand the school library profession and the doors it may open for you. This school library management text will introduce you to and inform you about the profession, how to manage a library and its instructional program. I envy you as you begin this journey. I hope that my experiences will inform and inspire.

I did not intend to be a school librarian. In fact, I was enjoying my profession as a senior high school English teacher in rural Kansas. There were problems, though, and my husband saw what was inevitably coming and gave me good advice early in my career. We lived in a small rural Kansas community and with two young children and a husband just starting a new business after several years in military service, we were both extremely busy. My job was becoming very challenging, as I was teaching all the English and journalism classes in this rural high school—which meant I had six separate preparations each day (instead of the usual large school where one might teach four sections of senior English and two of sophomore with only two preps per day). In addition, I was a great believer in journaling and lots of written essays—lots and lots to grade. I was overwhelmed with papers and my own children were suffering.

CHOICES: Jeff suggested that, instead of completing the master's degree in English that I had started, I transfer to the library school and pursue being a school librarian. He didn't think it would be an easier job, but it wouldn't have the huge amount of preps and grading that accompanied teaching English in rural schools. We didn't realize that eventually I would be grading student research papers and projects along with my fellow teachers—because, of course, the job of a school librarian has evolved over time to take on more of that teaching role, as you will see discussed in this management book. I took his advice and began my MLS degree. It took me several summers, as I had to transfer from the nearby University of Kansas to Emporia State University, which was 90 miles away. However, I was extremely fortunate and within a couple of years I was hired to be the elementary librarian half-time in the same K–12 school and took over the half-time position as the 7th- and 8th-grade English teacher. It was the best thing that could have happened, as I was able to try out the library position in a small school (less than 200 kids) but keep my hand in at teaching English. Best of all, my own children were now going to the same school. So, we all went to school together for the next 13 years. What a blessing for my family.

Eventually I also took over the high school library and thus became the librarian for both levels. These facilities were at opposite ends of the K–12 complex, but fortunately for me both were well funded, and I had a full-time aide in both libraries. This transferred most of the clerical parts of the job over to my aides, and I spent my time teaching research skills and doing library professional work.

MENTORS: The superintendent in our district was an unusual man who had a passion for libraries. We three school librarians benefited so much from his interest and encouragement. He expected us to become professionally active and took us to see model libraries. During this time, I met Ruth Bell, director of the nationally known Blue Valley School District libraries in Overland Park, Kansas. I had not encountered her vision in my master's program; she saw the school librarian as the instructional leader in the school and the school library as the place where all the disciplines met in an open place to deliver integrated instructional experiences. This was an early vision of the learning commons approach we see today. I was profoundly affected by meeting her and seeing the program in the Blue Valley Schools.

With the encouragement of the superintendent, I began implementing those ideas in my schools and encouraged the other librarians in our district to do the same. We began presenting our programs and ideas at state and local library conferences. Our state librarian came to visit, bringing attention to the unusual program in our small district.

However, state politics did intrude; my small high school was closed and consolidated with the other high school in the district (20 miles away). My daughter's class was to be the last to graduate from our school, and the town was losing part of its identity. I had a serious decision to make: I was invited to take the full-time job as the librarian at the new combined high school or I could stay in my own school in a half-time elementary position. I really did not want to put someone else out of a job, but I wanted more than a half-time position.

CHANGES: Ruth Bell called to say, "I want you to come and work for me. We are opening a new elementary school and I want you to come on board this summer to buy the collection and begin collaborating with the principal to start your integrated program. You will have to interview with the principal, but I have no doubt you will be chosen."

And that, of course, is history! I interviewed with the principal, got the job, and spent the summer buying the collection and meeting with faculty to plan. At the first district librarians' meeting of the year, Ruth Bell gave each of us a copy of the original *Information Power* and said, "Read this and do what it says!" She, of course, was one of the authors and the program mirrored what she had already been requiring of her librarians. It was a halcyon time. I learned so much from her and the other librarians and the teachers in my school. My principal was a devotee of the Madeline Hunter method of instruction and design and a trainer for her organization. We had phenomenal staff development opportunities and started a peer coaching cadre, one of the first I had ever heard of in my state. My instructional skills were forever impacted by those years at Oak Hill School. We were honored to receive the Blue-Ribbon School Award and I went to Washington with my principal to the White House to receive that honor.

GROWING: While working at Blue Valley, I was asked to be a consultant for the National Library Power Project visiting and working with librarians in inner-city Philadelphia, Lincoln, Nebraska, rural Kentucky, and other sites. Coming from a life spent in rural and suburban Kansas, these experiences were life-changing for me. One library in Philadelphia was unheated and under the gymnasium. The librarian, when I visited, was working with students while wearing her coat, hat, and gloves in an almost empty library—but the students were there, and engaged. I still stand in awe of that librarian.

Because of that experience I started a charity of sorts, asking the children in my wealthy school to raise money to send new books to that school in Philadelphia and many others over the years. We would have fundraisers throughout the school year and in the spring, the students and I would pick out titles to send. We sent videos and letters so my students could get to know each other and develop a relationship. A few years later we found schools near us in inner-city Kansas City and a Native American reservation nearby, both in great need. Then we were able to meet the students in person when we took the books to their schools. We all benefited from this, and the parents in my school were very supportive.

In 2002, I had a decision to make. I had been working as a school librarian and teacher for 30 years in Kansas. The Blue Valley School District was offering a generous one-time retirement package to teachers who had enough retirement points.

My district had won the AASL School Library Media Program of the Year award (SLMPY) and my school had been honored with a visit to the White House to receive the Blue-Ribbon School award for excellence. However, things were changing. The principal retired; some teachers opted to stay home with young children, and Ruth Bell also retired. Going forward would be a dissimilar experience. I was ready for a change.

I had just finished a second master's degree in school administration and wanted to do something different, something that would have a broader effect on student learning. I loved our profession and still wanted to give back to school libraries, but in a new role.

LEADERSHIP: Winning the SLMPY award gave my school's library much national exposure. Visitors came from many other libraries and people began to be interested in what I might have to say about school libraries and student learning. I began writing for publication, consulting, and presenting at state and national conferences. I became much more active in AASL as a result and was asked to run for president. To my surprise, I actually won! After being elected, I remember going to the ALA midwinter conference and meeting David Loertscher, Barbara Stripling, and Ken Haycock, who were members of the AASL Executive Board that year. It was amazing. Those icons were real and were talking to me! What to do after retiring from my school library became a challenging choice.

While I was still working as a full-time librarian, I took a very part-time job as a consulting editor for Libraries Unlimited. I enjoyed finding books that would really help practitioners do their job better. As a school librarian

I was always frustrated that many professional books were too much theory and not enough practical application to be immediately valuable. Many were just clever lessons that had no real application to curriculum and student learning needs. They were not based on educational research at all. There had to be a common ground and those were the kind of books I enjoyed finding.

At the time of my retirement, Libraries Unlimited was located in Denver, Colorado, and they were looking for a full-time editor for their school library and teacher books. Ken Haycock, whom I had met when he was AASL president and I was his president-elect, was on the board of the company and had (without my knowledge) recommended me for the job. I will always be indebted to him for that.

My decision to take the district's early retirement option, combined with my still wanting to work in the school library field, and a trip to Denver for an interview, resulted in my being offered the job. I needed the summer to decide; I was used to having the summers off! Libraries Unlimited gave me that time. That summer I did interview for two library director positions in local school districts (both great opportunities), but in the end, it seemed that the opportunity to affect the school library profession and student learning more broadly was greater at Libraries Unlimited. So I became an editor.

Twenty-five years later, I have never regretted that decision. Editing gave me the freedom to become much more active in ALA and AASL, as well as the opportunity to travel and meet and visit school libraries and librarians across the country and indeed worldwide. I have learned so much from those encounters and my authors over the years. It has been such a great privilege to read the work of Jean Donham, Carol Kuhlthau, Leslie Maniotes, Vi Harada, Blanche Woolls, David Loertscher, Helen Adams, Danny Callison, Deb Levitov, Mike Eisenberg, Barbara Stripling, Leslie Preddy, Carl Harvey, and so many, many more. To have the opportunity to read and comment on their work out of my own experience has been such an honor and truly a graduate studies program in school librarianship extraordinaire!

I do believe that the hundreds of books that I have critiqued and guided into publication over the years have made a difference to our profession. I also am aware that my greatest asset as an editor has always been my years of practice. Reviewing a proposal or proofreading a manuscript, I always read it through the eyes of a successful practitioner. Even though I left the practice long ago, I still look through that filter. Will this work? Will it help students learn? Is it doable and possible given curriculum and schedules, or not? Nothing can replace those wonderful years with students. It has made all the difference in my career.

In your present education program or in your current position, you know that school librarians have much to offer. As expert teachers and information specialists, you and they can have a phenomenal impact on student learning. School librarians are lifelong learners. It is my greatest hope that they will see the need to broaden their effect. Publish. Speak. Travel. Visit. Consult. You have unusual experience and a stance—a very broad unique look at schools and student learning—that needs to be heard and shared. It is up to you to do just that.

Sharon Coatney

Acknowledgments

From the first to the seventh edition, many persons have been essential to its continuation. Among them are the publishers: Bohdan Wynar, David Loertscher, Ron Maas, and David Paige; graduate assistants: Bonnie Black, Sandi Bianculli Miller, Wendy Bethune, Jo Falcon, Dale David, and Janice Gilmore; and co-authors: Sharon Coatney, Ann Weeks, Joyce Valenza, and April Dawkins.

From the beginning, this textbook was crafted from experiences with students as a building-level school librarian. It was intended to allow those in my university classes to read about management and related research before class before discussing and applying management concepts in class. They added their life experiences, helping me improve my perceptions of what they would need when they left the class.

Textbooks continue when faculty members teaching school library management offer helpful suggestions for revisions and additions and when they adopt a textbook for their classes. Thank you for making this seventh edition possible. Thank you to those professionals who recognized my name badge at conferences and admitted keeping their text as a reference in their library office.

Thank you to the students who will use this volume to determine how to manage this essential space and contents in their school buildings, how they will plan to work with all of the teachers and all of the students all of the time assisting and collaborating to help their teachers teach and their students learn, how they will manage resources to meet every student's needs while engaging with teachers and their curriculum to create meaningful units of instruction.

Thank you to students when they become practitioners for meeting the challenges: to encourage students not only to learn to read but also to enjoy reading; to know how to find information and evaluate it for its accuracy; and to apply it to their life skills and, by combining what they learn, to create new information. Thank you most of all for meeting your greatest challenge to ensure that every student continues to have free and open access to information in all its formats and that every student becomes a responsible citizen in a democracy.

Blanche Woolls

April and Joyce would like to thank Blanche for allowing us to contribute in the continuation of the long tradition of this textbook.

All of us (Blanche, Joyce, and April) also acknowledge the many aspiring school librarians who have been in our classrooms and who become creative, reflective practitioners and outstanding educators. We are indeed fortunate to play a role in growing a next generation of librarians who enter practice with an innovator's mindset and a commitment to engaging learners in rich literacy and inquiry experiences.

We would like to thank all the expert library practitioners who generously contributed to our text. Thanks to:

- K.C. Boyd, librarian at Jefferson Middle School Academy in Washington, DC for her middle-school "Day in the Life"

- Carolyn Foote, retired high school librarian and blogger in Texas, for sharing her expertise on designing library spaces in her "Top Tips for School Library Design."

- Sarah Justice, school library media coordinator at Rosman Middle and High School in Transylvania County, NC, for her middle/high school "Day in the Life."

- Debra Kachel, former district library supervisor and librarian, affiliate faculty member Antioch University in Washington, for her Elevator Pitch Template and her Top Tips on Advocacy.

- Diana Rendina, blogger and media specialist/teacher librarian at Tampa Preparatory School in Florida, for her Top Makerspace Tips.

- Shannon McClintock Miller, Director of Innovation, Technology, and Library Media at the Van Meter School in Iowa, for her elementary school "Day in the Life."

- Melissa Thom, blogger and librarian at Bristol Middle School in West Hartford, Connecticut, for her tips on leading a reading culture.

- Jaclyn Schildkraut, expert on mass shootings and school safety trainer, for her content on safety and security in the United States.

Joyce would like to thank Springshare for their generous support of remote learning and professional development by facilitating the launch of the School Library NJ and School Library HQ LibGuides during the COVID-19 pandemic and its continuation in service of the school library learning community.

Introduction

Several years ago, during a long airport layover, one of the authors struck up a conversation with a charming young woman who shared her immigration story. As an infant in 1975, Julia was airlifted out of Saigon during the final days of the Vietnam War. She described how she was now traveling around the country building a franchise, leading the emerging brewery restaurant movement. When I said, "Wow, Julia, you really think outside the box," Julia responded, "What made you ever think there's a box?"

The fact is school librarians all work under constraints. School librarians respect national standards and core values and common beliefs. While school librarians operate under the hierarchical structures that define American schooling and various degrees of scheduling and budget limitations, by employing a whole-school lens they can look for the problems and invent solutions. School librarians must see beyond the obstacles of *boxes* that may not really exist and celebrate opportunities. School librarians have the capacity to abandon old notions and leverage our talents to better serve and lead. High-quality technologies for curation, creation, communication, and collaboration are widely available and largely free. The library's resources and the school librarians' instructional voices can be embedded into digital learning and made ubiquitously available, meeting their communities anywhere they live, play, and work.

As you read, keep in mind the fifth law, that "a library is a growing organism" (*The Five Laws of Library Science,* Shiyali Ramamrita Ranganathan, 1931).

Generations of librarians have considered Ranganathan's document a foundation or a framework for the profession. But it's Ranganathan's fifth law that resonates most profoundly as this text is updated for school librarians. When a school library continues to grow, so does the learning community it serves. This is a critical moment in time when radical change is possible and necessary. Hopefully, this text inspires you to consider how and when it is important for you to "hit the start button" and consider innovation.

This new edition emphasizes two threads throughout: leadership and innovation. Innovation is not only possible from the position of school librarian: in a period of radical shift, it is an essential element of the job and the possibilities for leadership as a school librarian are unlimited. Leadership allows growth and innovation to happen.

In addition to its content, each chapter suggests "Essential Questions," shares a list of "Key Takeaways," and presents "Challenges to Promote Growth" for use in library information science (LIS) classrooms, workshops, or to prompt reflection and inspire planning. At the end of this book, you will also find "Additional Resources" such as the dynamic playlists that Joyce uses with her own LIS students, as well as links to the School Librarian Headquarters (HQ) LibGuide that Joyce and April maintain for the profession (https://schoollibrarynj.libguides.com/Librarians/home).

The first chapter in Part I, "In the Beginning," explains the profession of school librarianship for anyone from the eager elementary student to the undergraduate who is ready to choose a school library education program. A typical day in a school library is described with four scenarios: an elementary, middle, high school library and a situation in which the librarian manages multiple schools, in this case a middle and a high school. Chapter 1 also offers options for choosing a professional preparation program.

Chapter 2 provides a short history of both education and school libraries through the 20th century, moving into the present day with the impact of pandemic-era learning, growing equity issues in information access; the availability of emerging technologies for curating, communicating, and sharing knowledge; and strategies for discerning truth.

Chapter 3 details steps for acquiring the required credentials for professional practice and offers suggestions for finding, applying for, and accepting a position.

Part II, "Going to Work," begins with Chapter 4, which suggests what the new librarian meeting a new faculty, facility, administration, and students might do (and might not do) to make an initial impact and begin to stage growth that first week on the job.

Chapter 5 presents the role of the librarian in the school's education program, beginning with the traditional role in improving students' reading. It moves to analyzing teaching methods, allowing the librarian to become a leader in helping improve teacher assignments and understand the learner, the curriculum, and inquiry learning. The school librarian, in the roles of teacher and instructional partner, teaches all kinds of literacies, moving out of the library and into the classroom, and organizing and leading in the use of makerspaces and other new technologies and trends.

Evaluation and assessment are covered in Chapter 6. These areas include qualitative and quantitative measures, a variety of standard assessment strategies, the importance of evidence-based practice, and opportunities for action research.

In Chapter 7 this volume addresses the business side of management, describing a model that can inform the ways in which school librarians engage in the administrative aspects of their job. This chapter explores the processes of strategic planning, developing budgets within the constraints of a school district, exploring alternative funding, and advocating for a schedule that allows both access and opportunity for students. Information is also included to guide development and revision of policy statements.

Chapter 8 discusses libraries as welcoming, learner-centered third spaces and includes advice on planning small changes; redesigning the library based on learner needs; moving into a new library; and, in general, thinking flexibly and creatively about space. The chapter explores trends brought about by digital resources and changes in the workplace, as well as creating space for such activities such as makerspaces; production; and more active, more collaborative learning.

Curating your collection to grow with the needs of your community is the focus of Chapter 9. This chapter discusses the extension of the collection beyond the traditional print collection, the life cycle of your collection, and the tasks associated with curation such as evaluation, acquisition, and deselection or weeding. Additionally, the development and revision of a selection and reconsideration policy is discussed along with the need to safeguard intellectual freedom. The protection of student privacy rights is explored through the federal laws that should guide the development of a library privacy policy. Intellectual property, copyright, and fair use are introduced in this chapter and expanded upon in Chapter 11.

Managing personnel, examined in Chapter 10, includes analyzing your leadership and group participation style to help you become a better leader. "Managing" also includes relationships with administrators and teachers as well as students and anyone who may be working in the library as paid staff or volunteers. One aspect of personnel management that is often overlooked is the library's role in the community and other types of librarians and their libraries.

Part III describes what "keeping up" looks like on the ground.

Chapter 11 addresses your role as an information specialist and leader. It offers advice on the thoughtful integration of technologies to support learning, communication, and creativity. It also discusses intellectual property, digital citizenship and leadership, digital curation, and digital libraries, as well as keeping up with edtech innovations.

Chapter 12 introduces the leadership role of the school librarian as an instructional partner in professional development, beginning with personal learning networks and professional learning communities, and covering engagement in social networks and online communities of practice as well as the journals, magazines, and professional associations with which librarians should be familiar. We discuss the librarian's role in developing and coordinating teacher professional development and relationships with other technology professionals. The chapter introduces a wide variety of strategies for keeping up, including webinars, blogs, workshops, institutes, and social media leaders.

The title of Chapter 13 is "Advocacy," but this chapter offers a business-like marketing approach to presenting the library to the school and community. Advocacy includes descriptions of activism with the school librarian becoming a participant in the political process, something that is essential if for no other reason than to provide a good model to other teachers and students. A short discussion features the potential of the school librarian as politician and closes with the role of the school librarian advocating in the global community.

Chapter 14 discusses the importance of future thinking. It addresses change and the diffusion of innovation, and we believe it functions as a hopeful call to action for new professionals.

After the content chapters, you will find a helpful list of "Additional Resources" along with the appendices that have been referred to throughout the book. These additional resources are intended to keep this textbook fresh and up-to-date by providing links to evolving information.

Part I
In the Beginning

1
Becoming a School Librarian

Understand that the right to choose your own path is a sacred privilege.
Use it. Dwell in possibility.

—Oprah Winfrey

Essential Questions

- What competencies and dispositions should a school librarian candidate develop?
- What factors should an aspiring school librarian consider in selecting a preparation program?
- What does the day-to-day life of a librarian look like at each educational level?

People choose a school library career for a variety of reasons. Some are aspirational, others a bit more practical. Among the aspirational reasons:

- Students remember their school librarian as an inspiring educator and wish to pay it forward by making a similar impact on young people.
- Parents may be inspired by the influence of an exemplary librarian in their own children's schools.
- Library paraprofessionals who have admired the role of their supervising librarian may choose to continue their education toward professional certification.
- Dedicated teachers may wish to extend their influence by serving the full school population, reaching beyond their single classrooms. They want to help learners learn and they want to help teachers

teach. Not only do they love books, they may also be ready to assume a leadership role in building schoolwide reading cultures and encouraging the growth of information and media-literate citizens.

- Dedicated educators who appreciate the value of emerging technologies, digital resources, and innovative pedagogical strategies want to share their vision for integrating those tools schoolwide to address and support a growing number of literacies to enhance teaching and learning.

- Dedicated educators may wish to function in not merely one, but all five of the critical roles defined by the American Association of School Librarians (AASL): teacher, leader, instructional partner, information specialist, and program administrator.

- Dedicated educators see in a school library position a way to develop a schoolwide lens through which they can identify and solve problems, innovate, and effect positive change.

Among the best reasons to become a school librarian is that your professional vision aligns closely with the Common Beliefs central to school library practice as described by our national association, the American Association of School Librarians:

1. The school library is a unique and essential part of a learning community.

2. Qualified school librarians lead effective school libraries.

3. Learners should be prepared for college, career, and life.

4. Reading is the core of personal and academic competency.

5. Intellectual freedom is every learner's right.

6. Information technologies must be appropriately integrated and equitably available.[1]

Choosing This Career

Sometimes this career decision is inspired and encouraged by memories of interactions during one's early school years where a school librarian encouraged the joy of reading and helped in the regular discovery of those *perfect-for-you* books. Those interactions likely also involved vivid memories of information professionals engaging with and guiding students through assigned research or inquiry projects, integrating a variety of new search and communication tools while also encouraging more lifewide investigations, perhaps relating to which family pet to choose and later which college or technical school to attend.

In many cases, school librarians are in unique positions to function as equity warriors, introducing students who have never used (or have limited or no access to) public libraries to a universe of resources in a wide range of media, including the digital tools they need to build knowledge and creatively communicate their learning. Alert to community-wide needs, school librarians scout for and share apps that, for instance, help immigrant learners and their families communicate more effectively; school librarians also support students with learning differences, ensure digital access to all families, provide safe havens at lunch and throughout the school day, and build critical bridges supporting college and career preparedness.

The effective school librarian does not build a program in isolation. Whatever the reason for choosing this role, the work cannot be solitary. School librarians serve entire learning communities: students, teachers, administrators, and parents. The interests, experiences, and skills, as well as the needs, of all of these stakeholders must be identified and considered in designing a truly user- and learner-centered library program.

Librarians must understand their communities: the variety of ethnicities and cultures as well as the socioeconomic situations they serve. Are students' homes in urban, rural, or suburban spaces? What do the homes look like? How many students rely on school breakfasts and lunches? Is the community home to a growing number of immigrant groups? Which languages do students and their families speak? Do some of the students come from families who are transient or displaced? What types of businesses and services are available to your communities?

Beyond demographics, it is helpful to understand levels of connectivity at home. Many of your students are likely to be highly connected with multiple personal devices—in fact, uncomfortable without them. Is that the case for every student? What does the wireless situation and the laptop or tablet situation look like at home?

It is also important to know what students bring into the library. What previous experiences might be packed in or absent from their invisible backpacks? What do their lives look like when you do not see them? Are students busily programmed into sports teams, clubs, travel, and play dates? Are some responsible for caring for younger siblings? What do families typically do on weekends? Where do they typically vacation?

In understanding the needs of the faculty, it is helpful to consider how many different approaches to teaching, curriculum, and assessment today's veteran teachers have faced. Often it seems that just as one pedagogical or curricular trend or technology is mastered, others are imposed to replace them. Even after years of experience, teachers may feel unprepared. Following two years of pandemic learning, teachers may find themselves needing to deal with a variety of collateral issues, while considering how they might continue to apply what many have all learned about teaching in remote and hybrid settings.

New teachers enter our schools with various levels of preparation. Some new teachers emerge from formal teacher preparation programs, holding degrees in education as well as in their specialties, whereas others, often because of local professional shortages, may find themselves adjusting to unfamiliar classroom settings prior to attaining the full requirements for licensure. Regardless, new teachers of all sorts may have not been introduced to the role of a school librarian as a professional partner and co-teacher. As an instructional partner, a school librarian can significantly contribute to easing the stress and load of a new teacher's challenging first year.

Your school library, its resources, and its program will be designed and implemented at all times to help students learn and help teachers teach. In their K–12 careers, students may learn to solve for X and balance a chemical equation. The highly transferable skills embedded in their information literacy experiences are likely to serve them well beyond the classroom. To become informed adults and active citizens of our country and our world, students need to be able to negotiate truth across a variety of media platforms, read laterally, interrogate social media feeds, and connect with information beyond potential echo chambers. They need to learn how to work effectively with others, acknowledging and respecting differences as they build and share their new knowledge and their creative efforts.

School librarians model an approach to collaboration by co-teaching both in the library and in the classroom. They accomplish this by designing, implementing, and helping to assess engaging units of instruction and by keeping up with promising emerging educational trends, tools, and innovations. Digital opportunities expand communities, allowing librarians to help connect students and teachers with global experts and collaborators. If this type of instructional and pedagogical leadership appeals to you, then this is the profession for you.

Where Do You Belong?

Although you may not have a great number of options in your very first employment setting, getting that first job can be achievement enough! In addition to simply choosing a career as a school librarian, you will eventually need to choose the type of library that best suits your interests and talents. In some ways and for some new professionals, this is a bit like the blind man and the elephant: you may not yet be able to imagine the whole animal. Some new school librarians maintain a clear image of the library they remember best or the one in which they have volunteered as a definition of what a *school library* looks like. But school libraries, as part of larger institutions, districts, and communities, vary in their levels of support and funding, as does their place in those larger cultures.

The degree you are pursuing or the program in which you are enrolled will likely lead to K–12 certification. You will need to consider differences between private and public schools in all their variety and you will also need to consider whether your preferred grade level—your *sweet spot*—is primary, elementary, intermediate, middle, or high school. You will want to try to visit a variety of schools during the course of your program as well as after you enter your practice. In fact, the school in which you land your first position may likely not be the only school in which you work. Be alert to opportunities, especially opportunities for growth. The following scenarios should help you envision your potential future role across a variety of grade-level settings.

A Day in the Life of an Elementary School Librarian

As the alarm goes off at 5:00 a.m., I wake up thinking of all the exciting things that will be happening at school today. Before I get ready, I get a little exercise in, fold laundry, unload the dishwasher, and get my high-schooler off to his lifting for football.

My social media and email alerts start going off as I get ready, so I check through those to catch up on ideas from other teacher librarians and educators around the world, and of course, check in with my school email, too. There are two emails from my building principals letting me know we are approved to have the book fair delivered early next week during our conferences.

Every day before I head into school, I check my Google calendar and write my daily schedule on a clipboard I carry with me through the day. I have it handy no matter where I am in the building. I grab my lunch and load up my book tote with a few new titles I picked up from the local bookstore last night. I have been looking to supplement our elementary science curriculum, so I am very excited about a few new ones I found during my search.

On my way to school, I get a text from my second-grade teacher friend, Tracy. She is starting a project today with her students where they will be researching plants and flowers in PebbleGo using a choice board I created last night. She wondered if I would have time to pop in to discuss our new community garden project. The plan is to create posters sharing their research using PixelArt and turn those into interactive StickTogether posters representing the garden.

I love arriving at school early to take care of library business before the school day starts. Today, I have a few boxes of new books from Follett to open and I need to get my order in for some other new books too. I use Titlewave to generate my list while paying close attention to the reviews attached to each title.

I am greeted by lots of smiling faces at school early asking if they can help carry my books into the library and if I am bringing robots to their class again. It's going to be a great day!

My library assistant and I kick off the day by going around to the classrooms to pick up returned books in the book crates outside of every teacher's door. This gives us a chance to check the books in before the students and teachers start coming to the library for their weekly checkout time.

Not long after book pick-up, the students and teachers start coming to their library for checkout time. Each class comes for 15 minutes each week with their classroom teacher to find and check out new books. This checkout time is mainly run by my library associate, freeing me to plan, collaborate, and co-teach with classroom teachers.

After stopping to booktalk a few new titles, I set off with my backpack and rolling cart full of robots, teaching materials, and a 3D printer for a morning full of amazing projects with several of our elementary classrooms. Today I am working with the third-grade teachers on their immigration unit. We plan to schedule a virtual visit with an Ellis Island National Park ranger.

As the day comes to a close, I shelve a few books and put things away. Tomorrow, we have a special virtual author visit for our Dot Day Celebration. I set up the video station in the library so I am ready to Zoom into each classroom with the author. It will be a fun day.

At 3:45 p.m., I go down to the elementary collaboration space to join our Girls Who Code club. We meet every other week to learn more about coding and to practice our skills with tools like Scratch. We have around 20 girls from 3rd to 12th grade in our coding club.

On the way home, I listen to one of the Battle of the Book titles on audio so I am ready to write questions in the spring for our contest group. I think about my day and just smile.

I am so happy to be an elementary teacher librarian.

—Shannon McClintock Miller, Van Meter (Iowa)
School, a rural school district

A Day in the Life of a Middle School Librarian

I'm a school librarian and it's the best job on the planet.

My day begins very early: 5:00 a.m. to be exact. From 5:00 to 5:30 a.m., I lie in bed, reading social media posts, the *Washington Post*, and email that was delivered overnight. It is this time in the morning where I chart out my day of tasks and to-do's. At 6:00 a.m., I jump into the shower and listen to *The Joe Madison Show* on Sirius XM radio. The civil rights activist, who reminds me so much of my late father, is outspoken and patiently breaks down the politics of the day for listeners. After greeting my niece and nephew and wishing them a good day at school, I'm in my truck at 6:45 a.m.

I have a long commute to work to my school located in southwest Washington, DC. Even though I don't need to sign in until 8:15 a.m., the needs of my students and DMV traffic encourage me to arrive at work early every morning. I toggle among listening to Madison, listening to voicemails, and sending voice texts to friends/family.

I arrive at school at 7:30 a.m., sit in my truck, and read the principal's morning bulletin. I periodically wave and greet students as they walk into the building. Also, this is the time when I determine if I can join a common planning meeting in person or virtually with teachers throughout the day. For me, it's imperative that I be aware of what is taking place academically and socially/emotionally for the students. Once I enter the building at 7:45 a.m., I'm greeted by zero-period students who arrive early and want to enter the library media center early. Students follow me down the hallway to the center and brief me on what's taken place in their lives since the day when I last saw them. Once all of the doors of the library are open, students head off to the fiction or nonfiction rooms to quietly read, check out books, or complete homework from the previous day. Another group heads into the makerspace lab to engage in Minecraft and take-n-make activities. Students are relatively quiet, with some getting in some precious last-minute sleep before the day begins. When the advisory warning bell rings, a flurry of students heads out of the center to begin the day.

During the 25-minute advisory period, students continue to come to the library to check out books. Sometimes the entire advisory class will visit and sometimes it will be groups of three to five students. This period goes by so fast, often I'm barely able to fully support students who want to locate resources during this period. When the bell rings, I shift into classroom teacher mode. This year I was assigned a class to support keeping the elective classes in the building down to a count of 23 students per class. Though this was not a task I initially welcomed, I accepted the responsibility of teaching students media-related content that would help them transition into 9th grade. The students I serve are a curious, energetic, and opinionated group of eighth-graders. I used a variety of resources to help teach a lesson that the students would enjoy: the News Literacy Project, Common Sense Education, *Washington Post*, The Grio, local and national news television channels.

After I dismiss my second-period class, I will push into classrooms to support teachers/students. Sometimes this is done in person, sometimes it's virtual. Support can range from reinforcing independent reading to project-based activities where students access technology. The DCPS Library Department invests in Follett Destiny and Sora, which heavily supports our emphasis on independent reading. The Library Department invests in BrainPop, PebbleGo, and Newsela, and we have the opportunity to access Britannica, Gale, Tumblebooks, and more through the DC Public Library. These resources help support instruction, as my school is a one-to-one school where students carry a tablet to each class. If I'm not scheduled to visit a class, students will flow down to the library normally toward the end of the period to check out books and receive one-on-one support in identifying that special book for them.

Lunch periods are hectic mainly because I float among three spaces: the library lobby, the fiction room, and the makerspace lab. Students are able to eat in the fiction room and they enjoy it. Many of these students, even pre-COVID, enjoyed the calm and quiet atmosphere of the library where they read while eating or chatting with a small group of friends. For these students, the lunch room is too noisy and overstimulating and the library meets their personal needs. After these students eat, they join students in the makerspace lab and participate in the weekly activity creating or making an artifact that they get to take home. Other students will continue their Minecraft explorations and builds while others will sit in the comfy chairs and read. Sometimes I have to put my counselor cap on and give advice . . . sometimes welcomed and sometimes not. Middle schoolers are still learning about themselves, finding their voice in the world through a physical body that changes every day. In some cases, I've served as referee to "friend" groups who have experienced some level of conflict. Again, this is normal; these students are in middle school and they are growing up. On an average day, the library will attract up to 40 students and spread them out safely in all spaces in the center. While monitoring students, I try to shelve books, respond to email, and prepare for the next project or library activity.

I normally try to take my lunch after the students' lunch periods but last year found myself eating on the run. Time was spent pushing into classes or opening up earlier for seventh and eighth periods due to student demand. These last two periods are designated as open makerspace periods where students who have completed work in the classroom can visit. Students enjoy this access because they are completing research-based assignments for class, catching up on required reading, or wrapping up monthly holiday/observation projects for the library program. Often I have six activities taking place at the same time with students from all grades and classes working independently. I circle the room and check in with students, to see if they need help or support on completing an assignment or project. I play radio-version pop and hip-hop music, which makes my students extremely happy as they bop around the room while completing their tasks. Sometimes students who need a break from the classroom will visit during this time as well. I have books that I use as bibliotherapy for many of my students who just need a little more support from a staff member, a special comfy chair/sofa for them to sit on, and calming music. My spaceship chairs and tables are a favorite location in my nonfiction room.

My day ends with dismissing students back to their classrooms five minutes before the last bell of the day. I quickly scan my pictures from the day and decide which ones will be posted to Twitter, Instagram, or Facebook. If the students were working on a project, I'd usually create a TikTok to celebrate them and their determination to complete a project or activity. I do a quick cleanup of all project materials and help my custodian bring the center back to its normal appearance before the dismissal bell at 3:15 p.m. During dismissal, I sit behind my circulation desk in the library lobby. The eighth-graders dismiss from my lobby to the 7th Street exit where the Metro buses wait for them and where I bid them goodnight daily. I usually joke and kid with these students a lot because in June, I will sadly bid them goodbye and wish them well as they begin high school. I take great pride in conversing with these students because I have had one of the most special relationships with them. I met them when they were wide-eyed little fifth-graders, taking a tour of the building and making the decision to attend Jefferson as a sixth-grader. I have watched them grow academically, physically, and emotionally. I view this as a special opportunity that only a few staff members have in the building. I'm going to miss them.

At 3:30 p.m., I lock my library doors and head out of the 7th Street exit. There are always a couple of kids in the parking lot waiting for rides and talking to staff. I talk to a couple of students as I head to my truck and wish them goodnight, be safe, and see you in the morning. As I drive to the expressway, I see many of the students heading to the Metro, local grocery store, or a local eatery, laughing, playing, and just being kids. I check my email as I listen to 2000s rap and R&B and catch up on phone calls during stop-and-go traffic. My day is full and eventful in my library media center. No day is the same and I wouldn't trade it for anything else in the world.

—K.C. Boyd, Jefferson Middle School Academy, Washington DC
Public Schools, an urban school district

A Day in the Life of a High School Librarian

I approach the big glass front doors at 7:30 a.m., greeting a group of waiting students. I love the active buzz of our library in the morning. Nearly every day, these early-morning "regulars" visit before homeroom to complete or print homework, get some last-minute help with a deadline project, or simply check in with friends.

After checking the digital schedule listing teachers who have requested and booked library space and my time on the iPad at the circulation desk, I make sure that the large dry-erase board in the front of the library shares an up-to-date listing of visiting classes and that I am ready for scheduled informal meetings or professional development. Students and faculty often rush in to check "the board" before home-room to see if their classes are scheduled, where they are scheduled, or simply to see if they face Day 1 or Day 2 in our block schedule sequence.

The board is not the only visual highlight. This library is filled with student art, carefully installed by our highly collaborative Art Department that uses our space as a rotating gallery.

A couple of our student volunteers offer greetings as they assume places behind the desk, automatically checking books in, handling any early book or tech check-outs, peeking in the workroom for the excitement of any new book boxes to unpack or the potential of snacks. One of them eagerly pitches me an idea for a new display on apocalyptic fiction.

First on the official agenda is Senior Capstone. I always look forward to consult-ing with these students individually on possible strategies for communicating the results of their semester-long "*passion*" research projects. Today we attempt to make connections with experts we are identifying via LinkedIn and Twitter. That is followed by a visit from the ELL teacher for a brainstorming session to plan engaging lessons for a large group of newly arrived English language learners and to collaborate on a LibGuide to engage with their parents.

As the day progresses, I work with the scheduled small and large groups who arrive with their own devices, helping them understand where they will be meeting and how they might reconfigure the flexible furniture to best meet their needs for research, collaboration, planning, meeting with remote experts, or presentation. Our drama and music teachers pop in with a small group of students, researching 1930s costumes for an upcoming production of *Guys and Dolls*. After we grabbed a few books, I suggested we create a collaborative Wakelet "mood board" to support their work with both costumes and props. Before they left, I got that curation started, invit-ing my colleagues in as collaborators.

During the three lunch periods, I meet with groups of teachers for one of our "Lunch and Learn" tech sessions, in the smaller of our presentation areas. This week we are brainstorming how we might mine open educational resources (OER) portals to discover quality resources to incorporate into curricula.

After lunch, I support the AP English students through their lit-crit research using a LibGuide collaboratively developed with their teacher. The normal stream of users returns materials and equipment at the circulation desk while students wait to check out greenscreens for production and iPads for their presentations. Study hall students are sitting at tables or in the informal seating area reading and working and chatting.

It's nearly budget time, so I find a little time for a Zoom meeting with one of our database vendors to discuss new offerings and pricing as I make decisions about which to continue and which to add in light of usage data and knowledge of upcoming student projects across disciplines and grade levels.

As the school day comes to an end, I review the materials I'll be sharing at the after-school social studies department meeting. The department chair asked me to ensure that all teachers in the department are aware of database integrations with the Canvas learning management system used by the entire faculty. I remember to straighten up a bit as I leave because the library space will be used for a school board meeting tonight. After dinner tonight, I'll revise discussion questions for tomorrow's after-school book club meeting.

—Joyce Valenza, Springfield Township High School, a suburban public school

A Day in the Life of a (Multi-School) Middle/High School Librarian

Me: Good morning!
Highschooler: *grumble*
Me: Good morning!
Highschooler 2: *grunt*
Me: Good morning!
Middle Schooler 1 and 2: "Mrs. Justice! They have hot chocolate in the cafeteria! Do you want us to get you one? We can get you one!"

That pretty much sums up what a day in the life of a middle and high school librarian is like. But seriously, working with both middle and high school students always makes for an exciting day.

The doors open at 7:30 a.m. for the early arrivals. Some students are returning or checking out books, while others are looking for a calm place to wait out the few minutes before the start of school. At 8:05 a.m., the day begins. The online Google Calendar shows what the day holds for the school library. The high school is on a block schedule, with each class lasting 80 minutes, while the middle school is on a modified five- to six-period schedule depending on the grade level. These various schedules mean that many classes overlap during library visits.

A cold Thursday in January is the prime example of a typical day. I arrive and unlock and prop open the library doors. I flip on the lights and stop to admire the amount of light now available since earlier in the week the custodian replaced the burned-out bulbs in the library stacks area. The bright and colorful walls create a welcoming space and the newly created displays beg readers to check out books. Before the bell rings and the announcements begin, a few students filter through. High school first period starts. Before the chaos of the day begins, I run to the art teacher's room for a brief planning meeting. We have started a multi-day project that incorporates the sewing machines in the maker area of the library. She is filming the fiber arts lesson for her National Board renewals, so we have been meeting on a daily basis to discuss the lesson's progress. We will start sewing in the library next week. At 8:30, the first rotation of sixth-graders enters the library for their weekly book circulation. Books are quickly exchanged, excuses are made about forgotten overdues, and finally the games and activities are pulled off the shelf. The sound of LEGOs being dug through and clicked together mixes with the sounds of a heated checkers game.

Sixth grade leaves, the bell rings for the end of high school first period, and the breakfast break begins. My two breakfast regulars come in with their food and head to the tables to enjoy a few minutes of quiet while they eat. High school second period begins and I take a few precious minutes to check email, get caught up on some tasks, and then dive into some clerical work. I'm in the middle of a book order and trying to figure out which titles are must-haves since my small budget is very tight this year. I am trying to replace some of the heavy wooden chairs at the tables and have worked out a deal with my principals so that each of us will pay a third for a few years to make this happen. Even though this deal will take part of my budget, I'm happy that I was finally able to get both the principals to sit down and agree to this compromise. But it does mean I have to be even more selective in book ordering for the next few years. After looking over the book order, I take the time to weed a few titles from the current collection. My Individual Growth Plan for this year includes upping the copyright date of the nonfiction section.

The bell rings for high school third period. The principal arrives and drops off some distance-learning students who are without a supervising teacher for the day. A loud rumble announces the arrival of the second group of sixth-graders. Once again, books are exchanged and games come out. One student is asking for a book that she saw on a Google search but she can't remember the name or author . . . just as the high school Spanish class enters for a scheduled BreakOut. I pass the sixth-grader to her teacher to get help searching the catalog and I focus on this new group of students. The library is home to six BreakOut Edu kits. I work with the teachers to find games that will enhance their curriculum and then set up the boxes for game play. Today's BreakOut is an ultimate collaboration because it plays off the strengths of both myself and the Spanish teacher. I am the gaming expert and she is the Spanish expert, so we work well together for this lesson. After their 45-minute time limit for game play expires, we break down what they learned, hand out prizes, and then the class departs. I quickly pack up the clues and boxes before the bell rings and the lunch crowd descends. Lunch trays appear, bagged lunches are unpacked, and multiple students ask, "Can I borrow your microwave?" The smell of ramen noodles permeates the air.

After lunch, the final sixth-grade group comes tumbling in and a scheduled group of ninth-graders enters the library for a second-semester library orientation. Orientation includes reminding students of the genrefied sections and pointing them toward the new books and books on display and teaching them how to use the self check-out computer. As they are let loose to explore the library, I am called into action. "Where are the true crime books?" "What's a good historical fiction book?" "Yes, I liked the schoolwide-read book, so maybe I should read another Alan Gratz book." Fifty-plus students bob and weave through the shelves finding books that call to them. Sixth grade leaves with treasures. Ninth grade leaves with a nonfiction and fiction book each. Some have found some new books to read while others have found comfort in old reliables like *Wimpy Kid*. I joke a bit with them over this and challenge them to branch out and be brave next visit. The bell rings and the official school day ends. Five minutes later, the after-school jam session starts setting up in the library. Fiddles, guitars, and banjos fill the air.

And so ends the day in the life of a middle and high school librarian. Every day is different and every day is planned for, but never turns out as planned. Of course, this narrative does not even include all the phone calls, student and teacher drop-ins for technology help, or the many other random interruptions. But every day brings new experiences and new lessons.

—Sarah Justice, Rosman Middle & High School, a rural school library shared between two schools in the Appalachian Mountains of North Carolina

School Librarian Competencies

What does it really take to experience the type of days described by these school librarians? This text will provide a far deeper dive into professional competencies as you move through the chapters, but here we give an overview of the *right stuff*. As a basic starting point, school librarians should certainly build their competencies around AASL's *National School Library Standards* and the five interconnected roles: teacher, leader, instructional partner, information specialist, and program administrator (AASL, 2018).

As an *information specialist*, the school librarian scouts for, introduces, and integrates promising technology tools into instructional design, encouraging and modeling how these tools might further the development of information literacy and critical thinking skills. School librarians must be ever open to discovery and making connections. On top of reviews and "best" lists, the school librarian assists in analyzing and evaluating digital tools, resources, and applications with knowledge of current intellectual property guidelines and the available labels that guide us in sharing and using Creative Commons content. School librarians should also develop shareable awareness of federal laws and regulations protecting children's privacy, such as the Family Educational Rights and Privacy Act (FERPA) and the Children's Online Privacy Protection Act (COPPA). These must be considered in the selection of apps and digital tools, especially for learners under the age of 13.

For students, librarians curate print and digital resources to meet their formal learning needs and appeal to their lifewide interests. For teachers, the information specialist digitally curates the great number of instructional portals and blogs and social media pointing to promising pedagogical strategies and curricular ideas and new strategies for assessment across the disciplines. The information specialist organizes and curates the growing number of open educational resources portals that can be a huge boost to teachers seeking instructional makeovers for their least favorite lessons. As the methods of teaching students continue to change, content for classroom instruction also evolves. Librarians help teachers adapt and develop curriculum for remote, hybrid, and flipped learning. In addition to maintaining their own websites, the librarian is embedded into classroom teachers' learning management systems.

As a *teacher*, a school librarian should possess outstanding teaching skills and model contagious enthusiasm for learning. This enthusiasm is essential for ensuring that they create a culture of literacy that will flow steadily from the library to the teachers and students. The librarian encourages reading for information, for understanding, and for pleasure across the many platforms on which stories and informational text now exist. The librarian ensures that learners are prepared with skills of critical thinking, engages in challenging inquiry experiences using information and media across formats, and actively practices the ethical creation and sharing of products of their new knowledge.

School librarians are school *leaders*. If the library program is going to continue to grow and change to serve the needs of a school, leadership skills are essential. As continual learners themselves, librarians listen to determine community needs. They keep up by actively engaging in local and global professional associations and online communities of practice. They seek opportunities to engage members of their own communities and build positive and productive relationships with all stakeholder groups.

Leadership in the area of advocacy is also critical. Advocacy becomes a far more effective practice when you understand that it is framed around addressing other people's problems. If administrators, teachers, parents, and members of the community are going to consider the school library an essential element of the learning mission of the school, the librarian must proactively gather and regularly present evidence of the library's value in the context of student learning. This evidence might be engagingly shared both informally in elevator pitches or during scheduled PTA/PTO (Parent Teacher Association or Organization) or school board meetings. This leadership role will be revisited throughout this volume, culminating in the final chapter.

As an *instructional partner*, the school librarian can play a critical role in enhancing learning by enhancing teaching. If teachers and the school librarian are to collaborate in designing and implementing instruction, the school librarian must be able to empathetically understand needs relating to teachers' preferred strategies, student differences, strategies relating to engagement, and possible assessments. The librarian's role is also critical in helping teachers prepare courses integrating the best available digital resources.

As a *program administrator*, the school librarian manages budgets, schedules, and staff (including volunteers); ensures access to resources; advocates on behalf of stakeholders; and establishes relationships with all of the stakeholder groups. In many ways, being a school librarian is like running a small business or organization. Like all good administrators, the most effective school librarians step back and evaluate their programs, questioning existing policies and procedures and strategies to discover whether they are operating as effectively and engagingly as they might. Incorporating a growth or innovator's mindset, you might ask questions such as: Why shouldn't we . . .? What would happen if . . .? What if we could . . .? As Chris Lehmann of Philadelphia's Science Leadership Academy frequently asks himself: What is the worst consequence of my best idea? We will return to the mindset of an innovator throughout this book, but these ideas are summarized in Appendix A, the Mindset for School Library Innovators poster.

As an administrator, it is important to be careful about your assumptions and to seek evidence of, by, and for your practice. Assumptions limit our abilities to consider new perspectives and opportunities. Based on evidence, school librarians collaboratively develop mission and vision statements, and establish goals as part of their strategic plans to ensure the growth of their programs. School library collections have grown to include a wide variety of formats and the librarian curates resources for their communities on a variety of platforms that are available ubiquitously. The school librarian's role continually evolves with shifts in information and communication landscapes. To be successful, today's new school librarian must embrace change. An interest in trying new things is essential because the skills necessary to manage teaching and learning are constantly evolving.

Before choosing the school library—the largest classroom in the school— as their preferred assignment, the new librarian should be willing to accept the multiple roles necessary for effecting positive change and be willing to embrace flexibility and innovation in choosing methods to help students achieve success.

While some of the preparation to assume these challenging and exciting responsibilities may begin at the undergraduate level, your full preparation usually means enrollment in an accredited graduate program. Choosing the right preparation program is an important first step.

Choosing a Pre-Service School Library Education Program

Programs to prepare school librarians are offered in schools of education and schools of library and information science at universities and colleges at both the undergraduate and graduate levels. Courses are selected by or assigned to students to help them meet the certification requirements, sometimes referred to as *credentials* or a *license*, for the state where they plan to teach. The credential or license is discussed in chapter 3.

Because persons attending institutions of higher education expect to be eligible for certification in a state upon graduation, university and college education programs respond to the certification requirements of their state and, whenever possible, also meet requirements for adjoining states. State requirements, therefore, dictate the components of programs that certify school librarians. For many states, the certification program remains competency based; for others, specific courses are described. Many states require a practicum, which varies from a certain number of hours or days divided between elementary and secondary schools to a specified amount of time in a single location. Some states require both a classroom teaching credential and the school library credential; others require successful teaching experience before granting school library certification. Additionally, some states require educators to take two Praxis (https://www.ets.org/praxis) exams, one measuring core educational knowledge and skills in reading, writing, and mathematics and another measuring content knowledge for their specialty.

For those who are already enrolled in a pre-service school library education program, this section may be unnecessary to read. However, if you began your program in one location and had to leave or delay finishing, this section should be helpful. It should also be helpful to professionals who are asked by interested prospective students about possible institutions to attend.

In the past, deciding where to go to earn certification as a librarian was based on the student's ability to attend in-person classes. Previous choices were limited by the proximity of the institutions and opportunities were not evenly distributed across the states.

Although this was steadily changing, the COVID-19 pandemic accelerated opportunities to attend higher education programs without leaving home. Possibilities opened by online programs make certification far more accessible and achievable for students across the country. Many colleges and universities continue to offer degrees through a combination of face-to-face sessions on campus combined with online experiences. In these programs, students may come to campus one or more times each semester and complete courses online. Other institutions offer programs completely online. As remote instruction becomes increasingly common in institutions of higher education, it is far easier to pursue both advanced degrees and continuing education experiences in the settings of your choice without leaving home.

If you are seeking information about potential programs, you will want to refer to two main sources:

- ALA's resource on Library Education & Licensing, which includes directories of library education programs (https://www.ala.org/aasl /about/ed/recruit/license)

- *School Library Connection*'s "State by State Certification" resources describing and linking to each state's requirements (https:// schoollibraryconnection.com/Glossary/StateCertifications/1959400 ?topicCenterId=0)

Choosing the right pre-service program requires consideration of a number of criteria. Although some undergraduate programs exist, most students will want to earn an ALA-accredited or AASL-recognized master's degree. If, over the course of their career, a student would like the flexibility of working across a range of libraries, as well as school libraries, an ALA-accredited master's degree is generally required. If the student plans to work in school libraries exclusively, they might alternatively consider a program that is recognized by the Council for the Accreditation of Educator Preparation (CAEP).

Some schools require the Graduate Record Examination (GRE) for admission; others do not. Some states require experience as an educator before a candidate can become a school librarian. Before entering a program, consider who will be teaching your courses. Will your instructors be primarily researchers or practitioners? What specific school librarian experience do the faculty members have?

To adequately prepare as an educator, it is essential that pre-service school librarians study teaching methods. Students who are in schools of library and information science complete the core elements of the library and information science (LIS) curriculum with others who are going to work in all types of information agencies. Those who work with children and young adults must understand the learning processes and learning styles of their clientele. If the student is not a certified teacher when beginning the school librarianship program, regardless of whether the program is situated in a school of education or information science, pre-service coursework should include educational psychology, pedagogy, teaching and engagement strategies, background in child development and learning differences, instructional design, knowledge of curriculum, selection of materials for youth, and instruction in leveraging promising emerging technologies for learning.

Some colleges and universities may require a teaching certification before admitting a student to the school librarian program. Others integrate pedagogy into the school library coursework. A program should include a practicum experience to allow the school librarian-in-training to teach in an actual school for a time period specified by state requirements.

Students in LIS programs who do take courses in a school of education will have an excellent opportunity to share with their fellow educator classmates the value of collaborating with a school librarian once they are placed in schools. They will also be given many opportunities to observe in what ways their classroom teacher colleagues are prepared.

School librarians are teachers *and* they are librarians. In schools with programs accredited by the American Library Association's Committee on Accreditation, school library students will take courses with students who are not seeking school library credentials but are planning to work in other types of libraries. Your introduction to other libraries will help you understand their role in the ecosystem, and you will be better able to work with your counterparts in public, academic, and other types of libraries once you are in your school.

Library science programs in both schools of education and schools of library and information science offer courses in children's and young adult materials; these courses are mandatory for librarians who will be certified across grades K–12. Because some districts include pre-kindergarten in their programs, if offered, a class in materials for the very young may also be desirable.

The wealth of youth-focused materials published each year makes it important to take courses covering each level. Further, the variety of types of youth-focused materials currently being published must be included in a school librarian's preparation. Pre-service school library students must be familiar with books across publication platforms and apps developed specifically for or appropriate for youth, as well as the wide variety of age-appropriate databases and digital tools. Programs should also engage pre-service students in understanding and evaluating the diversity of materials being published with an eye toward creating collections that are inclusive. Programs should also introduce students to the digital resources available for building and managing their programs and collections.

Beyond understanding resources for youth, knowledge of the K–12 curriculum, instructional design, and strategies for library integration, especially in the area of developing a culture of inquiry-based learning, should also be covered in the program. School librarians must learn how to work with curricula and teachers and how to blend materials in the library with materials in the classroom as well as those embedded in the schools' learning management systems.

Important elements to consider in selecting a preparation program are the variety of laboratory or practical experiences offered and the types of digital resources and tools modeled and embedded into the program. School librarian programs should evolve as the information and communication landscapes evolve and be on the forefront of emerging digital technologies. To promote new technology applications for workflow, communication, and learning, school librarians not only must be familiar with the platforms but also must have tested the technology and found it essential in the lives of students and teachers.

As you research pre-service LIS programs, it may be helpful to consider their reputation. In addition to consulting published lists of academic rankings, ask practicing school librarians which pre-service programs they would recommend. If they have hosted field-experience school librarians from a specific school, they can tell you how well prepared these students would be to join the staff. They may also be well enough acquainted with the current emphasis of their own alma mater to know if their school offers a curriculum that truly prepares new professionals for future practice. Learning about outstanding, forward-thinking programs will more likely prepare you to grow your own innovative and valued program once you are hired. When you have choices, choose to learn in the best possible program.

School librarianship has a brief history, but one that is worthy of review. The history of school librarians and their role in the education of students is covered in chapter 2.

Key Takeaways

- Effective school librarians assume a wide variety of key roles in school culture and student success.

- The role of school librarian can look very different depending on grade level and school settings.

- Choosing your preparation program is critically important and can determine the level of flexibility you experience in your career.

Challenges to Promote Growth

1. Find students in your current grade-level interest—elementary, middle, or high school—and ask them about their experiences with school librarians.
2. If you are able, interview students in courses preparing them for a leadership position in a school district, and ask them about their experiences with school librarians.
3. Scan AASL's *Knowledge Quest* blog posts relating to any of the designated topics and consider the scope of the activities the bloggers describe.
4. With geographic barriers removed, determine what criteria you would consider in selecting a certification or degree program.

Note

1. American Association of School Librarians. (2018). *National School Library Standards for Learners, School Librarians, and School Libraries*. Chicago, IL: ALA Editions, 11.

2
From Then to Now

Do the best you can until you know better. Then when you know better, do better.

—Maya Angelou

Essential Questions

- How has education changed over time in the United States?
- In what ways have school libraries paralleled, preceded, or fallen short of those changes?

Public education in the United States has changed greatly since the founding of the country. By the time of the American Revolution, some states had begun to fund public grammar schools; however, those schools were only open to white boys. With the founding of a democratic republic, many leaders realized that the United States needed educated citizens—but like civic participation, education was limited to white males with property, and wealth often determined access. Additionally, school libraries were slow in arriving on the scene in comparison to academic and public libraries. They began to appear in the United States only at the turn of the 20th century. This chapter discusses both education and school libraries then and now.

History of Education in the United States

American education has been, is, and always will be in a state of change. New theories are developed, refined, implemented (usually before they are tested adequately), and then discarded in a cycle that finds educators constantly reinventing wheels. Administrators accept innovation; teachers follow administrative leadership; and students become recipients of each educational teaching theory, mode, and method currently in vogue.

When an administrator becomes excited about a new trend or idea and tries to implement it without exploring the innovation fully, changes are often forced into practice in schools with little buy-in from teachers. The successes and failures of such educational innovations continue, but it is worth examining the process from the beginning.

In the first schools in the United States, education was individualized, with a headmaster asking students to copy materials. Students did not necessarily learn how to read or write independent of what they were copying. Schooling was labor-intensive and open only to those who could pay; the poor of our fledgling nation remained basically illiterate. However, for the masses, little formal education was necessary. Children would leave school to work in factories or on the family farm. The present-day "school year" was designed to allow students the summer free to work in agriculture.

Key Ideas and Theorists That Influenced American Education

- Lancasterian system
- Edward Thorndike
- John Dewey
- Booker T. Washington and Julius Rosenwald
- William Heard Kirkpatrick
- Maria Montessori
- The Winnetka Plan and The Dalton Plan
- Great Society
- Theodore Sizer

To overcome illiteracy in some of the larger cities, societies were formed to provide free education. These 19th-century societies adopted a method called the Lancasterian system, in which many students were taught at the same time. To maximize instruction, students were organized into groups based on ability. Joseph Lancaster taught older children who, in turn, drilled the younger ones. Students sat at desks lined up in large rooms where they observed their monitor, who would state a fact and write an example on a blackboard. Students copied the fact, spoke it, and drilled it until they "knew" it.

This system of instruction through monitors meant the headmaster was freed from working with one student at a time, and instead became responsible only for what was to be taught (by being written on the blackboard, copied, and drilled) and for training the first level of monitors. This type of instruction did require a trained teacher to plan the lessons, but ability grouping and rote learning became the norm.

Rural America had many one-room schools to serve the small communities throughout the states. The teacher taught all the curriculum to all of the "grades" in the school. Older students often helped teach or reinforce what they had already learned. Though this system involved more than simply copying and drilling information, it still depended on a single teacher, whose training and ability could range widely.

Before the passage of the Thirteenth Amendment in 1865, education of enslaved African Americans was prohibited by law. During the

Reconstruction era, under the auspices of the Bureau of Refugees, Freedmen, and Abandoned Lands (Freedmen's Bureau), some areas opened public schools for African Americans, but these schools were poorly funded and mostly ignored. With the rise of the Jim Crow laws in the 1870s, public education became legally racially segregated. The 1896 *Plessey v. Ferguson* ruling established separate public schools for black and white students. The result was a lack of financial support and resources for the black schools. One attempt to improve public education from 1915 to 1932 was the development of the Rosenwald schools, led by Booker T. Washington. Funded by the philanthropic efforts of Julius Rosenwald and matched by donations from local black communities, close to 5,000 schools were built to provide access to elementary education for rural black communities in the South. By 1928, one in every five rural schools for black students in the South was a Rosenwald school. In the 1920s and 1930s, Rosenwald funds in some states were used to pilot rural library service. After 1932, the school-building efforts of the Rosenwald fund ceased and African American public education was completely run through separate public local and state efforts.[1]

As the nation grew, various theories of education were developed, proclaimed, adopted, modified, and/or dismissed. The 20th century saw the creation of kindergarten, adjustments to the legal age for leaving school, and changes in the length of the school day and term. In the early part of the 20th century, the theories of Edward L. Thorndike and John Dewey predominated.

Thorndike believed that human nature, whether good or bad, depended on learning. He advocated a stimulus-response environment in which patterns of behavior could be established when a satisfying stimulus produced a satisfying response. Conversely, Dewey believed that education was life and that learners react to their environment, solving problems posed by their environment. These ideas led to the concept of direct instruction, so common in many schools in the 21st century. Teachers lecture, students read the textbook, and then students take a test to see if they have mastered the material.

In Dewey's Laboratory School at the University of Chicago, Lancaster's drill-and-practice approach disappeared along with straight rows of desks in classrooms. The modern-day approach of project learning was based on a revision of Dewey's theories by William Heard Kirkpatrick. In project learning, the teacher was responsible for beginning an activity, seeing that it was carried forward, and evaluating the results, but the actual learning was in the hands of the students, who defined how to execute the assignment and solve the problem.

Theorist Maria Montessori's work offered a private alternative to public day care and kindergarten. Montessori's focus was on the sensory perceptions of individual learners and allowing each child the freedom to investigate. The teacher provided relevant opportunities, encouraged independence, and allowed children to exercise and expand their inherent interest in learning. This foundational concept persists in some private as well as public schools today.

Individualized instruction returned in 1919 with the Winnetka Plan in Illinois and the Dalton Plan in Massachusetts. Students were tested, allowed to proceed at different rates depending on ability, self-tested, and retested to check the progress made. Although group work was acceptable, the emphasis was on individual learning.

One of the greatest impacts on education in the 20th century was the ebb and flow in school enrollments. In the 1950s, schools were built to accommodate the baby boomers, children born after World War II and often fathered by returning soldiers. In the 1960s, President Lyndon B. Johnson's Great Society programs instituted Head Start, provided free school lunches, and allocated funding for new teaching methods.

The Soviet Union's launch of the first Sputnik satellite in 1957 produced an upheaval in U.S. education based on fears of losing the "space race," which prompted Congress to provide funds for workshops, special programs, and institutes for training and retraining teachers. Funds also became available for materials and equipment to supplement classroom textbooks, especially in math, science, and foreign languages.

The *Brown v. Board of Education* decision in 1954 marked the end of the "separate but equal" policy of separate black and white schools. However, it took an additional year before an order was issued to enforce this unanimous decision of the Supreme Court. Desegregation of public schools was slow and met with fierce resistance. After additional Supreme Court rulings in 1968 and 1971 in two follow-up cases, the Court issued mandates with specific guidelines for implementation, along with guaranteeing the authority of the federal courts to enforce them.[2]

By the 1970s, it was apparent that enrollments were steadily decreasing. Neighborhoods changed as all the school-age children living there finished their basic education. In the late 1970s and early 1980s, many schools were closed and the buildings either demolished or sold to the community. Funds for education were drastically cut as legislators responded to citizens' opposition to heavy taxes.

The Coalition of Essential Schools (CES), a project organized in 1984 and cosponsored by the National Association of Secondary School Principals and the National Association of Independent Schools, was chaired by Theodore R. Sizer, a faculty member at Brown University. The nine common principles of the coalition were an intellectual focus, simple goals, universal goals, personalization, student as worker, student exhibitions, attitude, staff, and budget.[3] Students were to learn to use their minds and to master "essential skills" in school, with goals applying to all students. Teaching and learning were personalized, with students participating in the learning process rather than passively absorbing what the teacher delivered as instruction. Final high school performance became an exhibition of what had been learned. Although the CES no longer exists as a national organization, many schools still try to implement its principles.

At intervals, state and federal governments have become involved in education. In 1989, President George H. W. Bush convened the Education Summit with the nation's governors, and a set of national education goals were set. This framework, *America 2000,*[4] was designed to transform the United States into a "A Nation of Students" and make learning a lifelong endeavor.

Twenty years later, the National Governors Association began another effort to transform the nation's schools. This new effort reflected the 1990s and a society concerned about both the cost and quality of education and a commitment to accountability, but it was affected by momentous world events including the fall of the Berlin Wall, the breakup of the Soviet Union, the creation of the European Common Market, and the rapid expansion of technology with the advent of the Internet. The U.S. policy of free universal schooling, which began in the 19th century, intended to teach citizens to read, write, and do math, was followed by other nations—and some not only caught up with but also surpassed the achievements of U.S. students.

The Education Environment in the 21st Century

Challenges to schools in the current century have increased. The economy continues to play a prominent role, affecting the numbers of staff per pupil, the ability to purchase resources for schools, and the maintenance of school buildings and resources. The pressure imposed by state and national testing and its results, and its role in the evaluation of teaching, continues. The growth of the charter school movement has also contributed to the shifting of public funds away from traditional public schools. The COVID-19 pandemic caused unprecedented disruption in the lives of students even as their teachers moved to meet their classes and deliver instruction in unanticipated ways. The loss in educational experiences to students wrought by the pandemic is incalculable. The education environment today is more than ever a challenge to every educator, and solutions will require the best efforts of all.

The education environment following the pandemic is plagued by insecurities and, in many cases, continued loss of funding. Federal and state governments, in efforts to remediate some of the losses, provided funding for schools that could not or did not generate or institute any replacements for the loss of many "special" teachers such as art, music, librarians, and counselors; and the cancellation of special high school classes that drew only small numbers of students (among others). Despite these funding attempts, these losses have continued over the past two decades. The uncertainty of the situation makes it difficult for school district administrators to plan from one year to the next. Creating a budget and determining budget items require as much information as it is possible to gather.

One method of researching these situations is the use of *environmental scanning*, a term used to describe the gathering of statistics about key factors influencing the school district. The external setting includes political climate; economic condition of the nation, state, and city; primary and secondary cultures in the community; numbers of children to be educated; family structure, income, and educational background of parents; and geographic location.

The political climate of a neighborhood changes rapidly when the decreasing numbers of children to be educated signal the loss of enrollment, particularly in an elementary school. Often an effort begins to close such a school—although the tumult caused by parents whose children attend that school is often formidable. The economic condition in a location may be one that signals lower incomes and fewer businesses or industries. Parents in these communities may not feel they can change the situation. The opposite is found in other locations where parents and higher income levels lead them to establish school foundations and carry out fundraising activities to support positions in the school such as music, art, physical education, and a library. Bock[5] discusses how private schools have been joined by public schools in the effort to raise funds and offers the suggestion that if this fundraising can be done online, it will save much effort. He offers four websites to begin the process: Adopt a Classroom (www.adoptaclassroom.org), Digital Wish (www.digitalwish.com), DonorsChoose (www.donorschoose.org), and Schoola (www.schoola.com).

Internal factors include the economic condition of the schools; the staff and their educational backgrounds; facilities, materials, and equipment; and the administration. The students themselves, including their performance on tests, the numbers leaving before graduation, and numbers going to college, affect strategic planning. A major consideration is the general mobility of students. Schools in poorer communities must accommodate constant transfers of students for many reasons, ranging from the need to move before the rent is due to parents' job changes.

Moving farther into the 21st century, the world is witnessing what happens as an outcome of a pandemic. The statistics about children coming from homes where both parents worked[6] showed an increase in both male and female single-parent households from 2000 to 2010. In many cases, during the pandemic that single parent was able to work from home, but also was charged with greater responsibility for helping their children "attend" virtual classes and do their homework. In many cases, this was too great a challenge (for both parents and students), and the resulting loss of learning may be felt for many years to come.

For many children, school closures during the pandemic meant the end of important school programs such as after-school care, breakfasts, and snacks. In many areas, schools worked to establish ways to continue this provision of food from the school (often in concert with other community agencies and entities). In addition to the provision of digital resources and many other strategies to address equity, librarians took the opportunity to send requested books home with food deliveries.

Restructuring and Administration

Schools have undergone major restructuring, especially in leadership. Under school-based management or site-based management schemes, school programs have been decentralized and the decision-making process is undertaken by teachers, staff, and parents in individual buildings. No longer are central office administrators and staff making decisions across the entire district.

One of the reasons for this restructuring is the change in tenure and tasks of superintendents, who may be chosen to "fix" problems in a school district. Such fixes sometimes fail when those changes do not please some of the school staff and teachers, the community, or organizations such as labor unions within the community. In 1993, the longest tenure of a school superintendent in a major city in the United States was six years. The American Association of School Administrators (AASA) publishes studies every six years. Its 2000 study dispelled the fairly widespread notion that superintendents have a short tenure, maybe two and a half years. In fact, they usually have 14- to 17-year careers, but they work in two or three school districts, averaging five to six years in each. The 2020 AASA Decennial Study of the American School Superintendent reported that "the average tenure of superintendents was between 1 and 13 years with most superintendents serving 4 years in the same district."[7] A study by Grissom and Andersen[8] shortened that number of years to three in their study of superintendents in California schools. The challenges faced by superintendents may also describe the challenges of school librarians: energetic new leader assumes position with plans for revitalization, only to clash with a dysfunctional school board or impatient community.

The tasks facing many superintendents and assistant superintendents have become more business oriented. They now justify funding and seek outside sources of revenue, maintain buildings, negotiate with bargaining units, and oversee legal matters relating to students and teachers, among other tasks. They have little time to focus on curriculum and even less time to direct curricular reviews. In fact, one current idea is to replace the superintendent with a businessperson rather than an educator.

Standardized Testing

Another trend that is affecting schools and school staff is a redesign of the evaluation of student performance, placing it back in the hands of developers of standardized tests. "Developers of scholastic tests have inadvertently become the overseers of a very powerful instrument of education policy making: achievement tests."[9] This means that "local control over schools is also being lost to private organizations, namely test developers. Despite the significant and growing role that their products play in educational decisions, these testing companies face little government regulation or supervision . . . [being] governed by virtually no regulatory structures at either the federal or state levels."[10]

In the past, standardized achievement test developers created their tests on a generally similar curriculum scope and sequence not found in U.S. elementary and secondary educational programs because the nation did not have a national curriculum. In the past, the assumption underpinning mass testing was that the education and thought processes of students were similar. Haney and Madaus suggest that "the term *educational testing* is something of a malapropism, since most standardized testing has far less to do with the teaching of individual teachers and the learning of individual students than it does with the bureaucratic organization of schools."[11] The focus on No Child Left Behind and the Common Core State Standards (CCSS) reinforced the era of testing student performance. These have lost favor in many school districts and are being replaced. Attention paid to and subsequent increase in funding for charter schools has further reduced resources available for public education.

Challenges with Charter Schools, Home Schooling, and Vouchers

During the 1990s, an effort began to provide public funding for private education, long a greatly debated issue in the United States. One compromise was legislation for charter schools, a system in which private individuals are given the same funds per pupil for an approved school as would be given to the public school that the children would otherwise be attending. According to the U.S. Department of Education's National Center for Education Statistics,

> a *public charter school* is a publicly funded school that is typically governed by a group or organization under a legislative contract—a charter. . . . The charter exempts the school from certain state or local rules and regulations. . . . Between school years 2000–01 and 2017–18, the percentage of all public schools in the United States . . . that were charter schools increased from 2 to 7 percent, and the total number of charter schools increased from approximately 2,000 to 7,200.
>
> The percentage of all public school students who attended public charter schools increased from 1 to 6 percent between fall 2000 and fall 2017. During this period, public charter school enrollment increased steadily, from 0.4 million students in fall 2000 to 3.1 million students in fall 2017—an overall increase of 2.7 million students. In contrast, the number of students attending

traditional public schools increased by 1.3 million between fall 2000 and fall 2005, and then decreased by 0.7 million between fall 2005 and fall 2017, for a net increase of 0.6 million students.[12]

Charter schools, while publicly funded, are governed by a group or organization under a contract with the state. The charter exempts the school from some local or state rules and regulations. In return, charter schools must meet accountability standards, and their contracts are reviewed at intervals (usually every three to five years). If guidelines on curriculum and management or the established standards are not met, a charter school's contract may be revoked.

Although the first charter schools were privately funded, public school districts determined to initiate charter and magnet schools to keep education funds from the state within the district and to provide an attractive alternative to the traditional program. Administrators and teachers were given the freedom to develop what would be an attractive curriculum for parents and their children to keep those children in the local schools. Although charter schools were often touted as providing a better alternative to traditional public schools, often they are disproportionately segregated. In some states, charter schools are required to mirror the demographics of the local school district; however, this does not always happen.

Another alternative to traditional education has been homeschooling. Many parents have adopted homeschooling as an alternative because they feel they can offer more individualized instruction at home. They do not believe that a lock-step curriculum matches the learning styles of their children. Others homeschool so they can provide more religious training for their children.

Many students who are homeschooled take part in some school activities, such as band or chorus, and use materials from the school library. Meeting the needs of homeschooled children is a new challenge for the librarian.

Proposals to offer parents vouchers to send their children to a specific school, either public or private, come and go. Parents can take a voucher for the funds allocated for their child to any school: public, private, or even church-related.

Remote and Hybrid Learning

Online education is not a new concept. Correspondence courses were available to elementary students beginning at the end of the 19th century. As electronic transmission became available in the mid-20th century, students living on ranches in Australia were taught by radio. In Indiana, courses were made available by transmission from an airplane flying overhead. In 1994–1995, a public school, the Utah Electronic High School, offered supplemental courses, with much print-based correspondence.[13]

In September 2003, the National American Council for Online Learning (NACOL) was created. Then, only two years later, in October 2005, the name was changed to the International Association for K–12 Online Learning (iNACOL), and the membership now includes school districts, charter schools, and state education agencies, among others. They defined *online learning* as "education in which instruction and content are delivered primarily over the Internet."[14] Print-based correspondence was replaced by Internet-based components such as videocassettes and educational software programs with significant instructional content. Christensen, Horn, and Johnson (2008), in their book *Disrupting Class,* predicted that the majority of K–12 students would receive their education by online learning within the next decade.[15] iNACOL stated in 2011 that "online learning is becoming a common feature in public schools across the globe especially at the secondary level."[16] In 2006, Michigan required that all students have some form of online learning experience before graduating. Lincoln said that "requirements have been implemented to give Michigan students the skills and knowledge to succeed in the 21st century and drive the state's economic success in the global economy."[17] New Mexico, Alabama, and Florida have followed Michigan's lead.

The COVID-19 pandemic changed everything. Schools closed for in-class experiences and teachers were expected to create and present lessons in the online environment. The American Association of School Librarians (AASL) conducted several snapshot surveys throughout the pandemic to assess how school librarians adapted their services during the pandemic. The results, available at the *Knowledge Quest* website,[18] provide insight into what school librarians can contribute. What began as emergency remote learning became a way of life for teachers and learners.

History of School Libraries in the United States

As stated at the beginning of this chapter, the history of school libraries in the United States is somewhat shorter than that of other types of libraries. School libraries are indeed an educational innovation of the 20th century. The first professionally trained school librarian, Mary Kingsbury, was appointed in 1900.[19]

Prior to 1900, schools had built collections of books into libraries to the point that, in 1876, *Public Libraries in the United States* reported 826 schools of secondary rank with libraries containing nearly 1 million volumes, or a little over 1,000 volumes per library.[20] Between 1876 and 1900, statistics reported the number of volumes but not the numbers of high school libraries, so further comparisons are not possible.

Growth in the number of libraries was slow, and growth of the collections was even slower. In 1913, Edward D. Greenman wrote, "Of the 10,000 public high schools in the country at the present time, not more than 250 possess collections containing 3,000 volumes or over."[21] He continued, "The libraries are well managed, and are frequently under the supervision of a trained librarian. The students are given practical training in the use of the library, in cataloging, classification and in the value of reference books."[22]

The importance of school libraries was recognized when the American Library Association, which had been founded in 1876, created a School Library Section in 1914. This followed the first inclusion of school libraries in an ALA publication, the *Manual of Library Economy*, in 1913. The National Education Association had previously created a library section of its membership in 1896. The condition of school libraries was further described in 1915 by Mary E. Hall, the second person to be appointed a school librarian in the United States, when she was named to the Girls High School in Brooklyn in 1903. She described her "modern" high school library:

> To have as your visitors each day, from 500 to 700 boys and
> girls of all nationalities and all stations in life, to see them
> come eagerly crowding in, 100 or more every 40 minutes, and
> to realize that for four of the most important years of their lives

it is the opportunity of the library to have a real and lasting
influence upon each individual boy and girl, gives the librarian
a feeling that her calling is one of high privilege and great
responsibility.[23]

The activities were rapidly outgrowing a single reading room, and new facilities were being built that included a librarian's office or workroom and a
library classroom. Hall offered all that was available in new technologies to
her students:

> The library classroom adjoins the library reading room and
> should be fitted up to have as little of the regular classroom
> atmosphere as possible. It should be made quite as attractive as
> the reading room and have its interesting pictures on the walls,
> its growing plants and its library furniture. Chairs with tablet
> arms on which pupils can take notes, one or more tables around
> which a small class can gather with their teacher and look over
> beautiful illustrated editions or pass mounted pictures and
> postcards from one to another, should surely form a feature of
> this classroom. . . .
>   There should be cases for large mounted lithographs . . .
> for maps and charts, lantern slides, mounted pictures, and
> clippings. A radiopticon or lantern with the projectoscope in
> which a teacher can use not only lantern slides but postcards,
> pictures in books and magazines, etc. . . . For the English work
> and, indeed for German and French, a Victrola with records
> which make it possible for students to hear the English and
> other songs by famous singers, will help them to realize what a
> lyric poem is. . . . This room will be used by the librarian for all
> her classes in the use of reference books and library tools, it will
> constantly service teachers of history, Latin, German, French,
> and be a boon to the departments of physical and commercial
> geography. After school it will be a center for club work.
> Reading clubs can be made more interesting. . . . Classes will
> be scheduled for a regular class recitation there when a teacher
> wishes the aid of the room in awakening interest.[24]

Hall goes on to say that this library had come a long way from "the dreary
room with its glass cases and locked doors, its forbidding rows of unbroken
sets of standard authors, its rules and regulations calculated to discourage
any voluntary reading."[25]
  Despite the enthusiasm of Mary Hall and others, school libraries developed slowly. The impetus to expand secondary school libraries accelerated
in the mid-1920s, when regional accrediting agencies specified a high school
library with a trained librarian as a requirement for all schools seeking to
be accredited by their associations.

School Library Standards

- *Standard Library Organization and Equipment for Secondary Schools of Different Sizes,* 1920
- *Elementary School Library Standards,* 1925
- *School Libraries for Today and Tomorrow,* 1945

- *Standards for School Library Programs,* 1960
- *Standards for School Media Programs,* 1969
- *Media Programs: District and School,* 1975
- *Information Power,* 1988
- *Information Power: Building Partnerships for Learning,* 1998
- *Standards for the 21st Century Learner,* 2007
- *Empowering Learners: Guidelines for School Library Media Programs,* 2009
- *National School Library Standards for Learners, School Librarians, and School Libraries,* 2017

Although elementary school library standards were published in 1925, not many elementary schools had libraries or librarians. Even if monies were allocated for the purchase of library books, these books were kept in individual classroom collections and the size and quality of such collections varied greatly.

As mentioned earlier in this chapter, the Soviet Union's launch of the Sputnik satellite in the late 1950s prompted Congress to provide funds for materials and equipment to supplement classroom textbooks. Many school librarians were able to add to their collections to make these resources available to all teachers.

A Rutgers University professor, Mary Virginia Gaver, conducted two studies. The first, "Effectiveness of Centralized School Library Service (Phase 1) 1959–1960," reported the value of high school libraries. Her second, "Effectiveness of Centralized Library Service in Elementary Schools, 1963," researched that value in the elementary school. Her study was the basis of David Loertscher's doctoral dissertation in 1973 and the precursor of the Lance studies carried out at the beginning of the 21st century (discussed in chapter 6).

Several other events in the early 1960s had a great impact on the expansion of school libraries and the initiation of the concept of elementary school libraries in the United States. These are reported here because they are representative of the successful methods needed to improve school libraries and confirm the efforts of the school librarians who led with these developments. The first was the completion in 1960 of *Standards for School Library Programs,* which updated *School Libraries for Today and Tomorrow,* published in 1945.[26]

Immediately following the 1960 publication of *Standards,* the American Association of School Librarians received a grant from the Knapp Foundation to assist in the development of school libraries. Awarded in December 1962, the Knapp Foundation grant of $1.13 million was to be used for a five-year demonstration program to be conducted in three phases.

Another event that affected the development of school libraries was the publication in 1964 of a report by Mary Helen Mahar and Doris C. Holladay for the U.S. Office of Education showing that fewer than 50 percent of U.S. elementary schools had libraries.[27] The report attracted the interest of private industry, and additional materials were prepared to bring the plight of school libraries to the attention of the public.

These efforts in the early 1960s also caught the attention of Congress. Cora Paul Bomar, head supervisor in the Library and Instructional Materials Section of the North Carolina Department of Public Instruction (1951–1969), in her discussions with members of Congress, put on the "saddest face one could ever imagine" because she had "a vision of 10 million children going to 40,000 schools with no library."[28]

The lobbying efforts of the American Library Association's Washington office and the concentrated efforts of key school librarians across the country resulted in passage of the Elementary and Secondary Education Act (ESEA) in 1965. Funds were allocated in Title II specifically to purchase library materials. These funds were then combined with local initiatives and volunteer efforts to build school libraries in elementary buildings and expand libraries in secondary schools.

Modifications in this law occurred as federal funding guidelines were rewritten and categorical restrictions lessened. Librarians now competed with other programs not only for declining federal dollars but also for declining state and local funding. The monies spent for microcomputers further decreased funding available for other types of materials and equipment in school libraries; and in the early 1980s, the school library picture seemed bleak.

In the late 1980s and early 1990s, site-based management changes meant that many staffs did not include a school librarian as part of the essential programs for students. In other states, certification requirements came under review, and it was no longer considered necessary for the library staff person to hold a teacher certification.

Mid-decade, the DeWitt-Wallace/Reader's Digest Foundation funded a $40 million initiative to create model elementary and middle school libraries.[29] This Library Power project, administered by the AASL, involved 19 districts that received up to $1.2 million over three years to increase their collections, train staff, and improve facilities. Although the foundation ended this phase of funding in 1998, the impact of these models helped librarians make a case for strong school libraries.

For the past 30 years, progress in school libraries has been affected by the development of new technologies. School librarians who had added audiovisual resources to their practice in the 1960s and 70s adopted computers and software applications at the close of the 20th century. Not only was the card catalog replaced by the OPAC, but reference collections became largely available online. Digital resources became readily available in many areas, although economic disparity in school districts caused differing levels of access across the country.

At the beginning of the 21st century, teachers came under pressure to demonstrate student achievement through testing because of the No Child Left Behind Act and implementation of the Common Core State Standards curriculum, while also meeting the guidelines of the standards movement through the content areas. These pressures were very frustrating to teachers who needed help in understanding the CCSS and in keeping their students totally focused on the textbooks so they could pass the test. School librarians worked to help teachers understand and implement the new standards and to help change their approach to instruction as advocated by the CCSS. As with other "innovations," change in government administration can overturn previously mandated programs.

In short, school library standards have evolved over time just as education, information media, and technology have changed.

The School Library Environment Today

Much of the library environment today resembles that of the immediate past. The ease of use of Google, which offers free access to information, continues to reinforce a perception that libraries are less needed and that paying for resources in a library room is not necessary. Because many users are not aware of possible problems with, or even think to question, the accuracy of information they find, there is a hugely increased and critical need for librarians to teach how to determine the accuracy and relevance of information located almost anywhere. Questioning results and separating fact from falsehood have become difficult tasks in a world where social media allows everyone to share "information," making it more important than ever that librarians and teachers help students become critical consumers of information.

The most recent standards for school libraries provide guidance for meeting the challenges of an ever-evolving school and information environment. Published in 2018 by AASL, the *National School Library Standards for Learners, School Librarians, and School Libraries* provide guidance for what students should be learning, what and how school librarians teach and do, and how the school library should function to accomplish the important task of preparing students for the future.

One opportunity has tremendously accelerated school librarians' ability to collaborate with teachers. With the challenges of the COVID-19 pandemic, schools moved totally into an online environment. Teachers who were beginning to write ebooks or develop open-access materials for their textbooks in their courses found themselves adapting to the totally online environment. School librarians became even more necessary to help teachers find information, use it in accordance with copyright laws and issues, and move into a digital environment. This presented an opportunity for school librarians, who became essential in helping teachers to recreate their courses for new platforms.

> So, what exactly did school librarians do during COVID-19? Short answer, everything. Unlike most educators, school librarians are uniquely positioned to serve the entire student body, teaching and administrative staff, and the community at large. This provides them with the advantage of "connecting dots" and identifying gaps in their community. For some, this meant ensuring that students had access to technology and the Internet. For some, it meant creating resources to check in on students' well-being and emotional health. For some, it meant connecting families to community resources for food and employment information.[30]

School librarians had to determine ways to provide access to resources, services, and tools in this new environment. It was an extraordinary effort by all. Additionally, school librarians continue to advocate for equity of access for *all* students: providing resources in multiple formats as well as the tools needed for students to connect digitally.

As students returned to their physical schools after the pandemic, some of the activities that were successful will continue. The reliance of teachers, parents, and administrators on school librarians for access to technology and learning resources may lead to both greater responsibilities for school librarians and recognition of the invaluable role that school librarians play.

Key Takeaways

- Public education in the United States reflects and responds to changing social, political, and technological trends.

- The school library environment today has evolved beyond its traditional role of circulating print materials. It is an interactive, innovative, inclusive environment for students.

- Whether physical or digital, the library provides opportunities for students to achieve, learn, and grow, and develop a desire for lifelong learning.

Challenges to Promote Growth

1. Imagine the next set of standards. Project into the future. What predictions do you have for the upcoming changes? How does an understanding of the history of school libraries and public education help you to understand current and future practices and standards?
2. If you were to create a timeline of important, forward-thinking advances in school library history, what would be the top five entries on that timeline?

Notes

1. T. Hanchett. (n.d.). Rosenwald Schools. http://www.historysouth.org/rosenwaldhome

2. Legal Defense Fund. (1952, December 9). "What Was *Brown v. Board of Education*?" https://www.naacpldf.org/case-issue/landmark-brown-v-board-education

3. Theodore R. Sizer. (1986). "Rebuilding: First Steps by the Coalition of Essential Schools." *Phi Delta Kappan* 68 (September): 41.

4. U.S. Department of Education. (1991). *America 2000: An Education Strategy Sourcebook*. Washington, DC: U.S. Department of Education, 25.

5. Mike Bock. (2012). "Schools Tap into Online Fundraising to Expand Budgets." *Education Week* 32, no. 5 (September 26): 9.

6. U.S. Census Bureau, Housing and Household Economic Statistics Division, Fertility & Family Statistics Branch. (2006). "America's Families and Living Arrangements: 2006." https://www.census.gov/data/tables/2006/demo/families/families-living-arrangements.html

7. Meredith Mountford and Jayson W. Richardson. (2021). "Promoting Equity in the Modern Superintendency." *AASA Journal of Scholarship & Practice* 18, no. 3: 12.

8. Jason A. Grissom and Stephanie Andersen. (2012). "Why Superintendents Turn Over." *American Educational Research Journal* no. 6 (December): 1146–1147.

9. D. Monty Neill and Joe J. Medina. (1989). "Standardized Testing: Harmful to Educational Health." *Phi Delta Kappan* 71 (May): 688.

10. Richard J. Shavelson, Neil B. Carey, and Noreen M. Webb. (1990). "Indicators of Science Achievement: Options for a Powerful Policy Instrument." *Phi Delta Kappan* 72 (May): 692.

11. Walter Haney and George Madaus. (1989). "Searching for Alternatives to Standardized Tests: Whys, Whats, and Whithers." *Phi Delta Kappan* 71 (May): 684.

12. B. Hussar, J. Zhang, S. Hein, K. Wang, A. Roberts, J. Cui, M. Smith, F. Bullock Mann, A. Barmer, and R. Dilig. (2020). *The Condition of Education 2020* (NCES 2020-144, U.S. Department of Education). Washington, DC: National Center for Education Statistics. https://nces.ed.gov/pubsearch/pubsinfo. asp?pubid=2020144

13. DeLaina Tonks, Sarah Weston, David Wiley, and Michael K. Barbour. (2013). "'Opening' a New Kind of High School: The Story of the Open High School of Utah." *International Review of Research in Open & Distance Learning* 14, no. 1: 255–271.

14. International Association for Online Learning. (2011, April). "Fast Facts About Online Learning." https://aurora-institute.org/wp-content/uploads/fun-facts -about-online-learning.pdf

15. Clayton M. Christensen, Michael B. Horn, and Curtis W. Johnson. (2008). *Disrupting Class: How Disruptive Innovation Will Change the Way the World Learns*. New York: McGraw-Hill.

16. International Association for Online Learning, *supra* n. 14.

17. Margaret L. Lincoln, "Online Education in Schools." In Sue Alman, Christinger Tomer, and Margaret L. Lincoln, eds. (2012). *Designing Online Learning: A Primer for Librarians*. Santa Barbara, CA: Libraries Unlimited.

18. https://knowledgequest.aasl.org/tag/aasl-survey

19. Blanche Woolls. *Ideas for School Library Media Programs*. Castle Rock, CO: Hi Willow Research and Publishing, 1996.

20. U.S. Office of Education. (1876). *Public Libraries in the United States: Their History, Condition, and Management* (Special Report, Department of the Interior, Bureau of Education, Part I). Washington, DC: U.S. Government Printing Office, 1876, 58. Reprinted in Melvin M. Bowie. (1986). *Historic Documents of School Libraries*. Englewood, CO: Hi Willow Research and Publishing.

21. Edward D. Greenman. (1913). "The Development of Secondary School Libraries." *Library Journal* 38 (April): 184.

22. *Ibid.*, 184, 186.

23. Mary E. Hall. (1915). "The Development of the Modern High School Library." *Library Journal* 40 (September): 627.

24. *Ibid.*, 629.

25. *Ibid.*

26. American Association of School Librarians. (1960). *Standards for School Library Programs*. Chicago: American Library Association; Committee on Post-War Planning of the American Library Association. (1945). *School Libraries for Today and Tomorrow: Functions and Standards*. Chicago: American Library Association).

27. Mary Helen Mahar and Doris C. Holladay. (1964). *Statistics of Public School Libraries, 1960–61, Part 1, Basic Tables*. Washington, DC: U.S. Office of Education, 1964.

28. Cora Paul Bomar, quoted in Bertha M. Cheatham. (1986). "AASL: Momentous in Minneapolis." *School Library Journal* 33 (November): 38.

29. "Can Library Power Survive Without Its Chief Funder?" *School Library Journal* 43 (April 1977): 10.

30. Allison Mackley and Heather Lister. (2021). *School Librarians in the Second Wave: A Supplement and Follow-up to "School Librarians and the COVID Slide."* Every Library Institute. https://www.everylibraryinstitute.org /school_librarians_in_second_wave_report

3
Getting That Position

Your work is going to fill a large part of your life, and the only way to be truly satisfied is to do what you believe is great work. And the only way to do great work is to love what you do.

—Steve Jobs

Essential Questions

- What must you do to establish your credentials?
- What are the most effective strategies for getting your first professional position?

This chapter will help you think through your own professional preparation options, strategies for achieving accreditation, and ways of finding that first position. Being a school librarian may just be the best job in the school if you are well prepared to show your community what it should look like. Very often you have the freedom to refocus an inherited program and move it toward excellence by doing the very things you love doing. First, begin with the details involved in getting hired.

License/Credential to Practice

In almost all public schools, the librarian will need an educator's credential as well as a credential as a librarian. Requirements vary from state to state, so you will need to investigate the credentialing process if you choose to work in a state other than the one in which your preparation program was located or if your (likely online) program serves a national audience. Private schools may require only a teaching degree; some may require only a library degree. Many charter schools do not hire librarians at all.

Once upon a time, a student called one of the authors to discuss obtaining certification. This student had graduated but had neglected to apply for certification immediately. The reason given was that no one had ever made it clear that an application process existed and that using it was necessary. This person assumed that the college granting the degree would automatically send an application for certification when a student graduated (although this seems a little like assuming that one would automatically receive a driver's license after taking a driver's education course). Because most certification applications must be accompanied by payment of a processing fee, it is unlikely that such a process will occur automatically. A grant of certification may be accomplished through a variety of means.

The state department of education staff reviews the transcript of an applicant to determine whether the applicant's record meets state requirements. The school where you did your coursework may process the credential paperwork if they have been approved to do so by some accrediting body.

In addition to the formal course preparation, some states certify candidates based on their performance on a test the state has created or by accepting the results of a nationally prepared test such as the Praxis exam, which usually consists of one exam assessing core knowledge (reading, writing, and mathematics) and another assessing the candidate's subject specialty knowledge. Online practice tests and books can help you gain confidence with the types of questions presented on these exams. You may not want to wait till the very end of your program to register for or take these exams, as they may be a requirement for employment.

Some states require no specific college curriculum beyond teacher certification because such states recognize scores on a Praxis test as adequate evidence that an educator can work as a school librarian. In those states, an appropriate score on the Praxis exam serves to demonstrate competency.

State departments of education may grant certificates to persons with bachelor's degrees. The number of semester hours required at the undergraduate or graduate level varies greatly. Whereas some states require as little as 18 to 20 hours of library science at no specific level of instruction, others specify a master's degree as a requirement.

Such requirements may be located through each state's department of education. Some states have added a requirement for a competency test. Some preparation programs require their own competency assessments.

Every state handles the credentialing process differently, and you can usually find the requirements online. The sooner you apply after completing your prescribed coursework, the better, as many of these requirements change over time.

Because state requirements vary, the person in charge of the school library program at the pre-service university can best explain them. Competencies acquired in a program offered in one state may not automatically allow the graduate to be able to work as a school librarian in another state. Again, although some states require only a bachelor's degree, others require a master's. Some states grant simple out-of-state reciprocity, whereas other states offer a procedure for certified out-of-state teachers to become certified in the candidate's state of choice. Additional requirements may include a course in state history, completion of a higher-level degree, or passage of the aforementioned examinations. Specific requirements can be found on the teacher certification section of each state's department of education website.

While the American Association of School Librarians (AASL) officially adopted the professional title "school librarian" back in 2010, you may discover that the actual title of the credential varies across states.[1] The school librarian credential may alternately be referred to as *school library media specialist* or *coordinator*, *library teacher*, or *teacher librarian*. In some districts, titles have evolved to reflect librarians' growing responsibilities relating to technology integration. Recently, requirements as a technology specialist or instructional coordinator have been considered by some districts as adequate for running a school library. In these cases, the appointed person will likely lack the skills and dispositions for effective library practice.

Different types of credentials may be awarded depending upon the need for teachers within a state and the length of time before the credential expires. Credentials have such labels as emergency, temporary, or permanent. When the supply of candidates is inadequate to fill the positions available, persons may be able to begin working in a school library under an "emergency" credential. Often, those candidates have existing educational certification in another specialty. Graduates of undergraduate programs may receive a "temporary" certificate. Usually, persons who begin their careers with a temporary certificate must replace it with "permanent" certification within a specified period of time. Requirements for permanent certification also vary. Some states require teaching experience but no further education beyond a bachelor's degree, with some library instruction or passing a test; others demand a master's degree. Any certification may also require the holder to update the certification through continuing education at specified intervals.

Finally, many states require criminal background checks for licensure. States may also require self-reporting regarding convictions or teaching license suspension. In addition, schools or districts may require proof of up-to-date vaccinations and boosters for their new hires.

It is the responsibility of school librarians completing their programs of instruction to learn the requirements for certification and to apply for and receive their certificates as soon as those requirements have been met. Certification is an important credential to list on a résumé or an employment application. Employers may not consider résumés that do not list a date of achieved certification. Penalties may apply if the certification process is not completed in a timely fashion. In some states, one must complete the competency program in place when applying for the certificate. If certificate requirements change, it might be necessary to take more coursework or complete more requirements at a later date. Although these additional courses may be considered continuing professional education, it is preferable to choose continuing education experiences based on one's own needs and interests rather than on the need to make up some "deficiency" dictated by the state department of education.

One last factor may be—and will continue to be—critical in your own preparation. Whether your state has minimal or extensive requirements for earning the credential, you might examine those requirements to see if they fully prepare you for aspirational practice as a school librarian capable of leading a truly innovative library program. Examine position descriptions in your area. Do you possess the skills that will make you attractive for those positions? If you feel that you lack any particular skills, or feel that your current ability may not allow you to excel and lead a forward-thinking, innovative program, you might want to supplement your knowledge. Often skills in integrating new technologies and emerging pedagogical strategies can be obtained and enhanced through a growing array of free or inexpensive online professional development opportunities.

In fact, many states require continuing and documented professional development for all district educators following initial certification in order to obtain permanent certification or meet a professional growth requirement.

These opportunities include coursework in a higher education institution, attendance at conferences or webinars where you will be able to add to your knowledge and skills and earn certificates, or presentations in your own school district. Whatever opportunities await you, you will not only want to be a lifelong learner yourself, you will want to model that practice for your learning community.

How to Find a Job

Sometimes, finding a job is a matter of being in the right spot at the right time. Librarians within a district usually know when someone is leaving or about to retire before a position is posted.

The Lance and Kachel SLIDE study[2] used federal data to document a 20-percent decline in the ranks of school librarians over a period of 10 years. The researchers noted that the decline inequitably affected already marginalized populations. In some areas, reduced funding for education may mean that school librarians are furloughed or returned to classrooms, with the library turned over to clerical staff, or to volunteers, or (in some cases) closed. In other areas, you will find administrators actively seeking a highly prepared professional to lead a dynamic program. If you are already a classroom teacher, an administrator who knows of your excellence and interests may ask if you are willing to make a switch and offer support for your further library and information science (LIS) education.

Many universities providing the school library credential offer practicum or field experience programs to allow those without any classroom experience to try out their skills under the direction of an exemplary mentor. These experiences are often state-mandated. Such experiences can be enormously helpful if your mentor is a true model of the latest practices in planning and collaborating with teachers, integrating information literacy skills into instruction, doing digital curation, building collections, and building a reading culture. The practicum site can make a major difference in your professional growth, so it is critical that you investigate carefully to find the type of school and mentor who will push you to develop your own skills, allow you to contribute meaningfully, and in turn write solid recommendations for your professional portfolio. If possible, it is best to shop around for this placement to find appropriate fits. Checking out the prospective library's website may offer important clues about the program, its role in the learning culture of the school, and its focus and initiatives, as well as the technology expertise of the librarian.

What to Prepare for the Job Hunt

Next, the student should prepare a résumé and cover letter. Résumés should be carefully formatted, attractive, and professional looking. You will likely be required to upload these documents, as well as lists of references or reference letters, into a digital application system to facilitate online review of the candidates.

Before preparing these documents, *do your research*. Your documents must be focused on the specific position, and take into consideration the target school or district's mission, vision, focus, initiatives, and culture. Your résumé and cover letter should be up to date, and include contact information, educational background, and work experience, with emphasis on positions relating to education and libraries.

The cover letter should be customized, addressed to the prospective employer. Begin with how you heard about the job and why you decided to apply. This might give you an opportunity to briefly demonstrate your knowledge of the school or district. Follow up with an explanation of why you are particularly well suited for the position. Without rehashing every granular detail in your résumé, highlight your preparation, relevant abilities ("superpowers"), and driving interests as they relate to your potential contributions. As your first impression and potential foot in the door, this letter should be engaging and avoid jargon; of course, it must be closely proofread to assure that the reader will see that you are articulate and careful. Do your research and tailor the letter to demonstrate that you know at least a little about the school and community.

Your résumé should include listings of certifications, awards, and memberships in professional organizations. Brief descriptions of any related positions and responsibilities you have already fulfilled should also be included. Be sure to emphasize any experiences that demonstrate how you can both support and partner with classroom teachers. Consider listing any talents that might translate to your ability to sponsor clubs or extracurriculars. When possible, hyperlink elements of exemplary work to allow others to dig more deeply into your existing portfolio. You may also choose to link your résumé to your growing digital portfolio. It is important that your résumé prominently note your existing or upcoming state certification. Often résumés are initially sorted by qualifications, with reviewers considering only candidates with current or pending certification.

Résumés generally fit into three categories; you may want to be strategic in selecting the format that best highlights your strengths and stage of experience. You will find many models of effective use of these three résumé types online:

- Chronological résumés showcase your work experience, with the most recent positions at the beginning. If you are an entry-level job seeker or if you have been working in the field consistently, this traditional approach might be an appropriate choice.

- Functional résumés highlight skills and may be an appropriate choice for the candidate who has little formal school library experience or employment gaps; this is especially pertinent for people with highly relevant skills and talents outside the library or education fields. For instance, those who are shifting careers will want to highlight significant talents they have demonstrated in using technologies, writing successful grants, doing effective marketing, or their fluency in multiple languages, rather than burying those skills at the bottom of a timeline.

- Combination résumés balance both skills and experience. This hybrid approach may be the best choice for mid-career job seekers or highly qualified candidates who would benefit by shining a spotlight on exceptional professional accomplishments.

As a serious candidate for employment in a school, you will want to control your social media profile and ensure that employers see you at your professional best. Use your email signature to lead employers to your online professional profiles (on LinkedIn, for instance) and to leverage your website as your online portfolio. If you engage in professional networking online, you may choose to share your Twitter, Instagram, or other handles. Clean up any content you would not be proud to share professionally. Finally, most administrators want to know a little about the applicant's relevant interests and hobbies. One applicant might be chosen over another because of an ability to sponsor an extracurricular activity such as the school newscast, the tennis or debate team, the musical, or the newspaper. It may be beneficial to mention these special talents in your interview.

After the résumé is prepared and the placement file is complete, the student may begin the job search. Professors in a school library training program often have information about openings because school officials check with such training programs when they have jobs to fill. If the college or university provides a placement service, it will post any job openings sent to the placement office.

Many state library associations provide job hotlines. Although these may list more job openings for other types of libraries than for school libraries, they are a good first place to seek information. In addition, school library associations and state departments of education may offer listings.

Another job-search method used by some students is to request that their field experience or practicum experience be assigned in a school district where they might like to find a permanent position. This is positive for both sides. In addition to the potential advantage of getting a foot in the door, the prospective school librarian can assess the school district at the same time school district personnel are reviewing the competencies of the student. This is another reason to strategically select your field experience placement.

The network of school librarians is another source of information. These persons have immediate knowledge of resignations, transfers, long-term leaves, and retirements in the school district and may have information about neighboring districts as well.

Professional magazines and journals (especially their online feeds) provide information about openings in school districts. However, because school libraries are situated in the world of education, school listings are not usually posted on library-specific job boards. Online portals like REAP (https://www.usreap.net), a national teacher placement service, offer lists of school librarian openings by state from both school districts and private schools. State departments of education maintain online portals listing district openings. Job seekers also can talk with persons in federal agencies responsible for library programs. Special employment portals serve those posting and seeking positions in independent, international, and Department of Defense schools.

Professional association conferences are a source of information about job openings. Many students attend a state or national conference before they graduate, using that opportunity to talk with school library and other technology professionals about situations in various school districts. These experiences may aid the decision process by helping match skills to preferences. Many professional associations maintain their own digital lists of openings, allowing their members to post openings in their districts along with information about the actual position and how to apply. Of course, candidates will also want to keep their eyes on the employment section of their highly desired districts' websites.

Finally, openings for temporary positions occur when school librarians take sabbaticals or leaves of absence. Accepting a temporary position may lead to a permanent position in the district. When interviewing for these positions, it is wise to discover one's options. If you are called back for a second interview, it would be wise to ask about the possibility that this position will become permanent in the immediate or near future. Do others in the district wish to have a permanent library position? Will the school district accept your resignation if a permanent position opens in another location? The responses to these questions will help the job seeker to determine the possibility for permanent employment after a temporary position closes or ends. If you have established a good professional learning network (PLN), the connections in your network may also be useful in helping you find your dream job. Building such a network is discussed in greater depth in chapter 12.

Plan to keep your portfolio current. Join networks in your state and continually grow your network of professional inspiration. Depending on an entry-level credential is no longer an acceptable option. Think of yourself as you do your personal physician who, you hope, is constantly updating knowledge, skills, and practices.

Interviewing for the Position

Your preparation for landing the job begins immediately after you have made the interview appointment. The interview process goes both ways. While the school is conducting an interview for a librarian, the librarian applicant needs to be prepared to interview the school administrator and the staff and look carefully at the facility. Thorough preparation for an interview will help the applicant remain confident during this process.

Do not be surprised if your first interview, or subsequent visits, are virtual. These may require a little strategy in terms of how you appear online. Professionalism is key: consider your posture, your lighting, and what your setting says about you, and do your best to guard against technical issues or family interruptions.

After reviewing the criteria listed as essential for an application and interview and making any discreet inquiries of those working in the district or neighboring districts, the applicant can formulate a list of intelligent questions to ask about the specific school district. It is wise to research the district in much the same way the administrators will be checking the applicant. Just as the administrators attempt to determine whether the applicant will fit the district, applicants will want to know if the situation will suit them.

You will want to show you are invested in knowing about the community. Examine available data about demographics and academic standing. Check out available course catalogs. Also get a feel for the culture of the learning environment by exploring social media accounts and various teacher websites, and, of course the library website. See how you connect to vision, mission, and goal statements as well as special initiatives and events. And imagine the roles you might play as part of the team within that learning community.

Examine the school's website. Imagine how and where you might fit in with and use it. You will want to become familiar with the district's or school's vision, mission, and any major initiatives. Of course, dig just as deeply regarding the school library. Carefully review the library's web presence for a sense of how well supported the program is, which resources are available, and how integrated the library is into the learning culture of the school.

The principal of the school is a key person from whom to gather information. At this interview, try to find or create an opportunity to ask questions to determine the value an administrator places on having an excellent school library program. It is usually not too difficult to recognize when a principal is not interested in the library. Ask to be taken for a tour, and see what the principal points out to you when the door to the library is opened and when you walk through the facility.

You may ask some general questions about how well the library is supported and about what technologies are currently available or used in the school and about the administrator's perceptions of the librarian's role as a technology leader. Try to find out about any staff assigned to the library and their responsibilities. Do students or parents regularly volunteer?

Often, a dream job means seeking a dream principal who not only has a vision but will also encourage you to spread your wings. A great principal may be open to a major renovation or may even have been hired to reimagine a new school. Such a principal may be seeking an ally, as well as a leader, to place in this key position.

Principals may have some ideas about the atmosphere in a library, and their ideas are paramount in understanding what is expected from students. Although these days it is less likely, a principal interviewing you may share concern about noise in the library. If so, you may need to explain that noise does not mean students are out of control; students make constructive noise, which is not chaos but active learning. Experience, attitude, and abilities to manage a productive library space may come up in the interview, so you should be prepared to explore your vision for the types of learning activities that may fill a library with constructive buzz.

Applicants should always be on time for an interview. This means making sure of the location of the building, the amount of time it takes to arrive, and how difficult it will be to locate parking. An attempt to be calm and relaxed will fail if unexpected traffic rerouting, missed turns, or lack of a parking space delay arrival. Consider a rehearsal drive.

The interview process is designed to find out as much about the applicant as possible. One or more persons will be asking questions. The applicant should listen carefully to the questions and direct the reply to the person who posed the question, not to the entire review panel. Questions should be answered as positively as possible, with appropriate mention of personal skills. Although an applicant should appear interested and enthusiastic about the position, it is important to act naturally. Acknowledge when you are unsure about a response rather than attempting a clever guess. Share that you hope to learn more about the topic brought up.

The old adage "the clothes make the person" may be worthy of serious consideration when preparing for your job interview. First impressions matter. While standards for professional attire have grown a bit more casual, if an applicant really wants the job, this is not the time to try out an extreme fashion trend. This is a time to look professional while not being afraid to show a bit of your personal style.

The interviewers hope to learn a great deal about applicants: what kind of person they are, their skills, their thoughts on education issues, their vision, and perhaps a little of their philosophy of education. Practicing how to interview can help prospective school librarians formulate careful answers quickly. You will likely be asked to "Tell us a little about yourself" and invited to ask questions of your interviewer(s) at the end. Be natural, but prepare these responses in advance. In addition, video tools such as Flip may help you practice and reflect on your responses to commonly asked questions. It is now common to be faced with scenario questions about how you might handle a particular situation relating to instruction or student engagement. Be prepared to share instruction you were proud of designing or implementing. You will find a variety of question lists on the playlist that includes the AASL School Librarian Interview Question Matrix (see the Additional Resources). You will also find a list of typical school librarian interview questions in Appendix B.

You are likely going to be asked, "Do you have any questions for us?" Unless an employer brings it up, it is best to leave questions relating to salary, benefits, and other such logistics to a second interview or for the conversation that involves an offer. Instead, ask questions that reflect and relate to your research about the district and the position. You might ask your interviewers questions relating to their vision for the school or the library program. A prepared applicant who asks pertinent questions that reflect their existing interest and knowledge of the school or district can learn much about a position during the interview.

Look for the right moment to mention the portfolio you carry along (or be ready to share a shortened link to it for interviewers to easily access). You likely began a portfolio during your pre-service program. It might not be a bad idea to also have a book in your bag in case you are asked what you are currently reading. Be prepared to have grade-level reading recommendations in mind in case you are asked questions about what you might be excited to share with students.

Be prepared to share a favorite instructional partnership or inquiry project as well as favorite databases or details on how you integrate digital tools. You may be faced with hypothetical scenarios. You may be asked to share a vision for your own school library.

Following an interview, it is courteous to send a thank-you. Your letter or email note should remind the interviewers of who you are. An effective note references specifics from your interview and serves to remind the review team who you are. Consider including names of those who were on the panel and mention any positive ideas you might have developed as a result of the conversation. At this time, you can restate your interest in the position.

Successful candidates are often invited back for a second interview, and that interview may involve instruction. If you are invited back for a "trial teach," try to find out as much as you can about the class, grade level, any required lesson plan templates, the teacher's learning objectives, the time allotted, and the resources available, especially your technology options. You may also be expected to reflect on the effectiveness of your instruction. Consider this an opportunity to reflect about what went well and how you might authentically improve the instruction next time around.

Coping with Reality

While it feels great to get an offer, not every offer may be the right one for you. If you are already employed, of course, you are in a better position to be able to decline a job offer. You may want to consider your own deal breakers. Did you sense any red flags in the interview? Would you be unhappy working with a fixed schedule? Were any questions asked about book selection that were inconsistent with your philosophy? Was the salary offered professionally insulting?

In the present climate, school librarians are being asked to take positions with multischool assignments, and these may have very strange configurations. Such positions typically come with a heavy load of frustration.

Your professional vision of making a difference may be compromised by the fact that there is little time to do anything but manage the tasks necessary to keep the facility going.

If this is the only position available, try to determine if any change will be possible within the year or if the assignment could be changed in any way to increase the time spent in one school: for example, perhaps for four to six weeks in exchange for that same rotation to be made with the other school(s) in the mix. This could allow time to demonstrate the types of collaboration that make the school librarian essential in the building. Remember, the first professional job you accept will likely not be your last. A less-than-perfect position may provide experience to prepare you for the next, as well as get your foot in the door.

Some argue that taking a position as the only librarian in a district that shows little respect for or knowledge of the role of the school library and librarian in the education of students is in some way endorsing that situation. The view of administrators about the role of the library in the school is critical. If they assume that the function is largely the management of a collection of books, they may be satisfied if you are a well-organized person who is doing a fine job in a one-faceted program: simply buying books for the library. Such views are difficult to change unless you have excellent persuasive powers and plan evidence-based strategies to present a different role for the library. Such jobs may satisfy some state requirement for administrators and may function as first-job stepping stones, but they are unsustainable as careers, and will likely lead to burnout.

Getting your license to practice and finding a job will open the door to a school library career. Chapter 4 offers suggestions and early innovations for your first weeks on the job.

Key Takeaways

- Credentialing requirements vary across states and sometimes districts. Before you even begin a program, do your homework!

- Preparation is essential for the school library job applicant. Learn about the mission, vision, and culture of the place you are hoping to serve. Do your homework!

Challenges to Promote Growth

1. Compare the regulations and competencies for certification in your state with those of an adjoining state or state in which you might like to apply for certification. Estimate the amount of time it will take to complete those requirements and determine whether you could complete some of them in your present program.
2. Request an application for certification from your state department of education or locate one online. Carefully read the instructions and confirm the requirements for certification. What information must be included?

For example, is a physical examination required? What clearances are needed? What fees are assessed, and what method of payment is suggested? Are college transcripts necessary? To whom is the form to be submitted? What is the probable length of time between submission and return of the certificate?

3. Search for a school librarian job posting that you would consider. Using the requirements and skills listed in the posting as a guide, draft a cover letter and résumé. Share them with a critical friend for comments about clarity, completeness, design, and its ability to interest your potential employer.

4. Locate the placement office on your campus or its website. What services do they offer? How do they post potential positions?

5. Write a list of three talking points you want to emphasize in your interview, along with strategies for responding with them even if you are not asked about those matters directly.

6. Generate a list of questions you might ask the principal or members of the interview panel at the end of an interview.

7. Using a video tool such as Flip, practice your response to the inevitable question "Tell us a little about yourself." Evaluate your response for engagement, energy, and what you would want to hear more about from yourself as a candidate.

8. What are the deal breakers for that first offer? Consider any factors that would prevent you from accepting your first job. How might you graciously turn down an offer?

Notes

1. "AASL Reclaims Basic Terminology: School Librarian." (2010, January 26). *American Libraries Magazine.* https://americanlibrariesmagazine.org/blogs/the-scoop/aasl-reclaims-basic-terminology-school-librarian

2. Keith Curry Lance and Debra E. Kachel. (2021, July). *Perspectives on School Librarian Employment in the United States, 2009–10 to 2018–19.* SLIDE: The School Librarian Investigation—Decline or Evolution? https://libslide.org/publications/perspectives

Part II
Going to Work

4
Beginning the Job

Culture eats strategy for breakfast.

> —Peter Drucker, consultant, educator, and author, considered the architect of modern management

Essential Question

- In what ways might insights about the complex culture of a school inform how you lead and transform teaching and learning in and beyond our school libraries?

Getting Started

Certification credential and signed contract in hand, you are ready to begin your first professional job as a librarian, and you are bursting with ambitious ideas and the desire to launch many of them immediately. As you launch *some* of these ideas, recognize that to make a truly significant impact, you will need to learn about the organizational and political structure of the school district—its culture—and then to focus on the local school environment and its climate. You are about to enter a very specific culture with a multitude of moving parts. To be able to plan and implement strategies within the culture called *school*, it is critical to understand the people around you: how they behave and interact, as well as their beliefs, norms, values, and patterns of behavior.

Through your observations and conversations, you will also be learning about climate. *School climate* describes the way students and educators experience the school. A positive school climate is often characterized as an environment that fosters feelings of safety, belonging, and trust. As you build relationships and accumulate social capital, you will be able to create a positive learning culture in your library that can extend and enhance positive culture and climate schoolwide.

Entering a new school can be a bit daunting, especially if you are new to a career as an educator. School culture is not always obvious on the surface. It is often invisible, but always pervasive, so the more you know, the better able you will be to ensure that the school library program serves and engages the entire learning community.

Attack the obvious. There should be documents. Seek out local vision and mission statements, school improvement plans, strategic plans, scores on standardized assessments, portrait-of-a-graduate statements, relevant policy documents, and commitments to educational programs and initiatives. Carefully examine school and district websites on which you may find these and other documents to discern priorities.

Look, listen, and learn. You can begin by observing leadership strategies and relationships in the building. Remember that not every leader in your building will have an explicit role. Look for those who have influence as well as those who have titles. Listen to teachers as they talk about what is going on in their classrooms. Learn from what you see and hear. Attempting to institute and manage a program without understanding administrative and leadership practices or school culture may cause the school librarian to make unintentional missteps. Find out what is actually going on and learn who is supervising your work. Your initial meeting with the person who will supervise your work may be just a welcome meeting, but it may also help you learn about expectations for your performance.

Finding Out Who Supervises Your Work

You will also want to discover which specific building administrator is directly responsible for observing and supporting your work. When a school district has a coordinator or director of library programs (a situation more common in larger districts), it is a sign that the school district administration believes in the importance of the library program. It also ensures that building-level practitioners have knowledgeable administrative specialists to approach with questions specific to school libraries and their operation. You may have met that person during your interview.

Alternately, school librarians may be supervised and evaluated by administrators who have several other assignments and whose background may not include any library experience. If this is the case, you will need to connect with the other school librarians in your district to help you get oriented to your position in the school and within the district.

When no district-level library person exists, it is less likely that school librarians will meet regularly as a group for in-service sessions or that an advocate will speak up for library programs to higher administration. During the interview process, you may have been introduced to a librarian in the district who was assigned or stepped up to keep librarians informed; this person may even hold an information orientation at the beginning of the semester. You may also be assigned to a librarian in another school who will serve as your mentor. You will also likely be assigned a building mentor to help you acclimate locally.

As you gain experience, you will want to consider your own leadership role in the building and beyond. You may discover that no meetings are planned for the district's librarians. If this is your situation, you may address the leadership void by initiating district librarian meet-ups and collaborative initiatives.

This chapter presents a "who's who" of your stakeholders, beginning with an introduction to district administrative practice and the legal responsibility of the school board.

Finding Out About Your School Board

School boards are either appointed or elected. Appointed members may be selected by a public official such as the mayor; these members maintain their positions as long as the appointing politician wishes them to do so. When elected, members appear on the ballot in bipartisan elections or on a special ballot. Elected school board members serve at the pleasure of the voters of their community, and their decisions may be greatly influenced by community reactions. Individuals sometimes run for office to correct what they perceive as a problem, such as the actions of a current superintendent, the addition of a program to the curriculum, or the withdrawal of a program considered unnecessary or less necessary. The latter category may include programs begun with outside funds and discontinued when those funds are withdrawn or depleted. Beginning in 2021, an increase in school board involvement in book challenges surfaced nationally, regarding books both in the curriculum and on the shelves of school libraries. An increase in parents running for (and being elected to) school board positions allowed these persons to exert greater influence over curricular issues and materials.

School boards are legally responsible for setting policy for the school district. It is important to note that *policies* are generally board-approved legal documents developed in collaboration with the appropriate educator stakeholders (for instance, the district librarians). Policies may address a wide range of concerns, including the acceptable use of technology, selection of materials and material challenges, discarding of district materials, confidentiality of records, use of facilities, academic integrity, disaster planning, and acceptable use of personal digital devices. The librarian should become familiar with and be able to interpret and communicate about these public documents with members of the learning community. These documents are generally accessible on the school district website.

Because state sunshine laws mandate open meetings of public officials, school board meetings are open to the public. School librarians should plan to attend meetings to observe the actions taken, the positions chosen by individual members, and the general attitudes relating to local education issues. School board members are powerful individuals in the public education of children. Meetings of school boards are now far more transparent than they were historically. More and more, they are broadcast and archived online. Check to see if your school board offers remote attendance, livestreams, or video archives of their meetings. Later on, you may want to consider how you might volunteer to share your professional vision, innovations, and accomplishments as well as your students' creative efforts at future board meetings.

School board members review graduation requirements for high school students. Although state boards of education establish criteria for curricula within the state, a local school board may increase those requirements. For example, the state may require two semesters of physical education, and the local school board may include the additional requirement of being able to swim a prescribed distance.

School boards approve all budget allocations and confirm that monies are being spent as requested and approved. School boards are also responsible for purchasing and selling property owned by the school district. They must agree to the purchase of additional property and the construction of new buildings in places where the school population is growing. They also approve major renovation efforts supported by capital funding, such as updating school libraries. In some locations, school board members can vote in a tax on construction of new homes and apartments to ensure funding for the building of schools in those growing areas. It is the school board that must hire architects, approve plans, award jobs to contractors, and see that the building is built as specified. Board members must also agree to the closing of school buildings when enrollments decline, which are frequently contentious matters.

Finally, the school board is responsible for interviewing and selecting the superintendent, who then proposes the hiring of all administrators, teachers, and staff for board approval. School board members must ensure that state regulations are observed with regard to certification of employees. This may include ensuring that proper health tests are conducted and required vaccinations are documented, that police checks are done (some states now require confirmation that a prospective teacher has no arrest record), and that all teachers have the appropriate degrees and certificates.

While it may seem that you have little connection with the board at this stage in your tenure with the school district, you will soon want these powerful community members to understand and value the innovations you are about to implement. As the weeks and months pass, seek opportunities to share your successes with your board and garner their support.

Finding Out About Your Superintendent

As stated earlier, the superintendent is usually chosen by the school board, although in some locations this person is elected by community vote. State law may govern the superintendent's length of appointment. Such mandatory contracts provide the superintendent some protection from the whims of the community. Superintendents are responsible for the day-to-day management of the district program; the selection of administrators and teaching staff; the development and implementation of curriculum; and the continuation of the school district program, including maintenance of buildings. Management of the school program requires, among other things, creating, refining, and presenting the school budget for the approval of the school board.

Superintendents choose administrators to work with them. These administrators are assigned to the central office staff and to the building-level programs. Central office staff are responsible for special areas of the school program and assume districtwide responsibility in a particular function (e.g., art coordinator, elementary supervisor, curriculum supervisor, athletic director). Classroom teachers who may be assigned those functions are responsible first to their building principals and second to the coordinator of the specialized program. You will likely also make contact with a district-level curriculum coordinator.

New positions are emerging in many school districts. Your school's faculty may now include a variety of coaches. Instructional coaches function as building- or district-level professional developers introducing or helping educators hone established or emerging pedagogical strategies. Reading or literacy coaches work with students and classroom teachers to develop instruction, demonstrate effective pedagogy, and analyze achievement data to inform evidence-based literacy strategies. Technology coaches work with classroom teachers to integrate technology into the curriculum, model instruction, and offer support in keeping educators up to date with promising trends, applications, and best practices. In addition, your district likely also employs a technology coordinator or director whose responsibilities may include planning, purchasing, installing, and maintaining technologies in compliance with state and federal regulations across the district's buildings. Technology coordinators vary in the type of backgrounds they bring to the table. Some have backgrounds based in education; others may have backgrounds more directly connected to business or instructional technology (IT) work.

As a literacy, technology, learning, and information professional, you will need to understand and develop partnerships with all the coaches in your building. In some districts or schools a librarian might assume all or some of these roles. In others, you will discover that all of these potential collaborators are already present. You may even discover that some of them are stationed in your library space. And—importantly—you may find that responsibilities overlap. If this is the case, you may need to take the lead in mitigating potential turf issues and in establishing productive partnerships that best engage each educator's talents.

Although any superintendent may decide to restructure a school district, new superintendents often bring new vision and ideas for change. Some central office staff may be reassigned to broader areas of responsibility encompassing many functions, or they may be returned to a building-level position. The removal of the central staff person responsible for the school library program or the reassignment of someone who knows little about this area means that the new librarian will have to depend on another school librarian in the district to answer questions.

Superintendents must assure the school board that national and state requirements are being met. State and national pressures to increase testing, allegedly to demonstrate educational progress, combined with increased faculty accountability for student scores, encourages some teachers to "teach to the test." These outside influences affect both state and local curricula, and the superintendent is responsible to the school board for ensuring that such changes are addressed. In some states, local agencies are responsible for textbook adoption; in others, textbook adoption is decided at the state level.

Some superintendents seek and respond to teacher and administrator suggestions for improvements or requirements beyond those imposed by the state. For instance, teachers may consider it important for students to have additional writing experiences or complete a senior capstone project. These activities might then be added as district requirements with the approval of the school board.

The superintendent must be aware of trends in education so the district can offer the best possible education to all students. Many superintendents appreciate the quiet assistance of an information professional to make sure they are kept aware of new trends in education. Designing a LibGuide or website offering such resources as access to research, educational journals, curricular standards, and the like to specifically meet central office needs can very tangibly demonstrate your skills and build significant social capital. Such regular sharing positions the school librarian as an indispensable district-level partner.

Another responsibility of the superintendent is to see that facilities are maintained. Daily tasks in individual school buildings are the responsibility

of the principal, but any major changes must be approved by the superintendent, who makes recommendations to the school board. If a school library
is outdated or ineffectively designed and utilized, it is the principal who
brings proposals for renovation or new construction to the attention of the
superintendent.

The superintendent also develops and presents the district budget for
school board acceptance. How that budget is allotted directly affects the
school library. Some superintendents divide the budget into a per-pupil
allocation, with additional money given to special areas. That is, instructional funds are allocated with a certain number of dollars provided for each
student in a given grade or subject area for newly adopted textbooks (if
those books are provided by the district) and a supplemental amount ear-
marked for additional instructional materials. Art departments and school
library programs may receive amounts based on the number of pupils in the
building.

Under a site-based management approach, each building receives a
lump sum to be allocated by the principal or building committee or other
established local mechanisms. When a district employs site-based management, the school librarian should thoroughly investigate the funding devoted
to library services to confirm that the program will be supported and can
grow. The librarian's role in developing a budget is discussed in chapter 7.

Finding Out About Parents and Caregivers

While you have a lot to accomplish getting to know your *school* community, it is important to understand the larger community beyond the buildings and the environment to which your learners go home. Understanding
this broader context will help you anticipate and address less visible needs.
Understanding the needs of parents will help you understand and serve
your learners; it will also help you build critical social capital and support
for your program.

Some of this environmental scanning can happen without your leaving the building. Read the local newspaper. Check out any public community or parent Facebook groups and other online neighborhood platforms
(for instance, NextDoor). If you are not local, drive or walk around and
examine the various types of homes, businesses, signs of community organizations, religious institutions, and how people get around. Can you see
evidence of multiple languages spoken or shops that reflect multiple cultures served? Can you observe economic differences in terms of the types
of housing in the community? You might also develop a better understanding of where your students live by examining a few of the many
real estate sites that offer an overview of the various neighborhoods that
comprise the community.

Demographic data such as population trends, ethnic groups, and average household income are available online through a variety of sources,
including census reports (census.gov). Other sources of local data include
City-Data.com and The Educational Opportunity Project at Stanford University (edopportunity.org).

You will benefit greatly by exploring the most active community groups. If
your school has an active parent-teacher association or organization, plan to
join it. You can volunteer to share and present. During your first weeks on
the job, try to discover whether parents have assisted in the library in past

years and how best to communicate with those parents. Was there a parent who functioned as the volunteer coordinator? As you meet and grow allies, you may become more able to recruit parent help. Although working with volunteers is covered more thoroughly in chapter 10, the librarian would benefit by reaching out to invested parents, or other adults who have shown an interest in contributing, as early as possible.

Be conscious of the fact that some parents, especially those new to the country, may be in situations where they feel threatened and reluctant to share personal information. You can make a huge difference by connecting with and supporting these families, whose needs may not be recognized by other members of the school community.

During the 2020 pandemic, issues of equity surfaced that continue to this day. A June 2022 Pew Research Center report revealed that parents from lower-income households had greater concerns about the pandemic's negative impact on learning; unfortunately, despite efforts to address equity, the homework gap continues to exist. Teens from lower-income families were more often forced to complete homework on cellphones and to seek public wifi. Technology lending programs should address these equity issues.[1]

Schools in affluent districts may have some students from lower-income homes. This makes it imperative to learn about all the parents in your school. Your building-level administrators will have these statistics for you.

Finding Out About Your Building-Level Administrators

Building administrators include the principal, assistant principal(s), department heads or chairs, and lead teachers. Filling any of these positions may be solely the responsibility of the superintendent. In other instances, in the case of a department head, the person may be appointed by the principal or elected by the content-area teachers. Administrators at all levels manage their programs. Who reports to whom is a system worked out in the central office by the superintendent and staff, and the school librarian must be aware of this process to be successful in effecting change. In many high schools, it is important for the school librarian to be considered head of the library "department" in order to be considered for inclusion on curriculum committees and for other leadership roles. It may also be necessary for the librarian to demonstrate such leadership by volunteering for those key committees and getting a seat at the most critical decision-making tables.

Choices of textbooks may be dictated by a state or local list, but the classroom teacher determines methods of teaching, makes the choice of one textbook from the prescribed list for primary use, and approves the use of additional alternate materials. The new school librarian should become familiar with the curriculum at each grade level and content area and begin to examine any assigned texts that are heavily relied upon.

Building- or district-level alterations in curriculum can affect the school librarian's role as an instructional partner and co-teacher. Although textbooks, both print and digital, are still commonplace, additional digital content (purchased through the school library or municipal or state systems) plays increasingly important roles in today's classrooms. In addition, a growing array of open educational resources (OER) are available to be collaboratively chosen, curated, and created by librarians in partnership with classroom teachers. Often housed in learning management systems, this content is frequently more engaging, more current, more accessible, and more flexible than traditional texts.

The building of partnerships with your school administrators is essential to your success. Early on, the school librarian should assess the principal's perception of library programs in general as well as the program offered in the school. The principals' résumés or online profile and social media posts will offer clues about their backgrounds and interests. Knowing a principal's personal and professional interests can be useful. Knowing that the principal plays tennis, loves musical theater, or devours mysteries may offer opportunities for shared personal connections.

It may be even more important to know of and support your administrator's interest in educational initiatives, whether those initiatives are addressing schoolwide equity issues, initiating problem-based learning, improving literacy, furthering the Future Ready pledge, combating bullying, promoting academic honesty, or expanding digital leadership efforts. The librarian can support any and all such projects by supplying research and professional development, while demonstrating commitment to the success of the educational leadership team.

As you listen and observe, you will also develop a sense of your administrators' leadership styles and how administrators are viewed by the faculty and staff. Are these persons approachable? Do they encourage others to share and lead? Do they value inquiry-based learning? Importantly, are they proud to tour *their* library with distinguished visitors?

Finding Out About Your Teacher Colleagues

Your instructional success and your integration into the curriculum depend on the relationships you develop with the faculty. As an instructional partner, co-teacher, and information specialist, learning about your colleagues' needs is critical. You will not reach every teacher, every department, or every grade level in your first year or years on the job. Build relationships one teacher at a time.

If teachers are as yet unaware of how the librarian and library resources can enhance their teaching and learning, it may be that the former school librarian did not team with teachers. The first step is to quickly and convincingly create awareness. In contrast, you may find evidence of existing collaborative units, lesson plans, curriculum maps, calendars, or schedules on the library website. These will make the job of working with teachers much easier because you will be able to immediately identify your instant allies. Knowing the resources used, plans for presenting units of instruction, the roles and responsibilities of the teacher and the librarian, and the method of assessing previous student work can serve as a model for your upcoming involvement with your colleagues.

To respond to teachers' needs, the librarian has to understand their preferred pedagogical strategies as well as the curriculum. Do your potential teaching partners prefer to gamify their lessons, create choice boards, develop case-based scenarios, develop centers for small group learning, engage in problem- or project-based learning? Is inquiry-based learning valued? Some teachers may already use library resources frequently; others not so much. For those teachers who seldom use library resources, you might create unsolicited gifts in the form of annotated lists of resources on a website or a LibGuide shared via email.

What type of assessments do teachers design? Are those assessments engaging? Do they offer opportunities for choice and voice? Do they truly leverage appropriate digital tools for information use, creativity enhancement, and communication of knowledge? Do teachers prefer such student products as presentations, debates, simulations, or public service announcements? Are some of your teachers stuck in "report" mode?

What type of student work is celebrated? This question will lead you to major opportunities for collaboration and co-teaching. Investigate whether you are entering a school that encourages participation in Science Fair or National History Day or hosts its own literacy fair or art show. Do your third-graders annually engage in a living biography wax museum? Is *making* valued as a learning strategy or a focus of student assessment? Do students engage in the creation of authentic products or service learning projects?

Rather than add to teachers' already serious loads, you might begin by asking teachers which of their lessons or units are most in need of extreme makeovers. Partnering with classroom teachers to improve or enhance their assignments is the beginning of collaboration and will help you change faculty misconceptions of the role of the librarian in teaching and learning. After a few such successful partnerships, the word will spread and your "business" will grow.

The array of extracurricular activities available presents a lens on school interests and priorities. Your colleagues and your students are involved in and beyond the classroom. Determining who sponsors what may reveal important ways into the hearts of your new partners. Look for connections to such activities as the newspaper or newscast, the arts (including drama, poetry slams, art shows, book clubs, and Reading Olympics), sports, clubs, and technology initiatives. Look also for what might be missing: this might propel you into an impactful building-level contribution that leverages your special talents and may become one of the joys of your work.

In elementary schools especially, teachers may perceive that the role of the library is to provide teachers with preparation periods, rather than function as an essential component of classroom learning. If this misperception is evident in a school, over time, the school librarian may present the value of a different model that connects to and extends what is going on in the classroom. For instance, the school librarian may be able to plan a short collaborative project with one class using time created by putting two rooms together for book exchange. The displaced classes could visit the "finale" of this collaborative unit, showing teachers the value of a different model that connects to and extends what takes place in the classroom.

As will be discussed in chapter 11, teachers' emerging use of learning management systems and their growing interest in using OER to create and publish digital curriculum and texts present exciting opportunities for collaboration with school librarians whose strengths highlight curation. As information specialists, librarians not only have knowledge of the growing number of quality OER portals and other portals leading to excellent content, they also understand the affordances of the best curation and publishing platforms and have knowledge regarding best practices in the educational creative use and reuse of intellectual property, including copyright, fair use, Creative Commons, public domain, and Creative Commons Zero (CC0) licensing.

Finding Out About Additional Friends with Powers: School Facilitators

A new school librarian should build relationships with members of the staff who are critical facilitators beyond those discussed earlier in this chapter. You need to meet and learn the roles of school secretaries, custodians, carpenters, electricians, and teacher aides. These persons have significant institutional knowledge and talents and they know how to get things done. When they genuinely become your friends, they can easily analyze situations and facilitate solutions.

School secretaries can let you know the best times to contact the principal or which teachers are the biggest users of and advocates for the library. Custodians can help you rearrange the furniture when programming requires different configurations, and they can help you understand weeding procedures and proper disposal of weeded titles. They will notice and appreciate it when you and your students do small things to make their work easier. Carpenters can help rethink a round table and transform it into a high top. The people in the cafeteria may be able to save you a lunch if you need to keep the library open over the "regular" lunch periods.

A final group includes those teacher aides who are assigned to classrooms in schools. They are most often there to assist the teacher with students who have special needs. They will appreciate your taking an interest in them and in helping them carry out their assignments.

Finding Out About Your School Culture

School librarians bring to their new positions all their background experiences, their observations of other school librarians, their pre-service reading and learning, and their personal talents and skills, as well as their vision for what makes a library program effective. In some cases, they will discover that many of the elements of an effective program are already in place. In other cases, the librarian may accept a position in a program with significant room to grow.

As you begin a job, try to learn as much as possible about what has gone before, as well as procedures currently in place. If possible, visit before your actual start date. If you begin in the fall semester, try to get into the building in August. You may discover boxes of books and supplies that have arrived over the summer. You may be able to get a head start on unpacking, decorating, and creating a welcoming environment and informally meeting new professional colleagues and support staff.

As a newly hired school librarian, you have an opportunity to train a fresh lens on the culture to explore and stage positive change. Observe and ask questions before embarking on any major changes. As you observe in those first weeks, keep an eye out toward finding problems and imagining creative solutions, developing a preliminary set of goals and objectives. These goals and objectives and their action steps will be refined as you learn more about the needs of the learning community over your first year on the job, but initial projects worthy of planning will be evident from your first week in the school. Making an impact with small but thoughtful and visible changes at an early stage will attract curiosity, inspire interest in your program, and set the stage for the more formal planning to come as you observe and assess needs, gaps, and opportunities. More on formal planning is explored in chapter 7.

Finding Out About the Learning Environment

Look around. What message does the building itself share? Is it clean? Do people—including administrators—stop to pick up a stray piece of litter? Do the displays in the halls celebrate student work, student voice, student differences? Do people greet each other? Are there signs on the classroom doors that welcome students, or perhaps share what each teacher is currently reading?

Look around. What message does your new library space share? Does it tell the story you want it to tell? What impressions do visitors get when they first walk through the library's doors? Are they welcomed by your signage or bombarded by messages sharing what *not* to do? Do physical obstacles block the flow of traffic? Are the shelves jammed tight, or do they invite browsing and discovery? Are materials at your students' eye and reach levels? Do sight lines allow you to monitor the entire space? Does the furniture promote flexible use of the space for a variety of learning activities, including collaboration and creation?

Take a bit of time to observe use and seek out students who are willing to share their experiences with the space. Solicit suggestions. Enlist a few willing student or faculty volunteers, family, or friends to make suggestions during your early visits. Plan to make the statement that something fresh and exciting is going on and everyone can help make it happen in their library!

Even small changes, such as fresh posters and positive signage, will welcome students, share what they can do in their library, and set a learner-centered and engaging tone. Seek inspiration for displays on the many available school librarian blogs, Pinterest boards, Facebook groups, TikTok videos, and Instagram and Facebook posts. Be alert to design ideas beyond *libraryland,* perhaps in your favorite stores and coffee shops.

See what happens if you leave a puzzle or a board game on a couple of your tables. Look for a box of new books just waiting to be discovered and use them to create an informal display that invites engagement. Post a fun and provocative question on a prominently displayed whiteboard.

Create a display that features the principal, other building administrators, and key staff members and what they are reading or have read over the summer. Discover the names of the new teachers. Take their photos and try to uncover their hobbies, interests, and favorite books and films so you can introduce them on a bulletin board or display case. Encourage participation by sharing your own passions and preferences. This type of activity will help you get to know the colleagues who may be most in need of your partnership, and you will build instant social capital.

Moving furniture around changes any environment, especially when you create more flexible spaces to accommodate individuals and groups of various sizes. Before you engage in major rearranging, take a little time to observe traffic patterns and types of use. In the coming months, you will want to locate or create a floor plan and formally design larger changes. At this point, begin by talking with your stakeholders about their needs. Consider their dreams and your own dreams for the space. Small changes in seating and table arrangements can encourage collaboration, invite discovery of resources, and potentially reset the attitudes of those who used the facility in the past. If you feel a small reset is needed, then be a little playful with your rearrangement and observe the results.

Consider what really has to go and what might be easily accomplished. Ditch that tattered, no-longer-inviting storytime rug. Create corners with graphic novels or picture books. Set up a couple of activity stations or centers. Consider creating cozy nesting spaces, quiet corners for the student or two who simply want to sit and read. If you are considering adding a makerspace where one has not been before, take a few baby steps by gathering a few labeled and open storage bins. Begin seeking donations for such materials as LEGOs, duct tape, and other simple supplies. You are likely to find parents who are more than willing to share these resources on your first open school night.

Seek allies early. As you meet your new students, begin to recruit volunteers as well as potential tech squad members. Grow a few library ambassadors. The first teachers who stop by to say "hello" and the students who volunteer to help you early on are likely candidates because they are already interested in what is going on and what *might* be going on in their library. Volunteers are discussed more fully in chapter 10.

Always remember that you will want to document the changes you make. Take before-and-after photographs; perhaps you can tour the library with your phone and record a video of what things looked like the day you walked in. This type of evidence will become a critical baseline when you share the impact of your efforts in your upcoming, compelling reports. Be conscious of the fact that all of your actions move the library forward from a baseline that should be recorded.

As you begin the process of observing use and growing relationships, you will be gathering ideas for improving your physical space and planning change. Your immediate goal is to spread the word that something exciting and fresh is happening; that even beyond being the place where students might discover inviting books and learning resources and learn about information literacy, the library is a jointly owned learning space. Of course, the library you lead is about to become far more. It will be a place to engage, contribute, imagine, share, study, make, do, collaborate, and celebrate.

Finding Out About Your Digital Assets and Considering Other Front Doors

Your library has more than one front door. In addition to assessing your physical facility, you will want to assess your library's virtual presence. Does the school library have a website? How often is it refreshed? Is it a simple brochure, or is it truly an interactive destination? In what ways has the library or the former librarian used social media to connect with and engage the learning community? How often is the website updated? What evidence can be found of the collaborative efforts with classroom and some/most/all other teachers? Do library resources also appear on teachers' websites? Are they embedded on the learning management system as well as the school library website?

Beyond the curation and sharing of resources, is there digital evidence of partnerships in the form of instructional resources to support specific inquiry-based units on the website? Does the library website include evidence of student work? Keeping in mind any district policies regarding student photographs, does your digital presence celebrate students reading and creating and sharing their knowledge? How frequently do or will you refresh your website and post new content? Does the library have a social media presence, and does it exist in the spaces frequently visited by your community?

Beginning the job requires as much knowledge as possible about the facility beyond human and collection factors. The new librarian should identify available digital tools and hardware, learn about the librarian's responsibilities for these materials, and determine if those responsibilities extend beyond the library. When the pandemic forced schools to use remote and hybrid learning approaches, the equipment needed to support participation was quickly chosen, purchased, and distributed, with librarians often taking leading roles. Throughout the pandemic, and as schools resumed more normal programs, the responsibility for equitable distribution of technology such as laptops may have been assumed by the librarian. Will this role continue? Was this significant contribution documented?

Your faculty may rely on you to distribute hardware even before classes begin and you may need to be ready to do so. In addition to possible laptops and tablets, you will need to understand what equipment is part of your collection and how you will keep track of the distribution of such items as interactive whiteboards, cameras, tripods, virtual reality tools, and green screens and how to distribute these resources to students, teachers, and classrooms. Try to discover any strategies that already exist, both for tracking equipment and for managing potential repairs.

You will also want to assess your school's access to wifi. If your school does not have adequate wireless access, you need to discuss this immediately with an administrator. A variety of funds are available at all levels—municipal, local, state, and national—to provide equitable wifi access to schools.

Charging stations are an easy and inexpensive strategy for making new friends. Your learning community will be seeking multiple ways to recharge their devices (and themselves) and they will seek cozy, friendly places to do so. Check online vendor catalogs for attractive, inexpensive charging towers or kiosks or multiplug outlets or surge protectors. Point to these with fun signage.

As you learn about the curriculum, student interests, major inquiry projects, and celebrated events, begin to curate with the goal of making trusted digital resources not only ubiquitous, but also relied-on and essential tools for teaching and learning and personal exploration. If effort has not been exerted in this area before, students and teachers may rely only on the typical go-tos: Google and Wikipedia and YouTube. You may need to launch a campaign of discovery related to the many age-relevant, high-quality collections of reference sources, magazine and journal articles, ebooks and audiobooks, videos, apps, curricular content, and other media.

Begin with pushing what is already available. You will want to discover:

- Subscription databases already supported by the school and/or district
- Subscription databases available from the public library
- Subscription databases licensed through statewide contracts
- Subscription databases available from regional or municipal consortia
- Rich portals of OER to exploit

- Reliable age-appropriate websites and portals that support the curriculum as well as student interests

Database access should be 24/7, ubiquitous, accessible via mobile devices, and barrier-free. Students should be able to access these resources at school and at home and while waiting to get picked up from soccer practice. You will want to create a system that mitigates password barriers. Investigate statewide geolocation options. Consider all the important access points. Are you embedded on the spaces students use to access their assignments—the classroom teachers' websites or their learning management systems? Where is your library's landing page or "parking lot"? Will your online public access catalog (OPAC) host your learner- and teacher-centered curated collections, or will you use tools such as LibGuides and Google Sites and embed or link to your OPAC on these platforms? Can your curated suggestions be effectively accessed across the multiple devices used by your learning community?

It is important to ensure that students understand that there is a library ecosystem around them. Students should know about the physical and digital resources of the public libraries in the area and you should consider ways to facilitate that access, especially to the age-appropriate digital assets. In some cases (for instance, with ebook collections), school and public assets may be connected. High school students (and parents) might value knowing that many college libraries encourage visits from the community.

Increasing access to the potential array of digital resources will help you earn the endorsement of your teachers and students as you spread word of their value to teaching and learning. The bottom line will be the level of usage of these resources—their return on investment (ROI)—and, even more importantly, the evolution of the quality of inquiry and the products produced by the students. Digital resources are not inexpensive. They must earn their keep in terms of quality teaching and learning. School librarians are responsible for demonstrating this impact if they wish to keep and broaden the resources available. Most databases offer granular usage data and your vendors will help you run reports. This is another critical area in which you might collect and analyze data and share evidence of your impact. Again, it is important to establish a baseline assessment of database use in the first months of your practice.

Finding Out About Your OPAC

Nearly every library has an automation system to support collection building and circulation. If the system you inherit is unfamiliar, find someone (perhaps another librarian in the district) to introduce it to you. You will likely find multiple online tutorials for any OPAC platform. Once logged in, check to see if it is current and up to date. Does it include recently purchased resources? Are you using the latest version of the software? Figure out how to add new resources and print barcodes if your materials were not ordered pre-processed.

Your OPAC may be the most expensive piece of software in the building. Remember that the significant cost of your annual subscription likely includes customer and technical support. Do not be shy about phoning or emailing your questions. Vendors generally have highly responsive systems in place to address customer needs. If you do not have an OPAC, this may be a priority need worth addressing in your first strategic plan.

If you are familiar with the program, consider running a collection analysis. How inclusive is the OPAC of digital resources? Get a sense of the age, size, and focus of the collection. If you have time, look into performing an equity audit. Query students, especially any new volunteers, about their perceptions regarding the efficiency of the OPAC. Do they have links to it on their own devices? Where do they go to look for books and information if not in the OPAC?

Before school begins, you will have to get that OPAC ready for business. Make sure you have a devoted computer, updated software, a current login, and a barcode scanner to allow you to avoid typing in lengthy codes. If you cannot find these, ask around. If you have any aides, they are the people most likely to know. Have a note pad nearby just in case you need to do manual checkouts. If books have been returned over the summer, you may also want to check those in. You will also want to investigate how regular back-ups are created and where they are stored.

Among your first steps at the OPAC will be entering the school calendar with holidays and other closings noted. You will want to discover existing procedures for the circulation of books, equipment, and other materials. Learn about the checkout/circulation period and consider whether you want to keep it as it previously existed. A two-week circulation period is fairly typical. However, just because it has always been done that way does not mean that a procedure should be continued. Rather than investing a great deal of time in reminding students about overdues, consider lengthening loan periods to three or four weeks for materials not in constant demand. Placing materials to be used by entire classes on reserve or on overnight loans will increase their availability on a temporary basis. Similar strategies may be created for those high-demand titles that fly off the shelves.

At what point in an elementary-grade visit does book borrowing take place? Who is in charge of physically checking books out? While students can check materials out themselves, appointing one or two in the class to do this task will do much to increase their self-esteem. Hopefully students, particularly in the early grades, will not be restricted to a prescribed number of books. Are there any limits to the number of books and other materials teachers and parents may borrow?

You may also want to investigate procedures for late returns and damaged materials. Take a look at the OPAC to see if any special sections or collections or locations are present. This might offer early clues regarding student and teacher needs for specific materials, as well as major assignments. If you were left a library manual, perhaps on a LibGuide or website, all of these questions might be easier to answer. If you were not left a manual, start a folder with information to place in your manual later on in the year. There is no need to begin from scratch: you will discover multiple examples online to serve as templates.

Fines are always controversial. The authors of this book feel that fines present the school library as a punitive institution. Rather than teaching responsibility—a prime excuse offered for collecting fines—fines in fact promote clipping of pages or sneaking items through detection systems. In some instances, the librarian cannot actually use the funds collected for library purposes. Rather, they go into the district's general fund and are used for other purposes. Even if the money collected from overdue charges is used for the library, the cost to the library's image outweighs any advantage. You want to create an environment where citizenship is valued and students understand that keeping a book prevents others from accessing it. This behavior is not absolved by payment of a fine. Again, a school librarian new to the building may be able to reassess and begin the school year with a few new, less restrictive, less punitive policies. In its 2019 Resolution on Monetary Library Fines as a Form of Social Inequity, the American Library Association noted that "the imposition of monetary library fines creates a barrier to the provision of library and information services." The resolution encouraged libraries to "actively move towards eliminating" them.[2]

It is possible that you will be adding books to your OPAC that were ordered before the summer break. Look for boxes and files or digital records to upload. Locate purchase orders to check for completion. Copies of those will likely have to be sent to the central office. As you engage in administrative tasks, keep in mind how precious these early days in your new library are in building connections. As you establish priorities, consider whether focusing on resolving cataloging issues or manually entering gift book titles will send the wrong message to teachers and students who would benefit from the school librarian's leadership in more valuable endeavors that have a more direct impact on teaching and learning. If you face a serious processing backlog, you may want to seek volunteers for copy cataloging and preparing books for the shelves. You may also want to ensure that future new materials are ordered pre-processed with digital records. If you encounter a library without an OPAC, you will want to work toward getting one. Take your time and engage other librarians in your district or region as partners or advisers. If your budget does not allow purchase of a system, you may want to explore an emerging number of open-source software alternatives.

District-level material selection policies are discussed more fully in chapter 9. In your search for information during that first week, try to local a materials selection policy and review it as soon as possible. If no policy exists, or if it is not up to date, make a note to begin this process. Because policies are established at the district level, you will want to reach out to other librarians in the district to begin drafting one. At the time of this writing, book challenges were growing dramatically in schools across the country. The establishment of clear selection policies became even more essential in defending children's right to read. You may be the only one in the building serious about defending students' intellectual freedom.

Finding Out About Daily Operations

In addition to setting up your OPAC and reviewing circulation procedures, you will want to see if your life has been made easier (as mentioned earlier) by finding a library handbook or manual. It might be physical or online. It is possible that the previous librarian has left one and let you know where it is. If you cannot find one, it might be good to reach out with a text or email. Also, as mentioned earlier, if you do not have one, begin collecting the information to build one.

Whether you have a fixed or flexible schedule, you will also want to locate the physical or online versions of the library schedule from last year or last semester. If you have a flexible, responsive, or hybrid schedule, teachers will be contacting you very soon, so you will want to discover how the previous librarian planned and scheduled class time. If you are on a fixed schedule, you will want to discover what your rotation looks like, which classes are coming when, when you have blocks of time for administrative work, and when you are scheduled for lunch. If no templates exist, you may want to create a digital calendar for your visits or purchase a planner (which will likely live at the front desk and become essential). You may also want to share the daily schedule on a whiteboard posted in a visible space.

It is also possible that the previous librarian had access to a curriculum map or matrix that lists themes addressed and major assessments across grades and content areas. This will help you anticipate curricular needs and prepare to plan with teachers. If no such document exists, that might be an item to add to a future to-do list.

Finding Out About Library Staff

You have likely already learned about any full- or part-time staff in the school library and sought existing job descriptions for those positions. When job descriptions are not available, the school librarian should begin to develop them using one or several of the many existing models, some created by professional associations. New job descriptions, for yourself and for those who support you, should address necessary services and tasks, while permitting each person to feel self-worth and demonstrate their talents. This is best accomplished when school librarians match tasks to human competencies. In the case of a professional job description, seek aspirational and current models based on national standards. Both library staff and volunteers are discussed in depth in chapter 10.

In reality, many school libraries are one-person operations. Some share professionals between two or more schools. In others, a newly hired school librarian may find there are two library professionals or, in the case of a learning commons model, the staff may include any of an array of specialists in the school for technology integration and reading. Depending on the culture of the school and its space availability, teachers of the gifted or other special education educators, along with art and music and technology teachers, may also find their homes in the library. The guidance counselors may welcome a warm, less threatening atmosphere to help students removed from the principal's office.

The new librarian should meet with other professionals at the first opportunity to discuss their roles and interests in collaboration and co-teaching. Key meetings might be scheduled with the district technology director as well as your building's technology coach to discuss your vision and future partnerships in integrating learning technologies.

You will also want to learn more about device roll-outs, networks, filters and acceptable-use policies, media resources, learning management systems, and adoption of schoolwide software platforms (for instance, Google or Microsoft). As an information professional and an expert in learning resources, a school librarian's expertise and knowledge of technology applications can be critical to the school's awareness of promising new platforms and the school's continuing professional growth.

Finding Out About Your Students

If there is a student council or another sort of student leadership team, try to arrange a meeting with them through their faculty sponsor. Ask questions and listen thoughtfully to their reflections relating to their library as well as their vision for it. This is a quick way to begin to understand student needs and build coalitions, friendship, and trust with some of your most influential users. You might also conduct a survey or invite users to add to a growing wishlist on a whiteboard.

Among the first steps you might take in finding out about students is determining the methods used to admit students to the library. Some schools utilize a pass system. Passes are often signed by teachers, aides, administrators, or (in the case of lunch and study hall, for instance) distributed by members of the library staff. You should investigate whether the existing system presents unnecessary barriers to use. Some may argue that a relaxed pass system will overrun the library with students simply seeking a comfortable place to hang out, but this premise and judgment should be tested. An analysis of library use for one week will reveal whether students are using the facility for study or recreational reading, whether they are coming from a classroom or study hall, and whether or not their behavior affects the library's effectiveness.

You will also want to investigate when students are allowed to come to the library. Rigid scheduling of the library may mean that access is severely limited: for example, students can only attend once a week for 45 minutes. This limits so much of the library's potential for voluntary exploration and joyful discovery! The library exists to support both formal and informal learning and to celebrate literacies of all varieties. It belongs to the students and it should be as open and available to them as possible.

Your library is a culture within a culture. You will set a tone by the types of guidelines and expectations you establish. The goal is to help students understand what they can do in their library and how best to do those things. For a learner-centered library, you will want to establish a limited list of expectations that serve the community. Frame your expectations using positive language. Post your expectations so they do not appear to be arbitrary responses to a situation. If space is limited, guidelines may clarify how many students may come from each classroom for small-group study, lunch, or study hall.

In some libraries, guidelines describe possible disciplinary actions for intentional misuse of the space or its resources or behaviors that negatively affect the work, comfort, or safety of other community members. Often, the monitoring of a penalty is more troublesome than the action that prompted it, making such rules lose–lose situations. Keep in mind that developing ownership, by explaining how the library belongs to the users of the library and determines what they may do in their library, creates a far more productive environment than do lists of rules and penalties for infringements.

Among the documents the new school librarian might want to establish, continue, or edit are the mission and vision statements; guidelines for student aides and adult volunteers, circulation, and scheduling; and, in time, a strategic plan.

After determining the methods of access for students, scheduling, and procedures, new librarians will want to encourage students to join the library team. The librarian should find out whether students are already assigned to the library. These may include a tech team, after-school tutors, or perhaps National Honor Society students, who are often in search of meaningful community service. In those first days on the job, students who have worked in the library in the past might be eager to help with the distribution of resources, getting new books ready to go and creating dynamic welcoming displays.

An important consideration is determining which clubs or extracurriculars or events the previous librarians themselves sponsored. You do not want to unintentionally disappoint your Dungeons-and-Dragons fans or the devoted Book Club members, or overlook the every-semester Poetry Slam.

You do not want to be unprepared to host History Day, Science Fair, Reading Olympics, Dot Day, first chapter Fridays, or Wax Museum biographies. If there has been a book fair that students and parents look forward to each year, you may not want to lose either the momentum or the revenue of that tradition. So, ask around. Ask your students.

Finding out what students working in the library have done in the past will help you plan for the future. If your situation is that no students are returning with an interest in working in the library, begin a gentle recruitment effort. Students should feel a sense of pride in contributing to their library. Their service should be a memorable, meaningful, and enjoyable experience, one through which they might express their talents and creativity.

As students begin to join the team, librarians must realize that continually assigning students such dull tasks such as shelving books or reading shelves will not encourage them to remain and will not likely address your interest in providing them with rich opportunities for service learning. Students enjoy helping others use digital resources and learn how to navigate through new databases. They are very able at, and often love, opening boxes and preparing new books and other media for the shelf. Trusted students can help design and maintain websites, LibGuides, and other curation efforts. You will learn to treasure the student artists and designers on your team for their talents in helping you make the virtual and physical space more attractive. You might use additional, age-appropriate, and trusted social media experts to prepare and help you maintain your library's Facebook or Instagram presence. (Avoid this with students under the age of 13.) Consider encouraging your talented photographers to archive library events as well as those outside the library. Their work can be incorporated in your library reports and may also serve as fodder for reports that your administrators or central office create. Students might also create library orientation videos or public service announcements (PSAs) to promote services or the return of materials. Their digital contributions and experiences not only create a sense of pride, they also offer students memorable opportunities to prepare for their lives after school and may help them begin portfolios. The time of your library volunteers, or perhaps ambassadors, should be valued. Try, whenever possible, to ensure that student contributions are also learning experiences. For some examples of student volunteer activities, see Appendix C.

In a collaborative and creative physical space, teachers can expect "busy" noise. Plan techniques to encourage collaborative behaviors. School librarians might create zones of quiet and zones of moderate noise, and have private spaces where collaborative production and presentation can happen without disturbing others. Students and teachers learn the difference between constructive noise, a positive atmosphere, and chaos. When the environment engages with productive and purposeful noise, with opportunities to do, experience, create, and participate, students tend to get busy rather than become bored. They learn to appreciate a very different place in the school where they take ownership of their own learning and creativity as well as their behavior.

When Students Arrive

As a new school librarian, you will need to get a head start on making connections. Sometimes students are in the building before school actually begins. Athletes and band members, for instance, begin practice early to be ready for their first events. Student council or class leaders at the secondary level may be in the building to plan with their club sponsors or administrators. New students may visit with their parents to look around or try out their lockers. Should any of these students wander into the library, take the opportunity to introduce yourself. You might ask about their feelings about the library. If you sense their interest, see if you might reach out to them later about becoming a volunteer or a member of your tech squad. An avid reader might be interested in joining the Library Advisory Committee or your new book club. This is a good time to ask some questions and build some early student social capital as you prepare for the arrival of the rest of the student population.

Expectations for behavior in the library should be in place when school opens on the first day. It is also good practice to engage students in developing expectations or norms relating to library use during their early visits. Again, your goal is to create expectations that establish a positive and productive rather than punitive environment—one in which respect for others is the predominant consideration.

First impressions are crucial. Be yourself. Let your energy, enthusiasm, and personality shine. Your professional appearance and your *vibe* present an air of competence, emphasize the importance of the activities that will take place in the library, and invite co-conspirators.

Getting Ready for Orientation

In addition to meeting with regularly scheduled classes on a fixed schedule, or meeting classes with your classroom teacher partners on a flexible schedule, it is typical to host orientation for groups of students new to the school. Whether these are your incoming kindergartners, sixth-graders, ninth-graders, or a group of new English Language Learner (ELL) "neighbors," you will want to welcome them in a special way. Consider orientation an opportunity. You may want to share a few details, such as how to get to the library website, how to check out print books and ebooks, and which library apps are essential for their devices. You can present instruction in an engaging way: through digital and physical scavenger hunts, breakout rooms, center-based activities, and augmented reality tours. Many school library bloggers and social media colleagues regularly share their creative orientation strategies. Beyond the library basics, you will want to share even more important messages about who you are and what you stand for and what students can do in *their* library. Feel free to use or adapt the list found in Figure 4-1.

The following additional suggestions should be helpful to the new school librarian as students arrive.

- Be visible when students first enter the library. Greet your students and learn their names as quickly as possible. This demonstrates your interest in and respect for their presence in the library.

- Smile and connect. Students keenly read messages in your tone of voice, body language, and eye contact. You will discover that students read your expectations without needing to enforce them with your voice or words.

- Establish a reputation for being positive, fair, caring, empathetic, and flexible. Students should be the focus of attention.

- Acknowledge positive behavior. When it is necessary to address negative behavior, a private reminder or a redirect is more effective and more fair than directing public focus onto an issue.

11 THINGS TO KNOW ABOUT OUR LIBRARY

1. THIS IS **OUR** LIBRARY.

2. YOU HAVE A **VOICE** AND A **PLACE** HERE.

3. WE WANT YOU TO FEEL **SAFE** AND **COMFORTABLE** IN OUR LIBRARY.

4. WE WANT YOU TO **RETURN** (OFTEN).

5. WE LOOK FORWARD TO BUILDING A **LONG RELATIONSHIP** WITH YOU ACROSS YOUR CLASSES AND YOUR GRADE LEVELS.

6. THIS IS A PLACE FOR **LEARNING**, BOTH FORMAL (TO SUPPORT YOUR CLASSES) AND INFORMAL (TO SUPPORT YOUR **CURIOSITY**).

7. THERE ARE MANY DIFFERENT WAYS TO **"READ"** AND LEARN. *STORY* COMES IN MANY *CONTAINERS* AND WE WANT YOU TO ENJOY THEM ALL.

8. IT'S OKAY TO **TAKE A RISK** AND **BE PLAYFUL** IN YOUR LEARNING.

9. **TALK TO US.** (YOU CAN COMMUNICATE WITH YOUR LIBRARY IN MULTIPLE WAYS.) LET US KNOW ABOUT, LET US CONNECT YOU WITH WHAT YOU NEED.

10. THIS IS A PLACE TO **THINK, CREATE, SHARE AND GROW.**

11. **YOU** ARE THE **REASON WE ARE HERE**!

joyce valenza

Figure 4-1. 11 Things to Know about Our Library

- Be prepared for the students when they enter. Meet classes with well-developed plans. As you become familiar with the pace of visits, and as you develop your repertoire of instructional "tricks," this process will feel far less onerous.

- Demonstrate enthusiasm for your work. You have the most exciting job in the school. You are teaching in the largest classroom in the school. The possibilities for change and growth are limited only by your own imagination. Your enthusiasm will spread across the culture.

Having survived the first week on the job, the school librarian must begin to plan for the immediate future, for the remainder of the school year, and for the long-term future of the library program. The following chapters expand on these responsibilities.

Key Takeaways

- The library does not exist as an island. To be an innovative and effective leader, it is critical that you understand the culture of your district, school, and its stakeholders.

- In your first few weeks, you will want to discover and take stock of existing strategies, policies, guidelines, and procedures.

- In your first few weeks, begin to assess community needs across stakeholder groups. Seek problems that you can or might be able to address. Take pictures. Collect baseline data.

- Be kind to yourself in your first year. It takes time to build relationships. Nevertheless, make an initial impact with small but noticeable changes. Show your community that their library is going through a refresh and that their input in its improvement is valued and critical.

Challenges to Promote Growth

1. If you are unfamiliar with school district organization charts, search online for district organization charts to discover examples. Try to determine who is responsible for the school library program. How many supervisors might the school librarian have?
2. If possible, chat with an experienced school librarian about their first week on the job. If you are in a field experience, or a first job, compare that person's experiences with your own.
3. Review the school library websites of at least five schools and compare them for their ease of access, their clarity, their engagement, their links to resources, their connection to curriculum, and their efforts to promote reading and literacies, as well as the instructional voice of the librarian.
4. Begin to outline, create, or edit the website for your school library. Based on inspiration you may have gained from the reviews you did in item 3 of

this list and what you are learning about your community, establish links to resources you have found that would be useful to students and teachers.
5. Create your own poster of the positive activities that you (and your students) will be engaged in in the library. Perhaps begin with "Here we . . ." This would be a wonderful activity in which to engage your students!

Notes

1. Monica Anderson, Michelle Faverio, and Colleen McClain. (2022). "How Teens Navigate School During COVID-19." *Pew Research Center* (June 2). https://www.pewresearch.org/internet/2022/06/02/how-teens-navigate-school-during-covid-19

2. American Library Association. (2019). "Resolution on Monetary Library Fines as a Form of Social Inequity." Adopted by ALA Council January 28, 2019. https://www.ala.org/aboutala/sites/ala.org.aboutala/files/content/Resolution%20on%20Monetary%20Library%20Fines%20as%20a%20Form%20of%20Social%20Inequity-FINAL.pdf

5

The Education Program

Collaboration is important not just because it's a better way to learn. The spirit of collaboration is penetrating every institution and all of our lives. So learning to collaborate is part of equipping yourself for effectiveness, problem solving, innovation and life-long learning in an ever-changing networked economy.

—Don Tapscott

Essential Questions

- What roles do school librarians play in teaching of reading and the promotion of a culture of literacy?

- How can librarians improve instruction through modeling learner-centered teaching strategies and partnering with classroom teachers?

- How do school librarians integrate traditional and emerging literacies and inquiry skills into schoolwide teaching and learning?

This chapter explores the roles of the school librarian at the center of teaching and learning in the school. This centering requires a willingness to lead and share a vision and a plan for implementing change.

School librarians are integral to a rich K–12 learning experience. Librarians contribute by developing a schoolwide culture of reading; supporting reading instruction; integrating literacies of all sorts into the curriculum; fostering student curiosity, agency, and learner-centered inquiry; collaborating and co-teaching across curricula and grade levels; and positioning the library as a hub for formal and informal learning. A considerable body of research demonstrates the importance of a robust library program in boosting the achievement of students.

Reading

If students are to learn, grow, and enjoy school, they must be able to read and understand text. Knowing how to read goes beyond success in school. It is, of course, a lifelong skill that allows them to comprehend and interpret information and develop new understandings. First, our students learn to read, and then they read to learn.

A priority of school library programs has traditionally been the reading program. Henry Cecil and Willard Heaps, in their 1940 *School Library Service in the United States*, credit Governor DeWitt Clinton and William L. March of New York and Horace Mann of Massachusetts with traveling to Europe to bring back the best ideas for educating children to put into practice in the United States:

> These educational leaders and others of the day realized that the development of intelligent citizens depended not only upon teaching reading but also on providing reading opportunities. It was for the purpose of providing such opportunities that the school district libraries came into being.[1]

Reading is a complicated spectrum of skills, and experts do not agree on one specific "best" method for the teaching of reading. However, current research suggests that it is not as simple as a debate between phonics and whole language or the science of reading and balanced literacy. It has become a political issue sometimes referred to as "the Reading Wars." Many states and school districts have mandated a specific method for the teaching of reading, often with scripted curriculum. NCTE's Position Statement on "The Act of Reading: Instructional Foundations and Policy Guidelines" provides additional guidance about the elements necessary for effective reading instruction.[2]

As a librarian, you should advocate with parents, teachers, and administrators to support positive reading experiences outside of what is required for classroom instruction. Too often, adults complain that what children are reading lacks value or literary merit. Adults should model reading and help students become fluent readers. In their book, *The Joy of Reading*, Donalyn Miller and Teri Lesesne explain that "some adults want kids to read when the adults can control and define the reading conditions, but they don't trust kids to choose anything of value to read without their oversight. The skills and knowledge acquired through self-study like independent reading are often disregarded or ignored."[3] Be the voice that values all kinds of reading, including re-reading, graphic novels, audiobooks, magazines, print and digital books.

Students must be surrounded with a library collection that will be interesting to them and has a wide variety of books (print, digital, and audio) and other materials offering a vocabulary that they can read—not necessarily easily, but with the possibility of achieving meaning as they read. "When we inundate older struggling readers with superficial and lifeless reading and writing tasks that bear no resemblance to the reading and writing they encounter in the real world, we ensure their status as outsiders in the real literate community."[4]

School librarians should strive to create a schoolwide culture of reading. To build a culture of reading, we lead our communities by providing access to materials, encouraging opportunities to read beyond the curricular requirements, and supporting reading engagement and improvement. This culture of reading is created through deliberate effort, advocacy, and leadership.

Top Ten Tips for Building a Culture of Reading

1. Place students at the center. Empower them to plan programs and recommend new titles to add to the collection, and appoint student reading ambassadors to spread book joy every day.
2. Develop and maintain an up-to-date and diverse collection.
3. Expand your definition of *reading* to include various formats such as audiobooks and graphic novels, and include nonfiction and technical manuals.
4. Collaborate with all adults throughout the building. Encourage them to visibly share their reading lives via "currently reading _____" signs on their door/whiteboard and as part of their email signatures.
5. Schedule frequent author visits, whether in person, virtual, or prerecorded. Invite authors to record book talks via Flip (formerly Flipgrid).
6. Create book "floods" by providing wide access to books with Free Book Fridays and book swaps at the beginning and end of the year.
7. Encourage learners to develop and share their identity as readers. Plan and facilitate monthly lessons where students reflect on interests and habits. Create bookmojis.
8. Spread enthusiasm to get everyone talking about books! Reading culture should permeate every corner of your school. Engage with toilet talkers, one-minute classroom book talks, poetry zoom-bombing, first-chapter Fridays, and interactive displays, and broadcast "Live from the Library" regularly.
9. Read widely and frequently. Participate in publishing webinars to see what's coming. Utilize social media and follow hashtags such as #BookPosse. Attend conferences and form relationships with local independent bookstores.
10. Make curricular connections. Regularly infuse curriculum with engaging and provocative new titles.
    Bonus Tip
11. Remember the social aspect of reading. Start a book club that encourages school-wide participation, focus on Manga (or another popular genre), host poetry slams, encourage student reviews, and incorporate appropriate social media and tools such as Flipgrid for book talks.

Melissa Thom

Check out Melissa's webpage on Schoolwide Culture of Reading:
https://sites.google.com/melissathom.com/joyfullteacherlibrarian
/schoolwide-reading-culture

Most elementary teachers read aloud to classes daily. The experience of reading aloud should not end in elementary school. The activity presents effective modeling and helps students witness an adult's joy in reading and engages them in enjoying stories as a group as they are introduced to new authors and a variety of literature types. Librarians can be invaluable partners in helping teachers choose what to read, keeping them up to date with exciting new titles, and perhaps pushing them out of their usual comfort-zone, go-to books. Your recommendations to your teacher partners present opportunities for the introduction of diverse titles beyond classic children's literature and typical grade-level favorites. It is an opportunity to regularly inject into those classroom read-alouds a few "windows, mirrors, and sliding doors."

Although building diverse collections is discussed further in chapter 9, it is appropriate here to introduce the wisdom of Rudine Sims Bishop in her description of the importance of ensuring that students have access to books that offer them windows, mirrors, and sliding doors.

> Books are sometimes windows, offering views of worlds that may be real or imagined, familiar or strange. These windows are also sliding glass doors, and readers have only to walk through in imagination to become part of whatever world has been created and recreated by the author. When lighting conditions are just right, however, a window can also be a mirror. Literature transforms human experience and reflects it back to us, and in that reflection we can see our own lives and experiences as part of the larger human experience. Reading, then, becomes a means of self-affirmation, and readers often seek their mirrors in books.[5]

Middle and high school teachers might also be encouraged to read briefly to students at the beginning or the end of class if it is not their habit. Those who do regularly read aloud would welcome suggestions of quick reads from current news, as well as engaging biographies or other nonfiction, poetry, or short stories relevant to their courses. These can expand student understanding and promote feelings of empathy well beyond the impact of their standard texts. It also demonstrates their teacher's belief in the value and joy of reading.

It is important that students see their teachers and other adults in their lives as readers. In addition to encouraging teachers, administrators, and all of the school staff to share their favorite or current reads on signs or email signatures, librarians can lead school-wide initiatives such as Drop Everything and Read (DEAR) and sustained silent reading (SSR).

Librarians can support students who are reluctant or struggling readers, often with the support of the reading coach. As a team, the reading coach and librarian use many ways to invite more reluctant readers into the habit of reading. High-interest titles, literature about popular culture, and graphic novels may be highly effective entry points for some students. Audiobooks count as reading and can serve as an on-ramp to reading other formats. Discovering student interests and passions beyond the school day will offer strategies for connecting kids with books. Emerging artificial intelligence tools like Microsoft Reading Progress and Reading Coach present stigma-free approaches to developing students' reading fluency and pride in their growing abilities.

Quantitative dimensions ask us to consider the traditional reading levels of the text by using formulas such as the Flesh-Kinkaid, Dale Chall, or Lexile levels to determine the complexity of the text. Unfortunately, such formulas cannot determine the complexity of the text when taken in context, and most people read in context. These formulas strip out the language and rate the text without the context. Neither the difficulty of the concepts in the text nor the complexity of the grammar is rated by the formulas, so the true complexity of the text is not measured. Librarians can and may be required to rate books in their libraries by quantitative levels in some way, perhaps labeling them or giving teachers a relevant list. However, librarians need to intervene and help teachers and students find things that they can read but that they are also interested in reading. The American Association of School Librarians (AASL), in its Position Statement on Labeling Practices,[6] discourages the usage of labeling or arranging books by these scales and instead promotes unrestricted access. It is known that students can and do successfully read books above their tested reading levels if the content of the book is compelling for them. Previous studies show that children do not choose only "easy" books for their recreational reading. Much of what they choose is at or above their reading level.[7] In addition to the issues presented by labeling books by readability scales, librarians must consider labeling as it relates to student privacy and identity.

Ready Access to a Good Book Helps Improve Reading Skills

When Stephen Krashen revised his landmark publication *The Power of Reading* in 2004, he retained this paragraph:

> There is abundant evidence that literacy development can occur without formal instruction. Moreover, this evidence strongly suggests that reading is potent enough to do nearly the entire job alone.[8]

Almost 10 years later, in *Free Voluntary Reading*, Krashen noted once again that:

> the progress made in free voluntary reading over the last decade, since the completion of the second edition of *The Power of Reading* . . . is all good news: Free voluntary reading looks better and better and more powerful than ever. And the alternatives to free reading as a means of developing high levels of literacy look weaker than ever.[9]

Krashen reports the results of "read and test" studies, in which students read text with vocabulary that is unfamiliar to them. They were not told they would be given a vocabulary or spelling test. Rather, they were tested to see whether they learned any of the meanings of unfamiliar words. Acquisition of vocabulary and spelling occurred without skill-building or correction, which shows that literacy development can occur without instruction. Krashen summarized these results:

> In-school free reading studies and "out of school" self-reported free voluntary reading studies show that more reading results in better reading comprehension, writing style, vocabulary, spelling, and grammatical development.[10]

To apply these research findings in elementary schools, school librarians must allow as much free voluntary reading time as possible. A case can be made for using the entire time students are assigned to the school library to read and read and read. This research supports the value of having free voluntary reading in schools where students are assigned to the school library during the teacher's planning period.

Rather than attempting to teach some isolated library skill, you can teach reading by allowing students to read. Studies have shown that the amount of reading a student does is directly linked to achieving higher-order independent reading and that increased volume has been positively linked to increased reading comprehension, vocabulary, and writing skills.[11]

School librarians have little control over the funding for their school district, but they are responsible for their students having ready access to good books. Research confirms the need for a wide variety of materials to entice student interest in reading. Searching for funding to purchase good books may appear to be too daunting to address, but a start might be to find an organization or local group. Pointing out the need for good reading materials might become a fund-raising project for those groups. Although such projects must be undertaken with the knowledge and support of the principal, they will demonstrate and highlight the lack of materials in the collection and the effort being launched by the school librarian. Additional information about budgets and funding can be found in Chapter 7.

The connection between the amount of reading done and reading proficiency has been well known and accepted for a number of years. Less well known but of equal importance is the finding that more access to reading materials *leads* to more reading, and subsequently higher reading achievement, and can itself explain a great deal of variation in reading scores.[12]

McQuillan closes his book with this paragraph:

> There is now considerable evidence that the amount and
> quality of students' access to reading materials is substantively
> related to the amount of reading they engage in, which in turn
> is the most important determinant of reading achievement.
> Many students attend schools where the level of print access
> is abysmal, creating a true crisis in reading performance. . . .
> I do *not* wish to argue that simply providing books is all that is
> needed for schools to succeed. . . . But just as we would not ask
> a doctor to heal without medicine, so we should not ask teachers
> and schools to teach without the materials to do so.[13]

The challenge for every school librarian at every level is to provide a robust collection of reading materials (both print and digital), ensure equitable access for every student, and encourage and promote free voluntary reading for pleasure. This is in addition to the intensive work that will be necessary to acquire and integrate the correct materials at the right level of text complexity for each student into their planning for collaborative instruction with teachers in all areas of the curriculum in order to facilitate deep content knowledge and broad understandings.

Commercial Reading Incentive Programs and Suggestions to Encourage Reading

School librarians are often asked by their administrators to participate in and coordinate reading initiatives. In an effort to increase reading, schools may implement a commercial computerized reading incentive program. Houghton Mifflin Harcourt's *Reading Counts* and Renaissance's *Accelerated Reader* are the two industry leaders of this type of computerized reading program that has proliferated in the past. With these programs, students read from specific books, generally obtained from the core fiction collection of the school library. After reading the book, the students then take a computer test on what they just read. Points are awarded based on the number of correct answers and the length and difficulty of the book.

Although both the incentive industry and educators agree that these tests do not measure true comprehension or higher-order thinking skills, it is also established that they do measure basic recall and the amount of text that has been processed.

Disagreement about the effectiveness of these programs is often characterized with two major recurring themes: (1) teachers may use points to assign reading grades; and (2) reading is not connected to its misuse of the points and program intrinsic rewards, but instead an external reward is used to coerce reading as a means to get prizes. The literature has articles both in favor of and against the use of such external reward systems. Unfortunately, some of the research has been conducted by the program developers themselves rather than independent researchers, and it is not surprising that their research reports that such programs are effective.

Commercial incentive programs can become a real problem for or be a true boon to school librarians. On the positive side, libraries will generally require a larger and newer book collection to support the increased demand for and use of books. Administrators and parents who support these programs will generally provide funds to implement them. As long as the money is *in addition to* the amount needed to implement a balanced collection development policy, this is a way to grow a school library's collection. Initially, at least, the students will also tend to read a significantly larger number of books and visit the library more often in their quest for points. Teachers are likely to rely more heavily on the school librarian to support the reading program and to realize the importance of increased access opportunities for their students. Difficulties occur if the collection development policy is ignored when teachers (or parents) insist that only books available from and tested by these programs be added to the collection. Additionally, a school that makes a small initial investment in one of these programs may have very few quizzes. This can cause students to limit their selections to a small number of options, which will thus discourage reading choice based on interest. Students tend to game these quizzes. Once a school is firmly entrenched with an incentive program, school librarians may find that students will resist checking out books (even the brand-new fiction titles) unless a quiz is available because they cannot earn credit for reading them. An additional concern is that students will be limited to reading at certain levels in order to earn credit.

It is debatable whether extrinsic rewards provide the literacy development that reading alone can create. You can help teachers understand that the score from a computer test taken by their students does not necessarily indicate an understanding of the content of what has been read. Using the computerized reading program as a way of measuring reading practice and time on task may simplify record-keeping and verify that students have actually read books, which is something that self-reported reading logs do not do. Krashen reports: "Despite the popularity of [a reading management program], we must conclude that there is no real evidence supporting it, no real evidence that the additional tests and rewards add anything to the power of simply supplying access to high-quality and interesting reading material and providing time for children to read."[14] You may implement creative reading initiatives that are successful by keeping reading voluntary, linking it to intrinsic rewards, and maintaining a relationship with teachers to support a strong reading instruction program instead of supplanting it.

An article by Gilbert and Grover[15] adds ideas about making library resources available "when the library is closed," as it was during the pandemic. However, they detail many other creative ways to help you support reading, such as offering quality books and other sources like magazines placed in the cafeteria. Their mantra is to remove barriers to reading materials and provide as much continuous access as possible through expanding access in hallways and classrooms. It might even be possible to institute a program based on the concept of the "Little Free Libraries" that people have in their front yards, where you can take a book, donate a book, or return the book you borrowed.

Using booktalks to share books with students has long been an excellent way to encourage reading. A variety of digital applications facilitate these opportunities. For example, Microsoft's Flip and other digital storytelling tools allow for the creation of book trailers. Additionally, school librarians frequently utilize social media to promote reading, creating blogs, vlogs, and short clips on sites such as TikTok. Regardless of your background, AASL's Position Statement, "The School Librarian's Role in Reading," clarifies your responsibilities for leadership:

> As literacy leaders, school librarians are positioned to elevate the importance of reading as well as reading proficiency to support all learners' academic success. . . . The activities of school librarians in reading promotions, instruction, resources and services . . . are developed around six essential Shared Foundations—Inquire, Include, Collaborate, Curate, Explore, and Engage.[16]

You will also want to consult the AASL School Librarian's Role in Reading Toolkit.

Sharing with students is important, and booktalking is one way to share your collection. It is also important to share information when helping administrators and teachers keep up to date with research findings in professional journals.

Sharing Reading and Curriculum Research

No one doubts that the world is welcoming the advent of telecommunications to provide instantaneous access to information, but this merely intensifies the emphasis on reading and the emphasis teachers and school librarians must place on helping students learn to read. To understand most information on a computer screen, you must be able to read and interpret the language of the information. Students must know how to read, and they will learn when they are in schools with strong reading programs. Content-area studies cannot be realized until students become competent readers. Reading is basic. Research shows that reading programs are stronger when they are supported with an excellent collection of materials in the school library. Being aware of the research helps teachers learn best practices. School librarians should be aware of the latest research and share it with their administrators and teachers.

Fisher and Ivey[17] suggested that the traditional practice of assigning all students to read the same book at the same time results in a singularly unenthusiastic approach to the enjoyment of literature. Even high-achieving students take shortcuts just to finish assignments. You can help teachers move away from requiring students to read the same book by providing a list of quality options within a theme that allow choice of books of increasing text complexity. This will allow teachers to guide students in choosing appropriate-level texts, as well as allowing students choice and keeping them engaged. Research has shown that self-selected reading is twice as powerful as teacher-selected whole-class reads in increasing both motivation and comprehension.[18]

Because the school library has current and ongoing subscriptions to either hard-copy or online professional journals in the professional collection, school librarians should search the education research for results they can share with teachers. Teachers are often pressured to implement the current educational trend. "Keeping teachers informed will help them structure programs using the library."[19] Sharing research creates the opportunity for you, the librarian, to share in the implementation of a reading program, and everyone wins. When you work with teachers to improve reading proficiency, you are helping learners use their skills, resources, and tools to inquire, think critically, and gain knowledge. This moves beyond teaching reading to other areas of the curriculum.

The Education Program and the Curriculum

This section explores the role of the school library as the center and heart of collaborative teaching and learning in the school. It follows that the number-one task of a school librarian is to assist teachers in successfully turning units of curriculum into opportunities for student inquiry that will promote lifelong learning. Unit activities are planned with full knowledge of current teaching methods, an understanding of student learning differences, and knowledge of the curriculum and the types of assignments. Your goal is to collaboratively plan and co-teach units of instruction that encourage and enable student inquiry to take place. This means managing the library as a classroom with the knowledge that the librarian will sometimes need to go into that classroom (and others) to facilitate a co-teaching experience. To meet the teaching needs of teachers and the learning needs of students, you must understand how to teach, how teachers teach, and how students learn. You should strive to be an excellent teacher yourself, staying abreast of new technologies and new teaching methods and theories. As excellent researchers, school librarians are able to access and share current information with teachers and administration. You will be able to use those new learnings to model the best instruction and provide staff development opportunities for your fellow teachers. You will become the learning leaders—specialists—in the school. An excellent resource to consider in understanding this role of the school librarian is *Librarians as Learning Specialists* by Harada and Zmuda.[20]

Analyzing Teaching Methods

Despite the efforts of education leaders who suggest the need to use a variety of resources and teaching methods to accommodate students' different learning styles, many teachers rely on their textbooks and their lectures as their go-to teaching methods. However, the textbook model does not make use of what experts know about learner engagement and the wide variety of instructional design strategies and materials available as you work to reach every student. Moving beyond the textbook encourages teachers and librarians to plan experiences that will help teachers to expand curriculum experiences, incorporate emerging news, engage with media, and encourage individualized and group activities that will meet the needs of students and engage them in learning.

Teachers who anticipate student learning needs by incorporating a variety of methods make discoveries well beyond the text and are often very grateful for librarian partners. Planning curriculum-based inquiry projects with teachers to ensure that students can explore a topic of interest or embrace an interesting project, and report this learning or problem solution in a meaningful way, requires much more time than preparing a lecture and developing a test on the content. Librarians can also promote the idea of the Genius Hour[21] in their schools, which encourages students to make individual inquiries into topics of their choice. Either type of project is coordinated with the library staff to confirm the availability of library space and materials when activities move out of the classroom. Topics are expanded to permit students to conduct their research as individuals and in small groups.

Many teachers are better able to manage classroom-wide assignments than independent study or group projects, but you can help them manage individual projects and empower students to research topics of their individual choice. School librarians can help by suggesting alternatives to "Make a poster" or "Write a report" to show how students might creatively use their talents to demonstrate what they have learned. A link to a list of "50 or So Ways" can be found in the Additional Resources. These transform potentially boring presentations—as boring for the student carrying out the assignment as they will be to the audience who must view this result—into informative events. The interesting ways to present student findings grow exponentially with new technology applications. It is your responsibility to be informed and continually update their knowledge in order to pique student interest. Librarians can do much to encourage alternative teaching methods and materials for covering the curriculum.

For some students, visual or auditory media can enhance reading skills through strengthening decoding and contextual understanding. Visual and auditory media can provide access to content that might be above a students' current reading level. For example, a graphic novel about the discovery of DNA would provide introductory access to students of many levels through its use of visual context clues, where traditional text about the same topic may be intimidating for some students. You could also use a 3-D virtual model of DNA to better demonstrate its structure. Media resources like documentary films, virtual lab simulations, augmented reality resources, and non-fiction graphic novels can add new depth to lessons. Librarians should facilitate integration by selecting, linking to, and embedding relevant media on library and teachers' websites or in learning management systems.

Expanding projects requires extensive planning, but the rewards are well worth it. Working closely with teachers, librarians help plan units of work by agreeing on desired student outcomes and designing the unit of study; deciding on appropriate teaching methods; preparing activities related to the unit; helping teach the unit; deciding methods of testing; and, finally, helping score the products and assign the grades.

If examples are needed to show projects and how they are evaluated, see *Assessing for Learning: Librarians and Teachers as Partners.*[22] A wide variety of assessment models are also included in this volume.

Helping Enhance Teacher Assessments

Helping teachers improve their assessments will increase learning opportunities and make learning more interesting. It is easy to illustrate a boring assignment. A common use of the library for classroom assignments is the book report. At the elementary level, the assignment may be as unexciting as, "Read a book with at least 100 pages." From the management standpoint, this is simple. It does not take long for us to locate books with more than 100 pages. The assignment lacks creativity, and this is not lost on students. Furthermore, one book with 100 pages might look very different from another book with 100 pages, to say nothing of how we might count audiobook pages. Offering to help teachers design creative assessments that leverage personal choice, spark inquiry investigations, and engage learners in creative communication of their reading or learning becomes a major opportunity for librarians.

Librarians encourage a culture of academic honesty. This means that you teach and model media-appropriate attribution. You might simplify the process through the introduction of documentation tools, often embedded within the students' writing and research tools and databases. They should consider those outputs as a rough draft that may need tweaking. Students also need to consider that subject-area teachers, at the high school level and later in the various disciplines they will encounter in higher education, may prefer different documentation styles.

Too many librarians never see the final results of their support of inquiry projects. Assisting teachers in reading, viewing, or listening to the final projects and sharing responsibility in assessing the products of student inquiry are part of your curricular responsibilities. Collaboratively reviewing student projects allows you and your partner(s) to reflect on any necessary instructional tweaking for next time around and decide whether additional instruction may be needed to prepare students for the assessment as they become more efficient and ethical users and creators of ideas and information.

Understanding the Learner

As accomplished teachers themselves, school librarians must draw on their knowledge of learning theory and child development, as well as instructional design, to participate in designing instruction in collaboration with teachers. You have in-depth knowledge of literature for students of all ages and know just the age when a particular title is best used. You have in-depth knowledge of all types of learning materials available from the library and beyond, and you understand the needs of a wide variety of learners. You have knowledge of and lenses on both the grade-to-grade vertical alignment and disciplinary or class-to-class horizontal alignment of the curriculum.

The classroom or subject-area teacher will know their content and their students and be able to bring that knowledge of their preferred learning modalities and learning differences to the collaboration discussion. You will have expert knowledge of what materials are best to use with all types of learners, and you will have knowledge of the inquiry process, including searching, curating and communication skills, and you will have knowledge of emerging technologies and strategies, and so you will become invaluable to the planning process. In planning instruction, you should validate and respect the strengths and diverse perspectives of your students. Culturally responsive teaching approaches learning from an asset perspective rather than a deficit perspective, building on what students already know, rather than focusing on what they don't know. This approach requires that we know our students, their cultures, our resources, and our curriculum. Together the school librarian and teacher make a great team in planning the best learning experience for all students.

Understanding Curriculum

School librarians who have elementary teaching certification, or a subject specialty at the secondary level in addition to library certification, already know a good deal about curriculum. They may be highly knowledgeable about the relationship of the curriculum to the classroom. Most preparation programs for school librarians provide some experience in the development of curriculum units in coursework and in the practicum setting. In preparing to participate in curriculum collaborative planning, librarians must learn as much as possible about the curriculum in the local school.

Steps to Learn About Curriculum in Your Building

1. Review state-level standards for the curriculum being taught
2. Determine what textbooks are used and keep a copy of each in the library's collection
3. Collect information from teachers about content-based software programs that are used in teaching
4. Request and review school or district-level curriculum and pacing guides
5. Participate in curriculum committees such as department committees or grade-level committees

---

Begin this process by creating a collection of all textbooks used in the building, both commercially produced in hard copy and e-format and teacher-created e-textbooks. Librarians who review textbooks and other materials used by teachers can make serious inroads in co-planning the upcoming semester's instructional units. If you cannot collect texts, try to borrow copies from teachers as you begin to partner with them.

Some courses may not use formal texts, and curriculum may be based on an online program. In schools where librarians have already made an impact, subscription databases may function as texts. For instance, Gale, ABC-CLIO, Rosen, and Capstone products are seamlessly embedded in teachers' learning management systems and offer integrated functionality for such tasks as note-taking and documentation. You can make a huge difference in a teacher's success and confidence by introducing these attractive, engaging, dynamic, and continually updated tools into their instructional practice.

You will want to examine curriculum and pacing guides developed at the building and district levels and at the state department of public instruction. Collect state or national standards for student learning in all subject areas and alignment across grade levels. These will also be useful to teachers who need to know what has been covered in previous grade levels and subject courses and what will be covered in the future. An ever-growing variety of AASL crosswalks will help you connect the National School Library Standards with the standards of your classroom colleagues and instructional coaches. These documents allow you to speak the language of your collaborators and more directly meet their needs. As of the writing of this text, these crosswalks include the following, all of which are available as downloadable PDFs on the AASL National Standards portal (https://standards.aasl.org/project/crosswalks/):

- ASCD Whole Child Tenets
- Code with Google's CS First Curriculum (Statement of Alignment)
- Future Ready Framework
- ISTE Standards for Students and Educators
- Next Generation Science Standards (How to Read)

Throughout the year, you should expand on the projects reviewed during the first week in the building, determining what each teacher teaches and integrating the method of teaching, the materials needed beyond those provided in the classroom, and the probable use to be made of all types of resources available in the library and online.

One way to lead in curriculum development, and develop full-program awareness, is to volunteer to serve on text adoption or curriculum development committees. Being more aware of text contents facilitates your ability to directly connect your print and digital resources to your teacher-partners' needs. If digital texts are adopted, the librarian should work with the classroom teacher to ensure that all students have access. This may involve advocating with administrators regarding purchases for individual students or purchasing and loaning personal devices and wifi hotspots from the library. New procedures may have to be developed for these loans.

Librarians also serve on curriculum committees. By serving on these grade-level or subject-area committees, you will be better able to collaborate and provide library resources for the unit plans of all teachers. Meetings of such committees are frequently scheduled for after school and sometimes as summer projects. Managing time to participate in these meetings may be difficult if they occur during school hours, but you need a seat at these tables. Volunteering for these roles will determine whether inquiry and research become school-wide, grade-level, or department priorities. If necessary, try to arrange the coverage that will allow you to attend. Justifying this need emphasizes the importance of your involvement as an instructional partner. You need to develop an understanding that the library can be available with a professional replacement when you have critical responsibilities and contributions to make elsewhere.

Because of their responsibilities to teach all students and partner with all teachers, school librarians take a leadership role in developing and implementing curriculum. Librarians are in a unique position to suggest units that span grade levels and connect subject areas, emphasizing that learning does not fit in discrete boxes and ensuring that the instructional program is presented as an integrated whole rather than as separate, segregated components. This allows learners to make critical connections in their knowledge and apply real-life relevance to their studies.

The relationship of what is taught to your students' futures may become more apparent to the students who are tasked with designing their own learning. A *learner-centered program* is one that engages students in the process and addresses their needs and interests. Whenever possible, you will want to invite students to collaborate with the teacher and librarian team. Whenever possible, recognize the importance of student choice and student voice. Learner-centered opportunities may be furthered by offering choices in students' inquiry opportunities and choice of assessment options. For some fresh assessment ideas, visit the many school librarian and edtech bloggers and social media folks shared in the "Finding Your People" in the School Library HQ LibGuide as well as "50 (or So) Ways to Ditch Your Paper or Book Report," both found in the Additional Resources. The options for authentically communicating new knowledge have expanded dramatically with the emergence of free, easy-to-use, and professional-looking publishing and digital storytelling tools. More of these are explored in chapter 11.

These opportunities may be furthered by the use of pedagogical strategies such as digital choice boards, collaborative escape rooms such as BreakoutEDU and other game-based approaches, Hyperdocs, and learning centers or stations set up in classrooms and libraries or on the library's digital spaces. These will allow you to present students with choices for how they prefer to learn and communicate their learning. They also allow you to personalize and differentiate instruction. Additionally, library spaces may include informal makerspace opportunities and challenges introduced at library tables, or on displays and bulletin boards. Some librarians introduce the possibility of independent passion projects or lead learners to outside micro-credentialing, certificate, or badging programs.

Help teachers provide the kinds of experiences that students will translate into their immediate future and when they are adults. Faced with the often-required, narrow, test-driven curricular programs, teachers may feel they have limited opportunities to experiment with new strategies. Your role—school librarian as instructional partner—can encourage teachers to take a few risks and be more playful and joyful with their instruction. Your in-depth knowledge of what is being taught and what will be taught in each classroom provides opportunities to suggest combined learning experiences. The big-picture knowledge of all content standards enables you to see overlaps and repeated broad requirements, which can be streamlined and taught as one lesson, thus freeing up instructional time. Students working in makerspaces or participating in schoolwide Genius Hour projects can cross grade levels with an interest in a particular application. Methods for creating this environment in the library are described in *Social-Emotional Learning Using Makerspaces and Passion Projects*[23] and *Challenge-Based Learning in the School Library Makerspace.*[24] This is discussed in more detail later in this chapter.

You can help teachers remember to integrate critical thinking assessment to better prepare students for transferable lifelong and lifewide learning experiences. When curriculum is discussed, the librarian should be an aggressive advocate of expanding student learning into real-world experiences such as project- and problem-based learning, so as to place students' learning into the context of how they will function in the future. In planning learning activities, librarians should be advocates for equity relating to physical and intellectual access and assist in showing how instruction might be as inclusive as possible. Additionally, the librarian should work to integrate the learner framework from the *National School Library Standards* into collaborative projects.

Inquiry-Driven Learning

Inquiry is truly in the DNA of the librarian. The librarian helps teachers implement inquiry-driven learning with a focus on meaningful activities that will help students develop critical thinking skills and prepare them to transfer those skills to the problems they will encounter well after they graduate.

A variety of models exists to support inquiry as a learning strategy, including Carol Kuhlthau's research-based Six Principles of Constructivist Learning, based on the theories of Dewey Brunner, Vygotsky, Kelly, and Piaget. These principles underlie the guided inquiry process:

1. Children learn by being actively engaged in and reflecting on an experience.

2. Children learn by building on what they already know.

3. Children develop higher-order thinking through guidance at critical points in the learning process.

4. Children have different ways and modes of learning.

5. Children learn through social interaction with others.

6. Children learn through instruction and experience in accord with their cognitive development.[25]

When the librarian joins teachers in planning classroom assignments, it is easy to move into the inquiry process, especially when teachers are open to makeovers that may create more student engagement.

Making Inquiry Happen

Librarians can work with classroom teachers to scaffold projects that spark curiosity and guide students toward success. Kuhlthau, Maniotes, and Caspari (2007) offer a description of the inquiry approach:

> Inquiry is an approach to learning whereby students find and use a variety of sources of information and ideas to increase their own understanding of a problem, topic or issue of importance. It requires more than simply answering questions or getting a right answer. It espouses investigation, exploration, search, quest, research, pursuit, and study. It is enhanced by involvement with a community of learners, each learning from the other in social interaction.[26]

Inquiry-driven learning actively engages students in critical thinking and questioning. The approach has far longer "legs" in terms of transferability of growth dispositions and skills than the traditional report, which simply requires students to repeat knowledge that likely has already been covered by professional reference book writers. Instead of the traditional country report, an inquiry project may engage learners in determining which country they would prefer to visit based on criteria of their own choosing, and then have them creatively present and defend the reasons for their decisions using a communication tool of their choice.

In their article, "Making the Shift: From Traditional Research Assignments to Guiding Inquiry Learning," Leslie Maniotes and Carol Kuhlthau offer a strong rationale for the transition to inquiry:

- Inquiry promotes and supports academic research at all ages.

- Inquiry is learning-centered, not product-driven.

- Inquiry recognizes and supports the emotional aspect of learning.

- Inquiry is carefully and intentionally designed.

- Inquiry is driven by students' high level of questioning.

- Inquiry goes beyond low-level fact-finding to deep understanding.[27]

Partnering in the design of learning also involves developing assessments of student products. You can be actively involved in several ways:

- Ensuring that projects are learner-centered and that students are offered opportunities for choice and voice in their investigations and assessments.

- Ensuring that projects are inclusive and address needs for personalization and differentiation.

- Identifying and selecting from among the various methods of assessing student progress reported in the literature.

- Assuring that assessments of student progress include an analysis of students' ability to search for, evaluate, synthesize, creatively communicate, and ethically credit information from diverse sources.

- Working with students and teachers to reflect and make judgments about what was learned and what comes next.

- Planning collaborative inquiry-based units that foster authentic, learner-driven investigations.

Inquiry Learning Models

A variety of models offer inquiry scaffolding to help you work with partner teachers and learners in designing effective inquiry experiences. They include Guided Inquiry Design, the Stripling Inquiry Model, Framework of Skills for Inquiry Learning, and Big6 and the Super3.

Guided Inquiry Design® (GID)

The GID framework scaffolds the inquiry process in eight fluid and flexible phases—Open, Immerse, Explore, Identify, Gather, Create, Share, and Evaluate—that occur over time as students engage in and are guided through overlapping learning experiences (Figure 5-1). GID incorporates Kuhlthau's classic research in the information search process (ISP), acknowledging the stages that students experience in the ISP and suggesting when students need guidance and what type of guidance would be most helpful (https://guidedinquirydesign.com).

The Stripling Inquiry Model

The Stripling Inquiry Model, used in New York's Empire State Information Fluency Curriculum, is based on a model developed when Barbara Stripling worked with the Library of Congress Teachers with Primary Sources Program. Her six-phase model is recursive and reflective and encourages students through the stages of Connect, Wonder, Investigate, Construct, Express, and Reflect (https://nycdoe.libguides.com/c.php?g=944646&p=6809534). See figure 5-2 on the next page.

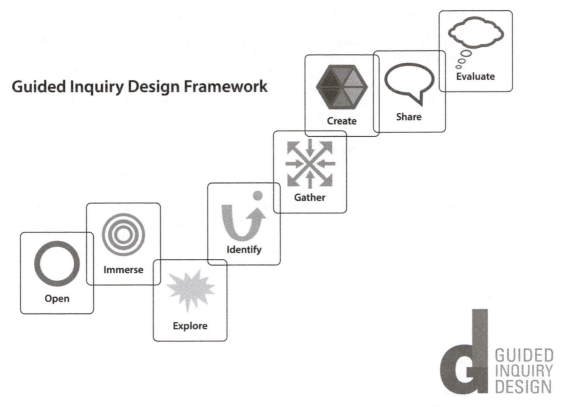

Figure 5-1. Guided Inquiry Design: A Framework for Inquiry in Your School (2012).

Reprinted with permission.

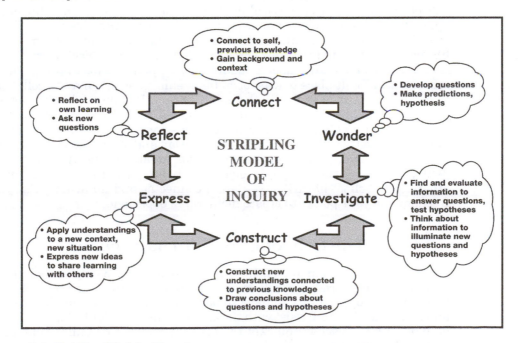

Figure 5-2. Stripling Model of Inquiry.

Barbara Stripling.

Framework of Skills for Inquiry Learning (FOSIL)

FOSIL, a model developed by Darryl Toerien from the United Kingdom, is based on Stripling's Model of Inquiry. The FOSIL Cycle of Inquiry for ages 4–18 (with a simplified version for younger children) uses double-headed arrows to represent students' inevitable moves backward and forward between the stages identified as Connect, Wonder, Investigate, Construct, Express, and Reflect. https://fosil.org.uk

Big6 and the Super3

Designed for K–12 students, the Big6 model, developed by Mike Eisenberg and Bob Berkowitz, describes how people of all ages might solve information problems. The Big6 model involves six phases: Task Definition, Information Seeking Strategies, Location and Access, Use of Information, Synthesis, and Evaluation. Each of those phases has two sub-stages. The Super3 echoes the Big6 stages in language accessible for younger students. https://thebig6.org

Beyond the Curriculum

In several ways, school librarians have more freedom than any other educator in the building. They are free to create and connect across grade and ability levels and across disciplines. In fact, they are free to create beyond the walls of the traditional program and the building. The school librarian is in a position to plan activities and events for students that reach beyond the curriculum. These can be helpful opportunities that may be hosted in the library before and after school and during lunch.

Schools may also have additional areas of student learning focus outside of the subject-based curriculum. Some schools adopt a leadership development model or place an emphasis on social and emotional learning. These school-wide cross-curricular initiatives provide opportunities for school librarians to initiate programs across grade levels and subject areas.

Activities for high school students may be planned for evenings; if the school is a difficult place to keep open for evenings, events may be collaboratively planned and hosted with the public library. Pajama nights for elementary school children, poetry slams, unplugged music nights, informal art galleries, and whole-community book discussions bring school and public librarians together. Global events like Dot Day and World Read Aloud Day, to name just two, present opportunities for greater connections with students, authors, experts, app developers, scholars, scientists, and so many others. As a school librarian, you are a connector and innovator. Use your freedom and your power to create memorable experiences.

The School Librarian as Teacher

Your participation in teaching a lesson and reviewing or helping to assess the final products will encourage teachers to plan units of work together. The opportunity to have someone help make teaching both easier and more effective and assist with the assessment of student progress should be irresistible. Teachers quickly realize that instruction can be enhanced and made more fun with the inclusion of a partner, and in fact, it is easier to take a few innovative risks when someone has your back. Students now have the skills of two teachers focused on their project rather than just one. While one teacher focuses on content, the other may focus on processes, dispositions, and skills. The investment you make in collaborative planning will be rewarded through development of strong teaching collegiality. Lessons are not one and done. Each time you collaborate, you have the opportunity to reflect with your teaching partners and make improvements that will result in richer learning experiences for your students.

It can be difficult to coordinate the collaboration of teachers who may not, at first, feel comfortable in joint teaching experiences or in setting their students free to learn independently and in small groups. Some teachers prefer to keep their doors closed. It requires the best efforts of the librarian to lead the teamwork to make this happen. You will not win every teacher over right away, but your base will grow bigger as the word of your valuable contributions spreads.

Formal Lesson Plans

Your classroom teacher colleagues are usually required to submit formal lesson plans to an administrator on a weekly or monthly basis. These are shared with substitute teachers when the classroom teacher is ill or away. Even if you are not required to provide lesson plans, the fact that you have recorded plans moves you from the "special" category into the role of teacher. Models of lessons are widely available and you will practice designing instruction in your pre-service coursework. The recorded plan book just indicates your plan of instruction.

While your school or district may use its own standard template, you can expect the typical components of a formal lesson plan to include:

Learning objectives: These must be built using verbs that are measurable and observable. There are several charts that list verbs associated with the various levels of Bloom's Taxonomy.[28] With his collaborators, Bloom created a framework for categorizing educational goals that has been applied by generations of teachers and college instructors. The Revised Bloom's Taxonomy describes activities moving in the following progression: Remember, Understand, Apply, Analyze, Evaluate, Create.[29] When possible, you want to move students from the base lower-level thinking skills verbs associated with Remember up to objectives that offer learners opportunities to Create, associated with higher-level thinking skills. Your choice of verbs is important in promoting the growth of learning. You will want to avoid the following verbs, as they are not measurable: Know, Comprehend, Understand, Appreciate, Familiarize, Study, Be Aware, Become Acquainted with, Gain Knowledge of, Cover, Learn, and Realize.

Lesson information: Grade level, content area(s), length of time needed, etc. If the lesson is part of a unit of instruction, how does this lesson fit into the sequence of the overall unit?

Learning standards or benchmarks: Include the AASL National Standards, your colleague's content area and grade-level standards, and standards that may be co-owned (for instance, ISTE's Learner Standards or the Future Ready Schools Framework). You may choose to link these for convenience, especially for your administrator.

Learning environment: How will you arrange instructional resources? Will students work independently, or in groups, or will the instruction be a large-group event? If there is more than one activity, how will you manage transitions and how much time will you allot to each? Are accommodations planned to address students with special needs? What equipment or materials are needed and where are they located?

Hook/lead-in: Learning cannot happen unless you engage or connect with learners. You can begin with a story or anecdote, a provocative question, a short video, a relevant primary source or object, a poll that might double as a formative assessment, or a quote to interpret.

Assessing previous knowledge or recap of a previous lesson: What strategies would you use to determine what students remember from previous learning? Might you plan some questions, use polling software, gamified feedback, or other such methods?

Materials or instructional resources: For inquiry-driven projects, these will likely include curated digital options, such as databases, news sources, portals, videos, your own tutorials, or textbook(s) or other reading materials. You might also include or point to scaffolds for note-taking and outlining. You will also need to consider options for communicating new knowledge (for instance, infographic, newsletter, timeline, storytelling, video creation, and other platforms for publishing and sharing).

Instructional activities/Guided or independent practice: How will you actively engage students in the learning activities? Will you vary small- and large-group interactions? Are you planning any gamification elements or conversation protocols?

Formative assessment or evaluation of what was learned: Assessment or evaluation could take the form of an exit ticket. You might ask students to respond with a variety of digital tools or using index cards, flip-chart paper, or graffiti on a whiteboard or whiteboard tables. A simple approach is a flipchart page divided into the following columns–with markers for students to use to leave a dot. You could ask students to reflect with a 3-2-1 response. While these are adaptable, one approach is to share: three things you learned today, two interesting facts or ideas about the lesson, one lingering question. (See the Exit Tickets/Backchannel Playlist in the Additional Resources.)

Wrap-up: How will you conclude or summarize the learning, perhaps with the help of your students? What final messages do you want students to take away, perhaps to prepare them for their next visit?

Anchor Charts

One helpful strategy in visualizing, reinforcing, and creating evidence of your instruction is the creation of *anchor charts*. Whether physically displayed on a flipchart in the library or digitally displayed in online instruction, these attractive lists make learning "sticky" and visible. By presenting visual reminders of what is being taught, anchor charts support instruction and reinforce learning, anchoring or holding it in place. They remind students of what they are currently learning and, when archived, can present powerful evidence of your instructional impact. Look for models of visual tools on sites like Pinterest.

Teaching All Kinds of Literacies

The responsibility for teaching research skills and information literacy has long been seen as a major role of the librarian. Ever-increasing quantities of content generated in all media formats expands the role of the school librarian as responsible for students' learning in multiple literacies. Maintaining our commitment to the "information" part of information literacy, school librarians consider skills and dispositions necessary for students as they learn, work, and play. These skills and dispositions can be incorporated across the curriculum and involve far more than simply locating information.

Among others, literacies include:

- Digital literacy
- Financial literacy
- Media literacy
- News literacy
- Visual literacy
- Global literacy
- Numeracy

As discussed further in chapter 11, students need a new vocabulary for news literacy and tools for fact-checking across social media platforms. The basic necessities include the ability to evaluate the presentation of data in infographics, strategies to determine if images have been manipulated, and to determine whether a video (e.g., of a politician) is really a deep fake. The librarian's role in these emerging literacies can easily be tied to the curriculum and applied across content areas.

The School Librarian in the Classroom and the School Library *as* a Classroom

School libraries are experiential learning hubs for their schools—places where students can explore, experience, and innovate. The school library is *your* classroom. What takes place in your classroom is up to you. This is your opportunity to create the type of learning space that supports innovative and inclusive teaching and learning. With a greater degree of freedom than many classroom teachers, you can create an environment that fosters the individual curiosity and growth of each of your students. Adopting new models of instruction and trying new strategies is an important part of your role as an innovator in your school.

Among the new models are libraries as learning commons and the inclusion of makerspaces in libraries. When it becomes a learning commons for the school, the library becomes a classroom for everyone and includes every teacher. Koechlin, Rosenfeld, and Loertscher describe the learning commons as a "new learning model":

> Schools must develop new relevant learning models in response to students who expect to learn in new ways using the technologies they use ubiquitously outside of school. The Learning Commons is a real world approach to creating such a new collaborative learning model for students and teachers.[30]

This learning commons library is scheduled to accommodate students engaged in a wide variety of activities planned by a different composition of collaborators. Art, music, physical education, and counselors (among others) join classroom teachers to work to initiate activities that are collaboratively planned. Once the curriculum, teaching, and student assignments have been determined, students go to work.

Librarians continue to offer instruction in locating resources in the online public access catalog (OPAC), navigating traditional print formats (reading tables of contents, consulting indexes), and strategies for effective searching of the web, as they guide students in ethically attributing credit across information formats, discovering perspective, and discerning "truth." Teaching students to discriminate between fact and fiction, truth and falsehood, is becoming an ever-more-important responsibility for the librarian.

Functioning as a classroom, the library offers access to the world, facilitating global connections with authors, politicians, journalists, scientists, and others, including students and teachers through interviews via Zoom or Google Meet. If such connections are in languages other than English, librarians may be able to demonstrate new tools for real-time translation and students may be able to practice their knowledge of a language they are studying.

Makerspaces offer opportunities for students to engage in hands-on activities that inspire creativity and innovation while fostering critical thinking, as well as design thinking. In addition to presenting informal learning experiences, makerspaces offer opportunities to link memorable hands-on, creative experiences to curriculum. Each school library's makerspace should be specifically designed to meet the needs of its students. Some makerspaces will be devoted to focus on digital media creation; others may focus on the arts or crafts. If the library is not a large space, the makerspace may simply be a small corner with wider use at a time other than the school day. In some schools activities scheduled for the makerspace are directly tied to curricula. For instance, if the third grade is studying types of bridges, the makerspace might facilitate activities that engage learners in building various types of bridges, perhaps presenting these opportunities as learning challenges.

In many schools, makerspaces regularly offer opportunities to address challenges. These challenges may be puzzles, or problems involving constructing vehicles, robots, bridges, or other physical solutions that solve a particular problem. Ideally, students might identify real problems to be solved and engage in a collaborative design thinking process around prototypes for solutions. In some cases, makerspaces contribute to larger community needs. The librarian is charged with helping students research, seek expert help if necessary, and find the appropriate materials to solve the challenge using design thinking skills and perseverance. As mentioned earlier, *Challenge-Based Learning in the School Library Makerspace* can support such activities.

Current Awareness and Research Support for Teachers and Administrators

Librarians can use their expertise by helping administrators and teachers search for and discover information to inform their practice and support their formal learning. The librarian ensures that administrators and teachers are aware of trends in education. When professional journals come into the library or are posted online, share articles with administrators and teachers who will benefit from them. Regularly glean tables of contents of journals that will interest your faculty and share any articles and links you discover with those who need them. You might simply share those tables of contents and invite recipients to circle articles of immediate interest. You might offer to help your colleagues set up professionally relevant news feeds.

Additionally, some of your administrators and faculty will likely be involved in graduate programs. You can support this learning as well as action research that addresses critical school needs. This is an area where you might more personally demonstrate your value. Do not wait to be asked. Regularly support your colleagues' current awareness and research.

School librarians may feel restricted in the face of a rigid curriculum centered around a need for students to score well on statewide testing or to match rigid standards. However, changes can be made if teachers are willing to collaborate on meaningful assignments. Small pilot programs may be implemented with teachers to see whether they result in improved engagement and learning for students.

Focus on the curriculum. When time is limited, it is most important to focus on working with teachers and students instead of administrative tasks. For instance, helping students complete projects at the end of the school year and doing preliminary planning for the next year are far more important than closing the library for inventory. Weigh the impact of your activities, and decide which will not be noticed or recognized or appreciated by your students, colleagues, and administrators.

Put teaching and learning first. Your teaching role is enhanced by collaborating with teachers and students and learning. You may feel better prepared for this work after examining the suggestions in chapter 6 on assessment and evaluation.

Key Takeaways

- The charge to the school librarian is to create a learning environment offering multiple opportunities for teachers and students to work and learn together.

- The more creative librarians are in planning, implementing, evaluating, and supporting curriculum with engaging resources, the more able they will be to enhance learning in their community and the more valuable they will be as a member of the instructional team.

Challenges to Promote Growth

1. Visit with an elementary classroom teacher and ask about working with students to improve reading. Try to determine in what ways the school librarian might work and plan with this teacher.
2. Choose a middle or high school teacher and discuss the concept of text complexity with that teacher. Curate a bibliography of books of varying levels of text complexity to use in helping students choose a book to read on an assigned theme. (If they are available, consider using tools like Novelist, Novelist K8, and TeachingBooks and available book award lists for support.)
3. Create a digital choice board for an instructional unit presenting choices for both inquiry topics and creative assessments.
4. Plan an integrated curricular lesson that will teach reading skills, inquiry skills, and required content-area curricular content. Create an anchor chart representing that lesson for learners.

Notes

1. Henry L. Cecil and Willard A. Heaps. (1940). *School Library Service in the United States: An Interpretative Survey*, p. 41. New York: H. W. Wilson. Reprinted in Melvin M. Bowie. (1986). *Historic Documents of School Libraries.* Englewood, CO: Hi Willow Research and Publishing.

2. National Council of Teachers of English. (2019, December 5). "The Act of Reading: Instructional Foundations and Policy Guidelines" (position statement). https://ncte.org/statement/the-act-of-reading

3. Donalyn Miller and Teri Lesesne. (2022). *The Joy of Reading.* Portsmouth, NH: Heinemann, p. 23.

4. Douglas Fisher and Gay Ivey. (2006). "Evaluating the Interventions for Struggling Adolescent Readers." *Journal of Adolescent & Adult Literacy* 50 (November): 182.

5. Rudine S. Bishop. (1990). "Mirrors, Windows, and Sliding Glass Doors." *Perspectives: Choosing and Using Books for the Classroom* 6, no. 3 (Summer): ix.

6. American Librarian Association. (2021, February 18). "Position Statement on Labeling Practices." https://www.ala.org/aasl/sites/ala.org.aasl/files/content /advocacy/statements/docs/AASL_Labeling_Practices_Position_Statement_2021a.pdf

7. Rachel L. Wadham and Terrell A. Young. (2015). *Integrating Children's Literature Through the Common Core State Standards.* Santa Barbara, CA: Libraries Unlimited.

8. Stephen Krashen. (2004). *The Power of Reading,* 2nd ed. Englewood, CO: Libraries Unlimited, p. 20.

9. Stephen Krashen. 2011. *Free Voluntary Reading.* Santa Barbara, CA: Libraries Unlimited, p. vii.

10. Krashen, *Power of Reading, supra* n. 8, p. 17.

11. R. L. Allington. (2012). *What Really Matters for Struggling Readers: Designing Research-Based Programs,* 3rd ed. Boston, MA: Pearson; W. G. Brozo, G. Shel, and K. Topping. (2007). "Engagement in Reading: Lessons Learned from Three PISA Countries." *Journal of Adolescent & Adult Literacy* 51, no. 4: 304–315; J. Cipielewski and K. E. Stanovich. (1992). "Predicting Growth in Reading Ability from Children's Exposure to Print." *Journal of Experimental Child Psychology* 54, no. 1: 74–89; S. D. Krashen. (1993). *The Power of Reading: Insights from the Research.* Englewood, CO: Libraries Unlimited.

12. Krashen, *Power of Reading, supra* n. 8, 13.

13. Jeff McQuillan. (1998). *The Literacy Crisis: False Claims, Real Solutions.* Portsmouth, NH: Heinemann, p. 86.

14. Krashen, *Power of Reading*, *supra* n. 8, 121.

15. Stacy Gilbert and Rachel Grover. (2020). "Branching Out: Promoting Reading and Providing Access When the Library Is Closed." *Knowledge Quest* 48 (May/June): 17–23.

16. American Librarian Association. (2020). "The School Librarian's Role in Reading." https://www.ala.org/aasl/sites/ala.org.aasl/files/content/advocacy/statements/docs/AASL_Position_Statement_RoleinReading_2020-01-25.pdf

17. Douglas Fisher and Gay Ivey. (2007). "Farewell to *A Farewell to Arms*: Deemphasizing the Whole-Class Novel." *Phi Delta Kappan* 88 (March): 494–497.

18. J. T. Guthrie and N. M. Humenick, "Motivating Students to Read: Evidence for Classroom Practices that Increase Reading Motivation and Achievement." In P. McCardle and V. Chhabra, eds. (2004). *The Voice of Evidence in Reading Research,* 329–354. Baltimore, MD: Brookes Publishing.

19. Anne DiPardo and Pat Schnack. (2003). "Partners in Reading, Partners in Life." *Educational Leadership* 60 (March): 56–58.

20. Violet Harada and Alison Zmuda. (2008). *Librarians as Learning Specialists.* Santa Barbara, CA: Libraries Unlimited.

21. Elizabeth Barrera Rush. (2017). *Bringing Genius Hour to Your Library: Implementing a Schoolwide Passion Project Program.* Santa Barbara, CA: Libraries Unlimited.

22. Violet H. Harada and Joan M. Yoshina. (2010). *Assessing for Learning: Librarians and Teachers as Partners*, 2nd ed. Santa Barbara, CA: Libraries Unlimited.

23. Julie Darling. (2021). *Social-Emotional Learning Using Makerspaces and Passion Projects.* New York: Routledge.

24. Colleen Graves, Aaron Graves, and Diana L. Redina. (2017). *Challenge-Based Learning in the School Library Makerspace.* Santa Barbara, CA: Libraries Unlimited.

25. Carol C. Kuhlthau. (1993). *Seeking Meaning: A Process Approach to Delivery and Information Service.* Norwood, NJ: Ablex, p. 25.

26. Carol C. Kuhlthau, Leslie K. Maniotes, and Ann K. Caspari. (2007). *Guided Inquiry: Learning in the 21st Century.* Santa Barbara, CA: Libraries Unlimited.

27. Leslie K. Maniotes and Carol C. Kuhlthau. (2014). "Making the Shift: From Traditional Research Assignments to Guiding Inquiry Learning." *Knowledge Quest* 43, no. 2 (November–December): 8–17.

28. B. S. Bloom (Ed.), with M. D. Engelhart, E. J. Furst, W. H. Hill, and D. R. Krathwohl. (1956). *Taxonomy of Educational Objectives: The Classification of Educational Goals. Handbook 1: Cognitive Domain.* New York: David McKay.

29. David R. Krathwohl. (2002). "A Revision of Bloom's Taxonomy: An Overview." *Theory into Practice* 41, no. 4: 212–218.

30. Carol Koechlin, Esther Rosenfeld, and David V. Loertscher. (2010). *Building a Learning Commons: A Guide for School Administrators and Learning Leadership Teams.* Salt Lake City, UT: Hi Willow Research and Publishing, 2.

6
Assessment and Evaluation

Neither better relations with our colleagues nor more preaching about the importance of information literacy will save our jobs. Data—that measurement of a library program's impact on student learning—isn't something we traditionally collect, or even know how to collect, but if we are to survive, it's the information we desperately need.

—Brian Kenney, former editor-in-chief of
School Library Journal

Essential Questions

- In what ways does evaluation of your program foster its growth?

- What types of evidence are most critical in advocacy?

- What types of evidence are most critical in informing your practice to promote innovation and growth?

Measurement, according to Brian Kenney, is the key to the survival of our profession and the essential proof of its value.[1] School librarians should be prepared to reflect on how much and in which specific ways their libraries serve their learning communities. How well does the library offer access to meet the information needs of students and teachers? School librarians must be prepared to assess how they improve students' inquiry skills and affect their learning in general. Using a growing array of assessment and evaluation tools, librarians can demonstrate exactly how and how much the presence of a well-supported library and a professional librarian is critical in the education of students. Librarians can also identify critical areas for growth and improvement of services, resources, and instruction. While all this may seem daunting, remember, you are going to spend a large part of your time discovering what works and observing, finding and analyzing the problems most worth addressing. You do not need to address growing every aspect of your program at once. You get to decide where to place your initial focus. This chapter considers your role as a reflective practitioner and how you might measure growth. It also explores how others will evaluate your program and your performance. Note that further information regarding evaluating specific aspects of your program (such as collection, facility, and staffing) are addressed in upcoming chapters.

Who Evaluates Your Work?

First, a question likely on top of your mind as a new librarian: How will your work be evaluated?

As mentioned previously, some of you will have the benefit of a district library supervisor who is also a school librarian and will mentor you and lead your "department." Generally, though, these people do not function as direct *line* supervisors, the ones who may assign duties and appraise your performance. In the best of all possible worlds, building administrators and superintendents would understand the complete potential for their library programs, especially their relationship to teaching and learning. Ideally, these administrators would have an effective means of evaluating this contribution to teaching, learning, and literacies, and the relationship of the library to the school's curriculum. However, not all administrators have had the type of pre-service instruction or any significant personal experience that would allow them to understand the role of a credentialed librarian. While it may seem that evaluation is difficult and time-consuming for an already overwhelmed school librarian with many other program facets to consider, the process will be a far more collegial event when your administrator is already a supporter of your program. As school leaders, program administrators, and educators, school librarians should regularly schedule chats with their principals to discuss their plans, their practice, and the role they play in teaching and learning and share the specific types of standards-based evaluation instruments that can help a librarian and their program grow.

When it is time to make program cuts in any school setting, the principal must believe in the value—in fact, the *necessity*—of the school library program. This is not something that is accomplished in one day. It is the result of continual efforts. Aside from its value to the reflective librarian who is interested in ensuring that the library program grows to meet community needs, program appraisal is essential to ensure that principals and superintendents recognize the worth of the library. Ongoing reporting of impacts and results is key.

Expect to be observed. The administrative team member assigned to you will generally set pre- and post-observation meetings with all educators in their buildings. Observations are often scheduled, but may happen as a drop-in. Because your teaching schedule may look different from those of classroom teachers, be proactive and invite administrators to observe a lesson of which you are particularly proud. It is always best to share one that involves your partnership with classroom teachers and furthers their curricular goals. You might choose a more formal lesson, rather than one of those frequent follow-up visits where students return to practice the research strategies you introduced earlier. You will likely be asked to share a fully developed lesson plan before your observation. You will also likely be asked to reflect on your effectiveness in your post-observation discussion. Serious administrators are very concerned about teacher growth and value thoughtful professional reflection.

In addition to regular formal observation and reporting, you as a new librarian seek opportunities to demonstrate your impact. In some schools, administrators often wander into the library. You will want to ensure that this is a regular habit. (Visits may happen more frequently when coffee is available.) When you engage in a promising co-teaching collaboration or event, invite an administrator to observe, or better yet, engage. If you are hosting a debate, ask an administrator to judge. If you host a poetry slam or a guest picture book share, invite an administrator to read. If you schedule a career event or an author visit, have your administrator share a welcome. If you host a current issues debate, invite an administrator as a judge.

Some states require educators to prepare annual student growth objectives (SGOs) based on the use of annual Specific, Measurable, Attainable, Relevant, and Time-bound (SMART) goal statements that can be set to help measure the academic achievements of students. Some states require professional growth objectives. When possible, seek examples of these from your mentors, local librarians you respect, or on the district or state website. These SGOs may become a cornerstone of your annual reports.

It is important to note that many schools engage in a districtwide assessment framework for all faculty that creates a shared vocabulary around improvement of pedagogical practice. A frequently used tool is Danielson's research-based Framework for Teaching evaluation.[2] Developed around teaching clusters, the instrument is aligned to standards and grounded in a constructionist view of learning and teaching. Its 22 components are organized into four domains helpful in considering and reflecting on the varied areas of competence that comprise the complexity of teaching: (1) planning and preparation, (2) classroom environment, (3) instruction, and (4) professional responsibilities. If your school uses an instrument related to the Danielson Framework, it is essential that you examine and prepare to address its domains, components, and elements in advance. Some districts either use or adapt the Danielson Framework to address the different criteria involved in evaluating educators who are not classroom teachers, such as counselors, coaches, and librarians.

Standards-Based Evaluation

Beyond those strategies used to evaluate educators and instruction, a variety of state and national tools also have categories to identify librarian-specific strengths and weaknesses, and thus can help you determine the effectiveness of the various aspects of your program. (See the Evaluation/Evidence-Based Practice Playlist in the Additional Resources.) First, you will want to check to see if your own state has an evaluation instrument. You can find a few examples of state instruments on that Evaluation/Evidence-Based Practice Playlist. Criteria in these instruments might be measured and described using both quantitative and qualitative measures.

Aligned with the *National School Library Standards for Learners, School Librarians, and School Libraries,* and available as a free download, the American Association of School Librarians (AASL) School Library Evaluation Checklist[3] was developed to help practitioners reflect and plan for growth, as they collaborate with their stakeholders and their administrators to "determine the areas where your school library is already strong and where you can begin to set goals for improvement year after year," across a variety of areas of responsibility:

- Instructional responsibilities
- Curriculum alignment
- Collection development
- Policy development
- Technology integration
- Advocacy and promotion of the effective use of the school library and its services
- Facilities and learning environment
- Management of personnel and resources
- Budget development
- Professional development

When shared with administrators, in addition to functioning as a tool for assessment, these instruments can build awareness of school librarians' multiple responsibilities at both the building and district levels as they relate to key commitments to each of the six Shared Foundations—Inquire, Include, Collaborate, Curate, Explore, and Engage. In addition, the AASL Evidence of Accomplishment[4] checklist presents a lengthy list of accomplishments worthy of documenting to demonstrate your efforts in supporting teaching and learning. This document is an essential tool in your efforts to evaluate your program. Remember to collaborate with your administrators in establishing priorities.

The Future Ready Librarians Framework, a tool related to the larger Future Ready Schools initiative, also offers a variety of criteria for evaluation, including the Librarian Self-Reflection Tool[5] which is organized around the Future Ready School "gears." You may also want to investigate the growing variety of crosswalks connecting AASL Standards to those of the International Society for Technology in Education (ISTE) and the Future Ready Framework, the Next Generation Science Standards, and Google's Computers First CF Curriculum. Connecting your standards to the standards of other groups facilitates their implementation for all involved. Crosswalks allow you to see connections and alignments among standards documents. They support you in understanding and speaking each other's language. If you can speak the language of the technology coach, the administrator, and the classroom teacher as you look at your own work, you can really see where the connections are and where you can amplify each other's work.

An additional evaluation measure that can be useful is the standards-based rubric contained in the application for the AASL's National School Library Program of the Year Award.[6] The criteria for this award detail a tried and proven way to examine a complete program and guide you as to the evidence to gather. Give yourself a few years to learn and grow professionally, and then you may want to consider establishing a credential as a National Board-certified educator. Informed by national and state initiatives, the National Board for Professional Teaching Standards: Library Media Standards[7] are highly regarded. Certification is often rewarded by school districts. The program is designed to generate and acknowledge ongoing improvement by describing and encouraging personal reflection on what accomplished school librarians should know and be able to do.

Evaluating and Reflecting on Your Own Work

Program evaluation is not only a road to program justification, it is very much a road to growth. It is very possible that you will enter your library every day feeling you are doing a fine (likely an exceptional) job. But can you document that *feeling* and share it with your stakeholders? Many librarians fall into "good enough" ruts, unable to see that their hunches, though they may be comforting, may not in fact be leading us in the most productive directions possible.

Brian Kenney describes one essential purpose for evaluating our programs: survival. Actually, though, librarians engage in evaluation of the school library program and its components for multiple reasons. The data they collect can demonstrate their value, and can inform their practice to make programs and services even more responsive to community needs and thus more valuable.

Evaluation is critical as a tool for advocacy, but perhaps the most important reason to gather and measure evidence is to focus and guide improvement. As professionals, librarians aspire to grow, and they recognize the value of continuous improvement for such growth. Evaluating evidence allows them to discover problems and identify issues. It informs their practice and promotes solution building and innovations. If you are going to ensure that your programs meet the evolving needs of—and ideally exceed the expectations of—your community, you need to continually conduct assessments and address change by planning for growth.

The school librarian may choose more global approaches or may choose to examine single program facets. The latter might include, for instance, the equity of physical access to the facility; the diversity and relevance of specific collections; the effectiveness of procedures relating to independent visits; and whether the library meets the needs of particular groups of learners, grade levels, or departments.

To examine program facets, the following list of questions may help you begin the process. The first two questions were posed by school library educator David V. Loertscher and are retained from previous versions of this text:

1. If you had 10 cents for each time you had helped a teacher design, implement, and assess an engaging inquiry-based curricular unit, what could you buy: a new laptop or an ice cream cone?

2. If you were arrested for participating in and helping to assess a student's learning or their social and emotional needs, would there be enough specific evidence to convict you?

3. If there were an award show in your district, would you be nominated to accept the coveted accolade of educator who best addressed their building's professional development needs in the category of information and communication technologies?

4. If the business office were to acknowledge the educator of the year best able to demonstrate return on investment (ROI) on their

resources based on evidence presented in an effective annual report, would you be in contention?

5. If there were significant fines for participating on the most critical school- or district-level committees, would you be in serious debt?

While these questions may appear exaggerated, and perhaps a little goofy, they point to potential examples of measurable evidence of school librarian achievement across the librarian's roles as teacher, instructional partner, information specialist, program administrator, and leader. They present just a little taste of how much there is to measure. As you begin to consider evidence, you need to consider which types of evidence are most compelling.

Simply saying that the school library program is essential to the learning environment in the school is not enough. Library programs that grow to meet needs are those that are regularly analyzed beyond the types of binary yes/no boxes found on checklists. These explorations require evidence. You will have to explore in which *specific* ways library services meet the mission and vision of your school and district. How does your library work to represent the established core values of the profession? In which ways do the librarian and the program work to live up to the aspirational criteria established by national and state standards documents? What efforts are taken to ensure that the library provides physical and intellectual equity of access to the resources students and teachers need?

For example, if a program objective is to support the searching of relevant and high-quality databases for research projects, the evaluation should not be a simple yes-or-no answer: "Yes, database searching has been added to library services." A better value statement tells how many searches were made for/by how many students; the number of students who received instruction in searching; the granular user data offered by vendor analytics; and, most importantly, the improved number of *relevant* references found. Data might be collected to see which subscription databases are more popular, to determine their ROI. Data might demonstrate that highly relevant yet underused databases may require promotion campaigns. Those campaigns should be followed up by tracking usage beyond an established baseline after your interventions.

In a time with so much focus on access to technology for online and hybrid instruction, a true understanding of access in relation to what has been called the *homework gap* is essential and a key function of the library. It is important to know for which students access to digital resources is available only through their school library, in order to ensure that they have access at appropriate times during the school day and to mitigate unfair gaps in at-home access. Are there students who have no devices at home other than a cell phone? Are they able to get to their public library in the evening? Must they use commercial spaces such as coffee houses, restaurants, or perhaps parking lots that offer free wifi? Will you need to work with the district to mitigate the homework gap by budgeting for technologies that students can check out to take home with them, including a plan for mobile hotspot lending?

On Counting

School librarians can count. You can count such things as the number of books checked out, the number of bodies through your door, the number of reference questions you have answered, the number of classes you taught or co-taught, the number of teachers with whom you have partnered, and the number of clicks your websites get, but do these data alone tell the full or real story of your library? Do the tables and charts you generate demonstrate your actual impact? While these outputs are often used to justify funding for materials and staffing, they may do little to communicate your contributions and the differences you make. Metrics should also describe that difference. Are your students asking better questions? Are they excitedly discovering new authors and genres? Are they thoughtfully engaging with high-quality sources, negotiating truth, synthesizing content from thoughtfully gathered sources, and ethically and creatively constructing and sharing new knowledge as global citizens?

Consider the image of a leaky faucet: precious water pours out, but much of it goes down the drain, unused and wasted. Data, in all its glorious forms, surrounds you, but many school librarians are not effectively capturing the obvious. When you begin to consider evidence of your practice as your own professional inquiry project, you may begin to identify the truly essential questions and get closer to answering and sharing with others the many ways in which you make a difference in improving teaching and learning and to what degree your efforts contribute value to the learning culture.

School district administrators may wish to compare all programs or any part of their library program at the local level, or they may wish to use data for the purpose of receiving approval by a regional accrediting agency. The most important evaluation strategies, especially if school library programs are to continue to exist and be led by credentialed librarians, require the gathering of data that demonstrates student learning gains, both formal and informal, connected to your professional interventions.

Defining Terms

The word *evaluate* itself is defined in several ways and the terms *evaluation* and *assessment* are frequently confused. According to one dictionary's definition of "evaluate": "When you evaluate, you judge the overall quality of a service, program or performance against established standards."[8] When you *assess*, you collect, examine, and use data to improve the current facets of a service, program, or performance, and judge its relationship to the needs of users (and sometimes non-users). Whereas assessment is diagnostic, formative, reflective, and focused on process, evaluation is summative and product-focused and can be comparative and judgmental.

The ultimate goal of assessment is to improve programs and services. Assessment requires documentation of the multiple aspects of a program. It can involve counting things, especially if the assessment is based upon some standards imposed by state law or evaluated by regional accrediting agencies. However, your ultimate evaluation should be based on far more than what you have in your collection or the number of times you offer special events or programs, or the observation of one lesson. For librarians, the most important aspects of evaluation and assessment should be the use of evidence to demonstrate their worth to and within the learning community.

To choose among data to collect will mean choosing whether the questions to be asked will gather either *quantitative* or *qualitative* data. Connaway and Radford explain these two types of data in the following way:

> Quantitative research methods "use measurements and statistics to transform empirical data into numbers and to develop mathematical models that quantify behavior."

Qualitative research methods "focus on observing events from the perspective of those involved and attempt to understand why individuals behave as they do."[9]

Simply put, quantitative evaluation collects numbers while qualitative evaluation collects answers to questions. Both have their pros and cons.

The Problem with Numbers

When not used thoughtfully, or when used without context, quantitative measures may result in one-dimensional perspectives. Quantity metrics are not always true measures of a program's reach and impact. Traditional *output measures*—tangible, countable evidence of what you produce—may include the number of teachers and students who come into the library each day, the number of materials that circulate, the percentage of the student body using the library at least once a month, and the like. These numbers may not show the more important picture; that is, output measures may not tell the full story. While low-hanging fruit, such as data like circulation statistics, may reveal what materials have moved out of the library, they may ignore the larger picture that includes in-library or digital use.

Additionally, when you rely on your OPACs for data, you may ignore the multiple access points and the various ways your stakeholders interact with your collections. Simple people-counting does not illustrate the types of uses a library experiences in the course of a day. Focusing on a district- or state-suggested arbitrary number of books per pupil in your library may encourage you to avoid weeding efforts that would result in a more attractive, more relevant, and more active collection. Administrators who emphasize counting things may have little or no context for what the numbers actually mean.

Better metrics connect quantity to quality. *Outcomes*, however, are usually less tangible. They connect to the value of your efforts to your stakeholders.

A major problem with quantitative evaluation is that, unless you intentionally create baselines, few yardsticks exist against which to compare numbers. When embarking on any planning efforts designed to make positive change, it's important to establish baselines. This is especially important—and exciting—for someone beginning a new position. *Baselines* are points of reference taken prior to an intervention or innovation that allow for comparisons. After you establish baselines, you can examine changes and report on the results of your innovations in more meaningful and contextually relevant ways. For instance, rather than simply reporting the number of books borrowed each school year, comparing the number of fiction titles borrowed by Mr. Smith's fifth-graders in fall vs. spring semesters, following your focused genre booktalking efforts, describes an outcome that may have far greater meaning.

During the COVID-19 pandemic, when access to print titles was limited, a useful data point might have been the number of students who made use of the ebook and audiobook collections and how many titles they borrowed, especially if there was a baseline of prior use. You might also have examined visits and engagements with your LibGuides, websites, and social media platforms, at the time the pandemic began and at regular points thereafter. These kinds of numbers would be useful in measuring against future data.

To justify your return on investment (ROI) in databases and show their value in specific curricular areas, it is important to regularly examine rather granular usage data made available by the database companies and publishers. It is easy to generate reports regarding who, how, when, and how long students are engaging with these platforms. For instance, you can examine data to establish and defend the value of JSTOR or Gale Literature Resource Center to support the 11th-grade literature criticism unit, or Gale In Context Elementary to support the 4th-grade students' ecosystem inquiry project. You may also need to go beyond the quantitative to interview or survey teachers and students about the value of these tools. Before making purchases, it is good practice to engage the grade levels and content areas in trials of products worthy of consideration to get feedback as well as buy-in and support.

Counting outputs will certainly confirm the physical use of the library. *Output* includes the number of teachers and students who come into the library each day, an estimate of the number of materials that circulate, the percentage of the student body using the library at least once a month, and other similar statistics. The better measure is the relationship of quantity to quality, although one may lead to the next. Consider how you might connect these numbers to increases in use or the photographs you collect to describe types of use.

It is important to note that these quantitative measures may not be *causal*. With the many variables present in nearly any problem, especially in education, specific quantitative data may not be directly tied to cause and effect. Qualitative measures may offer additional and perhaps richer data.

You might begin to measure *what is* against *what should be* or *what if we could?* based on both your evidence for practice (from your readings) as well as your own no-box thinking and inspirations, and calculate discrepancies. In some instances, these calculations can be translated into actual dollar amounts. Although this sounds as if it is a quantity count, it is not. The *what is* is a quantitative count of professional and staff attention time allocation to tasks, services, equipment, and materials available. The *what should be* outlines what is needed to provide quality for teachers and students and begins the process of determining how to make up the difference. The *what should be*s may be established by national standards and frameworks, as well as professional research and literature. These may help you decide what to measure.

Deciding What to Measure

As a school librarian you have the advantage of a whole-school lens. Unlike classroom teachers, you see students, teachers, and parents across grade levels, ability levels, and content areas. When you observe and listen, you will discover a number of needs worthy of addressing.

As a program administrator, you need to engage in assessment even if no one suggests it. As you observe each day, you will develop your own research questions. You will also identify the problems most worthy of innovative solutions, modeling inquiry and design thinking. Consider connecting those questions to the most pressing goals of your school and your administrators. Consider identifying the most pressing learning issues your students face.

At a time when researchers note a decline in students' reading for pleasure, you might wonder: How your efforts to create a reading culture in your school affect your students' genuine increase in reading for pleasure? Did the creation of a graphic novel corner in the library draw the attention and engagement of more readers? These answers help the librarian decide if an activity was successful and whether to continue the activity, to do more "selling" of the activity in the hopes of success, or to replace that activity with a different one.

Your measures may be quite focused. For instance, if you recognize in your first semester that students are struggling to locate age-relevant materials on genocides, you might explore the baseline or the *what is*, exploring the materials used or shared in previous semesters. Then consider your most effective intervention. You might curate a LibGuide or website or a collection in your online public access catalog (OPAC), being sure to include historical, global studies and news databases, as well as free, searchable primary source portals such as iWitness and the United States Holocaust Memorial Museum. If funding is available, you might draw up a small but focused book order. Collaborate with the classroom teachers to build your content and ensure that your resources and instruction are embedded in the materials shared with students on the learning management system or that the teachers' assignment materials—learning objectives, instruction, rubrics—are embedded into your own website. With the teacher(s), establish criteria to evaluate the quality of student work this semester against the work submitted in the semesters to come.

Evidence to Promote Growth

As leaders and program administrators, librarians should be interested in moving their programs forward and measuring their professional growth. This involves you in problem-solving. You will discover problems and you will want to discover solutions to address them. Needs assessments and strategic planning allow the professional to identify and focus on pressing problems and to set measurable goals for ways to address them. Planning your own *action research* projects (described in a later section) to discover programmatic needs and creating interventions to address those needs in the form of formal goals, objectives, and action steps may move you out of your comfort zone, but the end results will help chart the future of the library and allow you to demonstrate continual improvement and growth.

After a few years in a position, it is easy to fall into a bit of a professional rut, feeling you are doing a fine job. Try to avoid the notion of *good enough*. Many schools consider the importance of what Carol Dweck[10] describes as the "growth mindset" in her neuroscience research. People with a fixed mindset limit their opportunities and are often risk- and challenge-averse. Those with growth mindsets actively seek opportunity and challenge. Librarians are not chained to their current abilities. Mindsets can be changed. To encourage a mindset of growth, with yourselves and your adult and young learners, focus on the word "yet": You haven't mastered this skill or that challenge *yet*.

You can consider your library programs in similar terms as you look at the many components you have effectively considered as well as areas you can focus on for growth. When you establish baselines and priorities based on needs, you can create goals that move your programs forward. Evaluation is an important step in the strategic planning process. As an effective information professional, you will be evaluating the impact of your strategic planning.

How do school librarians really understand their impact on the learning community? A focus on evidence-based practice (EBP) aligns with your role as leader, prepared and positioned to "transform teaching and learning,"[11] Ross Todd argued that, for school librarians, EBP connects to two concepts:

> the conscientious, explicit and judicious use of current best evidence in making decisions about [school librarians'] performance. It is about using research evidence, coupled with professional expertise and reasoning, to implement learning interventions that are effective; and . . . [the school librarian's] daily efforts put some focus on effectiveness evaluation that gathers meaningful and systematic evidence on dimensions of teaching and learning that matter to the school and its support community.[12]

In Todd's[13] holistic conceptualization of EBP, librarians systematically and iteratively engage in research-derived evidence. In his model, Todd described a composition of three dynamic and iterative practices for understanding student needs and for employing research-based evidence to make decisions relating to improving instruction and services based on school goals. Todd delineated the following:

- Evidence *of* practice, as the foundational dimension in Todd's model, involves "the measured outcomes and impacts of practice, [and] is derived from systematically measured, primarily user-based data." Evidence of practice describes how and to what degree our interventions change the learning.

- Evidence *in* practice is the transformational dimension of practice that "focuses on reflective practitioners integrating available research evidence with deep knowledge and understanding derived from professional experience." This type of evidence involves "implementing measures to engage with local evidence to identify learning dilemmas, learning needs, and achievement gaps with the goal of making decisions that result in the continuous improvement of school library practices."

- Evidence *for* practice is an informational foundation of practice that includes the "existing formal research [that] provides the essential building blocks for professional practice." You will find this type of evidence to inform practice in scholarly as well as practitioner publications.[14]

Todd warns librarians against relying on the approach of simply pointing to state studies to justify the effectiveness or value of a library program. Instead, the more effective approach involves "crafting a compelling narrative that starts with local evidence of practice and links to the wider formal research evidence for practice."[15]

On Collecting Local Evidence of Practice

If you go through the day neglecting the evidence around you, you will ignore critical clues that might support your understanding of needs and, ultimately, your ability to innovate and improve your program. There are many simple ways to collect the valuable yet often ignored evidence that exists and flows around you.

A *Knowledge Quest* article titled "Evolving with Evidence: Leveraging New Tools for EBP,"[16] indicates that such evidence has never been easier to collect. A variety of traditional and digital strategies, both quantitative and qualitative, can be used to facilitate the collection of evidence.

Surveys can be easily constructed using tools such as Google Forms. While you may be tempted to create broad general surveys about your library, focused explorations can serve to directly address issues. For example, collecting evidence surrounding a pervasive plagiarism crisis using anonymous surveys, in collaboration with teachers in the English department, can assess the student climate of academic honesty in your building. You could continue to log any dramatic improvement after interventions with the faculty over two or more years of professional development. Another school-wide survey addressing students' response to teacher-developed rubrics can lead to very effective rethinking of the assessment strategy and successful professional development efforts.

Among the less formal strategies you might employ is the use of exit tickets. Popular with many classroom teachers, exit tickets can take a number of different forms and provide immediate, formative evidence of learning. For instance, at the end of a lesson, you might ask students to share three takeaways, or one lingering question, or the best sources discovered, or what they want to learn more about. These answers can take the form of exit-ticket graffiti responses on anonymous physical sticky notes, or flip chart notes. You might invite students to *dot* their level of understanding or answer a simple yes-or-no question on a printed or whiteboard Likert scale chart. If you have whiteboard tables and dry-erase markers, feedback might be left on desks. Photographs of these physical instruments collected after students leave allow you to analyze and compare responses over time and also present evidence of your efforts.

In addition to these physical strategies, a variety of interactive feedback or response tools (projected at the beginning of a lesson to assess prior knowledge, or the end of a lesson to assess learning) can be used to allow students to reflect on their knowledge or their learning digitally, across devices. Such tools include Padlet, Mentimeter, Nearpod, Slido, Kahoot!, AnswerGarden, and PearDeck. These tools allow for feedback using various question types (short answer, word clouds, multiple choice, etc.), and sometimes drawings. Video tools such as Flip can function as exit tickets or serve as reflections at various points in a project. In the case of NearPod and Kahoot!, you not only collect data, but might also engage students through gamification.

Some exit ticket ideas:

- Share three takeaways from today's class
- Share one lingering question
- What did you/your group accomplish this period/block?
- What were the best sources you discovered today?
- Which criteria did you use to evaluate your sources today?
- How might you apply what you learned today in a situation outside of school?
- I didn't understand . . .
- I would like to learn more about . . .
- I used to think . . . , but now I think . . .[17]

Regularly analyzing video exit interviews with graduating students will allow you to discover what they learned in their library, their experiences with the library website, and their perceptions of what was helpful and what might be improved about library service and instruction. Teachers may be especially delighted to share their seniors with the librarian at the end of the school year. Focus groups can be an excellent choice for gathering qualitative evidence and assessing a variety of aspects of your program because they allow the interviewer to observe levels of consensus and disagreement. Depending upon the questions you plan to explore, you will want to note the composition of your groups to ensure that your sample represents the diversity or the focus you need. If you moderate the group, be aware that your polite students may avoid sharing very negative responses. Nevertheless, gathered in small groups, students may feel less threatened than they might in private one-to-one conversations with adults.

Consider what you might most like to know from your rising fifth- or eighth- or ninth-graders. These questions may help you decide your focus:

- What have you learned during our years together?
- What have you learned about finding information?
- What are your favorite databases? Which ones have been the most useful and why?
- What does a quality source look like, and how do you know you've found one?
- What have you learned about communicating what you learned during your research?
- What have you learned about technology applications and their use from our library program?
- Have you learned anything that friends from other schools did not?
- Which resources did you use most often on our library website?
- What did you like about our library website?
- What would you improve about our library website?
- What parts of the research process are you most comfortable with?
- What parts of the research process do you feel are the most challenging?
- Which was your favorite research project and why?
- Which was your least favorite research project and why?
- When you go to high school, do you feel ready for high school research?
- If you plan to attend college, do you feel ready for university research?
- What is the one thing you most wish you could have changed about our library?
- What will you miss most about our library?
- Can you share a highlight or lowlight about your experiences in our library?[18]

Important note: Exit tickets or exit interviews are not just for instruction and not just for students. These strategies can yield rich data allowing you to learn about the effectiveness of your professional development workshops as well as events and programs. Remember to steer away from generic form-type questions when you design your surveys or prompts. Collect responses that have specific local relevance and support you in evaluation, improvement, and planning to meet needs.

Leveraging Your Camera for Evidence of Practice

Your camera is your friend. It will allow you to document the energy of your space and the multiple ways in which it engages your community. Take photos of your library meetings and events—author and expert visits, poetry slams, debates, wax figure biography presentations, one-book-one-school discussions, global collaborations—as well as your displays, bulletin boards, and anchor charts. Plan to store these collections of visual evidence on spaces like Flickr, Instagram, TikTok, and Facebook. Be conscious of the proper and permitted use of photographs of students. Some schools have an opt-out form for students whose parents do not want them to appear in photos; others require permissions from all students to allow use. It is also quite easy to shoot pictures of groups from the back without faces showing.

Photos and videos are excellent fodder for library reports and presentations and may also be valued by your building and central office administrators when their reports, calendars, and newsletters come due. It is quite possible that the library will be the only place in which the learning culture is systematically and visually documented. Your evidence collection may result in your prominence in district publications. You might use a video recording platform to collect student reflections around a particular question. Many librarians use social media to record and show what the culture looks like in their libraries. On the varied platforms, organize your content into playlists or channels to make it easier to retrieve. Consider embedding these playlists on your websites.

This visual evidence is just too good to lose, but it can be overwhelming to host events and keep on top of archiving them. You need not do all the collecting yourself. Assign students as your photographers. Give them cameras and have them take pictures when you know something important is happening in your library or around the school. If your students are older, ask them to use their phones and invite them in as collaborators on library platforms. Keep organized by creating albums or boards for different types of activities.

Assessing Student Learning

It is no secret that students today have lived much of their school lives in a testing culture. In many schools, high-stakes summative tests drive teaching as well as school calendars and, sometimes, teacher evaluation. During the *return to learning* following the COVID-19 pandemic, fear of learning loss, in some schools and districts, began to fuel assessments designed to determine needs for remediation. In contrast, the pandemic's impact led many teachers and administrators to consider rethinking stressful state assessments in favor of more frequent formative assessments that are more likely to directly inform instruction, more accurately meet learning needs, and better serve the social and emotional needs of learners.[19] As this text is being written (in late 2022), school librarians are seeing a culture of questioning what has been, consideration of radical change, and potential large-scale innovation in which school librarians will have opportunities to contribute and lead. At the same time, promising educational technologies offer a variety of ways to find out how and what students are actually learning and offer new strategies for diagnosing and addressing needs.

Data gathered in the many studies by Lance and colleagues at the Library Research Service demonstrate the importance of the school library and its staff in the achievement of student learning.[20] Despite the facts that these studies have been replicated across the states and that they present critical evidence, they may not resonate with those who make your local decisions. To make a local argument, you will likely need to demonstrate how you and your program affect and enhance teaching and learning at the school level where the focus is on individual students—what and how they are learning.

Harada and Yoshina explain that assessment is different from evaluation because assessment is "an ongoing activity that provides critical *formative* information about what the student is learning and how that learning is taking place."[21] Learners who are involved in their own assessment are learning in the process. It is essential to discuss assessing authentic learning and information literacy and how they are related to the content standards. Results would be difficult to discount if this research was conducted in your school.

The critical point is that school librarians should seize these opportunities to show how what is being taught as a part of inquiry-driven learning and information and digital literacy instruction reinforces and enhances classroom and lifelong learning and furthers the mission and vision of the learning community. When students approach assignments with enthusiasm, it is obvious, and these moments of engagement cry out to be documented. When the quality of students' creative work improves, the improvement should be made obvious. The bottom line is that teachers, administrators, and parents need to see how the classroom–library partnership targets stakeholder and schoolwide goals and priorities.

Among the types of tools that may be used to assess learning, plan for addressing issues, and make the connections more visible in both digital and physical formats are:

- Checklists or checkbrics
- Rubrics
- Portfolios
- Individual artifacts of student work
- Surveys
- Exit tickets
- Scaffolds or organizers
- Conferencing with individual or groups of students
- Reflective logs or blog posts
- Regular check-ins

Years ago, librarians seldom saw the final products or the summative assessments of an inquiry project. Learning management systems and document-sharing platforms (such as Google Drive, G Suite, or Classroom, and Microsoft Office 365 or Teams), or digital platforms for collecting sources and writing (such as Noodle Tools) make it possible to see, engage with, comment on, and collaborate with students as you formatively watch their works-in-progress grow. These opportunities also allow you to assess gaps in knowledge on the individual student, class, and school levels and offer support and interventions. Examining specific aspects of a project—for instance, choice of sources or development of a thesis—allows us to collaborate with classroom teachers on assessment and diagnose student issues with finding and using information. This lens also allows you to document your role in student growth across or between projects or over time.

Digital portfolio tools can be used to demonstrate growth over time. Such tools are often apps that allow you and your students to use cameras to gather and share artifacts of student inquiry and communication products, as well as their digitally recorded reflections or check-ins. You can also use these tools to share and celebrate student work with parents and the larger community.

New tools allow you to assess progress relating to reading and literacy, by tracking progress of individual students, groups, classes, or grades, while respecting students' privacy. Microsoft's Reading Progress and Reading Coach offer stigma-free assessments of reading fluency, saving educators from the tedious time needed for testing individual students while engaging readers in improving their own fluency. Tools such as Biblionasium, which plays well with Follett's Destiny, allow librarians to create, manage, and monitor student reading lists, logs, and challenges while encouraging independent reading.

Teachers sometimes get together with other teachers to authentically examine student work. Protocols, such as the Critical Friends Tuning Protocol initially developed by the Coalition of Essential Schools, allow educators to informally or formally analyze student responses to assignments including research prompts. These protocols might be used informally or during faculty or team meetings and can focus on key questions relating to the assignment. The protocol involves presentation of the work and the issues by the teacher, clarifying questions and discussion responses from the group which involve warm and cool feedback, and reflection that usually leads to a plan to refine the assignment. This type of local inquiry is a simple form of action research. Action research is an inquiry process for educators that should lead to improvement of practice.

Educators and Action Research

Action research involves the identification of authentic local issues and the collection of evidence with the goal of applying your findings and innovations in practice. You do not necessarily need an academic partner to engage in valuable action research; however, an educator or a collaborative group of educators may often actively participate in such research. Like any good inquiry project, action research begins with a research question. Development of the question is generally followed by a literature review and the process of designing the study, considering ethical issues, and getting permissions, especially when the study design engages human subjects. You then go about conducting your interventions or experiments in the field, collecting either qualitative or quantitative data. Once data is collected, it is organized by any noticeable patterns or trends and analyzed to determine or derive conclusions that you will likely want to share with colleagues. Often, one action research project will lead to more questions and further research.

A Canadian school library researcher and action research expert, Judith Sykes, explains action research:

> Action research is a process of defining a question related to one's practice, then designing, executing, reflecting upon, and changing that practice as a result. It combines studying and reviewing literature, collecting and analyzing quantitative and qualitative data, and structuring action plans to create continuous cycles of informed professional renewal. Individuals (educators or students), schools, school districts, and even states or provinces can adopt the methodology of action research. As such, it lends itself to mobilization—indeed, action and transformation—in enabling schools and school libraries to support and advance the learning of each student. Developing skills and strategies for formulating questions, amassing data, structuring events, and analyzing results can lead to profound professional renewal and more responsive service to the students and learning communities one serves.[22]

Canadian School Libraries (CSL) offers a rich Research Toolkit[23] to support the action research projects of practitioners. The process is briefly summarized in CSL's poster, Action Research Process for Teacher Librarians Made Simple (Figure 6-1).

CANADIAN
SCHOOL LIBRARIES

Action Research Process for Teacher Librarians Made Simple

✓ Consider your present program and the needs of learners today.

✓ Identify a target for improvement.

✓ Develop questions to guide your work.

✓ Imagine how you might achieve your target.

✓ Investigate what others have tried and develop your own plan.

✓ Try it out, adjust strategies if necessary and keep track of your evidence.

✓ Analyze and interpret your results.

✓ Prepare a summary report and share.

✓ Apply your findings to better address learning needs in your school library.

✓ Consider new questions to explore.

Tips for Getting Started

• Begin with your school/district goals.

• Align with a standard or theme or indicator from *Leading Learning: Standards of Practice for School Library Learning Commons in Canada*.

• Explore the research others have done. The Canadian School Libraries <u>Research Archive</u> makes scholarly and practitioner research from all Treasure Mountain Canada research symposiums accessible and searchable.

• Two heads are better than one. Find a collaborative partner or team to work with you.

• Visit the Canadian School Libraries <u>Research Toolkit</u> for more tips.

Figure 6-1. Treasure Mountain Canada: Action Research Process for Teacher Librarians Made Simple.

Canadian School Libraries. Reprinted with permission.

Exploration of the climate of academic honesty or integrity in your school with a collaborating teacher, as discussed earlier in this chapter, is an example of anonymous survey-based action research that could lead directly to strategies for positive change in your school, as well as a publication documenting the process. In addition to sharing the results of this and other reports of your research with relevant local stakeholders, school librarians who implement action research projects can report their findings in professional literature and at conferences. Having a knowledgeable person to help make sure the research is ethical and well designed and a statistician to help with analyzing the data collected can alleviate concerns that might arise when an action research study is carried out at the building level. Additionally, these efforts add to the body of research. What might be discovered during an local action research project can potentially benefit a much larger community of practice.

Documenting Your Role as Lead Teacher

As leaders of professional learning, librarians should document their contributions with evidence in a number of areas, including professional development as well as units of study. Exit tickets and surveys may also be used during or following professional development sessions. Similarly, as instructional partners, librarians might solicit feedback from or reflect with classroom teachers on the success of a lesson or unit and discuss potential improvements for future classes with a plan to measure the impact of these enhancements.

Among the most rewarding roles is the one you might play in supporting teachers and administrators researching pedagogical improvements, as well as those researching in their journeys pursuing new credentials or advanced degrees. You will want to capture data regarding these experiences and the materials you provide and recommend to support professional learning. Creating a LibGuide or website focused on educational research and tracking its visitors and engagement is one strategy for measuring impact. Your efforts in keeping administrators and teachers informed of new resources—physical materials, digital portals and tools, as well as the emerging wealth of open educational resources—demonstrates your critical contributions to the teaching culture of your school and will build your social capital as a collaborative educator.

Evidence for Practice

School librarians have been fortunate that a number of scholars, often professors in library and information science (LIS) programs, as well as LIS doctoral students, regularly conduct and share their research on school libraries. AASL's Community of Scholars (CoS), a steering committee within AASL's Educators of School Librarians Section (ESLS), was developed to support scholarship and networking in the field of school library research, and to highlight relevant research accomplishments. Additionally, such researchers as Keith Curry Lance regularly carry out funded research projects, with their work and models for future work archived on his Library Research Service website.[24] The following publications regularly contain research articles:

- School Library Research (SLR) (AASL), https://www.ala.org/aasl/pubs/slr

- Knowledge Quest (AASL), https://knowledgequest.aasl.org/category/kq-content

- School Libraries Worldwide (IASL), https://iasl-online.org/publications/slw/index.html

- School Library Connection (ABC-CLIO) https://www.abc-clio.com/product/SLCRW/#

In addition, AASL's Knowledge Quest blog,[25] written by practitioners, leaders, and LIS educators, regularly shares relevant experiences, trends, and new ideas across a wide variety of school library functions. You can search the ERIC database, often supported by state database licensing and available for free searching from the Department of Education (https://eric.ed.gov). You can search for references from EBSCO's Library and Information Science Abstracts. If you are associated with a university, you likely have access to *Library and Information Science Full Text*. Additionally, SJSU's LIS Wiki maintains a long list of scholarly LIS journals. You might also check out a curated Wakelet of professional journals and magazines.[26]

The need for more research is critical to support the value of school libraries in schools today and for us to better understand what works. Methods for testing must be designed with care to determine exactly who will be queried, which items will be measured, and what procedures will be used to acquire the needed information. Careful consideration must be given to the choice of statistical methods used to tabulate and analyze the responses. Furthermore, individual components of any library program should not be measured in isolation.

If you are interested in engaging in research, you might contact faculty in pre-service programs and partner with university researchers for whom research and publication are important to their success. If they are given the opportunity to use a school or a school district as a site to conduct research, they may welcome the chance. They can help set up the research methodology, create the questions for a survey, report the related research in the literature, and analyze the data they collect, thus adding to the body of research about school libraries.

Evaluation as an Awareness Device

Your efforts in evaluation can be particularly useful for those who have misunderstood the purpose of the library program. Many educators base their expectations on models they observed when they were in school, on examples seen in their children's schools, or on libraries and librarians they may have connected with in their student teaching or practicum experiences. In truth, those models may range from mediocre to exemplary. Many parents may have very limited awareness of the potential of the library to support family learning needs.

After your pre-service preparation, your partner teachers and your administrators add perceptions of what school libraries look like based on the schools in which they accepted positions and past programs they observed. Although some of these experiences may have provided excellent models, many did not. An effective evaluation designed with librarian, teacher, and administrator input can raise awareness, expectations, and enthusiasm for program use. Generating a list of services currently offered as well as some potential services to add can inform administrators and teachers of possible activities to offer in the library. Recently, school librarians have begun sharing these services as graphics in the form of *menus*. You can find a number of attractive examples of such menus using a simple Web image search. When you survey your teaching and administrator or parent community about awareness, make sure you speak the language of the audience and avoid library jargon. Focus these surveys on the specific users whom they are likely influence or have an impact on. For instance, evaluating interest in services such as weeding may not interest your teacher colleagues. Try to include a couple of open-ended response options to get a sense of services that may be needed, but are not listed on your menu. You might use the Future Ready and AASL checklists discussed earlier in this chapter to support your design of awareness surveys.

On the one hand, reporting back informs stakeholders who have not been using a service that the service is highly valued by others, and should inspire interest in exactly what that service is. On the other hand, a service that is recognized but not considered important can be either promoted, better explained, or considered for elimination.

Appraising the Facility

Your space and the story it tells are discussed at greater length in chapter 8. Perhaps the most important metric is how inviting your space is. Evaluating space has to do with a few important elements: how it is used or not used, how it might be used, and how inviting it is for users.

You might ask a group of students to tour the library as if they were going to write an article for a magazine. Ask them to use their cameras, record how they use the space, what works, and what they wish the space included. You can also take pictures and videos that relate to use of the space and traffic. As you read about and view images and videos of new or attractive spaces, consider creating a digital vision board for later reference.

You might conduct student and faculty surveys or focus groups relating to their use of, as well as their dreams for, their library space. Invite those who are most interested (perhaps members of your fledgling advisory group) to contribute to your vision board.

One quantitative analysis strategy is simply counting the number of students who are in the library and at what times they come. Learning what they do in the library and how they use it is also helpful. An effective space serves a variety of user needs. As you observe your new space, observe the patterns and how teachers, students, and coaches arrange themselves. Use may look different at various grade levels, in fixed versus flexible schedules, and at different times of the day. Is there room for readers, visiting classes, small-group work, presentation, and production? That will become apparent in how they arrange themselves in the current spaces.

Over the past several years, widespread use of personal devices like laptops and tablets allows us to reconsider space formerly devoted to labs. Bookshelves devoted to reference materials have become less necessary as reference tools and other resources have become more available in digital form. Reference and circulation desks are getting smaller and librarians are rethinking the need for large offices and workspaces for processing materials. As you evaluate your space, you will likely need to consider possibilities for opening the library for small-group learning spaces, makerspaces, or performance or presentation areas and to consider modifying the present facility as a learning commons for the school. This work will require planning and evidence. Having testimony from students and teachers will lessen the time it takes to gain buy-in by the administration. A well-documented need for a larger or differently configured facility will support repurposing the present library or, potentially, building an entirely new facility.

At the End of the Year: The Importance of Reporting

Your evaluation efforts should involve sharing the evidence of the progress you have made, evidence of the needs you wish to address, and plans for acting on the results. Even if no one asks you to do it, at the end of the year, write a report. You can certainly report more frequently and update your stakeholders using tools such as newsletters, but an annual report allows you to reflect on your accomplishments of the past year and solidify your plans for moving your program forward. It also allows you to share the many artifacts of practice you have been collecting. In addition,

- It ensures that others recognize the impact of your work on our learning culture.

- It forces you to reflect—to collect and share a rich array of evidence in the form of data, stories, student work, collaborations, photographs, and video.

- It proves the ROI of your program.

- It allows you to focus on both achievements and challenges and to set goals for program growth which you will revisit in your next reports.

- It presents you as a professional interested in the growth of your program and the success of the larger learning community.

As a new librarian reaching the conclusion of your first year on the job, like a veteran school librarian, you should be constructing and reporting on your goals, objectives, and action steps. Report on and celebrate your accomplishments using the evidence you have collected. In addition to quantitative data, include stories, photographs, and videos. Share quotes with any positive feedback you receive from parents, students, and teachers. In areas of concern, report those baselines, with a bit of analysis and your plan for moving forward to address the concerns. The analysis you present in your report should become your blueprint for growth for the year or years ahead.

Another example of evidence you will not want to waste comes in the form of informal, unsolicited feedback. Keep a *Nice Stuff* folder on your laptop. Over the course of years, fill that folder with the emails, scans of letters and thank-you notes, news clippings, and so on in which one of your stakeholders took the time to celebrate your work or express gratitude for a service or for a simple kindness. Share these quotes or artifacts in your reports (after getting permission to do so when appropriate).

Assessment and evaluation are key to managing an effective library program that is truly helping teachers teach and students learn. The degree to which this is happening throughout the school year provides the basis for growing the services offered, the materials selected, and the activities planned throughout the school year. Chapter 7 details the actual management of the school library.

Key Takeaways

- You cannot grow a program without first evaluating its components.

- Effective school library professionals use assessment strategies to reflect on their practice, ensure its relevance, and plan for growth and innovation.

- Sharing evidence of your practice is critical for increasing your impact and your professional visibility.

Challenges to Promote Growth

1. Meet with one or more school librarians to find out what program evaluations they have conducted in the past year and to whom they reported their findings. If no evaluation has been conducted recently, volunteer to help design and implement an evaluation project to test one component of the library program.
2. Discuss with a school principal the appraisal process being applied to the school library staff and services in that school.
3. Locate one or two articles to share with your principal on the role of the principal in evaluating the school library. Describe how you would share these articles with your principal when you first begin your job.
4. Decide on a service you would like to provide to students in your school and decide what quantitative measures and what qualitative measures you would use to determine its degree of success.
5. Examine AASL's School Librarian Evaluation Checklist and/or the Evidence of Accomplishments checklist (Appendix H of the National School Library Standards). Consider which of the Key Commitments or components you are on top of and which are most worthy of setting as goals for growth for the next semester. If you are currently working in a school, consider sharing the checklist with an administrator and setting up an appointment to discuss your checklist-related goals in a meeting.
6. If you are in a school or imagine yourself in a school that has taken the Future Ready (FR) pledge, examine the Future Ready School Librarian Self-Reflection Tool to consider your current strengths and areas of growth as they relate to the FR Learning Framework. Reflect on the personalized snapshot generated by the tool to assess your own needs for growth.
7. Embark on a digital safari for the best school librarian annual reports. You might do this as a class using a digital curation tool such as Wakelet. Consider which of these models does the best job assessing the program and planning for growth. Which are most likely to be read and valued?
8. Consider your field experience, actual position, or imagined dream library setting. Based on the needs you have identified through evidence, ask yourself "why shouldn't I" or "what would happen if?" Suggest at least one potential out-of-the-box innovation that might address the need as an action step.

Notes

1. Brian Kenney. (2007). "Getting It Together: Sure, Collaboration Is Good, But We Need Data—and We Need It Now." *School Library Journal* 53, no. 7: 9.
2. The Framework for Teaching. (n.d.). https://danielsongroup.org/framework
3. AASL. (n.d.). Evaluation Checklist. https://standards.aasl.org/project/evaluation

4. American Association of School Librarians. (2018). *National School Library Standards for Learners, School Librarians, and School Libraries.* Chicago: ALA, pp. 262–270.

5. All4Ed. (n.d.). "The Future Ready Schools® Librarian Self-Reflection Tool." https://futureready.org/the-future-ready-schools-librarian-self-reflection-tool

6. AASL. (n.d.). "National School Library of the Year Award." https://www.ala.org/aasl/awards/nsly

7. National Board for Professional Teaching Standards. (2012). "Library Media Standards, Second Edition." https://www.nbpts.org/wp-content/uploads/2021/09/ECYA-LM.pdf

8. "Evaluate." (n.d.). *Merriam-Webster.com Dictionary.* https://www.merriam-webster.com/dictionary/evaluate

9. Lynn Silipigni Connaway and Marie L. Radford. (2021). *Research Methods in Library and Information Science*, 7th ed. Santa Barbara, CA: Libraries Unlimited, p. 4.

10. Carol S. Dweck. (2016). *Mindset: The New Psychology of Success.* New York: Ballantine Books.

11. AASL. (2014, July 15). "AASL Transforms Learning with New Mission Statement and Strategic Plan." https://www.ala.org/news/press-releases/2014/07/aasl-transforms-learning-new-mission-statement-and-strategic-plan

12. Ross J. Todd. (2001). "A Sustainable Future for Teacher-Librarians: Inquiry Learning, Actions and Evidence." *Orana* 37, no. 3: 15.

13. Ross J. Todd. (2015). "Evidence-Based Practice and School Libraries: Interconnections of Evidence, Advocacy, and Actions." *Knowledge Quest* 43, no. 3 (January–February): 8–15.

14. *Ibid.*, 9–10.

15. *Ibid.*, 12.

16. Joyce Kasman Valenza. (2015). "Evolving with Evidence: Leveraging New Tools for EBP." *Knowledge Quest*, 43, no. 3 (January–February): 36–43.

17. *Ibid.*, 39.

18. *Ibid.*, 38–39.

19. Instructure. (2021). *The State of Assessment in K-12 Education: Study & Trends.* https://www.instructure.com/canvas/resources/k12/k12-school-districts-state-assessments-education-trends-study#main-content

20. Library Research Service. (n.d.). https://www.lrs.org/data-tools/school-libraries

21. Violet H. Harada and Joan M. Yoshina. (2015). *Assessing Learning: Librarians and Teachers as Partners.* Westport, CT: Libraries Unlimited, p. 1.

22. Judith Sykes. (2013). *Conducting Action Research to Evaluate Your School Library.* Santa Barbara, CA: Libraries Unlimited.

23. Canadian School Libraries. (n.d.). "Research Toolkit." https://www.canadianschoollibraries.ca/research-toolkit

24. Library Research Service. (n.d.). https://www.lrs.org/data-tools/school-libraries

25. *Knowledge Quest.* https://knowledgequest.aasl.org

26. Joyce Valenza Wakelet. https://tinyurl.com/schoollibraryjournals

7
Planning and Management for Growth

A goal without a plan is just a wish.

—Antoine de Saint-Exupéry, writer
and pioneering aviator

Essential Questions

- How is managing a school library different from managing a classroom?

- How is managing a school library similar to managing a small business?

- What are the steps in developing a strategic plan to most effectively create a school library that is dynamic and inclusive?

The management of school districts at the end of the first decade of 2000 was moving more into the realm of business than education. School of education training programs for administrators began to offer joint programs with their schools of business to add the Master of Business Administration to the Master of Science. Though this trend seems to have dwindled somewhat, it has brought the business approach to managing in schools.

Although school librarians are educators, equally responsible for all parts of the school's curriculum and for the learning of all students in their building, as program administrators they must also manage a many-faceted operation involving staff, materials, equipment, facility, and furnishings. These are covered in the chapters that follow. However, the library itself is a commodity and the inventory of the library has a very big price tag, as many districts learn when they are opening new schools or when they must rebuild after a disaster. It takes good planning and budgeting to manage this commodity, its inventory, and its upkeep, and the business of management requires different skills to make this all happen. This is a great deal more complex than managing a single classroom and its students. That complexity is often overlooked by administrators who may wonder why a clerk or a volunteer cannot replace a school librarian in their school.

Good school library management begins with a strategic planning process and the creation of a vision, mission, goals, and objectives. According to Barbara B. Moran and Claudia J. Morner,

> Strategic planning, then, is the systematic outcome of a thinking process that enables libraries and information centers to organize efforts necessary to carry out major decisions and to measure the results of these decisions against the expectations written into the plan. This is done through organized, systematic feedback and adjustments.[1]

When a district has a director of library programs, a vision, mission, goals, and objectives for the program may already be in place; if a district does not have a director of library programs, school librarians must create their own mission, goals, and objectives after they have defined the vision for their library in cooperation with other stakeholders: teachers, students, administrators, and parents.

The library program's shared vision grows out of the vision of the school and the school district and should align with both. This is the direction the library program will take for the future, defining where the library should be going, and as such it guides the development of the mission statement. The vision should be translated into a *mission statement*, a "short, succinct statement focusing on the purpose of the organization, its reason for existence, and what it hopes to accomplish."[2]

The library staff and the advisory committee members first discuss the school district's mission statement and also that of their school if it has its own mission statement. They then develop the library's mission as it relates to the school's mission and agree upon this statement. In the best of all possible worlds, the entire school will agree on the mission. Identifying the mission allows the formulation of objectives, policies, and eventually, the procedures and methods to provide services to meet needs.

Developing policy statements, goals, and objectives is the next step in the planning process. A sound library policy statement, if missing at the district level, is developed at the building level. This statement need not be redone each year, but it and the mission statement should be reviewed yearly.

Policy Statement and Needs Assessment

At the theoretical level, planning begins with a policy statement to describe library services. Two books can help in developing a school library policy. These two books, *School Media Policy Development* by Helen Adams[3] and Marian Karpisek's *Policymaking for School Library Media Programs*, were both written more than two decades ago, but if you can find copies, they have excellent information. Adams describes the argument for developing policies, the policy development process, and the political process for ensuring acceptance of established policies. In her book, Karpisek cites the following eight steps of policy writing:

1. Research: written manual, district and school policies, climate of the school

2. First draft: philosophy

3. Advisory committee consideration

4. Final draft: rewriting to incorporate advisory committee considerations

5. Advisory committee review of revisions

6. Administrative approval

7. Distribution to faculty and parents

8. Dissemination to students[4]

Those developing policies for exemplary library programs may come up against school practice. If principals use the library as the teacher preparation period in elementary school or for large numbers of students coming from study hall to the library in secondary school, the climate of the school will be different. Changing that schedule will require an acceptable plan for alternatives and full teacher support.

Once the basic policy has been determined, planning involves the identification of problems to be addressed. In this phase, objectives, policies, procedures, and methods are developed based on the needs of students and teachers. During this part of the planning process, school librarians also work directly with those who will actually carry out the plans, the library staff, any other teachers who may be assigned to the library area, and the advisory committee.

The advisory committee acts as an advocacy group, speaking for additional resources based on its awareness of needs. It is important to make the distinction that the advisory committee's role is to *advise*, not to approve. You are the trained professional, and you should be making the final decisions about the collection and the library program. The advisory committee provides input to test new ideas and interpret the results of any evaluation exercise to the appropriate audience. In a sense, the committee becomes an extension of library staff in recognizing needs.

For example, a committee member reports that new state social studies standards are being adopted. As a part of the needs assessment process, the standards are analyzed to find which topics, when matched to the collection, have print and digital resources available in the library and then which new resources should be added to the collection. If new materials are needed, and if new relevant databases have to be licensed, query social studies teachers for their suggestions relating to collection additions. You may know more about available database options. Arrange database trials. Share digital book lists hyperlinked to reviews or content previews. Ask teachers to prioritize materials to purchase. Although budget resources may be limited, try to order the most needed materials immediately. Perhaps the social studies staff is hoping to take advantage of new history databases to support an updated curriculum. Acquisition of user rights to additional databases will likely require supplementary funding to be added to budgetary priority listings. In some cases, a new program may bring in new money, so the financial responsibility may be shared with and supported by the social studies department at the district or building level.

As teachers in your building create open educational resources (OER) or plan to do so, you will have additional challenges. You will want to assist teachers' discoveries of available OER instructional portals and you will need to provide professional development to guide teachers through intellectual property concerns as they create with these new resources and integrate them into learning management systems.

After a needs assessment is conducted, courses of action are reviewed and needed items are prioritized for potential purchase. Needs might be small, such as a change in the placement of furniture to make it easier to handle new configurations for small-group use or to accommodate a maker-space. However, needs may be great if new uses of library space are to be implemented. Alternate strategies are determined in case the first course of action is not possible, and the pros and cons of each alternative are discussed.

The following returns to the example of a need for more materials in social studies. Because students are quick to use social media and the Internet to find information, the most effective strategy to support the new social studies need would be to ensure easy access to databases and other high-quality digital resources. Among the strategies you might employ in promoting the use of these digital resources are the following:

- Partnering with teachers to support students in using online resources effectively, ethically, and creatively

- Understanding how your school's filters may hinder research and being prepared to propose solutions to those barriers

- Helping teachers understand the benefits of using high-quality, grade-relevant online resources and offering strategies to teach students about responsible online searching

- Building parent awareness of the value of school-licensed database content, perhaps by introducing them at a PTA/PTO meeting and spreading the word in newsletters and on the library website

- Providing equity of access to students who lack home access to the Internet

- Assisting teachers in locating or developing open educational resources and OER search portals to include in their curricula

- Helping students find and ethically use reputable online resources

- Providing 24/7 access to online resources such as databases across student-used devices

- Researching and connecting with speakers from the local community, and beyond, who can help bring social studies to life.

At each step of solving a problem, alternatives may be reviewed in terms of cost accountability while keeping in mind the focus on program objectives. Development of your program goals and objectives follows the needs assessment.

Goals and Objectives

Goals and objectives written after a needs assessment process define the library role in meeting the needs of users as it relates to the school curriculum. The objectives should be clear, and the reasons (basis for your choices) should be recorded. You need to develop clear rationales for the goals and objectives you choose for your strategic plan. If one of your goals is to increase the circulation of books in your library, you should be able to articulate why that is important. Is it just so you can say you have high circulation? Probably not. Your true reason is that the more students read, the greater their academic achievement will be. Activities or strategies to meet the objectives will depend on your level of participation in curriculum planning. It is essential that you seek and accept leadership in this process, becoming an integral part of classroom planning, participating in the development of all strategies and alternatives and articulating the reasons for final choices. This planning will make it easier to adjust the strategies later if they appear to be failing. You should record this process, perhaps in a log, to help recall successful activities as well as the outcomes of revisions. These successes can be reported to the advisory committee, teachers, or administrators in monthly or yearly status reports. Sharing examples of successful implementation of objectives can encourage other teachers to follow your lead. Recording changes or planning to use a previously successful strategy will help anyone who wishes to implement similar plans.

Organizing

In the process of strategic planning, school librarians organize the efforts that are necessary to carry out major decisions. In the organizing process, collaborating with teachers is logical because you have full knowledge of the curriculum, the way teachers teach, the assignments they give and the activities they plan in classrooms, and the support teachers will require from the library. These activities, whether conducted in the library or elsewhere, affect management because the different forms of instruction and the assignments that necessitate use of resources—both in the library and outside the library walls through its online resources—require much more planning and organizing than in the past. School librarians perform a variety of roles, ranging from merely being consulted to collaborating fully with the design and implementation of classroom units of instruction. Organizing teaching for inquiry-based learning units could go across the curriculum and include the entire school. This type of teaching, particularly when it involves many teachers and many curriculum areas, requires the particular organizational skills of the librarian.

While organizing, decisions are made about who should do what work, the activities the work entails, and the facilities available to accomplish the task. What is the nature of the library's involvement in the teaching activities? The librarian and the teachers must agree on work division and work assignment, and activities should be allocated between classrooms and the library during the organizing process. Returning to the example of the social studies project, a first activity is selection of new materials, and teachers are asked to review materials for purchase. As the librarian, you should set up a system for previewing, and receipt of items and their subsequent distribution to and return from teachers should be automatic. Clerical and professional staff should carry out the process. Again, websites and possible databases are reviewed for their availability, continued relevance, and usefulness.

A next step in organizing is to review the unit to see exactly where activities involve library staff. What will take place in the classroom and what will take place in the library? When will materials such as new databases and information available on the Internet be introduced and linked to the library website? What about access to materials? Are they only available on devices in the library? Where can students find access to a wifi network? What can students do if they do not have technology access at home?

As the time to begin the unit grows nearer, those involved must decide how to divide the teaching of the unit, define what research skills are required, and detail what reference sources and materials will be used so that involvement of the library and the library staff can be scheduled. This review continues throughout the unit so that library staff and use of the library as a classroom are available whenever needed.

At the beginning, decisions must be made about when and where the assignments will be introduced, how many sessions students might need in the library, how much actual research time will be allocated, and when the assignment will be due. Responsibility for each activity is assigned to the appropriate person or persons. Care is taken to ensure that the activities continue as planned and that the appropriate resources are available. This stage involves matching the plan books of the teacher and librarian with the library schedule.

Systematic Feedback and Adjustments

To meet the guidelines of Moran's and Morner's previously noted planning definition, school librarians must constantly evaluate the process, particularly as it applies to student learning. Did the unit work as planned? When, where, and how were the activities performed? Were they performed in accordance with the plans? To answer these questions, those involved must check progress during the unit and hold follow-up sessions. How well did students perform on evaluation exercises? Were sufficient resources available? What activities did teachers and students consider the most successful? Any final reports, comparisons with other units, costs, and projected budget needs are a part of the planning process. Finally, the librarian and teachers must ask whether the activity met the learning goals.

Planning for Growth

Planning for one week at a time is better than no planning at all. However, a school library program will be far more likely to grow its effectiveness and impact if the librarian creates a forward-thinking, well-documented aspirational plan. For too long, librarians have neglected to set goals and objectives beyond a single semester. Such short-term planning limits the ability to set priorities for major purchases that will continue the progress of the program beyond a single school year. For this reason, school librarians should develop a three- to five-year plan, which formalizes goals, objectives, action steps, and metrics. In this plan, all components of the library program should be listed with an indication of "what is" and "what should be," taking into account all necessary additions to the program—staff, equipment, materials, and/or facilities. Additions or modifications to the present situation should be proposed somewhere in the first, second, third, or fifth year, with a budget analysis for each activity. Check the School Library HQ in the Additional Resources for a sample five-year plan. As many districts have adopted Future Ready Schools, you might also consider creating a strategic plan using the Future Ready framework. You will find multiple templates online that adapt the framework into a multi-year plan. The advisory committee and principal, as well as any others who are interested, might be provided a printed copy of the three- or five-year plan, but it should be maintained primarily as a digital copy to allow changes which will affect the plan in the future to be made throughout the year.

For planning large projects, school librarians can learn from project planners who develop a timeline. One simple timeline is the Gantt chart, which displays tasks on the left side with the timeline across the top or bottom. The timeline is flexible, depending on the time allocated for completion of the project. The chart shown in Figure 7-1 was developed as a planning chart for creating a new makerspace in a library. Many other timelines and templates can be found online and in this book's Additional Resources.

	Sep	Oct	Nov	Dec	Jan	Feb	Mar	Apr	May	Jun	Jul	Aug
Elicit administrative approval	■											
Establish ongoing, collaborative input from teachers and students	■	■	■	■	■	■	■					
Develop mission/vision for new MS		■										
Select equipment and furniture			■	■	■							
Plan layout including storage and access to electrical facilities			■	■	■							
Determine supplies			■	■	■							
Plan budget			■	■	■							
Share budget and plans with stakeholders to elicit feedback					■	■						
Secure funding					■	■						
Order equipment and furniture							■					
Order supplies							■					
Plan promotion and marketing							■					
Determine scheduling and access							■					
Process new materials, equipment, and furniture								■				
Install and test new equipment								■				
Develop safety protocols								■				
Train staff and volunteers on new equipment								■				
Design sample lessons and activities									■	■		
Send out publicity									■	■		
Begin teacher trainings									■			
Hold open house for teachers												■
Hold open house for students												■
Hold open house for parents and community												■
Welcome students												■

Figure 7-1. Gantt Chart for Creating a New Makerspace (MS) in a Library.

April Dawkins.

The Gantt chart is helpful because one can see immediately where a project stands in relation to the schedule. When deadlines are not met, additional resources may be allocated if the opening date appears to be in jeopardy.

The final step of the chart is the turnkey date. At this time, "keys" should be turned over and the project completed. The purpose of such an exercise is to establish a timeline for a long-term project. However, the school librarian must also be able to manage time on a day-to-day basis.

Scheduling the School Library

The facility must be scheduled for maximum use by students and teachers: as individuals, as small groups, and as entire classes. Scheduling and monitoring access to the library is a major task requiring careful management of space, size, and time. The size of the actual space available in the library and the way the library is configured define the numbers of students who can fit into the space. To lessen the chance of gridlock, the needs of students/classes/activities are carefully reviewed and assigned. The ability to manage a schedule for the library also requires keeping that scheduling flexible rather than rigid.

Time management is a particularly difficult skill to acquire in any school, where the potential for sudden needs to arise is commonplace. However, it is more likely to be a challenge in an elementary school, where the facility is often smaller than in those in a middle or high school. The school librarian, more than other teachers, must be prepared for interruptions. On any day, a student or small group from a classroom needs information immediately because of an event that has just occurred. Elementary students may enter the library enthusiastically and find the librarian conducting a story time with the kindergarteners. Working this special need into the day is easier when teachers know they should give a little advance notice.

Capturing the "teachable" moment involves the library as often as or more often than any other area of the school. Perhaps this is one of the most compelling reasons to provide free access to the library rather than limiting access because of a rigid schedule of classes. Students and teachers with information needs must have these needs met at the earliest possible moment. Most high schools have full-time staff and libraries that are large enough to accommodate both full classes and small groups. This is not as often true in elementary schools, so creating a flexible schedule will be a challenge. Sometimes this can be done by seeing two classes from one level in the library at the same time for book exchange and silent reading or listening to a story. If they are studying a topic, booktalking some books on that part of the curriculum can encourage research. When this works, a time slot is freed for a different use of the library. Creative thinking with teachers and administrators involved can generate other ideas to test flexible scheduling. It will not be easy when the elementary teachers' planning time is built around "special" subjects, such as music, art, physical education, computer literacy, and the library. When library time is used as planning time for teachers, an administrator arranges scheduling, and the school librarian works to find additional time slots for spontaneous use of the library and its resources. Some advocates argue that unless elementary teachers are scheduled to bring their classes to the library, they will not do so, and they do not object to a strictly scheduled plan. If this seems to be the attitude of teachers, a short book exchange time can be scheduled regularly so that students who finish their books quickly can return them.

Consider using The American Association of School Librarians (AASL) Position Statement supporting flexible or responsive scheduling to advocate for change. Although a fixed schedule may ensure that you see all students, a responsive schedule ensures that activities in the library are closely tied to activities in the classroom, "responsive to the learning community's needs" and allows for flexibility in student access.[5]

When a rigid or shared schedule is in place, the librarian must plan activities to help change this use of the library. It will take the endorsement of the advisory committee and detailed, careful, curriculum-related planning with one or more teachers. If a class activity has been planned for a full semester, it may be possible to exclude other classes from the library for their regular schedule for a special culminating event for one class. For example, students in a class focusing on the study of early settlers in the Northeast may build one or two houses in the library for a week's activities, sharing this project with the entire school. This will not be easy to achieve, but if such an event is successful with one class, other teachers will want their students to have a similar opportunity. This encourages teachers to recognize that the library is a research center rather than a free period.

The fixed-versus-flexible debate continues. Both positions have their merits: a fixed schedule guarantees that young children have frequent access to the library and a responsive schedule allows the librarian to provide more curriculum-driven lessons and activities. In some elementary schools, a combination of fixed and flexible schedules are used, with younger grades maintaining a fixed library schedule and upper elementary grades using a more flexible schedule. To advocate for better learning for your students, begin discussing a move toward responsive scheduling which will allow you to provide on-demand services. If your school has followed a fixed schedule for some time, it may take several years to complete this shift to a more responsive schedule. AASL supports this move through its School Library Scheduling Position Statement, which says: "Scheduling of classes should allow flexible, open, unrestricted, and equitable access on an as-needed basis to facilitate just-in-time research, training, and utilization of technology with instruction from the school librarian and the content-area educator."[6] With the support of your administration and classroom teachers, you can suggest responsive scheduling for older students and maintenance of a fixed schedule for the younger ones. In the first year of a transition, you might only have a flexible schedule for fifth grade, for example.

Another typical scenario is that the librarian may be shared with one or more schools and paraprofessionals may be employed to do library story times and book checkout with the students when the librarian is at another location. In these cases, the librarian may be expected to do isolated skill instruction on the scheduled day at a facility. This scenario precludes the use of the library as a learning place. As discussed earlier regarding planning for use of the facility, the advisory committee can be helpful in suggesting an appropriate schedule for the library and the librarian that allows teachable moments and real learning to occur. Any emphasis on teaching students how to do research emphasizes the role of the library and the librarian and should lead teachers into collaborative unit planning.

At the secondary level, many students who have no study hall scheduled can come to the library only when their teachers bring an entire class. Other students have so many study halls scheduled that they use the library as a change of scene or social gathering spot. Both situations must be addressed. Students need opportunities to use the library during the day. Homeroom might provide access for those with no study hall scheduled. With the help of teachers and students, plan alternative activities especially for students who have nothing to study while using the library during study hall. Engaging them in completing online searches to expand information they are studying in their classrooms supports the curriculum. Asking students what they would like to do and helping them locate the resources and materials to do so will lessen the time it takes to plan such activities.

Additionally, many students are now taking online classes through virtual high schools or community colleges. Often these students are using the library space to complete their assignments. If these students are assigned to the library to complete their online courses, you will need to work with administration to determine how these students will be supervised so that you can continue your work as the librarian.

Those students, from elementary through high school, who come to the library with no apparent reason or assignment present excellent opportunities to encourage experiential learning and inquiry. You can help these students see the library as a place to explore their personal interests through makerspace activities, creative projects, technology playgrounds, passion-driven inquiry, or simply free choice in reading. In this instance, without directives or an assignment, students choose to read or engage in the activities that interest them.

Digital Calendars and Daily Plans

Classroom teachers are expected to maintain a daily plan (in either print or digital form) to post the goals and learning objectives of lessons and activities, and to share evaluations of progress through the units. As an educator, the school librarian maintains a similar record, although the daily plans may cover several classrooms rather than one. This plan book is a log of activities being planned, in progress, and being evaluated. It is a record of alternatives when the original plan is being revised. If the timing of a unit must be adjusted, the plan book shows the new schedule. In this record, the librarian shares goals, objectives, and activities and, finally, records progress. Keeping the plans as a digital calendar makes it easy to record revisions to the daily schedule and allows the librarian to link to relevant documents. When this calendar becomes available on the library website, teachers have immediate knowledge of open periods and can make their preliminary plans with an email message. Note that the plan may list activities of the librarian as well as activities in the school library that may be monitored by someone else. Teachers need to be specific in their emails as to their needs. Are they interested in signing up for the library space, which they will monitor, or do they also need to schedule the librarian's time? To reduce the number of emails, create an online form that covers the information you need to collaboratively plan with teachers and understand their needs. You can find many examples of these collaborative documents through an online search. Some of the information you might want when beginning the collaboration process includes:

- Information about the grade, class, subject, and goals of the project
- Timeline, including time in the library and due dates
- Resources/materials/technology/equipment required
- Project/assessment description and final product(s)

- Description of what the teacher wants the librarian to provide

- Type of space needed

The planning function is complemented by the budget needed to manage a school library. School librarians may not recognize or may forget that they are responsible for managing resources that would be extremely costly to replace. Only the coach with athletic equipment and the band and orchestra directors (when students' musical instruments are furnished by the school) come close to having such an inventory to control. These are actual "things" that must be kept working and must not be lost. The value of these is high, and their continued usefulness often depends upon the budget allocated to the school library. This is the true business side of management.

A great deal of this chapter relates to the budgeting process for the school district. School librarians need to learn as much as possible because

- School librarians need to be aware of the actual amounts in the budget for print and digital resources, processing supplies, technology, etc.

- Orders for materials must follow procedures and rules and often have dates affecting when these orders must be submitted and when they must have been received and invoices paid.

- Business managers often need help because purchases for the library are different from purchases for other classrooms within the district.

School district budgets are not secret. Anyone in the community should be able to see a copy of the district budget. However, these are often pages and pages of numbers that may seem very difficult to interpret. Depending on each state's funding model, there may or may not be specific funds allocated for purchase of library materials. Some funding models provide districts with a bulk amount for instructional materials which is intended for distribution over all curriculum areas. Local boards of education or even site-based decision making may determine the library's actual budget. If you are not aware of the actual amount budgeted for libraries, you may not receive all that was intended for the library. This is discussed later in the following section.

Budget

School librarians are usually given a budget. The size of this budget may vary from year to year. The management of a small budget may be more of a challenge to the school librarian as manager than a much larger amount of money.

A fundamental responsibility of the school librarian is to be a conscientious steward of financial resources. Regardless of the size of the budget—or whether there is an allocated budget or not—it is the job of the school librarian to be aware of the financial resources that are required to support a library program that is integral to learning and teaching in the school. School library programs expand or disintegrate depending on the amount of money regularly allocated in the school district budget for purchase of needed resources, staffing, technology, and equipment. District administrators plan the district budget and present it to the school board for approval.

Funding for school libraries generally is allocated either throughout the district on a per-pupil basis or is determined at the building level by the principal in each school. In districts that use the per-pupil allocation formula, the per-pupil dollar amount may vary by level—elementary, middle, or high school—and most establish a minimum level of funding so that very small schools (those with student populations of less than 200) are not negatively affected. In addition, special allocations often are made to address unique needs, such as schools with very old collections that require updating, schools in which the curriculum is changing significantly, new schools, or schools that require more access to technology because students' resources are limited at home. Per-pupil funding generally results in more equity of library resources and services across schools within a district.

Additionally, library funding may be included as part of a lump sum given to the school and then divided up through site-based decision making, or it might be done through a line-item budget. In a line-item budget, there may be several categories that provide funding for the library, such as for print books, technology, ebooks and databases, and library supplies. Line-item budgets can be a challenge to prepare, but they offer the librarian an opportunity to illustrate actual item costs and briefly share justifications for purchases. It is important for you to determine how your library's funds are allocated so that you can advocate for your students.

In the 1980s, many school districts moved toward school-based management, and many districts have continued this practice. Rather than allocating resources to schools based upon a per-pupil formula, funds are given to each school's principal, who (individually or with a school-based committee) decides how they will be disbursed within the building. In schools in which the principal or the site-based leadership team recognizes the value and importance of the library program to teachers and students, funding is often sufficient to support the program.

Unfortunately, in programs in which the principal and the librarian do not have a good working relationship or those in which the principal has low expectations for the library program, the support is insufficient to meet programmatic needs. Additionally, librarians working in site-based managed schools often cannot depend upon a consistent funding stream, which may make long-range planning difficult. Furthermore, changes in leadership within a school may result in radical changes to budget priorities.

With the passage of federal legislation, starting with the Elementary and Secondary Education Act in 1965 and then No Child Left Behind under the Bush administration, attempts have been made to address inequities in education. In 2015, there was a renewed potential for large sums of federal money to be allocated to states for education because of the Every Student Succeeds Act (ESSA). This encouraged school librarians to work to find out how administrators were anticipating using any funding within the school. School librarians were able to assume their leadership role to help establish the most need in the building that could be met with these funds. The librarian who has documented needs to support student learning and the curriculum can help expend such funds in the best and most impactful way possible and can also help evaluate the results of such application of funds. Each state and district developed plans for the expenditure of ESSA funds. It is important that you determine if those plans include the school library.

The Development of District Budgets

One analogy for budgets is to think of the district budget like a pie, with different programs, divisions, or initiatives each getting pieces of the pie. You need to know if the library gets a piece of the pie. If it does not receive sufficient funding from the district, the librarian may have to creatively bake a new pie. Whatever model the school district uses, you must understand that model and conform to its requirements whenever you have input into the budget process or when you are submitting items for purchase. You must always be ready to respond to requests for budget input. Consider keeping a running list of items for purchase that could be turned into an order at a moment's notice. You must be able to demonstrate that you have engaged in a planning process to show how the library contributes to meeting the curricular and personal information needs of teachers and students and what funding is needed to adequately support those needs. It is important for you to demonstrate why supporting the library program is a more cost-effective approach than replicating resources in individual classrooms or departments.

Conflicts arise out of the realities of the school district's financial situation, usually defined by local taxation, and the practical need to provide a wide variety of materials for students and teachers. These conflicts can occur at the district level, when the library budget is distributed from a central library budget, or in each school, if district funds are distributed to individual buildings. Because budget items for the library program are part of the total school district budget, funding requests compete with those from other units, such as academic requirements, art, athletics, and music programs. Site-managed budgets distributed in the local school will find the librarians' requests competing with the classroom teachers' requests as well as with requests from other programs.

Annual budgets for school districts are prepared early in one fiscal year for the next year's expenditures. Superintendents may request assistance from others who are asked for input, but the superintendents remain responsible for the final decision on items and amounts. The principal's staff and the superintendent's central office staff are usually included by demand rather than by request. An example of others involved would be negotiators for the teachers' bargaining unit if you live in a union state. All of these oversee preparation of the budget to make sure no budget decreases will necessitate personnel reductions and to confirm the inclusion of salary increases and other benefits.

Once the budget is prepared, the superintendent presents it to the local school board for approval. In some states, the state board of education grants final approval. In other states, voters are asked to pass a referendum for funding and budgets can be voted down by the members of the community. The amount of control exercised by local or state boards of education or by the voters in a referendum is in direct proportion to the amount of funds they control. In states where the major portion of education funding comes from state rather than local revenues, state officials maintain closer control over the local budget process than in states where most school funding is locally generated.

Regardless of how money is allocated for school library programs and where decisions are made, it is important for you to understand how budgets are created, how to find the funds allocated for purchases, and how and when to make those purchases. School librarians should locate the persons who can help with questions. In some districts, it will be the district library supervisor. In other districts, it may be a secretary or accountant in the school or the business manager in the central office.

Most states and districts use line-item descriptions. Budget processes as well as numbering of line items vary from state to state. Each line in the budget represents either the source of the revenue or the amount of funding that is allocated for each category. A school district's revenues can come from local property taxes, the state or federal government, proceeds from bond sales, sale of property, interest from investments or trust funds, grants, and/or rentals of facilities. Each source of revenue has a specific code.

The next pages of the budget include the expenditures. Most school budgets reflect the past year's budgeted and actual expenditures, the current year's budget with anticipated and actual expenditures, and a column to project the next year's budget. For example, in a budget being prepared for 2025, the first two columns would show the budgeted and actual expenditures for 2023. The middle two columns would show the budgeted amount for 2024 and the expenditures against that amount as of the date of budget preparation. The final column would show the anticipated budget for 2025.

The Fiscal Year

School districts' fiscal year usually matches the state government pattern. In some cases, the fiscal year begins on January 1 and ends on December 31. All orders for materials or services to be charged to a particular fiscal year must be placed after January 1 and received and paid for no later than December 31. If the fiscal year is July 1 to June 30, the accounting books will close on June 30, and all expenditures not cleared by that date will be charged to the next year's budget.

Business managers often require that all purchase orders be issued in enough time to receive the merchandise, confirm shipment of the appropriate items, and issue payment before the end of the fiscal year. In some cases, no purchase orders may be issued within four months of the end of the fiscal year, so that orders will be completed in ample time before closing the books. For many districts, purchases may be prohibited after a specific date, often in March. It is important that the librarian learn of this date in advance. School librarians seldom have large budgets, and any loss of funds can be painful. Items that require longer times for shipment should be ordered as early as possible. If vendors, jobbers, or publishers send orders in more than one shipment, it is important that all shipments be received before the end of the fiscal year so the invoice can be approved and paid with the current year's funds.

Some distributors will allow "fill up to" or "do not exceed" orders. If these options are available, the school librarian sets an upper expenditure limit for a specific order and the distributor ships as many items as can be purchased with the identified dollar amount. This approach ensures that no money from an order is lost because some items on an order are not available. If you are aware of an upcoming district budget freeze, you may want to quickly prepare an advance or standing-order purchase order from a trusted vendor to ensure that new materials can arrive after the freeze and to encumber existing funds. Using this strategy, you can prepay for upcoming publications.

The need to handle fiscal matters promptly is one of the reasons fiscal officers sometimes wish to limit the librarian to one or two book orders each year. Limiting orders seriously affects the librarian's ability to provide materials for students and teachers as needs arise. Working closely with business managers and clerical staff can help overcome this problem and allow for more flexible and responsive collection building.

It is wise for the librarian to be as supportive of the fiscal officer as possible. Most librarians are expected to present necessary buying information to the purchasing agent by submitting printed lists, online forms, school or district requisitions, or purchase orders. All forms must be completed accurately, from correct spelling and address for the supplier to correct spelling of author, title, publisher for books, and ISBN or ISSN for periodicals. Accurate item numbers for supplies, accurate model numbers for equipment, and accurate quantities desired, unit item costs, and item totals are essential. Any erroneous information on an order may cause an incorrect shipment or incorrect billing, which will necessitate additional correspondence from the business office for the return or exchange of items. This costs staff time in the accounting office and may lead the business manager to restrict the librarian's freedom to issue a requisition or purchase order.

Those school librarians who are allowed to order from a vendor using an electronic device may bypass the process of creating orders and submitting them to the business office. This ability should be treated as the perquisite that it is, and care should be taken to stay within budget limits for materials and to confirm all shipments when they arrive.

As more and more routine ordering is performed digitally, librarians need to be even more attentive about making sure that item numbers and other information are carefully and correctly submitted. The ease of ordering does not release the school librarian from writing specifications for purchases.

Acquiring Resources: The Purchasing Process

Many methods exist for acquiring resources for the school library. Although sometimes the library receives gifts, most additions to the collection must be selected, ordered, received, and paid for. A first step in the acquisition process is to select a source from which to purchase an item.

Purchasing Materials

In some school districts, purchase orders may be initiated by the school librarian and sent by the school office to the vendor. In other places, orders are submitted to a central office to be issued. Items purchased may be shipped directly to the school, or they may be sent to the central office. A document should be available showing exactly how and to whom orders are to be sent, but this document can be created if none exists. The school's office staff should be able to help develop this, or you may need to ask the principal from whom at the central office you can get this information.

Online purchase of books and other smaller items over the Internet is becoming commonplace. One can order from online bookstores such as Amazon or Barnes & Noble or from jobbers or aggregators using selection lists such as Follett School Solutions *TitleWave* and the lists offered by Mackin Library Services, which have access to the same information you would find in *Books in Print*. Equipment is usually more expensive, and you may want to learn how to order efficiently from a salesperson.

A purchase such as laptops for 200 students in a school is a very big order. It may be that a district wishes to have one brand of computer in every school, which could substantially lower the cost of a single item. A consortium may have a procurement list with established prices based upon large quantities. If it is up to individual schools or school districts, most states regulate the way things are purchased. Larger purchases are likely to be initiated at a higher level, perhaps by the district technology department or through district capital funds.

In many states, selection of a purchase source is based on a bid process when an item costs a specified amount. Most purchases are made through vendors who have been approved at the district or state level. However, for larger purchases you may be required to solicit bids for all items over a designated amount (perhaps $500). This means that suppliers bid to provide the material or equipment and the lowest bidder receives the order. This is often true of the jobber chosen to supply library resources.

A *jobber* or *aggregator* is a supplier who buys from a wide variety of manufacturers or publishers, so the librarian need send only one order for most resources. Individual publishers and suppliers may give a better discount, but this means that individual purchase orders must be sent. Business managers often prefer to order from a single source rather than send multiple orders to individual suppliers because of the cost of issuing payments. Once materials and suppliers have been determined, materials are ordered, using the process in place in the school district.

At present, most large school districts order by digital transmission. A purchase order is returned, often by email attachment, to the librarian to confirm receipt of the digital order. No matter how materials and equipment are ordered, great care must be taken in completing the ordering process.

As stated earlier, school librarians may now purchase from jobbers or aggregators who offer digital ordering, which is often as simple as checkmarking a box. The availability of all titles ordered will be confirmed, and the materials shipped and billed immediately. Many purchasing officers welcome this easy method of ordering. The school librarian sets a total price limit beyond which the jobber should not send further shipments. This ceiling on purchases allows the librarian to maximize quick-order opportunities.

Maintaining accurate records about your purchases is essential to creating a good relationship with your business manager and administrators. You should keep a running tally of your budget, copies of all of your purchase orders, and files with information about contracts or warranties. If you have centralized processing in your district, orders may be delivered to a central location where they are checked off against the purchase order and readied for distribution to your library. However, in many schools, orders are delivered directly to your school and you will be responsible for checking the shipments against the purchase order to ensure that the order is complete and in good condition. After checking the order, you will be responsible for notifying the business manager, providing the invoice, and confirming if anything is missing.

As noted at the beginning of this chapter, school district business managers do not always understand the specifics of the library world and will welcome assistance with selection and ordering. They may need help in selecting suppliers of materials, especially when the suppliers are not the more familiar sources of other educational items; in writing specifications for equipment; and in confirming that products ordered have been received. This is one way to make friends with those who handle funds for library programs.

Creating rapport with the business manager is as important as developing relationships with the administrators in the building and with the custodial staff. Remaining friends with these persons is easier if care is taken to make their jobs easier. One excellent way to do this is to notify them as soon as items are received and checked against the purchase order. This enables them to make full or partial payment to the supplier. Otherwise, the supplier continues to send bills and notices to the business manager.

Selecting Equipment

Selecting equipment is no longer the challenge it has been in the past. The need for computers continues to grow and although the prices vary, it is still a costly proposition for most district-level budgets. Libraries are investing less in heavy desktop computers as people move to more portable, personal devices. Cloud-based applications that run across devices simplify previous issues relating to installing and updating software. Physical formats for media have been largely supplanted by online media portals and licensed media databases. Reference information, magazines, and newspapers are widely available online, and librarians now face decisions about which formats are most useful for their communities and whether they need to purchase materials in multiple formats.

Libraries and classrooms today offer computers or other devices to access information while students are in the building. It is not uncommon for schools to have 1:1 rollouts of Chromebooks or iPads. These became even more common during the COVID-19 pandemic. It is also not uncommon for districts to purchase carts of devices for class use or for borrowing that are supervised, maintained, secured, and charged in the library. These carts and other methods of distributing laptops and tablets do not necessarily address equity issues if students do not have wifi access at home, a situation broadly described as the *homework gap*. When some students can access information and use digital tools on their personal iPads and cell phones, and others cannot, librarians must take the lead in advocating that all students get equitable access to the library's website, databases, and other digital resources. As government funds are allocated to states and cities to provide wireless access, issues relating to limited wifi access will be mitigated. Until then, efforts to provide or lend hotspot technology will facilitate use of devices at home.

For many new school librarians, the selection of equipment can be a challenge, especially if they feel unprepared to make these significant and expensive choices. Although the district or school may have a technology coordinator who assumes responsibility, school librarians should learn as much as possible, advocating for their users' needs in any decisions.

Cost Accountability and Return on Investment (ROI)

When advocating for your budget, you might be asked about the costs of the services you are providing. Some districts allocate library funding by providing a per-pupil dollar amount. In that situation, it is sometimes helpful to provide information about how much the resources and services provided by the library cost per patron. You may have an opportunity to discuss ROI in your annual reports or in school board presentations.

Cost Accountability

Examples of illustrating ROI might include proving the value of licensing a new database or purchasing a 3-D printer. To calculate the cost of equipment use, list the piece or pieces of equipment and their purchase prices. Divide these figures by the number of expected years of service and number of days of possible use and then the days by hours of expected use to arrive at a use-per-hour figure. For example, if a piece of equipment costs $2,700 and its life expectancy is three years of 180 days each year, or 540 days of use, and it is anticipated to be used five hours a day, the anticipated use would be 2,700 hours. The cost of use is $1.00 per hour, not counting any repair or replacement parts if the machine does not operate as anticipated. Alternatively, you may want to consider the per-student use or the use by varied groups of students. If you are considering illustrating use of a database, detailed analytics are easily accessible in the resource's administrative space. Your vendor can help you customize the reports you need.

Human costs include professional and clerical staff in the library. If the annual salary of the librarian is $60,000 and this person works 180 days per year and seven hours each day, both daily wage and hourly wage are easily calculated. To calculate the daily wage, divide the days worked per year into the yearly salary. This indicates that the librarian earns approximately $333 per day. Calculate the hourly wage by dividing the hours worked per day into the daily rate. This person's hourly wage is approximately $44 per hour. If the librarian spends 30 minutes cataloging and processing a new item, the cost for this is $22 in labor, not counting any costs for supplies. It would be difficult to defend this expenditure, because purchasing complete processing from a book jobber is much less costly. The time saved by ordering books fully processed frees the librarian to spend that time collaborating with teachers or teaching students. The cost for processing an item increases as the librarian moves up the salary scale.

Material costs are calculated based on their replacement cost, which rises with inflation. An annual average cost figure for books (even though these are no longer the major purchase item) may be calculated by adding the total of all purchase orders for books submitted in a fiscal year and then dividing by the number of books received. Both of these figures are easy to find on billing statements. Using the average cost of a book multiplied by the number of books that were lost, missing, or stolen from the library can show the replacement cost for a single year.

The approximate cost of a book can be used in another way: to show the total replacement value of the library and the amount of materials and equipment the librarian oversees. If a library has 20,000 items and an item costs an average of $24 to replace, the librarian oversees $480,000 in materials. Adding the cost of replacing equipment greatly increases this amount. Book, media, or equipment estimates can also be used to show students and their parents how valuable the library is to them. That is, if books have an average cost of $24 and 200 books are circulated each day for nine weeks, the value of the books circulated during one grading period is $216,000 (9 weeks × 5 days per week × $24 per book).

Librarians in single-person centers are often concerned about the time it takes to complete clerical tasks, reshelve books, or replace paper in printers. When a $44-per-hour person spends an hour shelving books, the cost to the district is very high compared with the $15 per hour paid for clerical staff to do that job. For some librarians, clerical tasks are somewhat rewarding in that they have a beginning and an end. However, as discussed earlier, when professionals are required to complete clerical tasks because they have no assistance, it is not cost-effective for the school or district. The greater loss, and one even more difficult to calculate, occurs when a professional is not available to collaborate with teachers. A librarian who is preoccupied with clerical tasks cannot help students find, analyze, and evaluate materials or assist teachers in locating materials to meet students' abilities or learning styles. Comparing the costs of time for professionals and clerical staff members can assist in this effort.

ROI

Perhaps more effective than providing cost analyses in advocating for your budget is to instead frame budget requests by explaining the potential ROI, an idea from the business world that explores profitability. It has been adapted in public libraries to examine the economic impact of the services that libraries provide. ROI looks at how much benefit is provided by an organization based on the dollars invested in it. While this has not been used to a great extent in school libraries, the public library ROI research can support your advocacy efforts. An ROI calculator was developed at Syracuse University to examine the impact of library services.[7] You might adapt this for use in advocating for your budget.

Many school administrators may not see developing budget requests as a function of the school librarian. As a result, many librarians have little opportunity to plan a budget or request funds. However, it is a fundamental responsibility of school librarians to assume a more proactive role and plan for their programs by quantifying the value and cost of services and differentiating among those that are strictly administrative and those that contribute to meeting the mission and goals of the school and are integral to learning and teaching. This process must take into account the present, the immediate future, and long-range plans. Unless you engage in long-range financial as well as program planning, carefully detailing the anticipated costs of necessary services, administrators will remain unaware of the costs of providing for the information needs of teachers and students. Needs and objectives must be established and proposed expenditures clarified. Success is more likely if the requests are presented in a structured format, not unlike the formal process of project proposal writing.

Top Ten Tips for Successful Grant Writing

1. Determine needs, identify funding sources, make sure your project aligns with the grant's eligibility criteria.
2. Align your budget with your narrative and activities.
3. Articulate the need and how you will measure success.
4. Follow the directions! Read the rubric and focus on the areas that can gain you the highest scores.
5. Format the proposal correctly: use required or approved fonts, spacing, margins, and page limits.
6. Obtain administrative support early and make sure you allow time for permissions and signatures.
7. Meet the deadline! (Is it a received-by date or a postmark/transmit date?)
8. Have someone unfamiliar with your project (preferably outside the library world) read your proposal to make sure it is easy to understand and free of jargon.
9. Include all requested documents and omit those not requested.
10. Proofread!

Writing Proposals to Expand Programs

It is the responsibility of the school district to provide the funds to support the library program. It is not appropriate for the district to expect the school librarian to be responsible for raising funds to build the book collection or provide digital resources. However, many school librarians consider fundraising options to enable them to offer special programs such as author visits or reading enrichment programs or to expand specific sections of the collection. One option for obtaining additional funding is to develop a carefully thought-out and well-documented proposal. The type of information you collect and the way you explain your needs can be used in approaching an outside agency or other individuals from whom you are seeking support. Potential funders include the principal, the school board, parents (individually or from the Parent Teacher Association/Organization), a foundation, or a state or federal agency as new funding is being allocated in this decade. Whether a funding request remains in the district or is sent to an outside agency, a proposal must be developed. If you have never written a full grant proposal before, you might want to start by developing some smaller funding projects through local grant programs or donation programs such as Donors Choose. The proposals for these are typically much simpler than for a larger grant program.

The remainder of this section discusses writing proposals for the school district or agencies that fund proposals directly related to school library programs. For someone who has never written a proposal for funding, this may seem an overwhelming task. If you know of librarians who have written project proposals, listening to their suggestions will be helpful. Five successful proposal writers have shared their ideas in a book titled *Librarian's Handbook for Seeking, Writing and Managing Grants*.[8] It covers everything from how to research possible funding sources through how to manage the grant when you have been successful.

Sometimes school librarians are invited to join other (perhaps larger) agencies, the public library, or a county-wide system to develop a broader proposal. For some agencies, collaboration is either encouraged or required. The expertise, experience, or other resources of a co-writers' group can also add value to your proposal.

Most project proposals include the following elements: a statement of needs or goals and objectives, a plan of action or activities and procedures anticipated, a timeline, an evaluation plan, information about facilities and other resources available to support the project, and a carefully planned budget with detailed budget notes that explain the anticipated expenditures. Additional items, such as applicable employment opportunity regulations, may be required if the proposal goes beyond the school district. Résumés of staff and consultants for the project also may be expected.

Developing the Statement of Needs

Few individuals are willing to allocate money without a needs statement. As children, we learn to justify additional allowance requests to our parents. As adults, personal budget decisions to make major purchases are based on a needs assessment. School librarians cannot expect additional funding without presenting a strong case of need. Needs are defined in a variety of ways. One approach is to read research studies that address the problem in your school. You can ask for funds to implement a program that has been demonstrated to address the problem. One example would be the purchase of a test preparation software program that will help students practice taking the PSAT or SAT exams for college admission.

Another effective way is to compare the resources available in your school with those of a similar school in the district or a nearby district where the student body is similar but achievement levels are higher. The difference in resources available could be suggested as a reason for the difference in achievement levels and would give you the opportunity to test the result of adding materials and equipment for student use. As chapter 9 details, analyzing the resource collection to determine how well it met the needs of a diverse student body is a critical undertaking.

The needs analysis process will be much more effective if the input comes from the advisory group rather than the librarian as a single individual who has identified the need. The composition of the group is very important. Funding agencies want to know if those to be served by the project helped identify needs and if those identified needs were used to help set the priorities. Proposal writers should cite the persons involved in the needs assessment process. In this case, administrators, teachers, and parents are most likely to be those who helped establish the needs because they know when students have problems with reading or in another area of the curriculum.

Although a librarian can say that the collection is inadequate in particular areas or to support particular programs, the statement is more powerful if teachers review the collection and determine that it is inadequate. Alternatively, students could compose lists of missing or inadequate materials for projects they have researched. It is a good time to have student and teacher input in the process because it is important for the assessment of needs to involve those directly or indirectly affected by the proposed project. It would be foolhardy to ask for an expanded collection of art books if the art teacher did not plan to use the books or make assignments that require students to use them. An assessment has strength when the missing information is available on a database that will help students learn they can find information in places other than Google. Consider soliciting suggestions for additions to the collection from students and faculty. This can easily be done with a Google form.

To confirm the participation of others in establishing needs, the proposal writer should list all meetings held and who attended, tests that were administered and their results, and any other relevant details. Participation may also be confirmed by letters of support, which should be appended to the body of the proposal. Once the need has been established, a goal should be stated and objectives for the project developed.

Preparing Goals and Objectives

An organization sending out requests for proposals (RFPs) may define a goal as measurable; if it does, then the goal must in fact be measurable. However, for the purposes of this book, the definition of a *goal* is a broad, general statement that is not measurable. Because a goal is such a broad statement, it is not always required for a project proposal. However, when a goal is required, it should be realistic. Consider requesting additional reading materials as an example of a goal. Trying to overcome all reading problems in an elementary school in a single year might be an unrealistic goal. If children are reading below grade level, or not reading at all, a few books and magazines added to the library collection will not alleviate the problem and the goal cannot be met.

Conversely, objectives must be measurable. They are designed to help address the needs that have been determined, and they should state the precise level of achievement anticipated and the length of time expected to be needed to achieve them. Objectives must be an outgrowth of the stated needs. They should describe where the school library program should be at the end of the grant time frame in relation to where the program is currently and who or what is involved in the project. The better the objectives are written, the easier it will be to prepare the evaluation later. For instance, an objective that attempts to increase reading scores will have to include the number of students, how much increase will occur, and the time frame within which the increase will occur. These elements are included in the objective.

Goals and objectives themselves may be evaluated when the proposal is reviewed. *Context evaluation* is the assessment of goals and objectives to see whether they are written in terms of the intended constituency of the project. For example, this evaluation reviews the number of students who will benefit from the project, for they should be part of the stated objectives. For the reading project, you might choose to work only with third-grade students for one year, and you would suggest that each student would raise reading scores by two years.

Objectives are often confused with activities. Rather than stating the expected or desired outcome, novice proposal writers often list the methods to achieve that outcome. These methods are activities rather than stated objectives, and they are a part of the plan of action.

Establishing the Plan of Action

The section of the proposal that states the plan of action, or proposed activities, describes the methods to be employed to meet the stated objectives and alleviate the needs. A general statement of the overall design of the project includes the population to be served, how the population will be selected, and how the project will be managed. But the activities themselves must be directed to the objectives, and the relationship must be clear. Activities designed to achieve the objectives must follow from the objectives. If the relationship between objective and activity is ambiguous, those reading the proposal may reject it. Most funding agencies and school administrators prefer projects with a step-by-step plan of realistic activities to meet the objectives and alleviate the need. The activity for third-graders might be to give them books to read that they will want to read and allow them unlimited access to these books.

When a project planner is unsure that proposed activities will meet objectives in the anticipated time frame, alternative plans of action may be presented. A rationale for each alternative may include a brief statement about why the first plan of action was proposed and how, when, or why it will be decided to use the alternative plan. If providing a large collection of reading materials does not seem to be encouraging children to read, providing more reading opportunities during the school day and asking parents to help children read more at night at home could be an alternative plan of action or even a second activity. Whenever possible, proposal writers should include relevant research supporting their choice from the array of possible activities.

As the project activities are described, a timeline for each of the activities may be presented. The timeline shows the sequence of separate activities that have gone before, what is in progress, and what will be done. This description enables the reviewers to understand how the activities are related—that is, if and when the initiation of one activity depends on the completion of another, when activities overlap, and the progress necessary for project completion.

Planning for Evaluation

After the activities have been designed, proposal writers must then determine the best methods to evaluate the activities to see whether they are indeed meeting the stated objectives. To do this, two kinds of evaluation are helpful: formative and summative. Formative evaluation processes occur throughout the life of the project. At each step, an evaluation may be made to see if the activities are accomplishing the planned improvements. If the project does not appear to be successful, an alternate plan of action may be put into place. Progress using the new activity will then be evaluated to see if it demonstrates more success than the previous plan. Formative evaluation further determines whether project progress is within the anticipated time period.

At the close of any project, a final, or summative, evaluation is conducted. At this time, each activity is evaluated to determine the degrees of progress made toward meeting the stated objectives. Proposal writers must detail the means by which they or their agency will verify for the funding source that the project has accomplished the objectives as stated and the degree to which the objectives have been met. Information to be collected must be described, methods to analyze the information must be outlined, and the degree of success that should be expected must be stated. With this example proposal, the obvious summative evaluation would be a reading test to see whether test scores have increased.

Proposal writing is often not an easy task, and many proposal writers seek help from persons in tests and measurements offices in colleges and universities and/or in local or state agencies to help define the evaluation procedures to be used after the project begins. Many funding agencies prefer the summative evaluation to be conducted by an outside evaluator to eliminate or modify the possibility of bias and add validity to the evaluation statements. When seeking project funding from outside agencies, choosing an outside evaluator—especially one highly regarded by the funding agency—may increase the likelihood of the project being approved. Someone not directly related to the project may be better able to objectively measure the degree of success. Certainly the evaluation is one of the most important aspects of project planning and should be given full attention.

Deciding the Dissemination

Many outside funding agencies may ask about how the results of the project, if funded, will be disseminated to the broader world. Even if this is not a specified requirement, the school librarian should be prepared to share the results of any project with all appropriate audiences. Just as government agencies and foundation staff need to know the degree of success of their investment, they anticipate credit for the contribution they made to the project. For locally funded projects, the school librarian reports project success to the superintendent and principal. They should be given material they can use for publicizing a successful project. It is no virtue to hide project success.

Funding agencies need good publicity to continue awarding money for projects; likewise, the school library is more likely to receive additional funds when successful projects are reported in the news media. Therefore, the librarian must carefully consider how to present information to appropriate audiences beyond the project. Sharing information may be done through letters sent home to parents or through full coverage in the news media, both newspapers and television. The school district may have a public relations director to handle this dissemination, or the librarian may need to send out press releases to reporters.

Information presented for publication must be well written, accurate, and complete. If photographs of students are submitted, permission for publication must be obtained from parents.

Finally, successful school library projects should be reported to the school library community through articles in professional journals and presentations at conferences and workshops. The librarian must share the outcomes of projects with other professionals so successful activities can be replicated in other school libraries. Publications of special interest to school librarians, as well as strategies for seeking leadership models on social media, are covered in chapter 12.

School librarians may be reluctant to make presentations. If you are the person in charge of the project, who developed the proposal with all its parts (the needs assessment, preparation of objectives, activities, evaluation, and dissemination), you are the best person to share how this happened and the results of the project. Even if the project did not meet its objectives, you will have some idea of how things could have been done differently. You need to share your expertise with your colleagues, and your professional associations may be the best place to do this. As you write the proposal, you should list all the ways information will be disseminated about the proposal.

Describing Local Resources

Project proposals should also describe the facilities where the project will be conducted. If the school or school district has excellent facilities in place to support project activities, there is a greater chance of success. Conversely, if an elaborate program is described but the school does not have adequate space for it, there is a greater likelihood of failure. Describing facilities and additional resources available—human, material, and electronic—will help the funding agency realize that the school librarian has a better chance of conducting a successful project. If special equipment is needed for the project, the equipment must become part of the project proposal, or the method of securing the equipment must be detailed in the project narrative and budget as in-kind equipment.

Proposal writers should list all resources that add credibility to what, or who, is being proposed. If a school librarian lacks long experience in the library world, assistance may be available from a district-level administrator. The community may be supporting the school librarian in some unique or special way, and if so this should be explained. Additional funding may be available for the project from other sources: the community, individuals, or the state department of education. This support should also be cited.

Personnel who work on the project must be listed. If they are available as in-kind contributions to the project, this means their salaries will be paid by the school district and will not be part of the cost charged to the project budget. All personnel to be added must be listed. Job titles, job descriptions, qualifications expected, and length of time assigned to the project must all be described. Résumés should be attached for all persons who are identified as part of the project staff. This includes project director, coordinator, consultants, clerical and technical staff, teachers, and evaluators. These résumés must be brief, and the activities and positions described in their backgrounds should be only those showing skills related directly to the project.

Before submitting a person's name as part of any project staff, proposal writers must secure permission from that individual. Most people are annoyed if their name is submitted without their permission. Often, an implication exists that these proposed project consultants or staff have approved the proposal in principle, even if they did not actually participate in writing it. Also, there is the danger of including someone's name in a proposal when that person is writing a proposal in response to the same request for proposals.

When competing for limited funds, the proposal writer should try to find out whether the project staff members under consideration are known to the funding agency. The agency may be more willing to fund a project if they recognize the capabilities of those directly involved. Also, the funding agency may insist on approval of the categories of persons to be hired, such as researchers, technicians, trainers, or clerical staff. Finally, many funding agencies are reluctant to approve the hiring of new persons for a project if there is no indication of how this staff will be continued or retained after the project is completed. School district administrators may find themselves obligated for any unemployment benefits for furloughed staff unless those people can be placed in other positions.

Building the Budget

The final part of project planning, the budget, includes the anticipated costs of the project, item by item. Government agencies provide a form to be completed. Often grant funding requires matching funds, so be sure to indicate how much matching funding is included in your budget and where it is coming from. If no form is provided, use the following list for some suggestions of items to be included:

- Personnel—any paid staff, consultants, or contractors. Include salary, stipend, honoraria, and fringe benefits (taxes)
- Travel—purpose, estimated cost
- Supplies and materials—office supplies, software, consumables, etc.
- Services—communication, copying, website development and hosting
- Spaces—conference facilities, training sites that must be rented
- Other—equipment such as virtual reality (VR) headsets, stipends for participants
- Overhead or indirect costs—percentage of grant funds given to district/university for administrative purposes (not always allowed)

These items can be used to verify that the information usually required is included in the project budget.

Two budget items that may cause unexpected problems are fringe benefits and overhead or indirect costs. Fringe benefits are part of salary statistics. The percentage figure used to calculate fringe benefits for proposed project personnel will be the same used for all school-district salaried staff. Fringe benefits for a district employee are determined by the monthly salary, percentage of time, and length of time of the project. That is, if a school librarian with a $2,000 monthly salary is to be employed half-time for six months, the project would show $1,000 X 6, or $6,000 for the project. If the school district has a fringe benefit package of 27 percent, $1,620 must be added to the project costs.

An overhead or indirect costs percentage may be set by school districts, universities, and private agencies. *Overhead* is an assessment of the use of staff, equipment, and facilities that will not be specifically included in the proposal budget. Examples of overhead are the preparation of purchase orders, checks for payment, bookkeeping, use of office furniture and equipment, heat and lighting, and computer use. The overhead costs are then added to the total costs for the project. This is sometimes discouraging to a proposal writer when the overhead costs add another charge to the project. It sometimes means cutting other parts of the project that seemed essential in order to submit a proposal that has a reasonable budget.

Some agencies, such as state departments of education, may prohibit assessment of overhead percentages or limit the amount that can be added. This should be determined before you begin the project proposal so that it is not an unexpected cost to the planning. If your district has a contract with the agency to which you are submitting the proposal, you will need to send a copy of that contract with your proposal.

If space or equipment is to be rented, those costs must be calculated. Consultant or contracted services also must be listed. Consultants may be paid a per diem amount rather than a salary, in which case fringe benefits need not be calculated. School librarians should keep in mind that telephone charges, mailing costs, duplicating fees, online database searches, and office supplies should be added to the budget if the school budget cannot absorb these additional charges. Finally, if the staff or consultants require travel funds, these must be included.

Proposal and grant-writing skills may help increase the budget, but just how much increase is needed? Also, a budget for one year is a narrow vision for the school library. The school librarian should plan for both the immediate and the extended future—and that plan should be written by as many as can be included in the process and then shared with the principal.

This chapter anticipates that the school librarian will manage the library using a business approach. This may be a difficult change because librarians have long considered their role to be acting as a guide to reading resources and helping students read and enjoy reading. In this current century, applying a business model means a strategic plan is developed for a longer period than one year. It explains the probable costs of activities and for needed resources and other expenditures. Developing a management attitude in providing access to information will set the stage for moving into a leadership role (which is discussed in the final chapter of this book, chapter 14). The next chapter, chapter 8, discusses the library space and housing of its contents.

Key Takeaways

- Planning is necessary to transform and improve your library program.

- Developing a strategic plan for growth and change in your library requires that you know your school community and first determine what the needs are in that community.

- Similar to running a small business, school librarians need to develop the skills to manage a budget, to make purchasing decisions, and to seek out additional funding when needed. Developing these skills will allow your library to grow to meet the changing needs of your students.

Challenges to Promote Growth

1. Review the planning book of a school librarian. Estimate the percentage of time spent (1) working with students, (2) planning with teachers, (3) performing administrative tasks, and (4) completing clerical tasks. Develop a pie chart to reflect the data you discover. Is there a category missing?
2. Using information from a school library, create a three- to five-year plan for improvement in chosen aspects of the entire program.
3. Review the literature published by the National Association of Secondary School Principals or the Association for Supervision and Curriculum Development to see what trends are being proposed there. Make an appointment to discuss these trends and their effect on the school library program with a principal to see what information is needed to help with understanding or implementation and any costs that might be incurred.
4. Given the following outline, draw a Gantt chart for closing a school library in two months and transferring the holdings to two other libraries. A suggested procedure is:

   Step 1.
   Weed the collection.

   Step 2.
   Review contents for integration into the other two collections.

   Step 3.
   Pull items from shelves, sorting for the two locations.

   Step 4.
   Create electronic records to match the sorted items.

   Step 5.
   Pack items.

   Step 6.
   Unpack items at new locations and shelve.

Step 7.
Check electronic records against items placed on shelves.

Step 8.
Add electronic records into existing OPAC, noting duplication.

5. Locate a grant for either collection development or special programming for a school library and work with a school librarian to write a proposal. AASL has several that you might consider: Innovative Reading Grant, Inspire Collection Development Grant, Inspire Special Event Grant (https://www.ala.org/aasl/awards).
6. As a committee or even class project, visit a local school district and ask to see a copy of their budget for the upcoming year. Note the sources of the district's income, whether from state or local taxes, federal grants, or rental of property. Then note the allocation of funds. What percentage of the budget is for salaries? See if any line items show more or less funding than they received the previous year.

Notes

1. Barbara B. Moran and Claudia J. Morner. (2018). *Library and Information Center Management*, 9th ed. Santa Barbara, CA: Libraries Unlimited, p. 81.

2. *Ibid.*, p. 91.

3. Helen R. Adams. (1986). *School Media Policy Development: A Practical Process for Small Districts*. Littleton, CO: Libraries Unlimited.

4. Marian Karpisek. (1989). *Policymaking for School Library Media Programs*. Chicago: American Library Association.

5. AASL. (rev. June 2019). "Position Statement on School Library Scheduling." https://www.ala.org/aasl/sites/ala.org.aasl/files/content/advocacy/statements/docs/AASL_Scheduling_Position_Statement.pdf

6. *Ibid*.

7. iSchool at Syracuse University. (n.d.). "True Value Calculator." https://truevalue.ischool.syr.edu/calculator

8. Sylvia D. Hall-Ellis et al. (2011). *Librarian's Handbook for Seeking, Writing, and Managing Grants*. Santa Barbara, CA: Libraries Unlimited.

8
Library Spaces

We never educate directly, but indirectly by means of the environment. Whether we permit chance environments to do the work, or whether we design environments for the purpose makes a great difference.
—John Dewey

Redesigning learning spaces isn't about decorating a space; it's about how design impacts the brain and ultimately student learning.
—Thomas Murray

Place matters in education—it always has and it always will.
—David Thornburg

Essential Questions

- What is the connection between physical space and learning?

- How can you design learner-centered, engaging, flexible libraries that become essential third spaces to our stakeholders?

- How might you document the transformations of your spaces and the impact of your efforts?

As the largest classroom in the school, your library space matters in terms of the message it sends to learners. It matters in terms of the invitation and opportunities it presents to learn both formally and informally. It matters in terms of its promotion of the active learning educators want to encourage. It matters because it may be the only safe space a child encounters in school.

Does your space promote community, inquiry, collaboration, creativity, and sharing? Does it entertain, delight, enchant? Does it address the interests and tastes of the young people it serves? Does their space invite and celebrate their contributions? Is it flexible and adaptable?

This chapter explores the story your space tells or the story it might tell. While Dewey's notion of environment is broader than simple space alone, Dewey believed that interaction with the environment is essential to learning.

Background Thinking on Spaces

Several learning experts have considered how learning spaces might/should evolve. Urban sociologist Ray Oldenburg's 1989 work, *The Great Good Place,*[1] described the importance of the third space. One's home life is the first space. The workplace is the second space. Third places are neutral public gathering places where people choose to congregate, and these third spaces contribute to everyone's lives. They are accessible, comfortable, familiar, and offer personal fulfillment and a sense of identity and connection beyond home and work. The role school libraries play as third spaces is valuable to consider as you think about making spaces that invite your young users. As environments that exist between classrooms and home, school libraries can fill these third-space functions as they support both formal and informal learning and exploration and welcome conversation and activity.

The American Association of School Librarians' (AASL's) *National Standards* emphasizes the importance of environment, and references the notion of school libraries as third spaces—in both their physical and virtual presence—in its first Common Belief:

> 1. The school library is a unique and essential part of a learning community.
> As a destination for on-site and virtual personalized learning, the school library is a vital connection between school and home. As the leader of this space and its functions, the school librarian ensures that the school library environment provides all members of the school community access to information and technology, connecting learning to real-world events. By providing access to an array of well-managed resources, school librarians enable academic knowledge to be linked to deep understanding.[2]

The groundbreaking ethnographic study *Hanging Out, Messing Around, and Geeking Out* (HOMAGO), originally released in 2010 and reissued in its 10th anniversary year, explored digital learning in libraries and museums around the country and developed a conceptual analysis represented in the study's title.[3] The connected learning, interest-driven, inclusive design of the YOUmedia Learning Labs,[4] found in libraries, museums, community centers, and schools, is based on the HOMAGO model. Consideration of young people's learning needs through this model serves as an inspiration for school library design that recognizes and respects the evolution of youth culture in its response to using and creating with technology.

YOUmedia Learning Labs are represented by the following hallmarks:

- Provide a balance of opportunities for hanging out, messing around, and geeking out (i.e., HOMAGO)

- Provide multiple ways for a diversity of youth to engage within the program space

- Prioritize a culture of equity, inclusion, and youth leadership
- Give access to tools, technology, and people who support learning, self-expression, creativity, critical thinking, and innovation
- Employ mentors who are dedicated to the YOUmedia approach
- Design clear pathways and opportunities that enable youth to apply skills in meaningful ways[5]

While school librarians may identify more with the geeking-out part of the model, you might do well to recognize the value of hanging out and messing around in the social and creative lives of young people.

Clearly, it's not just about the *stuff*. A piece in *American Libraries* shared a vision of how as spaces school libraries are transforming, as well as how they transform:

> School libraries are not merely places to get stuff. School libraries are more kitchen than grocery store. They are more *transformational* than *transactional*. Critical weeding and new design models make space for user-centered, "genrefied" collections and for messy, informal, self-directed learning. On any given day in a school library, you can hear the productive noise of collaborative invention—brainstorming, design, debate, production, storytelling, and presentation . . . What's happening in our third spaces—our participatory spaces—is powerful. In times and places of narrowed and narrowly assessed learning, school libraries are spaces where creativity is nurtured and allowed to flourish. The library is a place where it is safe to be different, where we can have conversations about social justice.[6]

In his book *From the Campfire to the Holodeck*, David Thornburg presents his model of primordial learning metaphors:

- Campfire spaces (home of traditional lectures and teacher-led stories)
- Watering holes (home to conversations and collaborative exchanges with peers)
- Caves (places for individual quiet reflection and experimentation)
- Life (places where students can apply what they have learned by building and sharing their authentic products)[7]

Thornburg advocates for balanced learning experiences that allow students to move seamlessly across all four metaphors, choosing the appropriate mode(s) of learning for the challenges or adventures at hand. Thornburg contends that space and place, as well as the appropriate technologies, are necessary to ensure the potential value of each metaphor in the holistic learning experience. Connecting with all four of the metaphors in Thornburg's well-respected model may require reconsideration of school and library design.

Educational design experts, and most educators, recognize that classroom design no longer need be traditional, "frontal," or desk-bound. In many cases classrooms continue to be bound by outdated practices that may have been defined by the original design of the building, rather than support a librarian's vision, mission, goals, and aspirations for teaching and learning. As you make decisions about library spaces, it is critical that you put pedagogy first. As you consider design, instead of focusing on which equipment or furniture to buy, you should first consider the types of learning activities you hope to see in your spaces and whether any design decisions will lead to meaningful outcomes. In other words, what will learning look like in the library, and how will you engage your communities? It is likely that many of your decisions will be associated with the experiential activities espoused by Dewey. It is also likely that you could sort each of these engaging activities into Thornburg's learning metaphors.

If you were to describe your list of activities, you should be able to use words prevalent across the literature of engagement in learning: relevant, choice-based, personalized, multimodal, authentic, problem-based, project-based, hands-on, active, playful, collaborative, inclusive, connected, social, shared, culturally responsive, equitable, and respectful of student voice and contribution. (See Figure 8-1 for a representation of such words.)

It is wise to begin with some of the documents mentioned earlier: school and district mission and vision statements, portraits of a graduate, school improvement plans. Not only will these offer aspirational vision and likely

Figure 8-1. Engagement Word Cloud.

Used by permission from Joyce Valenza.

connect to the words you chose, they will also show you as the vital member of the team you need to become. If your school is committed to the Future Ready Schools Framework, you may choose to consider space updates in relationship to the Future Ready frame Use of Space and Time and specifically connect your facility's plans to these two research-based elements:

> *Intentional and Inclusive Learning Space Design*: Designing learning spaces is about how design impacts the brain and learning, not about being pretty for Pinterest. Future ready educators understand that every child needs and deserves to know that they belong, both as a part of the class community and in the learning space itself. As such, schools are leveraging a research-based approach, that takes into consideration: (1) naturalness: considered the effects of lighting, temperature, and air quality, (2) individualization: considered the ownership and flexibility of the space, and (3) stimulation (appropriate level of): considered the complexity and color of the space. These inclusive spaces are culturally responsive and gender neutral.
>
> *Flexible Spaces for Responsive Instructional Pedagogy*: Future ready educators understand that the learning experience should drive the design of the space, not vice versa. Flexible spaces amplify a place for learners to explore, design, and create, as opposed to teacher-centric environments designed for consumption and regurgitation. Future ready spaces are designed to empower agency and active learning, not demand compliance or passive experiences. Flexible spaces often include various "zones," are mobile and fluid, allow for aspects of personalization, contain easily moveable furniture, and have seamless connectivity.[8]

Even though school libraries may remain locked into traditional physical spaces, they can be altered into more engaging learning spaces. Much change can happen inside those walls.

Changing Spaces

For several years, it has been less essential to physically visit the library to access physical library content. Post-pandemic, there are opportunities to leverage some of the unexpected collateral gains brought about or forced by the adoption of remote and hybrid strategies and lessons learned relating to access and equity. Heavy investments were made (or should have been made) to support 1:1 initiatives, and to build and promote ebook and audio collections as well as databases to support curricula. Since March 2020, and likely well before, librarians considered effective ways to connect school with home. Increasingly, librarians became an embedded presence on students' phones, tablets, and laptops. It is likely that more librarians also became embedded in their classroom teacher partners' existing or newly adopted learning management systems.

Outside libraries, the move away from the formal workspace and the related emergence of shared workspace environments present useful models of flexible, collaborative, co-working environments that leverage the use of personal devices and value cross-community and cross-industry conversations. In social distancing, at work and at school, some have also rediscovered the value and the joy of outdoor space. Patios, gardens, courtyards, and local parks extended their spaces when the weather cooperated. These patterns will affect students' professional futures.

Questions to ask include: Will more parents and students opt for hybrid learning experiences? What was learned about equity as it relates to technology, in terms of devices, in terms of infrastructure, in terms of physical access as well as books and print and all sorts of other materials as well? Have students developed tech fatigue after more than two years of being in front of screens? How well did librarians keep them engaged? How will librarians use their space to better inspire learning, connections, social and emotional growth, and productivity in the future?

Look outside your library for inspiration and consider how popular third spaces are designed. What makes coffee shops so inviting? How do shared or co-working spaces attract workers? How do children's museums engage visitors in their exhibits? How can you create library spaces that are the least institutional spaces in your schools, spaces that are more playful and less *schooly*? What are futurists forecasting about learning spaces: for K–12, for higher education, and for informal and life-wide learning?

Classroom designs are moving away from a focus on the front of the room and the instructor. Clusters of tables that fit together or circular tables inspire collaboration and encourage small-group conversations. Seating that can be easily moved, reconfigured, and connected supports multiple work purposes. Large spaces can be made to flourish with multiple focal points and informal-group reconfigurable workspaces, moving beyond traditional frontal designs with rows of formal seating. Also, you can see opportunities to connect with learning opportunities well beyond the walls of our buildings.

Top Ten Tips for Redesigning Your Library Facility

1. **Get to know those who use the library better**. Interview your students and faculty about their learning, reading, and study habits and what kinds of learning spaces inspire and support them. Include a variety of users. You can use one-on-one interviews, focus groups, written surveys, or even drawings to capture their ideas.

2. **Read about or brainstorm what your libraries might look like in five, 10, or 15 years**. What may be the same? What might be different? How can you "future proof" your space? Think outside the box of "school" or schooly design. What commercial spaces can you get ideas from?

3. **Observe your current space**. As though you were a scientist in a lab, simply observe where people go, how they move through the space, and what they gravitate toward to see how your space is currently used and what is popular.

4. **Think of your new space in terms of zones**, like David Thornburg writes about. What kinds of areas do you want to create for "watering holes," "cave spaces," "laboratory" spaces, etc.?

5. **Create a "name" for your new space**. This may not be the name on the door, but name your concept. This will help guide your design and any others who are helping you create it.

6. **Identify 10 key things you would like your space to accomplish or be**. Use this list as you design the space to keep your design choices aligned with your vision.

7. **Enlist a group of students** to assist with the design process and selection of furniture. Include them when you ask vendors for furniture samples or fabric or paint samples. Not only is it empowering for students, it also gives you valuable input into what students prefer and helps you avoid "schooly" choices.
8. **Focus on purpose** before any furniture or design decisions are made.
9. **Think "flexible"** when you select materials and furniture, so that the library can be future-proofed. Anything that moves, folds, or rolls will help the library be a vibrant space that can be repurposed quickly.
10. **Get creative!** The library is a unique space in the school that welcomes everyone. How can you make it more appealing? Student art? Podcast stations? Tech hubs? LEGO walls? Whiteboard walls? Comics walls? Build a space that people want to be in.

By Carolyn Foote, @Technolibrary

The Learning Commons Model

Among the popular models of rethinking library space is the learning commons. Building a new facility provides an opportunity for the librarian to remind teachers and administrators of educational trends that should be considered in planning the new school.

The terms *learning commons* or *information commons* have been adopted by a number of school districts and universities to describe a welcoming space in which multiple activities can go on as individuals, small groups, and full classes of students take part in a wide range of activities simultaneously. The concept of a collaborative space that can support many approaches to teaching and learning has been the expectation of a library facility for many years. As defined by David Loertscher, co-author of *The New Learning Commons*, the learning commons is "the center of social, cultural and learning in the school."[9]

Loertscher et al. describe five different components of their learning commons: the open commons, the experimental learning center, the virtual learning commons, the virtual open commons, and the virtual experimental learning center.[10] The first is an extension of the classroom, but it has an "expert" bar (similar to that area in a technical equipment store) where students and other adults, perhaps even volunteers, respond to technical questions. The experimental learning center is a space for everyone to try out new trends and ideas and is "the heart of professional development and school improvement initiatives." The virtual learning commons is for students to carry out projects or work on online learning assignments they get from an online learning course. The virtual experimental learning center "provides the glue that makes collaboration and school improvement work." These, when put together, build the school's learning center.

A larger library staff will allow, and even require, more enclosed spaces as other teaching staff members are moved into a learning commons. The guidance counselor will need an enclosed office to speak with students. The positive in this plan is that students need not sit on chairs outside the counselor's office with little to do but wait. They will have the entire library to browse while they are waiting.

If your district has adopted the learning commons model, these spaces will be a part of the planning. If you are hoping to create one in an existing facility, the arrangement of that facility must be flexible.

First Impressions

The school library should make a positive first impression on all visitors, but especially its primary users: students and teachers. The view when the door opens must be one that encourages visitors to enter the space with a positive attitude. Signage should be positive, with letters and graphics large enough to be helpful in locating areas and resources and inspiring use. Posters, pictures, bulletin boards, displays . . . all draw visitors into the library. Freshness counts! Connections with youth interests and youth culture count, too.

When your students and teachers open their library doors, they need to feel a sense of comfort that you want all visitors to share. The space should project the playful, collaborative atmosphere that Oldenburg described as third spaces. It should project the sense of *enchantment* that technology guru Guy Kawasaki defined as "the process of delighting people with a product, service, organization, or idea. The outcome of enchantment is voluntary, and long lasting support that is mutually beneficial."[11]

Step back and take new "first looks" into your spaces (whether occupied or not), to gain first impressions as if you were an outsider entering your library. This can better inform your understanding of your own space. Try to actually see the space as if for the first time. What do your shelves, displays, signage, lighting, colors, textures, acoustics, and seating say? As mentioned in chapter 1, does the signage focus on what learners *can do* in their library, rather than what is *forbidden*?

Is your environment learner- and teacher-friendly? How are students and teachers using the library? Where do people tend to congregate? Where do they choose to sit? Which areas are not being used? Are there barriers or obstacles to access? Do users bring their own devices? Photograph or videotape your space from a variety of different angles to make a record of how it is currently set up. This will help you evaluate user patterns, plan for change, and document improvements.

School librarians are responsible for the management of library spaces and their contents. These contents—the books, technology, resources, furniture, and other materials—are a sizable investment, a major responsibility, and creative opportunities. Regularly review the landscape and the flow of activities to see that your space is responsive to the needs of students and teachers and that it not only accommodates, but welcomes the varied activities that meet those needs.

Your initial observations may prompt you to rearrange and reorganize elements of the library. Early on, you may discover a need to revise or refresh the signage. You may discover crowded and ignored shelves for a pre-weeding evaluation or simple shifting. You may also discover that longer-term plans for remodeling or reconstruction are in order. One of the most important aspects of possible redesign will answer the question: Does this space have a culture of accessibility?

A Culture of Accessibility

Space in a library is arranged to meet the priorities of the school and the program. Space should be comfortable and welcoming. It should enable multiple activities to take place concurrently. It should also envision future needs and be flexible and easy to reconfigure to adapt to varied teaching styles, pedagogical events, types of student use (group and individual), and the use of digital devices. Furnishings should fit your users and attract them. They should fit *all* your users.

All users should be able to access your space both intellectually and physically. Web accessibility is discussed in chapter 11. Here accessibility as it relates to your space is discussed. It is important to note that not all physical disabilities are visible. You may have students whose epilepsy, autism, cancer, or deafness will be less obvious than the abilities of your students who enter in wheelchairs or with service animals.

Librarians should be familiar with the following two federal acts:

- Individuals with Disabilities Education Act (IDEA) (https://sites .ed.gov/idea), which describes free and appropriate education (FAPE) taking place in the least restrictive environment (LRE).

- Americans with Disabilities Act (ADA) (https://www.ada.gov), which "guarantees that people with disabilities have the same opportunities as everyone else to enjoy employment opportunities, purchase goods and services, and participate in state and local government programs." It is "a civil rights law that prohibits discrimination against individuals with disabilities in all areas of public life, including jobs, schools, transportation, and all public and private places that are open to the general public."

In planning a culture of accessibility or adapting your space to present the least restrictive learning environment, you will want to examine:

- Counter heights
- Bookshelves and displays
- Aisles between bookshelves and other static furniture
- Walkways
- Doors, entryways and exits, and security devices
- Seating in the various library zones
- Bookdrops

Syracuse University's Project ENABLE (Expanding Non-discriminatory Access By Librarians Everywhere) offers a wide variety of resources to support access. It includes a useful ADA Accessibility Checklist[12] aligned to library-specific uses.

Remember that accessibility matters to everyone. You need to consider factors like children's height and convenience of access in your spaces. For instance, if you choose to use all the space on your traditional high shelving, you are likely to notice that few users will stoop down to browse your bottom shelves and few users will reach to grab materials from those top shelves.

By making actual notes of the ambiance of the facility, you will become prepared to plan how to remedy any flaws you observed. You will be determining what changes can be made immediately, in the short term, and even in the distant future.

Engaging with Your Space

Although few school librarians imagine having the opportunity to design a completely new library during their professional careers, it helps to do the dreaming and consider reconceptualizing, reorganizing, and refreshing existing space. Making changes in the physical space can result in changing students', teachers', and administrators' perceptions about what can and should take place in the library. It signals that transformations are afoot. When the facility is flexible, and furnishings are movable, changes in space are simple and immediate.

In designing third spaces, it is helpful to consider the concept of *hygge*,[13] the Danish art of unexplainable coziness; it is the feeling of being relaxed and in the moment whether you are alone or connecting with friends. You need to try to create a sense of calm in the library. The vibe of the library is just as important, if not more important, than the decor. Consider what you might do to create a more enchanting or more *hygge* space. When possible, enlist talented students in decorating. Fill your space with student work. Your art-teacher colleagues will likely welcome rotating gallery space. Projects can certainly come from other subject-area classrooms as well. Three-dimensional student work will find happy temporary homes on your lower bookcases, tables, the circulation desk, or even on the floor. You could commission sculptures to represent Dewey numbers and genres. You may commission sketches for murals. You may even be able to persuade local artists to lend their talents. If you have glass doors, those murals may be created and re-created each month or seasonally with colorful window markers. Other changes to allow for a myriad of different activities and future uses you cannot yet imagine will take longer to recognize and analyze. Then you must give careful consideration to the factors that affect what will be happening in the space.

Nontraditional strategies can create engagement and connection. A simple weekly question on the whiteboard in the front of the library may present a poll for everyone to watch for new entries and responses (for instance, ask about favorite genres or new movies). Have students post sticky-note answers to questions in a display case. Your end-of-year question might be: "What was your *stickiest* learning experience this year?" Another popular display could be created by inviting seniors to share their post-graduation plans. Little puzzles and stuffed animals stationed at the front desk point of entry are ice-breakers and conversation starters. A convenient box of essentials to borrow, such as pens, bandage strips, tape, index cards, bookmarks, and (for teachers) inexpensive reading glasses, is an excellent strategy for making friends.

Engage students in working with you to create interactive displays or bulletin boards. You may even have a team of students help you search the web and curate ideas. Your school library colleagues frequently document their display ideas across social media. Remember to do the same to maintain a visual record of your efforts and to share at the end of the year.

Making Room for Making

Engagement can also include active learning experiences. One significant shift involves making spaces in libraries for creation. Library makerspaces are not one-size-fits-all solutions. They too should support the school's mission and vision and be conscious of what is and what is not going on across the building. Examine the curriculum to see areas where opportunities to learn by doing might connect to and enhance content-area instruction. In many makerspaces, the skills built by design thinking and developing an engineering "fail-forward" mindset are as or more important than the actual products created. In some schools, makerspace may be a recess activity or a behavioral reward as a de-escalation zone.

In terms of space, you will likely need cabinets and labeled boxes for storing materials. You may need a devoted lab or rely on your students' 1:1 devices. Your needs for space will vary depending on the focus and scope of the makerspace that will best serve your learning community.

In the case of one author's high school, a large area called the "airport wing" was devoted to the technology department's STEM making activities. With cameras, tripods, greenscreens, and an array of software, she focused the library's efforts on digital production and art.

Some makerspaces have a technology focus, others have more of a tinkering and building focus, and some include the arts. Among the types of activities frequently seen in libraries: coding, robotics, 3-D printing/modeling, circuits, sewing machines, yarn and knitting needles for fabric crafts, blocks, video and music production. While some libraries devote designated space for a formal makerspace, smaller stations and centers might work as makerspaces. Portable makerspaces can function on carts or even borrowable bags. During the pandemic, digital makerspaces emerged.

At Islip High School in New York, Gina Seymour focuses her Maker-Care program on "nurturing philanthropic qualities while benefiting organizations both local and global. Collaborating with service-based clubs in her school and cultivating partnerships with outside agencies, students carry out hands-on service projects taking an active role in making a difference in their community and the world."[14]

Advice on getting started with makerspaces is available from many sources. Diana Rendina's "Renovated Learning" website offers helpful suggestions—and check out her tips!

Top Ten Tips for Designing School Library Makerspaces

1. **Make a plan.** What are your goals for your makerspace? What does your school already have? Where will your space be located? When will students use it? How will you fund future supplies?
2. **Share your vision for your makerspace with as many constituents as possible.** People will want to support what you are doing, but they need to know about it first.
3. **Start where you are with what you have.** Did your science department give you a few bins of LEGOs? Start there. Did your PTA donate a cart and a bunch of recycled materials? Use them. Do not let perfect be the enemy of good: get started quickly and learn as you go. Your students will help guide you as to what comes next for your space.
4. **Try to find storage solutions early on.** You will need storage for supplies and for projects-in-progress. Initially, this could be a fancy cart or just some plastic tubs. Whatever form your storage solution takes, be sure to label all your supplies and organize like with like.
5. **Cardboard and recycled materials can make for amazing design experiences.** You can create endless design challenges with cardboard and other free source materials.
6. **Write grants and ask for donations.** There is plenty of funding out there for STEM, makerspaces, social-emotional learning, and other areas of concern that will fit in with what you are doing.

7. **Invest in reusable supplies.** For the longevity of your space, look into getting some supplies that can be reused again and again, such as LEGOs, K'nex, littleBits, and so on.
8. **Balance structured activities with open exploration.** Design challenges and workshops give students specific goals or parameters to work toward or within. Open exploration lets students use whatever materials they want for whatever projects they want. Offer both.
9. **Give students opportunities to share their projects.** Whether they use a presentation to the group, a Zoom call with another school, or a full-on afterschool Maker Fest/Fair, give students the opportunity to talk about their projects with others and share their learning.
10. **Include student voice in your space.** Listen to your students and ask them what they want to create. Be responsive to the needs of your community; your makerspace likely will not look exactly like another school's makerspaces, and that's fine. You and your students will build this makerspace together, and it will be a wonderful experience.

By Diana Rendina, RenovatedLearning.com

Factors That Affect Use of Space

A variety of external factors affect use of library space. These include attendance patterns, the daily schedule, the age and learning styles of students, reasons for using the library, staffing, and faculty usage. Assessing the functionality and relationship between the space and the program is critically important both when the librarian takes a new position and when any librarian starts a new year.

Students' attendance patterns have a definite impact on use of library space. Students who arrive and leave on buses may have limited time to come to the library before or after school. High school students may attend classes in one building for part of the day and go to another school for the remainder of the day. In such a case, a school population of 2,000 may have only 1,000 in attendance at any given time. If students have arranged their schedules so they can participate in internships, work–study programs, or jobs, they may need a space to study until they leave for those pursuits. In some schools a "late bus" accommodates students who participate in clubs and other extracurricular activities. When and how students arrive at school makes a difference for opening and closing the library; when students come to the library during the school day also affects the facilities.

Student schedules may dictate library use. In secondary schools following a block schedule, students attend four classes within a school day and may spend from 90 to 120 minutes in one class. During these extended periods, teachers may often choose to divide the period so instruction begins in the classroom and then allow students to move to the library for individual research or group work. Alternately, students may spend time in collaborative instruction with you and your classroom teacher colleague and spend the second half of the block engaged in guided inquiry or practice of skills. Younger students usually attend school for fewer hours, and they tend to be voracious readers. Space must be available to allow teaching, reference, and group work to go on in one area, while in another area students may arrive individually or in small groups throughout the day to browse or check out new reading materials. Scheduling is discussed in more detail in chapter 7, but to some degree fixed schedules will affect the availability of the library to students and teachers not in scheduled classes.

Usage is affected by the reasons students come to the library and the arrangement of spaces. If students are scheduled into the library to allow the teacher a preparation period, the size and arrangement of library spaces may or may not allow the use of parts of the library by others. When students come to the library independently, they should be able to choose the seating option in which they are most comfortable. They may need to work in small groups around a table or by gathering a few moveable cozy chairs. At the secondary level, study-hall students are often assigned to the library, ideally with a teacher assigned to the period or block.

Age and learning styles of students also affect how the facilities are arranged and the types or sizes of furniture that are needed. Some teachers prefer to teach in classrooms where students are at desks in rows, whereas other teachers like to have students sit in groups of four. Some students prefer the more structured environment while other students prefer the opposite. When teachers bring students to the library to teach, they may want a classroom to use or an arrangement that resembles a classroom. This could be the case for the first visit for a major inquiry project, which may be followed by visits that involve more independent or small-group work. For many secondary classes, group work will require opportunities to use small creation or conversation spaces. Some projects involve consultations with students in their small groups with the librarian as a partner. At other times, multiple classes might gather in larger areas for an author visit, a live web event, or a local or global collaboration with another school or library. All these scenarios require flexible furnishings for configuring flexible spaces.

The number of library staff and teacher spaces affects the size and arrangement of the library. Librarians are best located where students can not only see them but also can approach them immediately. Office or workroom-type space is useful for storing equipment and materials for processing and production. Many librarians are reconsidering the need for large offices and workrooms. With decreases in support staff, and attractively priced processing services, librarians are rethinking the need for a lot of workroom space and are repurposing those spaces for production studios, small-group work, consulting with students, planning with groups of teachers, and online conferencing. Front desks are also decreasing in size, freeing up significant library floor real estate.

The library may include a classroom or computer lab that can be used by classroom teachers or for instruction by the library staff members. The introduction of mobile or personal devices and 1:1 strategies diminishes the need for lab space in many libraries. Nevertheless, some activities may be accomplished more effectively in a technology-rich lab that serves multiple purposes: production, guided inquiry, skill practice, and so on. You might plan for attractive labs or smaller studio or collaboration rooms enclosed with glass to encourage cozy group work spaces that still allow adults to survey the action.

A separate work space or production area for teachers and students may be a valuable part of the library space because this area allows for discussions. Offices for reading teachers, technology support personnel, professional development staff members, curriculum coordinators, and/or literacy coaches may be incorporated into or adjacent to the library space.

The library may be used for teachers and/or staff meetings, or for professional development offerings for teachers, or for meetings of parent groups. Although the library space may be used by a variety of groups within the school community, it is critical to remember that the fundamental purpose of the library is to support teaching and learning—both formal and informal—for all stakeholders. Ideally, spaces should avoid official designations and be used flexibly as needs shift.

Creating Flexible Zones

While keeping in mind the varied users of the library, the school librarian begins by analyzing the range of activities that will happen in the space. The library environment should be flexible enough to allow students and teachers to access the right type of space at the time of need.

The research on school library facilities shows that people who liked their libraries gave such reasons as attractiveness, plentiful space, and flexible design. The library should be designed to support the full range of identifiable everyday activities, yet flexible enough to be easily reconfigured as programs, priorities, teaching practices, and technologies change. Depending upon age ranges and formal and informal learning needs, libraries should consider accommodating the following activities and needs and develop the spaces that will flexibly support them:

- Full-class visits for instruction and inquiry-based research
- Inquiry-based research
- Student presentations
- Storytelling/puppetry centers
- Lectures and formal presentations
- Webinars or online events: local and global collaborations
- Performances: poetry slams, local musicians
- Distance learning sessions
- College representative visits
- Club meetings
- Small-group visits: instruction and consultation
- Small-group collaboration: meeting, research, production, and sharing
- Large groups: author visits, class debates, simulations, and poster sessions
- Peer tutoring
- Centers or stations: for choice and exploration
- Professional development sessions
- Teacher collaboration and planning
- Individual visits: independent study, research, viewing, or listening
- Individual visits: students escaping or seeking "safe" spaces
- Cozy nooks: quiet reading and reflection

- Displays and galleries: student art and work

- Display and shelving: books, graphic novel corners, holidays, genre themes, etc.

- Shelving: resources of multiple formats for appropriate age groups served

- Digital creativity zones: audio/video/podcasting/studio production

- Augmented, virtual, and immersive reality experiences

- Charging stations: mobile devices and laptops

- Desktop computer labs to supplement student 1:1 devices

- Online public access catalog (OPAC)

- Checkout/circulation: self- or staff-facilitated

- Printing and copying

- Work space: library staff and volunteers

- Office space: library staff

- Makerspace activities: tinkering, hands-on learning

- Playful building areas: LEGO walls, magnetic poetry centers, board games

- Easy access to sink and cleaning supplies

- Workstations: coding, 3D printing, and production

- Special collections and displays

- Yearbook signings

- Celebrations: honor society inductions, athletic signing days

- Materials/supplies to facilitate student production and creation

- Materials/supplies for students, teachers, and parents

- Service point: centrally located and absolutely approachable!

You will also need to consider traffic flow as well as spaces for things that will not or should not be accessible by the community. Secure storage is needed to protect valuable equipment and charge technology. Storage will also be needed for stackable chairs that accommodate meetings and events.

Your own checklist may vary depending on grade levels, the size of your facility, and existing use patterns. As you consider the activities listed above, consider the types of flexible zones that might house them. If you consider the constraints and affordances of the spaces you plan, you will see which zones might serve multiple purposes; for instance, the presentation space may also be used for instruction or professional development. Shelves may become gallery spaces, presentation spaces, or workspaces. Cushions may become collaborative tables. Making can happen all over the place. In spite of all your planning, you may discover that your students will define your furniture and spaces as alternate affordances, using them in ways you did not expect, envision, or imagine. Some spaces require serious dedication of square footage and others might merely require a shelf. Consider which zones will be used occasionally and which will be used regularly as you outline your plan.

Rearranging Your Facility

Rethinking and reorganizing can be an exciting challenge, a major opportunity, as well as a great deal of fun to visualize. This is the perfect time to ask, "What if we . . . ?" and "Why shouldn't we . . . ?"

As you approach a space reorganization effort, you might increase the excitement by inviting an advisory team of stakeholders, parents, teachers, and students with serious interest in helping. Create *with* your community, not just *for* your community. You can share your Pinterest vision board with student volunteers to collect ideas from within and from outside the library community. In one such project, students sought beautiful ideas for furniture, color, texture, and comfort and discussed their discoveries in design team meetings. Tools such as Pinterest, Wakelet, Padlet, and Pearltrees may be very useful in curating design discoveries in different categories. An obvious and visible way to increase excitement and interest is a physical cork/bulletin board that invites sharing of ideas. You might ask students to vote on their favorite ideas, perhaps by marking them with adhesive dots.

As you investigate user needs, expand your original group. Enlisting teachers and students in planning to meet their future needs creates advocates and supporters who will help define the library. Interview or survey teachers and students about what currently works, what doesn't work, and their dreams for using their library. In your interviews, ask about how they use technology for both school and personal tasks, which devices they prefer to use, and what types of technologies they wish they had access to. In addition to interviews and surveys, recognize the power of your camera in recording existing use patterns as visual evidence of what works and what doesn't.

You might also invite students to use their own cameras to create and share videos about the stories their library currently tells. Flip would also serve as an effective tool. Use simple prompts for the video. For instance, you might ask students to:

1. Share a tour that demonstrates how they currently use their library.

2. Share a brief video essay describing their dreams for how they might experience their library in the future.

3. Describe the activities they like to experience in their library. What resources should be available? How do they prefer to sit when they are reading, learning, searching, and interacting with friends?

In addition to creating a visual baseline, these images and videos will allow you to see and share your *before* and *after* improvements in reports and at board meetings. Of course, once projects are complete, you will want to conduct surveys as well.

If you are planning a more ambitious reorganization and moving more than a few pieces of furniture, you may want to visualize a plan initially to avoid time-consuming errors and unnecessary heavy lifting. As you develop your plans, remember that flexibility is critical. When shelving and interactive whiteboards are on caster wheels, your options for easily rearranging and redefining space expand.

Start with a rough drawing to brainstorm and sketch your big ideas. Roughly note where the zones you desire might be located. As the vision develops, move on to measure and place the elements of your vision. If you are lucky, you will find a floor plan online, in a filing cabinet, or in your administrator's office. If you cannot locate a floor plan, measure your space before you plot. Although you can always work with pencil, ruler, and graph paper or a simple drawing program, online design tools can inspire creativity, allow you to see what works and what doesn't, and help you more formally share your before-and-after vision with others.

Among the popular free tools for design are:

- Library Store Virtual Room Designer https://www.thelibrarystore .com/library_layouts

- Scholastic Class Setup Tool http://teacher.scholastic.com/tools/class _setup/index.html

- Visual Paradigm Library Floor Pan https://online.visual-paradigm .com/diagrams/templates/floor-plan/library-floor-plan/

- Classroom Architect http://classroom.4teachers.org

- Kaplan Floor Planner https://www.kaplanco.com/resources /floorPlanner.asp

- EdrawMax Floor Plan Maker https://www.edrawmax.com/floor -plan-maker

- Floorplanner https://floorplanner.com

- Sketchup Free https://www.sketchup.com/plans-and-pricing/sketchup -free

These tools are listed in the Facilities/Spaces Playlist and in the School-LibrarianHQ LibGuide found in the Additional Resources.

Using your grid or your online design tool, place tables and chairs, exits and entrances, doors and partitions. As you plan, make sure you allot sufficient space among all furnishings and the surrounding shelves to meet ADA guidelines. Are there barriers to address? Do sight lines allow you to supervise every area of the space? Where will the librarian and other staff be stationed? How many classes might you accommodate at one time? Do you need spaces for drop-in students or groups or study halls? Where will circulation take place? Consider the ways students will access the catalog. Will they use their personal devices or a central computer or permanently displayed tablets? Where and when will students be able to charge their devices?

Review any proposed changes and determine which configuration is best to allow for all of the relevant space uses on the zone checklist. Determine costs associated with the rearrangement. Is furniture being added? Is it flexible and able to serve multiple purposes? Are more electrical outlets and charging stations required? Does your district have carpenters and electricians who might be enlisted in your cause?

If you have yet to appoint an advisory committee, this is a perfect time to invite them to review the suggestions. Students and teachers may be helpful in spotting issues and generating potential ideas for improvements based on your vision. Because the information landscape is continually shifting, you must continue to rethink library spaces and what is essential and how space is devoted/assigned.

- The availability of digital reference resources that require no shelf space, are easier to share universally, and are more frequently updated has changed the way librarians approach the need for reference space and the purchase of large, multi-volume sets.

- The move away from desktop computers to personal devices (laptops, tablets, smartphones) allows you to rethink space formerly used for desktop labs. How might you rethink and revamp those labs for production, collaboration, and other purposes?

- The need for "loaner" laptops on charging carts may require an allocation of secure storage space.

- The focus on copy-cataloging and pre-processed materials may make devoting large spaces to processing less necessary.

- The availability of the OPAC on phones, tablets, and laptops may lessen the need for multiple, permanent look-up stations.

- The makerspace movement requires flexible technology-rich space that promotes design and coding as well as building materials, and a dynamic array of materials to engage in hands-on learning experiences. It will also require attractive storage strategies.

- The potential that some of your instruction will continue to be online or hybrid may increase the need for individual student spaces rather than entire-class spaces.

As stated earlier, librarians should keep careful records as facilities are arranged. Before-and-after photos will demonstrate your planning and innovation and their impact on the community. Teachers and students may quickly forget how the library looked before, and administrators should be alerted and engaged in celebrating your successful accomplishments in engaging your community. Your carefully planned modifications should be documented visually on reports to administrators because they demonstrate your leadership.

Although few school librarians have the opportunity to engage in design completely from scratch, all school librarians have opportunities to ensure that their spaces meet or exceed the needs of their learning communities. Analyze whether your initial rearrangement efforts satisfy needs or are merely temporary fixes. When they require more attention, a remodel of the facility may be required.

Remodeling the Facility

School library facilities are scheduled for remodeling for a variety of reasons. When school librarians advocate for and successfully lead such projects, they become an integral part of the remodeling efforts. Otherwise, they must try to oversee as much of the planning as possible.

In undertaking a remodeling project, many of the factors listed in the discussion of what you see in a library when you open the door and of rearranging a library may be applied to remodeling the library. The areas outlined in the preceding section on flexible zones should be considered for inclusion in a remodeled facility. Of course, this is a basic list; more ambitious areas may be added to the plan if money is available to do so. Funding is almost always a deciding factor.

Remodeling is not always costly. Non-load-bearing walls can often be removed by district or building staff; such renovations do not always require the hiring of an architect and a construction crew. Developing positive relationships with district carpenters and electricians can result in very exciting projects. You can enlist the district carpenters to transform traditional round tables into café-style high tops for a new digital workspace resembling a coffee shop. Carpenters can create countertops that fit beautifully over a long reference shelf and mount a large monitor on an arm that swivels between the new production space and the existing instructional area. Electricians can move access to power beyond the walls. District painters can create an accent wall. Students can collaborate on choosing colors for paint and any fabrics. The art teacher can encourage students to help design signage and perhaps design murals for the walls. Add casters to smaller shelving units to make them movable. Collaboration with faculty and students emphasizes their ownership of the space.

When more elaborate renovation is necessary, planning, documentation, and justification are essential. These projects are usually funded at the district level with capital funds, used to maintain buildings and purchase furniture, technology, and equipment. If the renovation is major, an architect is hired before the process begins. Form should follow function. It is essential that library staff members work with the architects designing the renovated space to develop an understanding of how the space will be used. When a full-blown remodeling project is being planned, the librarian should look carefully at the entire building. If a larger building project is in the works, it may make more sense to move the library to a new location than to remodel the existing, ineffective space.

Renovations are sometimes needed to repair previous design missteps. Examples of this include raising the floor for a sunken story pit in the center of a facility, a window wall that makes sunlight a challenge to students as well as the collection, balconies in two-story libraries, and open-plan facilities that encourage frequent walk-throughs by students with no need to be in the library.

Buildings are sometimes expanded. Old, inefficient buildings are sometimes leveled or retrofitted. Population increases create the need for new buildings. If you are lucky enough to start your vision from scratch, get involved in locating the best place in the building for a library and help the administration and the architects understand how this new space aligns with your vision. Architects and superintendents may not be aware of what spaces should be in a new facility and what spaces might be problematic.

Areas that support leisure reading with comfortable chairs will both reinforce the importance of reading and encourage students to come to the library to find materials to respond to their personal interests as well as their curricular needs. Younger children may need different types of areas and different types of seating for group work and storytelling. Some students with special needs may require quiet areas that are less likely to present distractions. Some areas may be designated for recreational reading, viewing, and listening, but other areas should be available for quiet study. Circulation of materials and borrowing and returning of materials and equipment tend to be noisy activities and thus should be located near the entrance. In choosing furniture, the district, or your state, may have lists of approved vendors that meet a variety of codes. Though it might be tempting, you may not be allowed to bring in furniture from a thrift or discount shop. A list of library furniture, shelving, and supply vendors, and access to their catalogs, are included in the School Librarian HQ LibGuide Facilities/ Spaces Playlist found in the Additional Resources. One of the reasons that it is important to attend library conferences is that conferences are great places to meet vendors and see some of their products.

Perimeter shelving and island shelving on casters make far more sense than rows and rows of heavy, immovable shelving. This frees the center of the library for multiple purposes and accommodates changing needs. Movable shelving can also be used to separate and define areas, expand or contract specific sections or displays of the print collection, or be pushed against the wall to accommodate larger groups. To accommodate community events, multi-class events, and larger meetings, a closet storage area with a rolling cart is incredibly useful.

While some librarians will prefer an attached library classroom, others do not. A library classroom may become problematic when sight lines are limited and no staff is available to monitor the main space if the librarian is teaching in the classroom. Strategically displayed mirrors can help, and glass walls are a great solution. Whiteboards on wheels can be useful to define more flexible spaces. When there is no formal divider to indicate discrete learning spaces, tables and chairs provide a classroom-like setting for both the librarian and teachers who want to teach in the library.

Librarians often assume the responsibility of providing devices for students and storing replacement devices to exchange when one is malfunctioning. At the end of the semester or the school year, the library may be the place where these can be locked away when the school is not open.

Opening a remodeled school library facility is a cause for celebration. It is a time to invite the library community to visit and to acknowledge any and all who have had a part in the planning. Those before-and-after pictures may be projected during the entire celebration.

Planning New Facilities

If or when a new school building is being planned, school librarians must find a way to make their voices heard. If the district has a central office staff member who is a librarian supervising other librarians, or if a school librarian has been appointed to the new building, they will be working with the architects on the plans. When neither of those persons are in the district, other school librarians need to form a committee to oversee this process as much as possible.

Architects may have their own ideas about what a school library should be, and some may have existing plans in mind. You can exercise your leadership skills and organize the team of school librarians to show interest in the project and to offer suggestions if at all possible. It will be no surprise that school librarians from other schools in the district will be interested in what is going to be created as an information center. Volunteering and making your interest known to the superintendent could be the easiest way to join in the excitement of planning a new facility.

Without librarian input, a well-meaning architect might design a library that is functionally impossible for one person to manage, or make recommendations based upon their previous school library experiences (perhaps in the 1980s and 1990s) or their familiarity with public or academic libraries, which serve different populations and different purposes. Gentle suggestions from a group of informed school librarians may help an architect see the challenges of a huge sunken circulation desk area in the middle of the library.

If you are going to be the school librarian assigned to the school and you are not initially invited to the table, find a way to connect. Your vision or mood boards or photographs and videos recording use and your users' dreams of future use will help you express your vision for the user experience and allow you to engage in the design process.

When school librarians have the chance to help build a new facility, they should visit several sites to review what other librarians consider the strengths and weaknesses of their designs. Taking the principal and one or two teachers with you on at least one of these visits allows you to affirm the important areas to be included in your plan. It is especially important to ask, "What would you do differently now?" Bear in mind that what works well in one location may not work well in another. However, knowledge of what did not work in one location could be useful in communicating with architects to rethink something similar in their plans. In addition to physical visits, school librarians are fortunate that many who have gone before generously share their own mood and vision boards (Pinterest is a gold mine!), and document their projects in their blog and social media posts.

Spend a little time learning the language of architects. Learn to read blueprints to consider what indicates a major support to the floors above, because those will affect the different types of use and traffic patterns. Note potential blind spots, storage issues, acoustics, lighting, and aesthetics. Form is important, but the final product is so much more glorious when the artistic statement connects with, supports, and enhances function, vision, mission, and purpose.

Architects designing schools tend to have limited opportunities to exercise creativity in designing classrooms, cafeterias, offices, gymnasiums, auditoriums, and band rooms. They may see the library as the place to make an artistic statement. Your voice is essential in ensuring that these aspirational visions do not result in dysfunctional libraries. Your voice as an expert must stress suggestions for truly functional learner-centered spaces.

When you meet with the architects, make sure they are aware of and interested in the philosophy of service for the library. If the building is new or the project involves a major reconsideration of space, this is the time to discuss the placement of the library in the building to ensure that it is accessible to all students. Other considerations may include proximity to cafeteria aromas or noise from the gym.

Architects need to know the number of students and teachers to be served, numbers relating to materials and equipment to be housed, and the areas needed for specific activities (as discussed earlier), which may include storage areas and professional work space. Electrical outlets, needed for all equipment, should be flexibly accessible and are critical for all students and teachers who will need to recharge their devices. The library should be a place to recharge in multiple ways.

Lighting and acoustics are important considerations. Architects and contractors should be aware of and consult standards documents to ensure that they meet requirements specific to library spaces. While sunlight sometimes presents an issue, you do want a space that feels light and open and incorporates natural light and views if you have them. Glass architectural walls present well-lit, inviting spaces and serve to separate smaller collaborative spaces while facilitating supervision.

The seating areas, storage areas, shelving to house collections, and production room should be fully described. A separate, but flexible, classroom may be a priority if the library has more than one person on the staff who will be teaching a large group of students. In addition, the architect may need to be reminded of such factors as climate control, acoustics, carpeting, movable walls, movable shelving, ceiling treatment, windows, doors, communication lines, and safety.

Architects may not want your detailed floor plans. You will want to share the most critical elements of your vision, including, of course, the importance of flexibility and the relationship of one area to another. For example, if the meeting spaces have to be where the librarian can oversee them, this must be specified. If there are noisy areas such as a circulation desk, question their relationship to quiet reading areas. The architects should know of the need for any areas to house 3-D printers; the need for sinks for students to clean up from a makerspace experience or for processing materials or hosting events; where cabinets might be needed; where receptacles must be placed; and so on. In addition, consider which spaces are best carpeted and which might be better served by tile or sheet flooring.

Architects design, draw blueprints, and return with the plans for further review. It is important to understand what is shown in the blueprint. A square in the middle of the plan probably indicates a load-bearing pillar. If it is placed directly in front of the circulation desk, rearrangement of the area may be necessary. As stated earlier, care must be taken to see that no blind spots are built into the arrangement. Be aware of traffic patterns, areas, and furniture that may cause discipline or safety problems. Architects need to justify attempts to beautify with balconies that are challenging to manage and invite flying books and secret meetings. Dramatic lighting fixtures that do not shed enough light may be beautiful, but will discourage readers. The librarian should discuss any serious concerns. If direct communication is not possible, with logical justification and open communication, your administrator should be able to intervene with the school board and the architect.

The school board approves construction plans. When bids for building are far higher than anticipated, cuts must be made from the original design. It is imperative that the school librarian review the proposed alterations to participate in selecting the sacrifices or suggesting compromises to mitigate negative impacts on the vision.

With the support of the architect and the construction team, you should be able to take pictures of the building process that you can display during the festivities of celebrating the opening of a new school.

Storing and Moving a School Library

Your collection may have to be moved during a remodel. If you have significant advance notice, weed to ensure that you fill your new facility with the materials you are most proud to share. If remodeling is in progress during the school year, much of the collection may be stored.

You will need to plan storage for your entire library. Ask your administrator to discuss your plan for safe storage. Before closing the library at the end of the previous year, decide which important items and equipment will be needed while the collection is stored and move them to a classroom or another accessible area. Keep the most-used materials out of storage, because you will expect to continue to provide service, perhaps with a "library on a cart." Equipment can be reassigned to classrooms or storage areas throughout the building if you label everything "Library." This way you can ensure that your equipment does not permanently find its way into other school spaces or become hidden beyond your ability to find. Seek safe places for your valuable laptop carts and other electronic equipment so that your colleagues do not "borrow" them permanently.

Consider how you will pack and label your collection of materials for logical and easy unpacking. If you enlist the help of volunteers, they will need guidance. The best strategy for moving items from shelves is to transfer them onto moving carts rather than putting them in boxes. It will greatly help the school staff if they are doing the move because they can roll trucks and carts around easily. This will ensure that the contents are visible and ready to be reshelved. If you are not able to borrow enough carts from other schools, the tremendous boost in ease of the move would justify renting them. Whether you use carts or boxes, label them with the section where they belong and the beginning and ending call numbers or fiction letters. Numbering the boxes or carts will help you with unpacking. If you use boxes, invest in banker's boxes or use boxes from professional moving companies. Avoid large boxes that will be too heavy to move, and do *not* overpack. It will be easier for movers if your boxes are the same size because they stack easily. Place books to protect their spines. Label boxes top and bottom and put arrows on the side to indicate which side goes up and which side down. Label each box on its top and side. Colorful dots help to code and identify materials for various sections of the library. Keep a master list of your codes in case you forget that yellow is nonfiction. The best advice of all is to *weed before you pack*.

When school populations decline or shift from one area to another or schools close, school librarians are assigned the task of closing libraries. This involves sending collections, furniture, and equipment to a central warehouse or distributing them among other schools. Before any distribution, the librarian should weed the collection to avoid sending unattractive, dated titles to another collection. When a district has a library supervisor, this person will typically be involved in a redistribution.

If the contents are to go to other schools in the district, the librarian plans the shift after taking a careful inventory at each library: both the closing library and the receiving library or libraries. Equal distribution may not be a case of "one for School A," "one for School B," "one for School C"; redistribution should be done on the basis of need and existing collections.

Collections, furniture, and equipment should be carefully scrutinized and the old, irrelevant, and broken removed. Certainly the librarian will analyze the materials collection for duplication at other schools. It may be preferable to keep materials in a central location where other librarians can pick only titles of use in their collections rather than to send cartons of unneeded materials to another school.

Branding Your Space

Once settled into your library, you can think about branding or refreshing the branding of your space and the zones within it. You may be very happy with the name *library*. While the term *media specialist* is an old one, abandoned by the American Library Association in 2010, many states have stuck with it, and you may want to call your space a *media center*. Other common options are *information center*, *learning hub*, *learning commons*, *information commons*, and *libratory*. Engage your students in the naming of those inside spaces. If you or your students choose a recognized name such as *Creative Commons*, you must clear it with the owners of that name. Carolyn Foote[15] engaged her students in naming the various zones in her library. Among the student-inspired spaces was the *Juice Bar,* a clever mix of a Starbucks café and an Apple Genius bar. Additional suggestions for branding your space can be found in *Elevating the School Library: Building Positive Perceptions through Brand Behavior* by Susan Ballard and Sara Kelly Johns.[16]

On a Serious Note: Safety

This text is being written in 2022, a year rife with trauma in which librarians have far greater consciousness of safety in library spaces. Educators have learned a lot about reaching users beyond the library walls and sharing spaces to allow others greater opportunities for social distancing. Librarians have ensured equity for distance learning by distributing hardware and growing and promoting digital collections. As students returned to face-to-face learning, libraries have presented a safe and welcoming space. In many ways, libraries have been the glue, adapting services and spaces as needs evolved. It is no longer possible to discuss our facilities without addressing safety.

At a panel discussion during a recent School Library Journal summit, the superintendents were asked: "If you had to pick an issue that is on the very top of your mind, what would it be?" Without skipping a beat, all three responded "safety." Of course, post-pandemic, that word takes on a deeper meaning; everyone must now prepare for a wider range of threats.

For decades, adults and students in schools have been preparing for the possibility of an active shooter threat. Several years ago, one of the authors found herself in the middle of this terrifying situation. Unlike many other intruder situations in the news, this one resulted in only one casualty. Nevertheless, it changed the lives of everyone present and altered the way everyone in the building considered the safety of the school's spaces.

To briefly describe the incident: Students and teachers near the science hallway heard pops as they transitioned to classes between blocks. Those in the hallway saw a fellow student with a gun. Almost immediately, a lockdown alert sounded on the announcement system. Faculty grabbed students casually passing in the halls. Many students and several teachers hid in the library while the young man shot up the science hall and moved through the school, eventually taking his life in front of the library's glass doors. It took two full minutes to secure the tricky lock on the library door, which that student eventually tried. Immediately following the incident, library personnel were instructed to cover the glass doors with construction paper to obscure the scene from students' view.

Anyone in this situation is likely to ask questions afterward: How can librarians prepare the safest plan of action? How should cell phones be handled? What is the best possible place to hide? Why did the doors not have shades? What's the best way to communicate with each other? As uncomfortable as it might be, it is wise to think about these questions, and others specific to your own physical space and how people move around it, in advance.

Safety and Security in the United States

Public mass shootings, particularly those events that occur at educational institutions, have generated widespread public concern about safety and security in the United States. Although in the context of the national crime picture, mass shootings are statistically rare events, their frequency is on the rise.[17] Their episodic and random nature, however, has highlighted that no community or location type—including libraries—is immune to such violence. For instance, during the April 20, 1999, mass shooting at Columbine High School in Jefferson County, Colorado, 10 of the 13 individuals who lost their lives were killed in the building's library; 12 others were injured.[18] Similarly, on November 20, 2014, a graduate of Florida State University in Tallahassee, Florida, opened fire at the entrance of the campus's library, wounding three.[19]

These two events highlight the importance of libraries and those who staff them having a plan in the event a danger (not solely limited to an active shooter) makes its way onto the campus. Depending on the location of the threat on campus, deploying a lockdown procedure may be the best option.[20] Lockdowns are used to build distance between a threat and its intended targets by deploying door locks, which have been found to be the most successful life-saving device in an active attacker situation.[21] In instances where one cannot lock the doors (e.g., not having the necessary keys), alternate strategies such as barricading may be used. Once the doors are locked, the lights should be turned off to provide added concealment, and occupants moved out of sight of any interior or corridor windows. Silence should also be maintained to avoid calling any attention to the location.

Importantly, there may be instances in which alternative strategies are necessary, such as in cases where the threat breaches the barrier and is now in the location actively threatening individuals; the attack itself also may start in the library. Evacuating the space to a safe location may be an option, while defending oneself may be necessary as a last resort. Importantly, librarians should consult with their school administrators and law enforcement officials as to what the desired plan for their respective space is, as different buildings will pose different environmental challenges (i.e., location of exits, furniture placement and mobility). Ensuring that the plan is not only understood but also regularly practiced by way of drills is also critical to ensuring that it is used effectively during times of crisis.[22]

By Jaclyn Schildkraut, expert on mass shootings and school safety trainer

Attention must be paid to safety issues with any facility. The school's overall safety plan will describe how to deal with a variety of building safety situations, including such natural hazards as floods, storms, and fires; technological hazards; chemical hazards, such as propane, ammonia, and chlorine; and such human-caused hazards as intruders, civil disturbance, or terrorism.

Although few of you will have the opportunity to engage in a full library redesign with architects, you can point to issues of concern that you observe regarding safety and security. If your doors do not lock easily, investigate the procedure for initiating a work order. Ask your principal if you might order blinds for your doors and windows. Develop and share a plan for where students might be safest in a variety of situations should no feasible plan already exist.

Libraries are soft targets. They are all physically different, and they require different room-level safety plans. You will want to make sure that those who need it have a floor plan of your library. You will want to get a copy of any emergency plans and discuss issues relating to your specific space with your administrators. Keep those plans visible and handy. Plans should consider multiple situations that may involve evacuation, hiding, and potentially taking action. Of course, your school/district will share guidelines and training as well.

To end on a positive note, libraries are third-space havens for children and young adults who need a break from trauma and may need to temporarily escape from the stress and pressures of school. Libraries are safe and peaceful places for socializing, social and emotional support. Be an adult who greets them by name. You will also host children who do not have a table of friends waiting for them in the cafeteria. You will have students who just do not fit socially. Sometimes these will be English-language learners who have not yet found a comfortable crew. Sometimes, these students will be deep thinkers or just children who look and think a little bit differently. In your library—no, in *their* library—these students will find peace, and they will often discover each other. Be conscious of the fact that you may be the only adult in their lives who provides a space where they are not judged or pressured. Offer them space, as well as opportunities to contribute, collaborate, and lead. These students grow up with especially fond memories of the roles libraries have played in their lives. They remember your name. You will read about those memories in the reflections of many well-known authors, artists, and leaders. Be that person and offer them that safe space.

Ensuring the Integrity of Library Space

One of the issues you will face in leading in the largest classroom in school is ensuring that the library is used to serve its mission. Because of its size and seating, administrators may need your space to spread students out for testing or, should it again be needed, social distancing. There may be requests to close your facility after school for meetings or professional development sessions.

Your space may be used by parent and community groups beyond school hours. You may want to secure personal items and valuables and consider how open you want equipment such as your copy machine to be when you are not there, even for such informal and apparently innocuous activities as parents waiting for their teens who are in driver training sessions or after-school clubs. You may need to weigh the social capital benefits of this community access.

There are side benefits of having once-a-month faculty meetings in the library: this will guarantee that every teacher will see the library at least once a month and allow you to display new items, equipment, or do an elevator speech about a new service as faculty members gather. These uses for both inside and outside groups can bring attention to the library's value. However, they are not in keeping with the library's mission.

Counselors and administrators may see the library as a place to send disruptive students or a place for students who are waiting for parents to pick them up for appointments. It is not a place to park students who have an excuse to miss physical education or who wait for a school bus to take them to an afternoon at a technical school. Some members of the faculty or administration may have their eyes on what they perceive as lesser used storage or office spaces.

As with any challenge, making a student's time in the library a positive experience will, after a while, demonstrate that it is not a place to punish students because they are enjoying their time. You want to be a team player, especially as a first-year librarian, but you also want to protect the library space allotted for teaching and learning and consider its most flexible future and the exciting plans you are likely making.

Staying Positive

As a new librarian, making an immediate difference will be important. Begin making those little tweaks. Use of new posters, interactive displays using QR codes, fun whiteboard surveys, the inclusion and celebration of student art, the decluttering of shelves, face-out shelving, rotating displays, shifting furniture, and the installation of a little green with flowers and plants can happen immediately.

Any space can be transformed slowly. While some ideas may be a bit of a reach, many small shifts are immediately doable. Schools are changing and so are the ways students learn and teachers teach, and the ways librarians provide their services. If you find yourself stuck in a routine, a little redecoration/refresh project can be a big boost.

Seek inspiration from other libraries, including public and academic libraries: those you visit and those that share images on their websites, in their blog posts, and across social media. Look at design books and vendors' catalogs, and examine school and library architects' websites. Reach beyond *libraryland* for design trends found in new businesses, coffee shops, bookstores, museums, and co-working spaces. Check to see if the district painters might be available to refresh the walls and ceiling. Virtually tour some of the examples of creatively designed spaces in the LibGuide[23] the New York City School Library System maintains on the Robin Hood Library Initiative. This partnership was developed "to improve city schools by helping to fund the construction of libraries in some of the city's poorest elementary schools."

Consider the opportunities your space offers to make a difference. Design spaces that invite students, teachers, and your community. Make sure the library is an important highlight of the tour your principal offers visitors. It should be a place people want to visit and to which they want to return. Dream, innovate, and engage. Consider what will come next.

This chapter detailed the types of new library spaces needed as libraries are rearranged and their contents change. Chapter 9 addresses building and maintaining your collection(s).

Key Takeaways

- Your space conveys the story of what you consider to be important in your school library. Will it be about people or about stuff?

- In a time of radical change, you have opportunities to radically rethink how your space serves your community.

Challenges to Promote Growth

1. Visit one or more school libraries. Analyze the atmosphere and vibe you feel when you first open the door. What draws the user into the library? What is less welcoming? Note the signage in the library. Is it positive or negative? How does it help users find their way in the library and help them locate places they need to go to find both resources and places to study?
2. Using graph paper or one of the available digital design tools, redesign a floor plan for your dream school library. As you design, consider both engagement and accessibility.
3. Embark on a digital safari for design ideas for school libraries. Look for full-blown designs or elements like seating, shelving, tables, makerspace setups and contents, even colors. You might do this as a class using a digital curation tool like Wakelet. Consider which of these ideas will have the most impact. Which are most doable? How will you plan for their access or implementation?

4. What metaphorical spaces might you apply to your dream library facility in addition to those listed in Thornburg's primordial model?
5. Visit a few other third spaces: coffee shops, parks, meet-up facilities, and so on. Describe any takeaways you find that might be applicable to school library space.
6. Examine the setup of a school library with an eye toward safety. What specific suggestions might you share with an administrator who is creating a safety plan for all school spaces?

Notes

1. Ray Oldenburg. (1999). *The Great Good Place: Cafes, Coffee Shops, Bookstores, Bars, Hair Salons, and Other Hangouts at the Heart of a Community*. Boston: Da Capo Press.

2. AASL. (n.d.). *National School Library Standards,* "Common Beliefs." https://standards.aasl.org/beliefs

3. Mizuko Ito et al. (2019). *Hanging Out, Messing Around, and Geeking Out: Kids Living and Learning with New Media,* 10th anniversary ed. Cambridge, MA: MIT Press.

4. YOUmedia Learning Labs Network. (n.d.). Home page. https://youmedia.org

5. YOUmedia Learning Labs Network. (n.d.). About. https://youmedia.org/about

6. Joyce Kasman Valenza. (2016, March 1). "School Libraries Transform." *American Libraries.* https://americanlibrariesmagazine.org/2016/03/01/school-libraries-transform

7. David Thornburg. (2014). *From the Campfire to the Holodeck: Creating Engaging and Powerful 21st Century Learning Environments*. New York: John Wiley & Sons.

8. All4Ed. (n.d.). "Use of Space and Time." https://futureready.org/ourwork/future-ready-frameworks/use-of-space-and-time

9. David V. Loertscher, Carol Koechlin, and Sandi Zwaan. (2011). *The New Learning Commons: Where Learners Win! Reinventing School Libraries and Computer Labs,* 2d ed. Salt Lake City, UT: Learning Commons Press.

10. *Ibid.*

11. Guy Kawasaki. (2015). *The Art of Enchantment*: *The Art of Changing Hearts, Minds and Actions.* New York: Penguin.

12. Syracuse University. (n.d.). "ADA Library Accessibility Checklist." https://projectenable.syr.edu/data/ADA_Accessibility_Checklist4.pdf

13. Merriam-Webster. (2021, January). "What Does *Hygge* Mean?" https://www.merriam-webster.com/words-at-play/what-does-hygge-mean

14. Gina Seymour. (n.d.). "The Compassionate Maker." https://ginaseymour.com/compassionatemaker

15. Carolyn Foote. (n.d.). "Library Design: Continuing Conversations." *Not So Distant Future.* https://www.slideshare.net/technolibrary/librarydesigntcea2013combo

16. Susan D. Ballard and Sara Kelly Johns. (Forthcoming). *Elevating the School Library: Building Positive Perceptions through Brand Behavior.* Chicago, IL: AASL/ALA Editions.

17. Jaclyn Schildkraut. (2021, July 15). "Can Mass Shootings Be Stopped? To Address the Problem, We Must Better Understand the Phenomenon." Regional Gun Violence Research Consortium, Rockefeller Institute of Government. https://rockinst.org/issue-area/2021-can-mass-shootings-be-stopped

18. Columbine Review Commission. (2001, May). *The report of Governor Bill Owens' Columbine Review Commission.* https://schoolshooters.info/sites/default/files/Columbine%20-%20Governor's%20Commission%20Report.pdf

19. Sean Rossman. (2014, November 20). "Shooting at Strozier Library Stuns Florida State." *Tallahassee Democrat.* https://www.tallahassee.com/story/news/local/fsu-news/2014/11/20/shooting-strozier-library-stuns-florida-state/70040320

20. Jaclyn Schildkraut and Amanda B. Nickerson. (2022). *Lockdown Drills: Connecting Research and Best Practices for School Administrators, Teachers, and Parents*. Cambridge, MA: MIT Press.

21. Sandy Hook Advisory Commission. (2015, March 6). *Final Report of the Sandy Hook Advisory Commission*. Hartford, CT. Author. https://portal.ct.gov/-/media/Malloy-Archive/Sandy-Hook-Advisory-Commission/SHAC_Final_Report_3-6-2015.pdf

22. Jaclyn Schildkraut and Amanda B. Nickerson. (2022). *Lockdown Drills: Connecting Research and Best Practices for School Administrators, Teachers, and Parents*. Cambridge, MA: MIT Press.

23. New York City School Library System. (n.d.). "Robin Hood L!brary Initiative." https://nycdoe.libguides.com/RH

9
Curating Your Collection for Growth

It's not the size of your collection that matters. It's what you do with it that really counts.

—Jennifer LaGarde

Essential Questions

- What are the essential components of policies to build an inclusive, vibrant collection for your community and protect the right to access information?

- How do you evaluate and improve your collection throughout the life cycle of your library?

- How do you ensure that the books you carefully select are discoverable by students at the moment of need?

At this time in this century, the traditional responsibility of information professionals in all types of libraries to identify, evaluate, acquire, and organize information resources has expanded. Meeting the needs of students and ensuring their free access to information has become even more essential. This chapter suggests the need for reviewing a collection development policy, or writing a policy if none exists that covers the traditional responsibilities and discusses new opportunities facing school librarians today. Protecting students' rights to information and protecting their privacy and the privacy of all users of the school's materials remain obligations. The chapter ends with information on building and maintaining the collection, organizing it for distribution, and selecting materials for the collection.

The Collection: Moving Beyond Print

In the past, collections were primarily in print and nonprint formats; however, the expansion of resources made possible by advances in technology now makes information available to users in libraries, schools, offices, and homes and requires new approaches to the management of information. Library users expect information to be available to them beyond the walls of the physical space and accessible 24/7.

These expectations for access to information and the opportunities for providing it increase the need for school librarians to ensure that library users have access. Creative solutions for equitable access are needed when budgets are constrained. You will need to advocate on behalf of students who do not have access to devices or wifi at home. The school library should provide a bridge to cross the digital divide.

Technology used to access information creates new challenges for school librarians, who need to be prepared to provide access to information. When a cell phone is their only device, show students how to access the library's information using phone apps. Building a wireless school will be less challenging as more funds are received from federal and other sources. Finding ways to provide each student with a device to access information has become easier since the COVID-19 pandemic because students had to obtain such devices for their online classes. Access to information is the highest priority if students are going to become effective citizens in a democracy.

Discovering the digital resources of their local public library, students with access are able to make use of digital content from both school and public libraries on their personal devices. Adults who travel often park near a public library to use their wireless device to read email. Students can also have this option for online access when schools are closed if wifi is made available throughout their communities.

The explosion of digital information has made collection development more challenging, as well as more exciting, and it provides opportunities to teach students about evaluation and curation. Technology has exponentially increased both the amount of information available and the means of accessing information; it has also made the process of identifying, evaluating, and disseminating appropriate resources more challenging. The school librarian's responsibility for helping students, teachers, parents, and administrators to effectively seek, evaluate, synthesize, and use the information they find online, as well as in print resources, has never been greater or more important. The responsibility of the librarian to assist both young people and adults in determining whether online information is accurate, reliable, and authentic cannot be overstated in a time when it is difficult to determine what is fake and what is accurate information.

In addition, new questions must be addressed, such as the most appropriate and cost-effective formats for various parts of the collection. Answers to these questions will vary in different schools; librarians will need to think about them in their own contexts. Should all resources in the sciences be digital? Are any hardbound reference books still needed? What print journals should be ordered when most periodical resources used by students are available in databases? If primarily digital resources are purchased, what does this decision mean for hardware purchases and maintenance? What ramifications must be considered when a decision is made to purchase primarily digital resources in communities where few families have access to broadband connectivity in their homes? How are physical and intellectual access to information provided when computer hardware is not regularly updated and kept in good repair and/or computer networks are not reliable? What databases are available from state purchases? When is it desirable to use funds to participate in collaborative purchasing of a collection of digital databases, and when is it best to limit individual resources that more closely support the curriculum of the individual school? How does the school librarian ensure that students do not choose to plagiarize information from the Internet or digital resources when it is so easy to "cut and paste" other people's intellectual property? This chapter focuses on the development of your overall collection, and a closer examination of digital resources and technology appears in chapter 11.

The Life Cycle of Your Collection

It is useful to think of your collection as a living organism that is constantly in a state of growth and change. The diagram in Figure 9-1 is helpful in examining that cycle.

To develop and maintain a vibrant collection, you must continually move through a cycle of needs assessment, selection, acquisition/deselection, and evaluation. During needs assessment, you should be involved in understanding the community in which you serve—both at the school and the community it serves. Only after becoming knowledgeable about both the curriculum and the students you will be serving in your school can you determine the needs of your stakeholders. Although the arrows in this diagram move in one direction, it is sometimes necessary to go back to a previous stage to make informed decisions. Evaluation can take place at multiple points in the cycle, but is especially useful in determining if your collection can meet the needs you have identified. This chapter examines the stages of the collection life cycle.

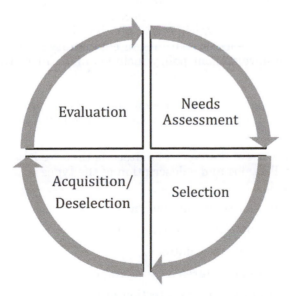

Figure 9-1. Collection Life Cycle.

April Dawkins.

Selection and Reconsideration Policies

In most schools and districts, selection of materials for the library collection is guided by policies and procedures. Policies, which are usually developed and implemented at the district level, provide broad guidelines explaining the role of the school library and librarian in the process. These policies may have a variety of names, such as materials selection policy, collection development policy, or instructional materials policy. Selection policies should be reviewed by and approved by the school board; if they are, that is noted in the policy for anyone to read. Many school districts will have a fully developed collection policy, which was created by library staff members within their district and approved by their school board. This policy generally is included in a policies and procedures manual that is available either physically or online in each school. When considering accepting a job in a new district, it is wise to inquire about the availability of such a collection policy. If one is in place, you should review it to see if the content is still valid or if it should be updated. If the district has no guide for its library collections and none seems to be available in your school, a first step is to create such a policy. Regardless of whether the school board approves your statement, preparing it allows you to document priorities and methods of selecting materials and to have it available if questions arise.

School librarians who have had materials questioned will admit that the experience is usually very frightening. Most school libraries have a single person in charge, and that person feels very isolated when a parent, community member, or fellow teacher questions the availability of a certain item for students. Having a selection policy available for the complaining person to read, as well as implementing the procedure they are asked to follow to lodge the complaint, should allow time to notify the principal. You may need to remind the principal that the superintendent should also be told that a resource in the library is being questioned and by whom.

Selection policies are essential because they explain the process followed and the priorities established before any material is purchased or accepted as a gift and placed in the library collection. The policy communicates the selection steps followed, which is useful when items in the collection are questioned by other teachers, parents, or community members.

A collection development policy includes much more than the process for selecting materials. It also generally includes:

- Information about the mission and goals of the school district and often its priorities and how these statements are reflected in the library program.

- An overview of the types of materials that are included in building-level collections and a description of the types of materials that are excluded.

- Guidelines for selecting materials.

- A description of the acquisition process.

- Information about donations.

- Policies and procedures for weeding collections.

- Statements regarding protection of intellectual freedom, including censorship and the process for reconsideration of materials.

- Information about preservation and archiving of materials.

- Information about when and by whom the policy is reviewed and updated.

If the district or building in which a school librarian is working does not have such a set of policies and procedures, it is a worthwhile but time-consuming job to develop these. If you are working with your district to develop or revise your policy, you will want to consult the American Library Association's (ALA's) Selection and Reconsideration Policy Toolkit for Public, Academic, and School Libraries,[1] which can be found on the ALA website. The toolkit provides essential components and sample language for inclusion in your new policy.

The collection development policy has several components: goals and objectives, materials to be included or excluded, selection guidelines, the acquisition process, policy for donations, circulation of materials, and weeding of the collection. The following box suggests 10 steps to help you create your policy:

Ten Steps to Creating a Selection Policy That Matters[2]

Here are some areas you should include and some questions you should consider during your policy-writing/revising process.

Does your policy include your library's mission?
You always want to include your mission. It can be used to justify your purchases and your decisions to retain materials in the collection if they are called into question.

Is there a section with a statement or explanation of the purpose of the policy and the school library's role in supporting intellectual freedom?
This is a great section that explains why selection is so important and why intellectual freedom and unfettered access to materials are essential rights of all students. This section is an opportunity to explain the difference between selection and censorship. This is your chance to promote the Library Bill of Rights.

Who is ultimately responsible for the selection of materials for the library?
If you are revising your district's selection policy, you will want to make sure the section on responsibility clearly states the importance of your role as the professional expert in selection.

What are the procedures, including the use of reviewing sources, that will be followed in selecting materials?
You will want to review any processes involved in selecting materials. Is there a role and opportunity for student, parent, faculty, and staff input? Unfortunately, in some policies and procedures the students are never even mentioned! Student access and input should be front and center in your policy. Another area of concern is the review and vetting of materials to determine if they should be added to the collection. Try to avoid including a list of acceptable reviewing sources or a minimum number of positive reviews. While sometimes helpful, this can also become a barrier for materials reflecting diverse cultures and viewpoints that might not be reviewed in traditional trade publications. If you want to include a list, make sure it is broad and suggested (rather than required) and that it includes nontraditional sources for review such as blogs.

Does your policy reflect more than just a print collection and provide guidance for nonprint materials, databases, and digital curation?
You are not just collecting print books any more. Your policy should reflect that and be flexible enough to allow for acquisition and use of new formats as they arise.

How are potentially controversial materials selected?
It is important to acknowledge in your policy that sometimes materials may cover sensitive or controversial topics and that you have procedures for selecting such materials. You want to make sure these materials are not automatically excluded from consideration.

How are gifts and donations handled?
It is wonderful to receive a donation or a gift, but it is important for you to have clearly outlined in your policy that any gifts and donations will go through the same selection procedures as other materials. You want to make it clear that being donated does not mean an item will automatically be added to the collection or kept forever. You definitely do not want to end up with someone's entire *National Geographic* magazine collection from 1900 on!

What are the procedures for maintaining the collection and removing outdated, worn, or inaccurate items?
Weeding . . . it can be controversial, but it is vitally necessary. This is one topic that those outside of the library really do not understand. Why are school librarians throwing away books?! Use this opportunity to explain why it is important to maintain the collection and remove materials. You should also explain why most of those weeded materials should not be passed on to classrooms.

Is there information that outlines the policy and procedures for reconsideration of materials?
Provide a general overview about removing materials from the collection, including the need for a formal procedure and review process. The reconsideration procedures themselves will have to undergo special review. They are typically in a separate section at the end of the selection policy.

Is a timeline or guidance provided for revising the policy itself?
All policies should include a date of adoption and guidelines for revising the policy. If this is a district-level policy, does your district allow individual school-level policies? If not, is the district policy broad enough to be applicable to all types of schools in your district?

As you are revising or writing your policy, keep in mind that its purpose is to provide access to quality resources and information for students. Are there procedures or guidelines in your policy that might be barriers to student access? Explore other school and district selection policies to see how these issues have been and are currently being handled.

Procedural questions about circulation of materials, management of the catalog, and purchasing are usually not delineated in the broader district policy. You will want to see if there is a procedure manual that provides such information or work with other school librarians within your district to develop those guidelines. Another area which is often only briefly mentioned in these policies is weeding of the collection. You will want to have or develop clear procedures for deselection of items and how they are to be handled once removed from the collection.

Which items may circulate, the number of items that may circulate, and the length of time they circulate are all procedures that may be determined at the district level, or you may be able to set those limits within your school. When the school takes responsibility for providing devices to students, these may be stored and circulated in the library. Are items checked out for two weeks or a full semester? What happens when items are lost or broken? How many items may a student check out of the library?

Decisions about placing limits on the number of items that can be checked out at one time by any user, student, teacher, or another person must be carefully made. In an age in which so many resources are available online, many teachers and students may believe that there are few reasons to actually visit the physical library. By allowing more items to be checked out at a time, you encourage patrons to make use of the collection you have curated.

Teachers are usually granted an extended period, and if your students are expected to take ownership of their library, they should be allowed to use the information found there until someone else needs it or until the end of the semester. Checking resources out for a full semester makes students exercise responsibility to bring it back when someone else does need it. It obviates the need to send overdue notices—which must be sent only to the student in such a way that neither teachers nor parents know what the student has overdue. It is an extraordinary way to teach both how to share with others and civic responsibility for peers.

Limiting the number of books that can be checked out by elementary students who are just learning to read and by students in higher grades who wish to check out books to read for pleasure is particularly troubling. As students take part in more outside activities such as sports, clubs, and music classes, they have even less time for recreational reading. As many obstacles to reading as possible must be removed, including eliminating fines and extending circulation periods.

In addition to the concerns a librarian should have in limiting access to the information available in collections, charging fines for overdue materials is also a very bad public relations move. These materials are purchased with funds from taxes the community pays and should be as accessible as possible. Charging overdue fines to a student who is on free breakfast and lunch forces an uncomfortable choice on that student, who may quickly become reluctant to take materials from the library if the book becomes overdue after two weeks or something happens to the book. For more support in moving away from fines, take a look at the Interpretation of the Library Bill of Rights[3] related to economic barriers to access. It provides good information on which to base your argument.

When the school librarian has a well-developed collection policy and adheres to its guidelines, it might seem that no one would ever object to any item in the library collection. However, far too many people think they should have a say in what other people's children should be able or allowed to read, and thus they raise a challenge. In some cases this is an orchestrated effort on the part of groups. No matter why or where, it is best to be prepared to withstand a challenge.

Intellectual Freedom and the Right to Access Information

Students have the right to access information and they have the right to have their use of school library materials protected. Among the rights not specifically enumerated in the U.S. Constitution is intellectual freedom. However, when considering the First Amendment right to free speech, judges have interpreted that right to include intellectual freedom. Courts have said that to engage in free speech, you must be able to receive information that informs your speech. This right to receive information is a corollary to the right of free speech. It extends the right of free speech beyond those who are the speakers to those who are the listeners or receivers of information.

Students in our schools are almost all minors. Throughout history, questions have arisen concerning what rights minors hold as compared to adults. Because of the Supreme Court ruling in *Tinker v. Des Moines*, First Amendment rights have been extended to minors allowing them free expression. This ruling became the basis for extending civil rights protection to minors within public schools. With the *Tinker* decision, the Supreme Court declared that students and teachers do not "shed their constitutional rights to freedom of speech or expression at the schoolhouse gate."[4]

The Supreme Court has ruled in only one censorship case directly pertaining to school libraries: *Board of Education, Island Trees Union Free School District v. Pico* (1982). An organized conservative group challenged the inclusion of nine books in the district's school libraries. Despite the recommendation to retain the book by a reconsideration committee made up of both parents and faculty, the local school board chose to remove the books from junior and high school libraries in the district. The Supreme Court justices sent *Pico* back to a lower court for retrial. Faced with growing litigation costs, the school board voted to return the books to the shelves. Currently, *Pico* is the first and only Supreme Court decision to take up and consider a minor's right to receive information. Unfortunately, the written opinions of the nine justices have been difficult for lower courts and school boards to interpret. One reason is that all nine of the justices wrote and released opinions on the decision to send the case back for retrial—and those opinions reveal a wide range of views.

Privacy and Intellectual Freedom

Just as intellectual freedom is not mentioned in the Constitution, neither is privacy. In a *Harvard Law Review* article published in 1890, Supreme Court Justices Warren and Brandeis examined the idea of the right to privacy as including "the protection of the person, and for securing to the individual . . . the **right to be let alone** [emphasis added]."[5] You might ask, what does the right to privacy have to do with the First Amendment freedoms of speech and expression? Because the right to receive information has been interpreted as part of the right to free speech, it has also been used to protect the right to privacy. If they are to learn, read, and share information freely, privacy is extremely necessary to protect students' free exploration of ideas and topics that might create embarrassment or expose them to judgment.

The right to privacy for children in public schools is protected through several federal laws. You will want to become familiar with the Family Educational Rights and Privacy Act (FERPA), the Child Internet Protection Act (CIPA), and Children's Online Privacy Protection Act (COPPA). FERPA, enacted in 1974, protects the confidentiality of "education records" in K–12 and postsecondary schools that receive federal funding. The law allows parents to inspect or review records and request changes where they find inaccuracies. FERPA applies to "education records" and defines them as "those records, files, documents, and other materials which (i) contain information directly related to a student; and (ii) are maintained by an educational agency or institution or by a person acting for such agency or institution."[6]

Both CIPA and COPPA are intended to protect children while using the Internet. CIPA (2000) applies when a school, district, or library has received E-rate funds. With receipt of such funds, the entity must certify that it has an Internet safety policy along with filtering of content. The issue of privacy comes into play because the Internet safety policy is required to include monitoring of Internet activities.[7] COPPA was first passed in 1998 and revised in 2012. The provisions of this law require that websites or online services obtain parental consent before collecting data on children under the age of 13. Additionally, any information collected must be "for the use and benefit of the school, and for no other commercial purpose."[8]

Although its Code of Ethics has included protection of the right to privacy and confidentiality for some time, ALA has placed greater emphasis on the privacy of patrons in recent years. In 2019, ALA amended the Library Bill of Rights by adding its first new provision since 1980. Article VII states, "All people, regardless of origin, age, background, or views, possess a right to privacy and confidentiality in their library use. Libraries should advocate for, educate about, and protect people's privacy, safeguarding all library use data, including personally identifiable information."[9] This article is seen as having particular importance to school libraries; as stated by Helen Adams, "with the addition of Article VII, students in K–12 public schools are promised the right of privacy and confidentiality in their library use. Adding the core values of privacy and confidentiality to one of the profession's foundational documents places school librarians in a stronger position from which to advocate for and educate about library privacy for minors."[10]

FERPA has perhaps the greatest implications for school libraries because of its provisions relating to parental access to educational records. If school library management systems have the ability to keep patron checkout histories, these records could be subject to review by parents. As protectors of student privacy, you should work with district-level leadership to safeguard student privacy by disabling checkout histories whenever possible. This removes the burden of providing a list of previous checkouts if school librarians are asked for them—there simply will be no history to share. If someone wants access to currently checked-out materials, library privacy policies should determine the decisions that are made.

CIPA and COPPA primarily deal with Internet usage and have fewer implications and ramifications for school libraries and reading. However, librarians often incorporate technology tools into lessons. Therefore, before using any website, app, or online tool that collects personally identifiable information from students, educators in schools and school districts need to evaluate that site's use policies. A useful tool for this is to examine the user agreements and policies for each site. However, this is often difficult, as these user agreements are long and filled with sometimes difficult legal terminology. Common Sense's Privacy Program[11] does have a searchable database of privacy evaluations for many commonly used technology tools as well as resources to conduct your own privacy evaluations.

In addition to CIPA, COPPA, and FERPA, most states have laws about privacy of library records. For example, North Carolina state statutes §§ 125-18 and 125-19 are about libraries. North Carolina law states that:

> A library shall not disclose any library record that identifies
> a person as having requested or obtained specific materials,

information, or services, or as otherwise having used the library, except as provided for in subsection (b).

(b) Exceptions.—Library records may be disclosed in the following instances:

(1) When necessary for the reasonable operation of the library;
(2) Upon written consent of the user; or
(3) Pursuant to subpoena, court order, or where otherwise required by law.[12]

In North Carolina, the law defines a *library* as any library established by the state and specifically mentions libraries created by school districts. This means that school libraries in public schools are bound by law to protect student privacy. Each state has its own laws. To help you discover your state's privacy laws related to school libraries, ALA created "State Privacy Laws Regarding Library Records,"[13] a site which also has useful information about how to respond to law-enforcement requests for user information.

Although the laws provide some guidance for school librarians when it comes to patron privacy and confidentiality, protecting the privacy of your students extends beyond record-keeping and Internet safety. Other areas for consideration include the way you distribute overdue notices; the use of surveillance cameras within the school library; checkout procedures at the circulation desk; the collection of student information through digital resources and tools; and training of school staff, library staff, and volunteers about student privacy. All of these topics related to student privacy should be explored and used to develop student privacy policies specifically related to school libraries.

Often, school districts have privacy policies that are only applicable to student electronic data and Internet usage and do not consider the privacy protections that should be in place for the school library. ALA provides some guidance in this area through its Privacy Resources for Students and Minors webpage.[14] They provide guidelines as well as a helpful checklist. Their guidelines provide ideas about the importance of privacy, developing policies, conducting a privacy audit of your library, collection and retention of user data, using data encryption, how data is shared, using learning management systems, and the role of digital literacy. The checklist provides practical action steps that a school librarian might take in an evaluation of how well student privacy is protected in their library. Although ALA does not currently have examples of school library privacy policies on their website, they do have examples from both public and academic libraries that might be helpful in developing school library policies.

Because school librarians work with minors, privacy is often a complicated issue. School librarians must work to protect the privacy of *all* children in their schools, from very young children to those who are newly adult. An example of the difficulty in serving all students is considering at what age parents will no longer receive information about overdue or lost books. As children grow older, privacy becomes more integral to their development as individual human beings. You must balance supporting a child's intellectual and academic growth with their emotional and social growth. Librarians are called on to respect the ethics of the library profession as well as the rights of parents and students. This often leads to difficult decisions. Designing policies guided by both practicality and principles will help to make your decision making easier.

A major problem for school librarians has been the necessity to try to filter information from the Internet, thus limiting access to information. Defending the collection—whether print, electronic, or transmitted—is a continuing obligation of the school librarian, but that role has become more complex with the introduction of electronic sources which have not been vetted by the school or district. On-site materials are carefully selected to meet the needs of teachers and students in the school. One, two, or more persons lodging complaints about items should not be allowed to prohibit use by others in the school. Parents may request that their child not be allowed to read, listen to, or view materials on evolution or holidays, for example, but the materials remain in the collection. With a selection policy in place and a procedure to follow in case of complaint, the school librarian's response to pressures can be more organized and less stressful.

What to Do in Case of a Challenge

Although specifics on what to do in case of a challenge may not appear in the actual policy, the existence of a reconsideration process should at least be mentioned there. The procedures and forms may be located in a procedures manual; you should know what that manual says and make sure your administration understands the procedures as well. See the text box for ideas to help you in revising or creating your reconsideration guidelines.

Creating Reconsideration Policies That Matter[15]

Do the reconsideration procedures include guiding principles while undergoing a challenge?
Your policies and procedures should include statements about diversity of content, formats, and ideas, the right to access information, and the freedom to read. Inclusion of Library Bill of Rights and the Freedom to Read Statement of the American Library Association is a great idea. These guiding principles might be included in the selection policy or as part of the reconsideration procedures. For a good outline of what to include, take a look at the *Selection & Reconsideration Toolkit for Public, School, and Academic Libraries* (http://www.ala.org/tools/challengesupport/selectionpolicytoolkit).

Do your procedures include information on how to handle an informal/oral complaint versus a formal/written complaint?
A parent, teacher or administrator may voice a concern about an item in the library collection without wishing to go through the formal process for reconsideration. You should be prepared to discuss informal concerns with parents, patrons, teachers, administrators—well, anyone who might say they are uncomfortable with an item in your collection. The policies and procedures for reconsideration should be shared during this conversation. However, an honest, open, and respectful conversation will often lead to resolution of the complaint without a formal reconsideration process taking place. But, be sure that your policy explicitly states that an item cannot be removed without a formal request for reconsideration being submitted and a complete process being undertaken.

Is there information about the timeline to be followed?
You really don't want things to drag on forever. Therefore, your procedures should include a timeline for response to a complaint, committee proceedings, and final determination. Keep the timeline reasonable and remember that committee members will need to obtain and read the challenged

material in its entirety prior to discussion. Your procedures might also include a clause that stipulates challenged materials cannot be challenged again within a certain time frame (maybe 5 years).

Is there information about who to contact in your school, district, as well as external resources for support?

The procedures should include who within your school and district should receive copies of the request for reconsideration and who is ultimately in charge of the reconsideration process. It's also helpful to keep school district public relations or media contacts in the loop about potential challenges and outcomes from reconsideration proceedings so that they may field any press questions. Information about challenges and reconsidered materials is subject to Freedom of Information Act (FOIA) requests. Therefore, it's important to determine where information about challenges is housed in your district. Additionally, you will want to know about the resources available to you through your state library, your state school library organization, and ALA's Office for Intellectual Freedom.

Is there information included about who has the standing to challenge content in the library or as part of the curriculum?

Within the policy, you'll want to include who can actually challenge materials that are part of the curriculum or in the library collection. Some of this may be determined by state law. However, when your district can make the determination, you'll want to weigh the costs and benefits of either limiting who has standing to challenge or keeping it pretty open. Some districts allow any citizen to file a request for reconsideration. Other districts limit this by allowing only parents of children within the district to request reconsideration of materials.

Is there a clear, easy-to-complete reconsideration form? Does the reconsideration form include the following information: What is being challenged and why? What is the outcome the complainant wishes from the reconsideration process?

Make sure you have a publicly accessible reconsideration form that can be completed and submitted. The form should include contact information for the complainant, information about the item for which reconsideration is being requested, and why the request is being made. The form should include clear directions about where the form should be submitted and the timeline for an initial response to the request. Be sure to include a question asking what the complainant wants to happen to the material, but I don't suggest including a list of options for this. Leave that up to the committee to decide.

Does the policy explain how challenged materials are to be handled while the challenge is being considered?

The policy should include a statement that challenged materials will remain in use and available until the conclusion of the reconsideration process. Limiting access during the process is an infringement on student intellectual and academic freedom.

Does the policy explain composition of the reconsideration committee and procedures the committee should follow at both the school and district level?

The policy should outline basic membership of the reconsideration committee for both the school and district levels. Typically, the committee is comprised of the school librarian, the principal or other administrative representative, teacher representatives, and even student representatives (particularly in upper grades). Additionally, the policy should explain what the committee should do to reconsider the material in question: reading it, discussion, voting, etc.

Does the policy outline the role of the school librarian during the reconsideration committee proceedings, and what is the role of the complainant?

Often, the policy will designate the school librarian as the chair of the school-level reconsideration committee. You'll want to know that ahead of time. As the school librarian, you are often the main spokesperson for intellectual freedom and the students' right to read. This should be the cornerstone of your role in the committee proceedings. Additionally, the procedures should clearly state if this is a public or private committee meeting and if the complainant has the opportunity to either submit a statement, attend the meeting, or participate in the proceedings in any way other than the initial written request for reconsideration.

Do the policy and procedures provide guidelines for notification of the complainant after a decision is made?
It's always good to have a plan about how to notify the person who made the challenge. It's even better to have sample letters ready to go. You won't need to panic or worry about being eloquent if you already have an outline of what to include at the very least. Your procedures should also determine from whom that letter should come. Should it be the chair of the reconsideration committee, which might be you as the librarian, or your principal?

Final things to consider
Policies are only as good as those who follow them. Plan to meet with your school's administration at the start of each school year to review important policies. Each fall, I met with my principal to talk about three things: the place of the library in the overall school budget; copyright and fair use and teacher use of video materials; and a review of the selection policy and reconsideration process.

It's important that you and your administration are on the same page when handling challenges to instructional materials both in the classroom and in the library. Many of the school library discussion forums include stories of principals arbitrarily removing materials from school libraries because of parent complaints. However, this is what gets administrators and school districts into hot water. When officials subvert their own policies and procedures, they open themselves up to litigation. Follow the process, and they are unlikely to face a lawsuit about infringing on students' First Amendment rights to access information.

Additionally, make sure that your school (or school district's) selection and reconsideration policies are publicly available on your school and district websites. The public needs to know how and why you are selecting content and the importance of protecting student access to information. Often just understanding the difference between parents' rights to make decisions about their own child as opposed to inhibiting access for all children is all it will take to prevent a challenge.

Many complaints begin informally with a simple statement of concern about the content of a specific library item. This is your opportunity to have a productive conversation about the concern, your selection process, the mission of your library to serve all patrons, and the rights of parents to limit access by their own children. The conversation may also include asking the person with the complaint if they have reviewed or read the material in its entirety. If their concerns are not alleviated following your conversation, they need to be given the reconsideration form and the selection policy to read. Be sure to notify your school administration about this interaction so that they are aware and so that they can notify district office personnel.

When the complaint is from a parent, try to get to the basic reason for the complaint. It may be something other than what appears on the surface. A parent who objects to a book on a list given to students to be read over the summer may be objecting to the assignment itself if, for example, that student is expected to work over the summer to save for college tuition. In other cases, some books are called into question at times by organizations and people are sent to the school to lodge the complaint. When this happens, these persons will be prepared to do battle.

Sometimes a fellow teacher may question the choice of something in the library. This is especially troubling because librarians and teachers work side-by-side to teach students. These queries are treated as they would be for any other person with a complaint, following the same process. Teachers may also suggest the purchase of a book for the library that you question. This is an interesting situation. A long-ago study of censorship in school libraries found that the greatest censorship was exercised by the school librarian who allowed personal bias to prevail in choices. Reviews of books by other school librarians can offer some assistance in these cases; these are discussed later in this chapter. Another source is the service offered by ALA.

The ALA's Office for Intellectual Freedom has staff trained to answer inquiries from a school librarian who is dealing with a challenge to materials either in the school library or to inclusion in the curriculum. This office will respond quickly to any question and provide support as you shepherd the challenged material through the reconsideration process. Further, state library and school library associations have intellectual freedom committees whose members can offer assistance, both when selections are questioned and in developing a selection policy when none exists. Your policy statement is your basis for protecting the privacy and intellectual freedom rights of your students.

This issue became more complex as a result of the passage of CIPA in 2001. As stated earlier, CIPA is a federal law enacted by the U.S. Congress to address concerns about access to offensive content over the Internet on school and library computers. CIPA imposes certain types of requirements on any school or library that receives funding for Internet access or internal connections from the E-rate program—a program that makes certain communications technology more affordable for eligible schools and libraries. In early 2001, the Federal Communications Commission issued rules implementing CIPA.

What CIPA Requires

Schools and libraries subject to CIPA may not receive the discounts offered by the E-rate program unless they certify that they have an Internet safety policy that includes technology protection measures. The protection measures must block or filter Internet access to pictures that are: (a) obscene; (b) child pornography; or (c) harmful to minors (for computers that are accessed by minors).

Schools and libraries subject to CIPA are required to adopt and implement an Internet safety policy addressing: (a) access by minors to inappropriate matter on the Internet; (b) the safety and security of minors when using electronic mail, chat rooms, and other forms of direct electronic communications; (c) unauthorized access, including so-called "hacking," and other unlawful activities by minors online; (d) unauthorized disclosure, use, and dissemination of personal information regarding minors; and (e) measures restricting minors' access to materials harmful to them. The policy must also include teaching students about digital safety and citizenship. Before adopting this Internet safety policy, schools and libraries must provide reasonable notice and hold at least one public hearing or meeting to address the proposal.

Schools and libraries are required to certify that they have their safety policies and technology in place before receiving E-rate funding. CIPA does not affect E-rate funding for schools and libraries receiving discounts only for telecommunications, such as telephone service.

An authorized person may disable the blocking or filtering measure during use by an adult to enable access for bona fide research or other lawful purposes. Often, school librarians are given override control to allow access to sites that have been blocked that should be accessible to teachers or students. CIPA does not require the tracking of Internet use by minors or adults. For more information, see the CIPA information on the Federal Trade Commission website.

Although filters are helpful in preventing students from accessing potentially harmful content on the web, they also create a false sense of security. Because filters are in place, students may not learn how to navigate the Internet as it exists outside of a protected environment. Teachers and students must learn how to make use of information found on the Internet if they are going to be informed members of present-day society. Prohibiting student use of the Internet—a valuable resource—is unthinkable. Although requirements of filtering software may appear to answer a major concern of some parents and others in local communities, they do not, and the installation of a filtering system does not solve the problem. Filtering programs miss the problems inherent in using such a solution; they simply delete text containing specified terms, regardless of the context or content. While others prohibit access to specific websites, they fail to stop access to any new malign websites that appear, and new websites appear every minute. Filters do not ensure limited access. Clever students can find inappropriate sites through their own ability to maneuver software. The best approach is to establish parent and student agreements (acceptable use policies) for Internet use. Students are given a password for their privilege, and they understand and agree to the regulations that are in place so they can keep their password and access.

As the school librarian, you can help students and teachers navigate the web by creating curated lists of sites for specific units of instruction. This saves students from unnecessarily wasting search time and perhaps even finding inaccurate information because the site has already been "selected" for the library collection. This is discussed further in chapter 12.

Copyright and Fair Use

School librarians are dedicated to preserving the rights of the school community regarding access to information. This carries with it the need to expend an equal amount of effort on preserving the rights of the authors and creators, producers, and publishers of the information purchased for the library collection. This requires the development of policies to explain the protections afforded by copyright law, trademarks, and even patents and how to monitor adherence to these policies.

Copyright is a legal concept that safeguards the intellectual work of a creator. Copyright law is difficult to understand for most people except copyright lawmakers, lawyers who defend creators and abusers, and judges who make the final decisions in court cases. It is sometimes difficult for school librarians to have enough accurate information to convince administrators, teachers, and students that, as a law, copyright restrictions must be obeyed. In an attempt to save money or because of a lack of funds, educators might engage in copying of materials while mistakenly assuming that such copying falls under the fair use exception.

What exactly is fair use? *Fair use* is a legal doctrine that promotes freedom of expression by permitting the unlicensed use of copyright-protected works in certain circumstances. Section 107 of the Copyright Act provides the statutory framework for determining whether something meets fair use criteria. It identifies certain types of uses—such as criticism, comment, news reporting, teaching, scholarship, and research—as examples of activities that may qualify as fair use. Chapter 11 provides more guidance on the details of fair use.

Librarians in academic, public, and school libraries are the first line of defense for the free flow of information. To continue this flow, the creators, authors, illustrators, editors, publishers, and producers of that information must be protected so they will be willing to continue writing, illustrating, editing, publishing, and producing. This will become more difficult as more information becomes available online.

The ease with which online information may be shared with a very large audience worldwide, downloaded, and reused makes that information very vulnerable. To help your learning community engage in ethical use of information, it is imperative that you keep current about what is legal and what is not. One-time use of material for classroom instruction is legal because schools are considered nonprofit users for educational purposes, under the doctrine of fair use. Considering fair use also means considering loss of revenue for authors and producers—truly a never-ending cycle. Having updated information means staying current on copyright changes and not getting lost outside the cycle.

Because few educators, including school librarians, truly understand copyright law, this is an opportunity for the librarian to take a leading role. Reading in the educational and library literature, attending conferences when copyright is a part of the programming, and making an effort to understand the law and any changes to it are just the beginning. School librarians must also explain any changes and point out any violations to colleagues, and this is never easy. Working with teachers and administrators to keep them informed helps remind them of the correct and legal use of materials.

Because you are the go-to professional for issues relating to intellectual property, you will want to alert administrators and other stakeholders to potential issues. For instance, while it may be a tricky conversation, administrators may not be aware of restrictions relating to showing films during instructional time that are used for entertainment or reward. You will need to review district policy and pursue public performance licensing if necessary.

Many of our students are creators beyond the classroom. Both students and teachers may be unaware that everything online is protected by copyright unless explicitly labeled otherwise. Make sure all students and staff have access to resources for discovering Creative Commons content and media and open educational resources. Encourage students and teachers who want to use copyrighted material to carefully examine fair use guidelines and pursue permission when unsure if the use can be considered fair. Rather than be a gatekeeper, teach and model the ethical usage, remixing, and creation of online content for your students and teachers.

Trademarks have made headlines in recent years, as celebrities trademark any of a variety of things in their lives that often just seem silly. However, major sports teams consider their trademarked logos their intellectual property. The Pittsburgh Pirates would not want a local high school team using the signature "P" on their ball caps even if the high school team was called the Pirates. Copying an image that is a registered trademark, such as the shape of a Coca-Cola bottle, can be as much a violation of intellectual property as copying a copyrighted paragraph.

Finally, one needs to be aware of how a teacher, teachers, or a group of students creating a project to solve a problem with a machine or other invention might need to get patent rights to protect their creativity. This is not a simple process and certainly not one that any school librarian can get through easily. However, it is important for the school librarian to know that getting a patent is a process that students might want to use. An excellent book, *Intellectual Property and Information Rights for Librarians,*[16] which covers copyright, trademarks, and patents, may be available in your university or local public library.

Preservation and Archival Functions

Another component of the school library policy deals with preservation and archival functions. As items become more and more digitized, the need for physical storage space within the library becomes less critical. The ability to store information online continues to expand. Students and teachers carry flash drives with as much information stored there as one used to need a mainframe computer to hold. *Data curation* requires the management of all kinds of data as long as it has interest for school library users for their use as scholars and for their education. For example, local historical materials including pamphlets, photographs, and oral histories can be preserved digitally. Pictures of one year's activities in a school may also be preserved in digital form for the future. These materials should be available through the school library's website. An additional consideration is the need to make sure these archival materials are discoverable within your catalog so that they can be used.

Building and Maintaining the Resource Collection

Management of the on-site collection includes the organization and circulation of materials. Organization is the first consideration, because materials must be identified in some way for students and teachers to be able to locate them. Your collection is only as good as your students' ability to discover what is in it. Discoverability is key.

Organizing Information

Any collection must be organized in such a way that it allows users to easily find what they need. For book materials, commercial cataloging and processing are available, and the best choice for a given situation should be based on full information. Options for cataloging materials range from original cataloging and inputting electronic records to receiving cataloging from a bibliographic utility (usually very expensive), the district center, or the jobber who fills the order.

You should remember that the purpose of organizing the collection is to *provide access to the contents for users.* Often, cataloging and classification courses are taught in library and information science programs with a major emphasis on such details as the number of spaces after a punctuation mark;

thus, the process becomes more important than the product. Although the organization of a collection should be consistent with the national standards for cataloging rules and subject headings (particularly if the library is part of a consortium or a district with many schools), these rules must be adjusted to fit the situation.

The most efficient method is to purchase materials with electronic records shipped with the order and bar codes in place on the item. These records can then be downloaded into the open public access catalog (OPAC); often records are downloaded directly from the vendor. Books and other materials may come already bar-coded for immediate placement in circulation.

Another source for cataloging and processing services is from school districts or intermediate units with centralized processing centers. Materials are ordered centrally, shipped to the processing center where records are entered into the district's database, and then sent to individual buildings.

Typically, school libraries are organized by the Dewey Decimal Classification system with fiction pulled out and perhaps biographies or short stories as well. It depends on what is best for your students and your library. With the popularity of graphic novels and manga, many school libraries are choosing to pull them from fiction and the 700s to have them as a separate collection. Dewey has some historically problematic classifications which are slowly being rectified. For instance, the Dewey system uses the 200s for religion. Six of the ten Dewey categories in the 200s are for subjects related to Christianity. The other four categories are supposed to contain the rest of the religions of the world. Even worse, Dewey relegates religious information about Black people into a single area: 299.6, which is for "religions originating among Black Africans and people of Black African descent." Many people are working to decolonize the Dewey system, but there are other ways to organize, including genrefication.

Genrefication places books into broad categories. Often school librarians choose to genrefy their fiction collection and not their nonfiction because nonfiction is already in broad categories based on Dewey. There are many different ways to genrefy, and many vendors are now supporting genrefication of collections in the development of their MARC records. In deciding if you want to genrefy a collection, you will want to weigh the time commitment to make the transition against the benefits of a potentially more browsable collection for students. For more information about genrefying your collection, explore the information in school library publications and available from your OPAC's vendor. Follett, Mackin, and other vendors offer resources and advice for genrefying your collection.[17]

Evaluating Your Collection

Determining the effectiveness of your collection is an ongoing process. You must know who you are serving and the curriculum in your school. You will want to conduct analyses of your collection: either the whole collection or specific portions of your collection. Whole-collection analysis can be done relatively easily using resources provided by some of the major vendors. Both Mackin and Follett have collection analysis tools. Follett's Titlewise analysis is very simple to use, especially if you use Follett Destiny as your catalog. However, if you do not use Destiny, you can obtain a Follett Title-Wave account and upload your MARC records into Titlewise for an analysis. The whole-collection analysis should provide you with a breakdown of collection age, types of materials, and circulation statistics by Dewey section or genre section if you have a genrefied collection.

In addition to the standard results of the collection analysis, you will want to look at the diversity of your collection. This is a more difficult process, but Follett and Mackin are working to make it an easier task. Both of these vendors are now including diversity analysis as part of their reporting; however, the analysis is primarily based on subject headings and keywords and the analysis is only as good as the MARC records they have in their databases. You should consider conducting a targeted diversity analysis on key components of your collection; for example, you could do a diversity audit of your biographies. For support in developing your diversity audit procedures, look at the blog series "Doing a YA Collection Diversity Audit" by Karen Jensen.[18]

Acquisition: Selecting Materials

Selection of resources in libraries is often covered in library and information science programs in one or more courses. School librarians may have taken children's and youth literature in one or two courses and they may have discussed materials to support the curriculum in another course. However, before discussing the selection of resources—a high-priority activity for the library staff—school librarians need to understand that they are not totally and solely responsible for this. Rather, some of these choices belong to library users, including administrators, teachers, students, and (whenever possible) parents. School librarians who select a collection with little or no input from users may find that the resulting range of materials is too narrow. At other times, it is even more helpful to be able to consult with teachers, parents, or students who are knowledgeable about technology before choosing a new technology. You will want to create a method for your stakeholders to provide recommendations or requests for new additions to your collection. A simple Google form is one easy way to collect this information.

It is important to remember that you are not just selecting print materials for your collection. You will also be curating a collection that includes equipment for use in the school and for checkout, such as green screens, tripods, and multimedia equipment. You might create special collections that meet the needs of specific stakeholders. You could have a library of items that are consumable or reusable. Examples of consumable items are materials used for making, such as buttons, seeds, or yarn. Reusable items might include specialty cake pans, gardening tools, LEGOs, ozobots, or augmented reality devices. Many of these items are things that would be useful for a makerspace, but during the pandemic some school libraries converted their makerspaces to "takerspaces," creating kits with making activities that could be checked out. You might also have kits that include a print book and a playaway (audiobook device). Think beyond the traditional print book when you are deciding what your users need access to. Also, do not forget that to create these takeaway kits, you will need packaging for storage and catalog records that encourage discoverability.

Although providing a core or basic collection is the first step in collection development, more important is selecting the remaining materials that must be chosen to fit the school's curriculum. Guides to building a core collection include *Children's Catalog*, *Middle and Junior High School Catalog*, and *Senior High Core Collection*, which are published in hardbound volumes or available as a database through H.W. Wilson. These databases contain carefully selected entries of book titles and are helpful to school librarians not only in establishing a core collection but also in reviewing materials for retention or discard. These tools represent research and professional experience by experts in the school library field. However, the standard selection tools may be cost prohibitive as useful after selecting the core because many of the materials listed are out of print.

Meeting curriculum needs is a major criterion for placing items in the collection. Librarians can begin to address this task by carefully reviewing the textbooks and review journals in the curriculum area used by each teacher, finding out the length of time any unit is taught and to how many students, discovering what teaching method is used, and finding out what the research assignments are likely to be.

A bibliography of materials in the collection can be obtained by searching the OPAC for specific subject headings. If the resulting bibliography does not appear to have relevant titles or titles at the ability or interest level of the students in the course, additional materials must be purchased. As a temporary measure, materials may be requested from other libraries in the area.

Current review periodicals such as *Booklist*, *Bulletin for the Center of Children's Books*, *School Library Journal*, and *School Library Connection* review new publications. Follett's TitleWave lists books with full bibliographic information, cost, and ISBN. This program also provides reviews from periodical sources. One can ask to have lists created by subject, grade level, and places where the item is reviewed. Because all reviews in *Booklist* are for recommended titles, asking for resources that have been cited in that periodical gives a choice of only recommended resources. Testimonials and reviews are featured to help with selection in a way that was not dreamed of in the past. Because smaller publishers are often not reviewed by the major reviewing publications, you will also want to look outside of the traditional reviewing literature to find diverse content. There are many well-established blogs and other websites that provide reviews of materials you might want to consider for your collection.

While highly valuable to the curriculum, databases can be expensive choices. These items really need some preview by teachers so you can be sure they will be used. You can request access to a database for a review period, provide that information to teachers, and then request their perspective on whether the database is worth the subscription cost. Vendors offer access through licenses for their databases. Sometimes these licenses are offered through the state department of education for all schools and the state library for all public libraries. In other states, this is a responsibility of each individual school or each school district. License agreements for multiple use become pertinent if they are limited to a small number of users rather than being assigned to an entire set of users.

Online references should have full-text and image files of current information that can be downloaded, and users can manipulate these for research reports; however, this makes it very easy for a student to copy rather than create. Efforts to reduce plagiarism become a part of managing this resource. Helping teachers plan research assignments that use the research process as a way for students to create products that reflect their work is an important role for the school librarian. The ease of cutting and pasting—and even taking a whole paper written and posted on the Internet—can make plagiarism appealing and easy. Carefully developed assignments to build critical thinking skills will make it very difficult for any student to plagiarize.

Software to encourage academic honesty and help students cite materials that need to be attributed are available at a range of price points or free.

Curating the Web

Information located on the Internet does not resemble the information that librarians have traditionally anticipated as a part of the selection process. It is not something that will be purchased, processed, and stored for future use on a shelf. However, information from the Internet, available to students and teachers, becomes a part of the library collection. How to choose the best from the Internet and how to keep what is not appropriate from coming into the library is a major subject of discussion among all types of librarians and their communities. Further information about curating the web and making your curation discoverable is provided in chapter 11 on technology.

Deselection of Materials (Weeding)

As stated earlier, materials in disrepair and materials that are outdated, irrelevant, and inaccurate should be removed from the collection; this is called *weeding*. Weeding is perhaps as important as selecting additional materials for a collection. A smaller, more attractive collection of relevant, up-to-date materials on the shelves, particularly when hardcover materials are less likely to be of interest, is more important to students and teachers. Many school librarians find themselves able to reduce shelving to create alternative spaces in the library when unused materials are weeded. Your selection policy should include your weeding criteria, available to show to anyone who objects when you are discarding materials. Many teachers, parents, and even administrators are shocked when they think something is going to be discarded. Sharing the reasons for these discards will help them understand the process. A quick overview of why to weed materials is provided in Figure 9-2.

In addition to those reasons provided in Figure 10-1, there are several other factors which justify collection re-evaluation and deselection:

- Changes in the curriculum require revision of the focus of the collection.
- Materials must be repaired or replaced if in poor condition.
- Shelves should appear attractive and inviting to users.
- Items counted as holdings should represent useful resources.
- Students and teachers should have access to the best possible collection of materials.
- Unused hard-copy materials should be replaced by online resources.
- Materials should be replaced if they are out of date or inaccurate.
- Reading levels should be appropriate for students in the building.

Just Weed It!

Library Girl's Tips For Keeping Your Collection...

IF THE ANSWER'S NO... IT'S GOT TO GO!

F Does it **FOSTER** a Love of Reading? The books in your library should help students see themselves as readers and make them want to read MORE.

R Does it **REFLECT** your diverse population? Every student in your school should be able to see themselves in your collection.

E Does it reflect an **EQUITABLE** global view? Your collection should represent a variety of view points and encourage global connections.

S Does it **SUPPORT** the curricula? Your collection should be age & developmentally appropriate AND it should support the learning goals of your school.

H Is it a **HIGH-QUALITY** text? Your collection should be made up of materials that connect your students and teachers to up to date and accurate information.

ORIGINAL IMAGE BY @JENNIFERLAGARDE
WWW.LIBRARYGIRL.NET

Figure 9-2. Just Weed It.

Deselection is a continual process. For hard-copy items, each item is reviewed as it circulates. Students and teachers can judge whether the material was helpful to them and, if not, why not. The staff should conduct a thorough evaluation of the entire collection at least once every three years.

The school librarian is responsible for reviewing the collection for compliance with the selection policy. As with the selection process, deselection must be regulated by the selection policy, not by personal bias.

Materials judged to be below or above the reading levels of students in the building, or those that treat subject areas shifted to another grade level, may be sent to another building. Retaining titles that might be useful in the future is usually not a good plan. It would be easier for the receiving school to return the materials if the situation is reversed or changes.

Materials in need of repair or replacement should be closely evaluated. Consider carefully if the information in this book is only available there or if it might be located online. Books may be sent to a bindery if the paper is of good quality and the information is important. In-house repair of materials must be reviewed to see that the costs of labor and materials do not exceed the cost of rebinding an item. Attention should be paid to the attractiveness of an in-house repair versus a new purchase of a similar book.

Finally, materials must be evaluated for retention or withdrawal. Old, worn-out materials must be discarded. Out-of-date materials should be removed unless they have great historical value. Duplicate titles may be reassessed if demand for the item has slackened. Biographies not linked to curriculum or of persons unknown to the present generation should not be retained.

Outdated materials may be almost anything in science and technology with a copyright date more than five years old. In fact, to answer one of the questions at the beginning of this section, consideration might be given to purchasing only electronic science resources. Psychology, history, business, and education materials become dated in 10 years. In fiction, certain authors and topics may lose their appeal to an age group. An author read by high school students 15 years ago may be devoured by elementary students today.

Many districts and schools have weeding guidelines in place, and you need to find out if your district has any requirements or restrictions. These guidelines should also provide instruction about how weeded materials should be discarded. Equipment may have to be picked up by the district. Books may be stamped as discarded and placed in the trash. Before deciding to allow discarded materials to be donated to classrooms, students, or other organizations, you should determine if those materials are in such poor condition or so outdated that they will do more harm than good. Many of the guidelines for these decisions are based on the CREW method from the Texas State Library and Archives Commission.[19]

A final caution concerns the destination of withdrawn items. If the reason for withdrawal is a change in grade level or curriculum, the librarian may wish to relocate these items to another library. If they are old, in poor condition, or contain out-of-date information, they should be destroyed. Less fortunate school librarians in poorly funded schools will not find them useful even if their collections were destroyed by hurricanes or fires or they are managing a library in a developing nation. Useless to one is useless to all.

If state standards require a certain number of materials in the collection or if the school administration insists that a large number of items and materials be kept, a separate list could be maintained for these useless materials. They would still be listed as part of the collection but stored out of sight until they can be discarded. In some states, software and databases may be counted as equivalents for materials. It is hoped that school librarians in states with arbitrary numbers for judging a collection can work to get such regulations altered or removed.

It would be difficult to try to justify keeping newspaper files unless it is the local newspaper, which is, one hopes, indexed. Most magazines are available in full text on databases.

Equipment can be evaluated with two criteria: use and repair record. Equipment that is no longer used because of lack of appropriate software should be removed. Any piece of equipment should also be removed when repair costs exceed replacement costs. Keeping a repair record for each piece of equipment is essential to help in determining the reliability of the company manufacturing the equipment. A simple method is to make notations of the date of purchase and type of equipment. Each time the equipment fails to function, a record is made of the malfunction.

This chapter has presented the responsibility of the school librarian to provide access to information as well as manage the resources in the school library. Remember that you will be providing access to a wide variety of resources, not just books, and if an item is not useful or helpful, it's time to weed it! The next chapter, chapter 10, explains the need for managing personnel.

Key Takeaways

- Maintaining a vibrant, inclusive collection is an ongoing process.

- Your policies are essential in providing guidance for selection and deselection of materials.

- Making your collection accessible through your organization, shelving, and catalog descriptions is very important. Discoverability is the key to increasing student access.

Challenges to Promote Growth

1. Visit ALA's State Privacy Laws webpage (https://www.ala.org/advocacy/privacy/statelaws) to determine whether your state has a law related to confidentiality of records. Does your state law apply to school library records? Compare this to another state's law and decide which law would be more difficult to follow.
2. Ask one or more schools how they maintain confidentiality of library records.
3. Outline a talk you would present to your principal, teachers, and parents concerning your response to the requirements for confidentiality of library records in your school.
4. Investigate the strengths and weaknesses of the filtering systems offered to school and public libraries.
5. Interview two or more school librarians to see whether they have had any censorship questions/issues and, if so, how they responded.
6. Locate your school district's selection policy and compare it to what you have read in this chapter. If you are not currently working in a school, use the policy from the district where you live.

7. Conduct a targeted diversity audit of your collection. Suggested areas might be biographies or a specific genre. Explore the Inclusive Collections and Diversity Audits Playlist for more resources: https://schoollibrarynj.libguides.com/Librarians/collection

Notes

1. American Library Association. (2018, January). "Selection & Reconsideration Policy Toolkit for Public, School, & Academic Libraries." https//www.ala.org/tools/challengesupport/selectionpolicytoolkit

2. April M. Dawkins. (2018). "Ten Steps to Creating a Selection Policy that Matters." *School Library Connection* (October). https://schoollibraryconnection.com/content/article/2209716?topicCenterId=0&learningModuleId=2209716&view=Print

3. American Library Association. (1993/2019). "Economic Barriers to Information Access: An Interpretation of the Library Bill of Rights." https://www.ala.org/advocacy/intfreedom/librarybill/interpretations/economicbarriers

4. Theresa Chmara. (2021). "The Law Regarding Minors' First Amendment Rights to Access Information." In *Intellectual Freedom Manual,* 10th ed. Chicago: ALA, pp. 137–146.

5. Samuel D. Warren and Louis D. Brandeis. (1890). "The Right to Privacy." *Harvard Law Review* 4, no. 5: 193–220. https://doi.org/10.2307/1321160

6. 20 U.S.C. § 1232g—Family educational and privacy rights. https://www.govinfo.gov/content/pkg/USCODE-2011-title20/pdf/USCODE-2011-title20-chap31-subchapIII-part2.pdf

7. Federal Communications Commission. (2019, December 30). Children's Internet Protection Act (CIPA). https://www.fcc.gov/consumers/guides/childrens-internet-protection-act

8. Federal Trade Commission. (2017, June). "Children's Online Privacy Protection Rule: A Six-Step Compliance Plan for Your Business." https://www.ftc.gov/tips-advice/business-center/guidance/childrens-online-privacy-protection-rule-six-step-compliance#step4

9. American Library Association. (2019 revision). "Library Bill of Rights." https://www.ala.org/advocacy/intfreedom/librarybill

10. American Library Association. (2019, February 7). "New Library Bill of Rights Provision Recognizes and Defends Library Users' Privacy." https://www.ala.org/news/press-releases/2019/02/new-library-bill-rights-provision-recognizes-and-defends-library-users

11. Common Sense Media. (n.d.). "All Common Sense Privacy Evaluations." https://privacy.commonsense.org/evaluations/1

12. N.C. Gen. Stat. §§ 125-18, 125-19.

13. American Library Association. (2021, November). "State Laws Regarding Privacy Records." https://www.ala.org/advocacy/privacy/statelaws

14. American Library Association. (2021, October). "Students & Minors." https://www.ala.org/advocacy/privacy/students

15. April M. Dawkins. (2020). "Creating Reconsideration Policies That Matter." *School Library Connection* (March), entry 2209716. https://schoollibraryconnection.com/Content/Article/2209716

16. John Schlipp. (2019). *Intellectual Property and Information Rights for Librarians.* Santa Barbara, CA: Libraries Unlimited.

17. Follett. (2022). "Genre Solutions." https://www.follettlearning.com/books-materials/library/genre-solutions

18. Karen Jensen. (2017). "Doing a YA Collection Diversity Audit: Understanding Your Local Community (Part I)." *School Library Journal.* https://teenlibrariantoolbox.com/2017/11/01/doing-a-diversity-audit-understanding-your-local-community

19. Texas State Library and Archives Commission. (2012). *CREW: A Weeding Manual for Libraries.* https://www.tsl.texas.gov/ld/pubs/crew/index.html

10
Managing and Partnering with Personnel

There are people who make things happen, there are people who watch things happen, and there are people who wonder what happened. To be successful, you need to be a person who makes things happen.
—Jim Lovell

If you want to go fast, go alone. If you want to go far, go together.
—African proverb

Essential Questions

- How can you leverage your advisory committee to support the creation of an inclusive, innovative library?

- What are the keys to engaging with your varied stakeholders to build a collaborative community?

The title of this chapter is "Managing and Partnering with Personnel," and it may seem that "managing" is too strong for someone who will be "working collaboratively" with peers and students. However, a degree of management goes with working with others in many situations, and this skill is sometimes overlooked. Traditional practice taught in many preparation programs focuses on selecting materials, organizing collections, and using new technologies, among others, rather than managing. In fact, many librarians resist the thought that they need to learn how to manage. Nevertheless, managing and collaborating with people is one of the most important factors in a successful library program.

You must have the ability to manage what happens in the library and communicate expectations to everyone using the library. The librarian must assume responsibility for the management of library staff (when it exists) and any volunteers who are available to help in the library. Management is needed when working with teachers and students who use the library so that operation of the library runs smoothly. The successful school librarian possesses the management skills needed to interact with everyone in the school as well as parents and others throughout the wider community. These skills help create a community of users participating in learning in the library and eliminate the need for authoritarian postures. Thus, the librarian becomes a colleague of all rather than someone writing and imposing rules and regulations without stakeholder input.

Many school librarians act as solo librarians—the single managers of their library; they have no paid staff to manage. Because of this prospect, education programs for school librarians often provide only skeletal instruction in management skills, such as interpersonal skills for communication with those in the school (administrators, teachers, and students) and how to handle students who misbehave. However, you will have a variety of people collaborating in the library. The secret here is, from the first day in a new school, to help everyone understand that this is not your, but *their* library, and it is up to everyone to ensure that their library is readily available for use, that its facility and resources are the best available, and that coming to the library is a learning experience for all.

This begins with the principal, who may have been responsible for hiring the school librarian. The concept of the library as a learning center should be a part of the interview process. A brief description of the library either orally or in a handout is provided for staff and teachers who will be at the school at least one day before the students arrive. You might create this as a menu of services and resources. As the parents and other caregivers are asked if they can volunteer some of their time in the library, they are told exactly what this will entail, from helping open boxes of new books and checking the invoice to serving as an artist in residence in a school with irregular visits from an art teacher.

Finally, at the earliest opportunity the community is approached to see who can volunteer to help in many ways, including sharing their knowledge and expertise with students. A good way to start this process is to enlist an advisory committee.

The Library Advisory Committee

A library advisory committee is made up of members of the school community. Some are assigned by the principal; others volunteer or are asked to participate by the school librarian. The committee should include representatives of the teachers, the students, and perhaps a parent. If membership is chosen by the librarian, those selected should be a mix of advocates and perhaps one or two for whom such involvement may be an opportunity for them to learn more about what the library can do. The advisory committee's role is to advise and provide input on all aspects of the library. Their role is *not* to make final decisions about the collection or selection or removal of materials.

Classroom teachers may need to be reminded that the library is there to provide access to information for their classrooms and for the entire school. When they are asked to help develop the mission, policies, goals, and objectives for the library, they begin to understand your challenges. Funding requests for resources are no longer interpreted as support for the librarian only, but for enhancement of student learning.

If students from elementary school through high school are to believe the library is truly theirs, then they need to have representatives on the advisory committee. They will be able to present the student view of suggested resources, including digital resources, and critique rules for usage of the library from the standpoint of student access. They may be able to help solve problems in some way other than creating a rule that must be enforced. They can point out information needs that are not being met, and they can add comments about changes or needed changes they hear from their friends.

Having a parent involved brings in another point of view about resources needed and things that would be helpful for their children. Their reports of comments heard from their children or their children's friends can also be helpful. Most of all, they and other members of the advisory group can be useful advocates for the library program.

An advisory group meets regularly, as frequently as is practical but seldom more than once a month. They will have a clear purpose or charge, and all members must understand their roles. Each member should have an active assignment, so they consider their membership worthwhile. School librarians, in consultation with the school administration, set the parameters for the group. Advisory committee members should help establish the purpose of the group. All of this is much more easily accomplished when the principal is an active part of the advisory group.

The advisory committee might be interested in many areas of the library program. Members could help with reviewing the library mission statement as it flows from the school's mission and analyzing the information needs of library users. The advisory group can assist in advocating for budget additions to support this mission and identified needs. This takes some pressure off the librarian when requests exceed resources. Once an advisory committee has been formed, you can begin the initial step in planning how to manage by analyzing your leadership style.

Analyzing Your Leadership and Collaborative Style

Leadership takes many different forms and not all leaders lead in the same way. It is essential that you act as a leader in your school. After all, Leader is one of our five roles. The book *Leadership: Strategic Thinking, Decision Making, Communication, and Relationship Building* by Martin and Roberts is an excellent resource to use in examining how your leadership is threaded throughout the American Association of School Librarians' National Standards. They note that "the capstone for building relationships is growing stakeholder empowerment through shared responsibility."[1] All school librarians need to be leaders, but they will not all have the same leadership style. Self-analysis of your style determines how you will be most comfortable in situations where you need to lead. Not all situations require the same type of leadership, but you need to know when and how to move out of your comfort zone.

In 2016, Everhart and Johnston[2] proposed a theory of school librarian leadership and developed a conceptual model with confidence, communication, and relationships at its center. In this model, *confidence* includes confidence in one's abilities to teach, lead, and engage with technology. Everhart and Johnston point out that having confidence supports both communication and relationships. Confidence is necessary so that school librarians will take risks, try new things, and inspire others. Communication is essential for school librarians. Without good communication skills in a variety of formats, librarians cannot share their ideas with others either as teachers or advocates. Everhart and Johnston note that relationships involve connections between and among people. School librarians need to build those relationships both within and outside of their schools.

Building on Everhart and Johnston's model, Pamela Harland[3] created an updated model of school librarian leadership behaviors (Figure 10-1). The start of the map is education or the school librarian's professional preparation and each of the stops represents school librarian leadership behaviors and characteristics. Note that everything is interconnected and that everything connects to relationships.

Harland added vulnerability, risk-taking, and job crafting to the original model. *Vulnerability* requires you to engage in trust with your community and share your uncertainty. *Risk-taking* is a willingness to explore potential solutions to problems by trying and potentially failing. *Job crafting* is how you might work toward your strengths and adapt your skills to meet the needs of your community.

Relationship building is one key to leadership success. Understanding how you can contribute to the collaborative process and work within a group setting will help you to work with your strengths and bring out the strengths of others. The School Reform Initiative has developed an activity that can help you understand how your preferences may affect group dynamics. The preferences are referred to as compass points: North, South, East, and West. North is characterized by Acting, South by Caring, East by Speculating, and West by Attention to Detail. Each group needs all of the compass points to be effective. To learn more about the compass points, you can participate in an activity through the School Reform Initiative website.[4]

In the book *The Many Faces of School Library Leadership*,[5] readers are given a look at leadership from school library leaders with a combination of theory and practice. The various roles and their leadership components are described. After you have analyzed your leadership and group preference styles, you are ready to begin the process of managing those around you.

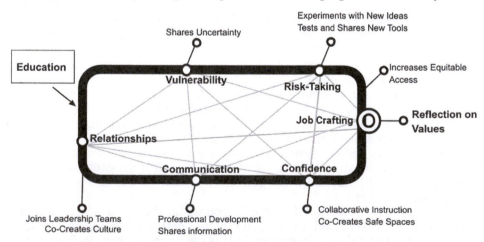

Figure 10-1. A Model of School Librarian Leadership Behaviors.

Pamela C. Harland. (2020). *An Investigation into the Leadership Behaviors of School Librarians: A Qualitative Study*. Plymouth State University. ProQuest Central; ProQuest Dissertations & Theses Global, Order No. 27669374. https://summit.plymouth.edu/bitstream/handle/20.500.12774/331/psu-etd-160.pdf?sequence=1&isAllowed=y

Library Staff

In the present economic climate, many schools operate with a single person assigned to the school library. In very large schools, the school library may have two or more professionals and paraprofessionals. Professional staff may include others who are not necessarily certified librarians, such as technology professionals. If reading specialists are assigned to the school, a good place for them to have an office and even classroom space is in the library.

One of the most important tasks of the librarian is to make sure staff members are working with a common goal and a common vision. Once the staff has established and accepted the goals and objectives, you must work to build a common vision of information and instructional services with the other teachers in the building, defining the role of the librarian as a part of the teaching staff. This is especially important as changes in curriculum or other requirements are put into place.

Tasks to be performed in the library have been developed over time by practitioners who manage library programs on a daily basis. However, in recent years these tasks have been changing with new technology and educational trends. The librarian leading the library is also responsible for helping faculty and staff prepare for advances in technology, learn about additions to the collection (such as new databases), implement new services (such as a makerspace), and develop new relationships with agencies outside the school.

When more than one professional is assigned to the library, each will expect the person in charge to direct their actions so they can complete their assigned tasks in a satisfactory manner. Such decisions may be group decisions. Nevertheless, all staff members, including students and volunteers who can work independently, should be allowed to establish how to do a job once the job has been defined. When improvement is needed, you will need to help staff understand the problem and how to solve it.

If the library is to run smoothly, job responsibilities should be assigned to specific personnel. The staff is then supervised to see that they carry out their duties efficiently and thoroughly. This is not always an easy job. Supervising personnel often means making decisions that may not be readily accepted by staff; at the same time, you have the responsibility of maintaining staff members' job satisfaction. It is important that you and anyone you supervise have a clear understanding about what the job entails.

Finally, if you have been given the responsibility of supervising staff, you will also be asked to evaluate staff performance. This is pleasant when staff is unusually competent, but a little more difficult if merit raises are given for outstanding performance. However, it is especially difficult if staff is poorly prepared or unable to fulfill their duties. Evaluation is based on standards of performance.

Standards-Based Evaluation

Standards and evaluation of school librarians were discussed previously in chapter 6, but as a potential supervisor of library staff, you will also need to engage in standards-based evaluation. Setting standards of performance and monitoring staff as they perform their jobs is a supervision and management task for the librarian. *Supervision* of personnel is the process of dealing with the persons who have been assigned the job responsibilities and evaluating performance and competencies individuals have for doing their jobs. Your involvement in evaluation and supervision of library staff will be determined by the line and staff organization of your school or school district. *Line relationships* refers to the hierarchy of authority within a school district. Line authority usually resides with the principal or a supervisor who has the power to hire. Staff relationships are usually supportive. An example is a district library supervisor who does not have the power to hire, but does have the ability to provide support.

Competencies directly define the personnel carrying out functions in the library. The degree to which you may participate in developing staff competencies or describing functions may be a product of the organization of the school district and the contracts binding personnel in that school district. When you, as manager, are assigned to evaluate other professionals working in the library, it is critical to be aware of these contracts, because they often have strict regulations and requirements for the evaluation of all personnel in the school district. Most school superintendents keep a copy of the union contract close at hand, and the school librarian's awareness and attention to following those rules becomes essential to the process.

In many school districts, state departments of education mandate personnel evaluation. For professional staff, the school district requirements may include evaluation of performance to determine reappointment or tenure. As suggested in chapter 3, the applicant should try to find out about evaluation steps to reappointment and tenure before accepting a position in a school district. You must research the process fully so you understand the process. After an initial evaluation, this will go forward to the principal or the district library director if one is in the district, and the personnel office. It is essential to obtain correct information about the latest policies or requirements in the state or district. Evaluation may continue to be required even after tenure or a continuing contract or license is granted.

Unfortunately, when you are tasked with providing input on the performance of a library staff member who is not meeting expectations, you will need to keep detailed records of deficiencies to build the steps for improvement, or, in the case of consistent lack of improvement, to support dismissal. You certainly hope that you will not need to dismiss personnel, but when such a situation occurs, the principal and the district library director will expect you to follow appropriate procedures. Dismissal requires a carefully documented record of tasks done incorrectly or not done at all. It is not a pleasant assignment, yet it is irresponsible to allow inefficient, ineffective, and even harmful employees to remain when the education of students is at stake.

Because clerical and technical staff members are seldom tenured, evaluation determines salary increases and continuation of position. Records must be maintained at all levels. Efficient staff must be rewarded, and merit pay raises often must be documented as carefully as refusals to grant merit pay raises. The dismissal of inefficient clerical and technical staff requires careful and thorough documentation just as with professional staff. In our litigious society, many persons who are dismissed will sue.

Hiring Staff

A school library management book ought to discuss the school librarian in a situation where staff is to be added to the library. In a situation where additional staff is needed for the library, you must clearly and closely analyze the factors that dictate requirements for more staff and prepare appropriate documentation to justify the positions. Administrators must be convinced of the need for a new or expanded position, especially in times when budgets are tight. The foundation established in the job description may become the justification for funding. Calculating actual costs of clerical tasks in relation to professional salary to establish cost accountability is one way to do this. The responsibilities for adding staff are described later in this chapter.

Larger school districts have a human resources department with staff and a director. In smaller districts, the hiring is assigned to a single person within another department of the district. These persons will be very knowledgeable about hiring teachers, but they may be much less familiar with the necessary competencies of the various persons working in school libraries; their vision of such a person's assignments, if based upon their past experiences, may be in dire need of an update. Writing job descriptions could become the school librarian's responsibility.

When the school librarian has the responsibility for recruiting and terminating personnel, the process for interviewing and hiring is usually a very well-established one, which the school librarian needs to learn if the responsibility for recruiting and terminating personnel lies with them. In any event, human resources personnel will welcome some help with interview questions, because (as previously noted) they may have very little experience with what is needed from a person who will be working in a school library. Developing a job description is helpful to make sure everyone is on the same page. The following box lists some tasks that might be included in a job description for a paraprofessional.

Job Description: Library Paraprofessional

Supervised by: Immediate Supervisor: Librarian; Building Supervisor
Principal Functions:

- Oversees library procedures and practices in support of the librarian
- Guides students in research in support of librarian's instructional program
- Manages accounts and budgets, contacts vendors, generates requisitions and purchase orders
- Experienced with Web tools and interactive classroom technologies
- Supports the librarian's instruction of students in new and emerging tools for research, storytelling, and publishing
- Maintains and helps manage library website and LibGuides
- Monitors and troubleshoots workstations, iPads/Chromebooks and functions as liaison with technology department to solve more serious computer issues. Ensures that technology is charged
- Monitors and troubleshoots fax and copy machines, scanners, digital and video equipment
- Manages library ebook/database accounts
- Maintains and updates library databases and spreadsheets
- Maintains and updates library procedures manual
- Maintains daily statistics documenting library use
- Contributes and aids in the preparation of library newsletter and in the year-end report which includes extensive statistical report generation
- Provides support to students and teachers in the operation and use of new and existing equipment
- Maintains weekly digital calendar for faculty and staff and schedule board

- Attends appropriate meetings, seminars, and workshops for continuing education
- Coordinates public relations with local media and library special events
- Answers student questions regarding library operations and basic research strategies
- Provides support to students and teachers in the operation and use of new and existing equipment and applications
- Supervises shipping, receiving, and processing of materials and supplies
- Supervises student and adult volunteers
- Manages circulation desk
- Ensures order of shelves and library physical space

In addition to this job description, it is essential that the person you add to your library staff shares your vision of what the library should and can be. You want your library to be a welcoming and active space; therefore, a new paraprofessional who does not agree with this perspective would not be a good working partner.

Another person who may be assigned to the library is the pre-professional or practicum student who is coming to learn about school libraries. Many universities and colleges need exemplary situations for placement of practicum or intern students.

Practicum Students

Supervision of practicum students from nearby colleges introduces the next generation of school librarians to the real world. Decisions on practicum placements are made in schools when the university faculty considers a program location that will provide a student with the best possible experience. This is a wonderful opportunity for you and your teaching staff as you provide these experiences.

The school librarian should allow the practicum student to carry out a wide variety of tasks and assignments and should work with teachers and students following best practices. If you have been asked to host a practicum student, confirm with teachers that they are willing to let the practicum student collaborate to help build a unit of instruction or other learning activity with their students. Practicum students often have specific assignments they must complete while working with you in your library. You will want to communicate with the faculty supervisor and practicum student to make sure you know what those assignments entail.

A faculty member will likely come from the university to see the student in action. Preparing a scenario that will allow the student to truly demonstrate skills learned is essential. The student will also anticipate receiving a letter of recommendation for the activities completed during the practicum. Finally, students seeking positions after graduation need the networking their practicum supervisor can offer.

Support Staff in the Library

All of the information about assigning work for professionals in the library applies equally to assigning tasks to support staff when school librarians are lucky enough to have nonprofessional staff assigned to the library. Some support staff may be library technicians who have had specialized training at a community college; these persons can carry out a wide variety of tasks. Other staff may be hired from the same pool of persons who are applying for secretarial positions in the school district. They will have little training or experience, if any at all, and you will need to teach them and help them acquire skills,

The range of skills and knowledge of support staff will be very wide, and they need to be asked about these skills before assigning them a task. The amount of training you will need to do will depend upon the responsibilities they have handled in the past and the years of experience they have had in any library. If multiple schools in your district have support staff, then the district might provide training specifically for library paraprofessionals.

Regardless of past experience and training of your staff, they must have one skill that they learn and use from the very beginning. It is extremely important that the support staff are welcoming to students and teachers and help to create a warm and open atmosphere.

Managing personnel may also be defined as getting along with the clientele. The next sections offer suggestions for managing students, teachers, administrators, parents, and volunteers. The chapter closes with suggestions for managing in the community that includes other libraries and librarians.

Students and Their Library

Students who consider the library "theirs" will work to see that it remains a pleasant place to visit and a welcome place to learn. They will see that this center for learning, creating, and sharing runs smoothly. Providing that "friendly place" with the freedom that should exist in the school library to allow students to explore their environment, learn from one another, work on joint projects, do committee work, and read or view or listen to materials recommended by their fellow students makes the position of school librarian a very pleasant one. Knowing when this interaction is moving from exploration and encouragement into mischief is a skill that may take practice to acquire, but it is crucial if you are to continue to allow students the freedom to explore.

The library is the only room in the school where every student can experience success. Although the librarian plans, integrates, and implements information, media, and digital literacy learning opportunities across curricula, there usually are no specific grades assigned to students for the activities introduced in the library. You will be expected to align your instruction with classroom concepts and grade-level competencies. You should have information and resources to support learners at all levels and to satisfy all interests. You should be available to give individual assistance to a student without drawing attention to the process. All students ask for help finding materials, and all students find something with which they can work, and in a true learning environment students help one another.

The cardinal rule is to place as few restrictions as possible on student use of resources. Limiting anything such as how many books can be taken home or how much time is allowed to search a database may seem to provide "equal" access, but it is frustrating to all. If the librarian's role is to encourage readers, avoid restrictions relating to numbers of materials borrowed. The real challenge is with books for beginning readers who will have read their library book before they get back to their room. To limit these students to the one or two books that they may check out for a week is discouraging their interest in reading. It helps if any rules or restrictions are understood by all, and the easiest way to do this is to have others involved in the decisions that establish those rules.

Students themselves can help establish rules if they have the opportunity. Students know when assignments require use of materials for a longer period of time. They can also help evaluate a plan to allow everyone to check out materials for a longer time, and they will help the school librarian manage getting resources back when someone else needs them because students have been involved in the planning for the process.

It is surprising just how capable students can be in solving problems with project-based learning and in meeting the challenges and opportunities presented in the school library makerspace. They can set the standards for digital citizenship and analyze why books are damaged or lost and make suggestions for solving these problems with physical items.

Librarians, when they assume the role of teacher, must follow the prescriptions for classroom management and effective teaching. Good planning with teachers for exciting instructional activities to carry out as a part of a unit means students will be interested and engaged. When students can do their assignments using their own plans for learning, whether as individuals or as a member of a group, they will be—and remain—interested and engaged. When the school librarian and the teacher are interested in what the students are doing, the students know this. Students are astute. They will be annoyed by busywork. Work with teachers and students to set objectives and develop authentic assessments. It will not be busy work if everyone helps plan what is going to be needed or produced and how it will be presented when it is finished.

Units should be planned with a variety of activities, including introduction to new materials, lively discussions, and interactive and independent activities; exercises that allow for movement and choice are also important. No one enjoys sitting for long periods of time, and the library is one room in the school that truly invites browsing and moving from one place to another.

The school librarian has full responsibility for the learning experiences of each student. The library belongs to each student. It is your responsibility to engage students in learning activities that they will enjoy, whether it is engaging with inquiry or finding the perfect read or introducing informal challenges in learning stations or interactive displays.

Teachers and the Library

Teachers will come under the "management" purview of the school librarian who introduces and models the effective use of new technologies appropriately. This management should become more of a partnership, with each taking an active role in making discoveries and connecting them with student needs. Managing and partnering with teachers is easily accomplished when you understand what teachers expect. You must listen to what teachers are concerned about and use that opportunity to collaborate on solutions. They have challenges that they can share with you, and your efforts in trying to resolve those challenges will be welcomed. One way to be successful is to anticipate teachers' needs and address them. Your success can often be defined as identifying your colleagues' problems and designing solutions. Asking which services teachers want and then offering those services will build social capital and trust.

You must communicate that the priority for the library is to be available for collaboration in planning and offering curriculum units of instruction. As an instructional partner, you provide classroom teachers with the help they need as they plan their instructional activities, and you are there through the instruction and as a part of the evaluation of the products of that collaboration.

Accessibility of resources when they are required is essential. Librarians keep a focus on the curriculum in every classroom throughout the year and encourage teachers to plan ahead for library needs, but help at the point of need must be given willingly and enthusiastically.

When working with your teacher colleagues, put as few restrictions as possible on library access. You should provide access to the library to as many students as possible and work collaboratively with teachers to ensure the best possible experiences for their students while they are in the library. You should welcome students sent to the library to work on group projects that might require space to create items as well as to work as teams to discuss their projects.

One way to help teachers understand the role of the library in instruction is to provide staff development for teachers in information sources, research methods, research in the field of education, and additions to the library. The librarian continues to provide in-service assistance that will help teachers gain technological skills they may be lacking with the new communication devices their students use with such great ease.

Helping teachers expand their skills without implying that they do not already have those skills is a successful management method. Overcoming teacher resistance is easier when teachers are involved in planning the in-service activity, because then the program will be based on teacher-developed needs.

When helping teachers, it is always a good idea to be empathetic. When colleagues return from absences such as health leaves or sabbaticals, spending extra time to help them catch up on rules and regulations that have changed in their absence or curricular changes being discussed will contribute to a positive atmosphere for all.

At times during the school year, teachers, administrators, and coaches may need to use the library space for purposes other than teaching and research. Sometimes more space is needed for activities and the library may serve as that space. You will need to balance providing access to library resources and services with acting as a team player in accommodating these needs. It is important that activities that restrict access to your library be minimized. It is important to engage in professional courtesy. You might be asked to cover a class when a substitute is not available or to accommodate athletes on a game day. Working with teachers who have responsibilities such as coaching, the yearbook, the prom, or a field trip will ease their teaching burden for that period of time and can make the day more educational for that teacher's classes. This does not mean that the library becomes a babysitting service, but rather that students are receiving the best possible use of their time in school. Building goodwill by accommodating these needs is important. One day when you need coverage in the library, they will return the favor. However, if this courtesy is misused, the problem should be addressed.

Finally, you should be willing to assist with extracurricular events. Think about the activities where your talents might be useful. Do you have an undergraduate degree in history? Think about volunteering to go along on the field trip to the local historical society. Were you a music major?

When the music teacher needs someone to attend the city choral festival with the school choir, you should volunteer if possible. Volunteering to go to the museum on the fifth-grade field trip provides an opportunity to talk with volunteer parents and observe what students are learning. Such tasks are not in the job description of the librarian, but they require a teacher-sponsor, and librarians are teachers too. Ignoring the opportunity to assist teachers makes collaboration more difficult later, when teachers use the library.

These approaches are equally important when working with coaches or other specialists on the staff. Learning the commonalities among these specialties means helping embed what they have to offer with classroom teachers. It helps students understand the reality of a real world that does not separate into units of time for music, art, and math . . . but for all students today who wear earbuds listening to music while they complete their homework, this is common practice!

Administrators and the Library

You can be your administrator's biggest asset. This section might be subtitled "How to Partner with Your Boss." Certainly, "managing" an administrator means getting along with those in authority in the school district. The focus here is on the building principal, but the methods and the suggestions for activities are equally applicable to working with the director of the library program and the district superintendent. It begins with a word of caution. If the only time a school librarian is in contact with an administrator is to complain about something, it will not take a very long time to find out that these persons will try to dodge any further encounters. This does not help the perception of the library and the librarian and is very harmful. It could even result in the program being closed, because that is an easy way to get rid of a problematic school librarian. A better stance is the philosophy that the best way to work with an administrator on challenges is not to go to the principal just to complain, but to identify both the problem and at least one potential solution when you meet with that person. Remember that principals bring their own talents and experiences to their position as the leader of a school, and you can help them by providing your skills and experiences to fill in their gaps in knowledge. The suggestions that follow are ways to be seen as an extremely competent and helpful person who is in charge of an indispensable program.

School librarians have management responsibility with their administrators. You should make regular reports to principals and other administrators to keep them informed of activities going on in the library and in the classroom, particularly those activities that increase student learning and add to the general instructional climate of the school. Principals have so many outside activities demanding their time that they have little time left over to focus on the well-being of the school staff. Keeping them informed of special events going on in classrooms is also helpful, both when the library is directly involved and also at other times when teachers may not have thought it important to inform the principal. Provide them with student-centered data that is easily digested and not too wordy.

When a principal does not support the library, it is often because they do not know the benefits of a thriving school library. It is important for you to interact and share all that you are doing in the library to support students and staff.

The school library program will prosper if you learn to plan with the principal. "Planning with the principal" does not mean discussing the titles of databases to which to subscribe. That is a professional task for which you have had training. Rather, planning with the principal should include providing a whole-school picture of students and teachers, as you are one of the few who have that viewpoint. Do not focus on small topics such as the continuing costs of new online reference services now replacing the book and periodical collections. Instead, focus on why these new resources are needed to increase student learning potential in the school.

This is a broad and somewhat different approach to the traditional relationship between principal and school librarian. Both touch the educational lives of every student through their interactions with students and teachers. However, the school librarian works with all the students, all the teachers, and all the curriculum all the time. Although principals want to do this too, they are frequently taken away to carry out other duties, often outside the building. This means librarians are in a unique position to keep principals informed when they are away from the school at those other functions. The teaching needs of teachers and the learning needs of students as they are carried out in the classrooms as well as the library then become continuing topics of discussion.

Successes are detailed in regular reports to the principal. This will help present the library program in such a way that the principal can speak highly of it to other principals. Too often in life, the complaints outweigh the compliments, yet, as stated earlier, complaining is not the way to influence a principal. Regular monthly reports on the use of the library and the positive learning experiences of students should outrank and outnumber any list of needs, great though they may be. Librarians also submit a yearly report, which is a compilation of the monthly statistics. If the librarian has developed a 3-, 5-, 10-, or even 15-year plan with the principal, this yearly report will cite progress toward each of the goals, point out what has not occurred, and present the plan for fulfilling this objective in the next one or two years. The year-end report should be concise, attractive, and easily understood.

Another type of report presents trends in education. You can provide helpful information to administrators and teachers about articles, research, and ideas that you come across either through the professional periodicals in your collection or through your online professional learning community. As you encounter information that is helpful, include it in your newsletter or forward links via email to those who would benefit. Making copies of articles or information taken from the Internet and sharing them with the principal provides up-to-date information. Sending abstracts from the latest important books can also help the principal maintain a high level of expertise in educational trends as they develop. This makes both you and your principal look good—an appealing perception in all circumstances.

The principal who participates in activity planning will better understand the role of the librarian and the amount of responsibility involved in managing a library. In evaluating performance, the principal must clearly recognize the dual role of the librarian as teacher and manager, and adjust the method of evaluation accordingly.

In some school districts, principals are administrators who are responsible for the day-to-day management of their building and also the discipline of students. This may limit the time they have available to visit classrooms except to evaluate teacher performances. Inviting the principal to read to students, listen to final reports of research projects, and help judge a poetry slam gives this official the opportunity to share in library activities with children. The principal's participation also gives your project more importance and provides a positive experience for students, library staff, and the principal.

As stated earlier, the school librarian has full responsibility for accomplishing as much as possible in the education of each student. Testing, recording, and reporting the role of the library in the educational progress of students will ultimately make the principal look good; and this is the best of all possible results in managing with the administrator.

The last group of community members to be addressed includes the members of the board of education or school board. As discussed in chapter 4, these persons are responsible for the school district. If the school district has someone in the superintendent's office who is responsible for the libraries, such as a director of library services, then communication with the school board begins there. However, if school librarians have no one on the board or in the superintendent's office who will present their case to the school board, the school librarians should form a committee and (with the permission of their principals) seek time on the school board agenda to make an annual report as a part of their "management" duties. This is different from the consideration of the school board members as a part of the community, which is discussed later in this chapter.

Parents and the Library

The librarian's relationship with parents is different from the relationship that parents have with classroom teachers. Parents sometimes overlook the impact that a librarian can have on the growth of their children. In order to confirm the role of the library in the education of students, the library should be featured as one of the "classrooms" on nights when parents come to the school to visit their students' classrooms.

You may think that you will see few parents because you are not classroom teachers, but this should not be the case. You should be ready and willing to invite parents into the library and also seek out opportunities to interact with parents. Welcoming parents into the library allows you to showcase the resources you provide, the engaging environment the students will experience, and the opportunities for pursuit of individual interests outside of the curriculum. The parent may also be interested in helping the library program and may become an advocate for the next budget request or the next effort to update materials or equipment. A parent may also be a potential volunteer in the library.

If your school has a parent organization such as a Parent Teacher Association or even parent booster clubs, you will want to partner with them in whole-school initiatives. They can become some of your biggest advocates. Sometimes parents will sponsor your book fair and provide volunteers to run it. They might help provide copies of books for a one-book/one-school initiative. You will want to know what their priorities are to see how you can further those interests.

An increasing number of parents are immigrants to the United States and may not be fluent in English. Consider partnering with community organizations and language teachers to provide translation services and other programs to support those parents. Helping children learn the steps to citizenship can help them help their parents. While similar services may be offered by the public library or other organizations, children can be the catalyst to start their parents considering the process.

Encourage parents to volunteer in the library and take on a variety of roles and tasks, including some of those clerical tasks that staff once did. They can help with book sales if the library holds these once a year. They can also use their skills in helping with makerspaces and in sharing their expertise when classroom content can make use of outside assistance. School librarians must remember that volunteers are not employees. The following describes their relationship with the school:

- Volunteers should be respected and valued.
- Volunteer availability may be inconsistent.
- Volunteers require training and direction.
- Volunteers should be matched with activities that spotlight their talents.

Much literature is available on the roles of parents and volunteers, especially on the role of parents as volunteers. Volunteers can be helpful, but there are a few things to keep in mind. As with any other regular visitor to a school, volunteers will most likely have to go through a background check or provide other information to gain approval for their visits. You have little control over this process or how long it takes for approval. You will need to take care to keep information about students confidential in the presence of volunteers.

A volunteer coordinator is essential to maintain the regular service of volunteers. Because they are volunteers, other important events—a sick child, an unexpected errand—will occasionally cause them to miss their scheduled time. The librarian cannot take time to make the telephone calls to get another volunteer for that day. This is more appropriately the task of a volunteer coordinator. It is almost impossible to expect volunteers to remain silent about interesting events in the library, but you must train them on student and school confidentiality matters.

Also, the librarian should be very careful not to leave a volunteer in charge of a group of students. The legal responsibility for students in most states lies with a professional who has teacher certification. A student injury while the professional is away from the library could cause much difficulty and perhaps legal action.

Volunteers, who are of great help in the library, can become excellent advocates. Communicate with your school's parent organization about volunteer needs so that they can help you to recruit. Offer to host their meetings. Set up opportunities for them to contribute to the library through gifting books, perhaps to recognize student birthdays or to honor a teacher. Resources that may be helpful in the management of volunteers are found in the Additional Resources.

Friends of the Library and Student Staff or Volunteers

School librarians may be aware of and even members of the "friends" group of the public library in their town. The national organization, United for Libraries, a division of the American Library Association, has been interested in encouraging friends of school libraries. A library friend organization may extend beyond the local parent-teacher organization in the school to include other members of the community. In some schools, these friends help with programs such as Junior Great Books; in other schools, they act in the same fundraising capacity as they do in the public library domain. More information about United for Libraries is available from ALA.

One librarian recruits his friends group from students in the school. These students are his library helpers or student assistants, for he has a very large school with a 12-month program and no clerical assistance. Student library staff can be volunteers, or they might be working in the library for course credit. If students act as volunteers, their activities should be tailored to the ages and interests of those students. Ideally, student contributions should not only support the library, but also contribute to their own learning and allow them to share and celebrate their talents while they engage in meaningful community service. If students are working in the library for credit, make sure your activities are aligned with curriculum that is related to information literacy. If your state does not have a curriculum, you will want to develop your own so that you are not having students engage in busy work. Brainstorm with your students about meaningful activities for volunteers and credit.

The Community and the Library

Keeping the community informed about the school and the school library was discussed earlier, but this is especially critical when school budgets are under scrutiny. The most important community members in relation to impact on the school district are the school board or trustees: namely, those individuals who hire the superintendent and oversee the budget, regulations, and policies applied to the school district. These persons make sure the district is meeting state guidelines, but they could add to those guidelines and requirements. For instance, the state may require a student to have one year of swimming, whereas the school board might think it more important to have two years of swimming rather than another form of physical activity.

The best way to develop a relationship with the school board is to keep them informed, and this is easier when an annual report is given of the status, activities, and achievements of school libraries with examples of learning activities and programming. If the principal invites school board members to visit the school, the school librarian can help plan the event and showcase the library as well as the activities going on in other classrooms.

School librarians should be willing to make presentations to local organizations, including service groups and churches. This allows the community to learn about school libraries and their importance in the education of students.

Included in the school library's community are any other types of libraries, whether academic or public. Though not all communities have an institution offering courses after high school, those that do should foster relationships among libraries.

Relationships with Other Types of Libraries

Libraries are ecosystems. They play different roles for our different needs at different points in our lives. We can demonstrate this for our communities. You might reach out to a local academic librarian to establish relationships on behalf of your high school students. When universities and school districts join forces, students are able to see that possibility in their lives. In fact, this begins with primary school and continues through high school, where students will understand why taking advanced placement classes in high school has a benefit when they do go to college. Introducing high school students to the community college shows them a way to continue their education while living at home, and many may take college classes while still in high school. Creating these experiences throughout the students' schooling makes finishing high school an expectation rather than school being something to leave as soon as possible.

Another benefit could be help from professors in conducting research studies, as described in chapter 6. Academic faculty in schools of education are required to research and report their findings as a part of their professional careers. They are often refused access to students in local schools because many administrators object to having students tested even more than they are with required state testing. However, they could assist in studies to analyze the value of the school library in the education of students.

The relationship between an academic community and a school district is often a less direct connection than that between the school district and the public library. Most cities have public libraries and most rural areas have some type of public library service, even if only by bookmobile.

Relationships between schools and public libraries have a long history of contact, communication, and cooperation. The length of time such cooperation continues and the degree or the depth of the relationship varies from year to year and from location to location. A public library at one time could have close communication with a school district and at another time no contact at all. In an 1876 speech, C. F. Adams, a trustee of the Quincy Public Library, noted: "Yet though the school and library stand on our main street, side by side, there is, so to speak, no bridge leading from one to the other."[6]

Adams ended his presentation with the following statement:

> I want very much indeed to see our really admirable Town
> Library become a more living element than it now is in our
> school system. . . . To enable you to do this, the trustees of the
> library have adopted a new rule, under which each of your
> schools may be made practically a branch library. The master
> can himself select and take from the library a number of
> volumes, and keep them on his desk for circulation among the
> scholars under his charge. . . . From that time, both schools and
> library would begin to do their full work together, and the last
> would become what it ought to be, the natural complement of
> the first—the People's College.[7]

Although school and public libraries complement each other, they differ in almost every area of facilities, management, clientele, and services. Schools should have their libraries located in the center of the building, accessible to all, whereas public libraries should be in the center of the greatest population movement, whether downtown or a branch. Public librarians report to a board of trustees, whereas school librarians report to their principal. The youth librarian at a public library reports to the director (another librarian), whereas the school librarian reports to the principal (an educator).

School libraries serve the students who are assigned to their attendance center; the students are a captive audience because they are sometimes sent or taken there during the teacher's contractual preparation period. In contrast, public librarians must seek out their clientele. A public library may serve a different geographic area than the school and may not be able to serve all the students attending a single school.

Librarians in schools exist to collaborate with classroom teachers to provide a learning environment and work with students to help them learn; the public library is more of a research library and community hub to serve the needs of its local clientele. Managing this relationship requires cooperation between the librarians in both settings.

You will want to share the topics and major projects and reading lists assigned at the school each year so materials can be made available to everyone who needs them—especially when the public library has a homework center in the library for those students who have both parents or other caregivers working and are not at home at the close of school. School librarians and teachers can advertise this safe location to students.

Sharing in the purchase of databases can stretch budgets when contracts allow for this type of use. Helping advertise programming at the public library, especially the summer reading program, and helping students who do not have one to get a library card prepares them to become lifelong users of the public library. Public librarians may have suggestions for joint funding proposals that could be written. Additionally, many school districts and public libraries are partnering to provide access to public library resources while using student identification information from the district.

School and public library boards often suggest combining these two entities. This is not a new idea, although many often think it is. An article by Bundy and Amey[8] describes what joint-use libraries should include and provides a list of planning success factors. It then expresses the need for evaluation and offers many suggestions for just how this evaluation should be implemented. The one evaluation that has never been confirmed is that any savings accrue with the combination. A strong resistance to the shared facility comes with the mixing of ages during the school day, which can be annoying for adults and, in some cases, has the potential for danger to students if adults are in the same areas.

School and public libraries are natural friends because they serve the same children. Among other opportunities, joint proposal writing provides a convenient mechanism for joining forces to interest a funding agency in helping to raise any required matching funds.

> No single library collection can or should attempt to meet all the needs of students in schools. Library services to students is the joint responsibility of school and public libraries with school library activities concentrating upon curriculum-oriented programs and the public library offering its wide range of reading and other varied program possibilities. Much has been done to solve the needs for materials and services for students. Much more can be accomplished if both agencies communicate and cooperate.[9]

Three divisions of the ALA—the Association of Library Services to Children, the American Association of School Librarians, and the Young Adult Library Services Association—worked together to create a *School and Public Library Collaboration Toolkit* (a link to this appears in the Additional Resources). This resource has many great ideas about building a collaborative relationship.

This chapter discussed analyzing leadership and collaboration styles so that the school librarian understands how to fulfill that role. Leading as suggested in this chapter improves the environment in the school and the community. The next part of this text covers keeping up in an ever-changing world.

Key Takeaways

- Every librarian should be a leader in their school by building relationships both within the building and in the broader community.

- You should take advantage of opportunities to provide input in hiring paraprofessional staff, additional library professional staff, or other professionals such as a technology or reading specialist.

- Relationships are the key to building trust and growing your program!

Challenges to Promote Growth

1. Discuss with school librarians how they have identified innovative solutions to issues related to any of the community stakeholders. Do you see any common themes emerging from what they share?
2. Outline a potential solution to an identified obstacle. Brainstorm how you might approach the presentation of your solution to your principal.
3. Brainstorm a list of student volunteer activities that are meaningful based on your library's needs and the needs of your students.
4. Visit the local public library and talk with the youth services librarian about the programs offered to their clientele who attend your school. What joint projects might you organize?
5. If appropriate, visit a local college library (community college) to see what resources might be available to your students and discuss their willingness to speak with high school students.
6. Complete the Compass Points activity described earlier in this chapter and determine what your direction is (North, South, East, West). For an online version of the activity to use with your own groups, use this link: https://bit.ly/3zJBpq1
7. Search the *Knowledge Quest* blog, as well as the other blogs listed on the School Library HQ Playlist in the Additional Resources, to identify strong examples of library leadership. Choose one that you feel best represents your approach to leadership or your aspirations for leadership to share with your classmates.

Notes

1. Ann M. Martin and Kathleen Riopelle Roberts. (2019). *Leadership: Strategic Thinking, Decision Making, Communication, and Relationship Building*. Chicago: American Library Association, p. xi.

2. Nancy Everhart and Melissa P. Johnston. (2016). "A Proposed Theory of School Librarian Leadership: A Meta-Ethnographic Approach." *School Library Research* 19. https://www.ala.org/aasl/sites/ala.org.aasl/files/content/aaslpubsandjournals/slr/vol19/SLR_ProposedTheory_V19.pdf

3. Pamela C. Harland. 2020. *An Investigation into the Leadership Behaviors of School Librarians: A Qualitative Study*. Plymouth State University. ProQuest Dissertations & Theses Global, Order No. 27669374. https://summit.plymouth.edu /bitstream/handle/20.500.12774/331/psu-etd-160.pdf?sequence=1&isAllowed=y. ProQuest Central

4. School Reform Initiative. (2017, March 30). *Compass Points: North, South, East, and West—An Exercise in Understanding Preferences in Group Work*. https://www .schoolreforminitiative.org/download/compass-points-north-south-east-and-west-an -exercise-in-understanding-preferences-in-group-work

5. Sharon Coatney and Violet Harada, eds. (2017). *The Many Faces of School Library Leadership*, 2nd ed. Santa Barbara, CA: Libraries Unlimited.

6. C. F. Adams. (1877). "The Public Library and the Public Schools." *American Library Journal* 1 (August 31): 438.

7. *Ibid.*, 441.

8. Alan Bundy and Larry Amey, "Libraries Like No Others: Evaluating the Performance and Progress of Joint Use Libraries." *Library Trends* 54 (Spring 2006): 501–518.

9. Esther B. Woolls. (1973). *Cooperative Library Services to Children in Public Libraries and Public School Systems in Selected Communities in Indiana*. PhD dissertation, Indiana University.

Part III
Keeping Up

11
Leading Through Technology

Technology will never replace great teachers, but in the hands of great teachers, it's transformational.

—George Couros

Essential Questions

- What is the role of the librarian as a technology leader in schools?
- How can school librarians integrate technology to transform teaching and learning?

From managing your online public access catalog (OPAC), likely the most expensive piece of software in your building, to integrating the best age- and curriculum-relevant databases and open educational resources (OER) into an inquiry unit, to scouting for the best apps to support instruction and student voice, to creating a dynamic virtual presence, to teaching students to negotiate truth on social media, to inspiring computational and design thinking with both high- and low-tech makerspace tools, to organizing virtual author visits and global collaborations . . . if you are a school librarian you will model the use of technology in a myriad of ways for teaching and learning.

In their role as leaders, program administrators, teachers, instructional partners, and information specialists, school librarians function as technology integration specialists, scouts, and equity warriors as they promote information, digital, news, and media literacies and celebrate stories in all their glorious emerging formats and on all their available platforms. School librarians have always been technology leaders, often first adopters of the essential platforms now regularly used in schools. This role is emphasized by national standards documents that directly connect your work to digital teaching and learning; growing thoughtful and kind digital citizens;

teaching strategies for finding, using, and sharing information; navigating the nuances of truth; collaborating beyond the walls of your buildings with a global learning community; and leveraging the tools of the time to communicate creatively and effectively.

If you are not interested in technology, school librarianship may be the wrong field for you. This chapter offers an overview of your potential roles in and opportunities for helping your learning community connect and grow.

Role of Librarians as Technology Leaders

The Competencies expressed in the American Association of School Librarians' (AASL's) Shared Foundations (Inquire, Include, Collaborate, Curate, Explore, and Engage), as well as the Domains (Think, Create, Share, and Grow), are explicitly aligned to the use of technology in a variety of Crosswalks,[1] including documents developed with International Society for Technology in Education (ISTE) Standards for Students and Educators, Future Ready Librarians, and Google CS First Curriculum. An additional Crosswalk aligns the ISTE Standards for Educators with the Future Ready Librarians Framework. When you need direction or evidence of your technology obligations to share with fellow educators and administrators, these documents not only present a road map for you, but also clarify the connections among your shared goals for digital-age learning and assert your roles in collaborative leadership.

Librarians have significant opportunities to innovate and transform uses and availability of technology. As digital scouts, librarians discover and help integrate technologies that work for the school's learning needs. They are the go-to professionals for guidance relating to intellectual property and its remix and reuse. They ensure digital access for all students. They ensure intellectual access with their digital presence, which might include choice boards and video tutorials. That access includes creating an engaging instructional web presence that is, in fact, the library's alternate front door.

A school librarian's technology expertise can encourage classroom teacher partners to take risks as they create opportunities to offer student choice and share student voice. This expertise offers opportunities to involve the entire school community in establishing authority and negotiating truth, participating in meaningful global collaborations and virtual learning events, and offering makerspace opportunities that engage students and meet curricular needs. As information and communication technology professionals, school librarians curate content and resources to inspire reading culture, facilitate inquiry, enhance creative workflow, and support technology-rich teaching. This chapter explores the many ways in which school librarians lead with technology,

During the COVID pandemic, school librarians' roles in digital learning became even clearer. As remote and hybrid learning became the norm, educators had to quickly adapt their practice to include learning management systems and video conferencing tools to supplant traditional face-to-face instruction. For many educators, the abrupt transition was a serious challenge. AASL's *Second Snapshot*[2] survey reported that 71.98% of librarians were offering technology support to learners, and more than 60% offered tech support to staff and parents. During the pandemic, AASL provided guidance for librarians in its *School Librarian Role in Pandemic Learning Conditions*.[3] That chart outlined the actions librarians should take for learning contexts ranging from face-to-face, socially distanced learning to blended (hybrid) learning, to fully online (distance) learning. In addition to their enhanced virtual presence, expanded ebook and audiobook collections, and establishment of a predominant role on schools' increasingly important learning management systems, librarians partnered with technology teams to distribute Chromebooks and lend wifi hotspots and other district-owned hardware.

Types of Technologies School Librarians Use and Integrate

This section explores some of the most popular software and applications used in school libraries. Note that before introducing any new tools, you will want to consider compliance with the Children's Online Privacy Protection Act (COPPA) for students under the age of 13 and consider whether the free tools you use collect student data.

For a list of free or inexpensive essentials for those new to edtech, see Appendix G: Desert Island App Picks. On the list are applications you will not want to go a day without. For instance, you will find yourself using Canva for any design or communication task and Wakelet for a myriad of curation tasks.

Note that many of the suggested tools have multiple affordances that facilitate their use across the categories. Just as your mobile phone is not merely a telephone, educators have discovered that a number of these tools have great flexibility beyond the original intentions of their developers.

Thinking About Software and Applications

A visit to the AASL, American Library Association (ALA), or ISTE conference exhibit floors can be an overwhelming experience in many ways, but perhaps the most exciting and confusing element is the array of edtech options available. Again, this is where your network can save the day. Librarians have been the champions of free and inexpensive software tools that can actually make a difference. Each year AASL's Best Digital Tools for Teaching and Learning review promising applications with regard to their learning qualities, congruence with our Shared Foundations, and compliance with federal privacy regulations. A number of reliable library and edtech bloggers concentrate their efforts on reviewing the best of the free tools. Your student volunteers are often happy to act as test-drivers. Additional sources of app reviews, lengthier lists of digital tools, and bloggers who regularly review apps are listed in the Additional Resources.

- School Library HQ: Apps & Digital Tools (including review sources)—https://schoollibrarynj.libguides.com/Librarians/techtools

- School Library HQ: Equity, Diversity, and Inclusion (EDI)—https://schoollibrarynj.libguides.com/Librarians/edi

- AASL Best Digital Tools for Teaching and Learning—https://www.ala.org/aasl/awards/best

- Richard Byrne's Free Technology for Teachers—https://www.freetech4teachers.com

- Monica Burns ClassTechTips—https://classtechtips.com

- Eric Curts' ControlAltAchieve—https://www.controlaltachieve.com

- Common Sense Education: EdTech Tools Search—https://www.commonsense.org/education/search
- Joyce Valenza's HyperDoc Curation Tool Petting Zoo—https://tinyurl.com/curationsituationshyperdoc
- Kristina Holzweiss crowdsource-curated two digital books:
  - *Epic eBook of Digital Tools and Apps—*https://tinyurl.com/epictoolapps
  - *A Digital Librarian's Survival Toolkit—*https://tinyurl.com/digitallibtoolkit

Software and their applications are major challenges to school librarians. Choosing from the vast array of digital tools available is inextricably linked with the need to teach students and remind teachers of the rights of those who produce these items and their ownership of intellectual property.

Intellectual Property

As an information professional, you will be the go-to person for instruction and guidance relating to effective and ethical use of intellectual property discussed briefly in Chapter 9. In days past, librarians were gatekeepers, telling students what they could not do when using the intellectual property of others. Rather than being associated predominantly with identifying plagiarism, today's school librarians will want to teach young creators to become true digital citizens who understand how best to use the works of others in building and sharing their own creative products. They also want to encourage students to let others know how and if they want their own original work or intellectual property to be reused or remixed to contribute to and enrich our shared culture.

You will be leading your learning community in understanding the categories into which the various types of intellectual property may be sorted. "Copyright and Creativity" was developed by three school librarians: Brittany Fleming, Julie Jamieson, and Jennifer Roth (see the Additional Resources for a link). Named an AASL Best Digital Tool for Teaching and Learning for 2022, "Copyright and Creativity" offers a suite of content for use across grade levels, including lesson plans, learning videos, visual aids, and a professional development course, all positively focused on how copyright and fair use work together to encourage creativity.

School librarians should be fairly familiar with the concept of copyright and respect for intellectual property. Principles relating to respect for digital authorship and creation are prevalent across national standards documents. For instance, the AASL National School Library Standards describe several relevant key competencies under the Shared Foundation, Engage: "Demonstrate safe, legal, and ethical creating and sharing of knowledge products independently while engaging in a community of practice and an interconnected world."[4]

Intellectual property can be sorted into a variety of categories with regard to the discovery, use, and remix of the creative work of others, and affect how students and teachers might choose to share their own creative work. These categories include copyright, Creative Commons licenses, public domain, and fair use.

Copyright

As discussed in chapter 9, copyright protects the rights of creators to display, reproduce, transmit, or modify their own work. However, copyright was not designed only to protect owners' rights. Copyright law is critical as it relates to education, the arts, and culture and in its support of the spread of knowledge and innovation. The rights of creators are balanced against the rights of users by the doctrine of fair use, and are further clarified by additional types of licensing, as explained later in this chapter.

Creative Commons

As both digital content users and creators, school librarians can truly celebrate the work of the emergence of the nonprofit Creative Commons (CC) and its development of CC licensing and public domain tools. CC respects intellectual property while it recognizes the new, more open cultural landscape, and makes it easier for creators to legally and ethically share and build on each others' work while ensuring appropriate, standardized attribution.

When a work is created in any type of tangible or digital form, it is automatically protected by copyright. Although that copyright is automatically applied and assumed to exist, you and your students as creators have every right to attach an additional CC license to your original creations. By doing so, the creator lets the community know whether and/or how the creator wants a work reused and remixed. A Creative Commons License Chooser guides that decision-making and generates a label to paste on or embed in the work. Links for the CC website and the Chooser appear in the Additional Resources.

BY Ⓘ Attribution: Credit must be given or attributed to the creator and any derivative works.

NC Ⓢ Noncommercial: Others may copy, distribute, display or perform the work for noncommercial purposes only.

ND ⊜ No Derivative Works: Others may use the work verbatim, but no derivatives or adaptations of the work are permitted

SA Ⓢ Share Alike: Adaptations must be shared under a license identical to the license governing the original work.

Six different license types combine the above-listed conditions. For instance, the license below, CC BY-NC-ND allows reusers to copy and distribute the content in any medium or format in unadapted form, for noncommercial purposes only, and only if attribution is given to the creator.

Creative Common Labels.

BY/NC/ND/SA and BY-NC-ND logos with text from https://creativecommons.org/licenses/

Because the CC licenses let you know explicitly how creators wish their work to be shared, no permission is necessary to reuse such work as long as licensing is noted and respected. Attribution or credit is required by most CC licenses.

Students need to understand the easily recognizable icons that represent the license options that are attached to images, songs, and other media. CC-licensed content is not always free for all uses. For instance, you would not be allowed to add a drum track to a song, recolor an image, or remix a video with a No Derivative Works license.

Creative Common Label for Public Domain.

https://creativecommons.org/licenses/

Two types of licensing are identified with CC0 licenses. *Public domain content* includes government content never covered by copyright and material for which copyright has expired. While not all content in the public domain is clearly labeled, the Public Domain mark (frequently used by museums, libraries, government agencies, and cultural heritage institutions) identifies creative works no longer restricted by copyright, making them more easily discoverable. You may use these materials without asking permission, but you should always use them with any identifiable attribution.

Creative Common Label for No Rights Reserved.

https://creativecommons.org/licenses/

CC0 offers creators the opportunity to waive their copyright and share their work in the most liberal way. The *CC0 No Rights Reserved license* allows creators—for instance, scientists and educators—to share their work without requiring attribution, thereby encouraging others to freely reuse or remix it for any purpose without copyright restriction. In other words, the creator opts out of copyright. Note that this is the *only* CC license for which no attribution is required.

CC licenses are for everyone. Your students need to know that young artists and producers have every right to make decisions and share information about how they would like or not like their own work to be shared, reused, remixed, or left alone. CC offers a license selection tool that generates a label to paste on or embed into creative work. For more information and for guidance, visit http://creativecommons.org/licenses. For help in deciding which type of license to attach to your or your students' original work, the CC's license chooser will generate a customized image to copy and paste, as well as an embed code.

A growing bounty of CC0 content, especially images, music, and video, is becoming available. Many CC0 portals are listed in the Additional Resources.

Fair Use

However fabulous CC and public domain content may be, sometimes you and your students will really need to use or share copyrighted material. Say you plan to comment on popular media or current events. For instance, you may plan to critique the portrayal of Native Americans in commercial films. You will likely want to "quote" commercial films such as *Pocahontas* and *Dances with Wolves*. If you are reviewing a book, you may want to share its cover art. You may use copyrighted content without asking permission **if** you believe that your use falls under the doctrine known as "fair use." Fair use is a little complicated, but it is important that students learn to make fair use distinctions and decisions.

In general, when you *transform* original content, *repurpose* it, and *add value* to it in your own remix, you may be able to claim the use as fair. *Fair use* is the right to use copyrighted material without permission or payment, although attribution is always necessary.

In making a fair use decision, courts consider the following guidelines:

- The purpose and character of the use.

- The nature of the copyrighted work.

- The amount or portion used.

- The effect the use has on the potential market value of the copyrighted work.

- Whether the material used was appropriate in kind and amount given the nature of the original work and the use.

- Whether the unlicensed use was transformative. Was the reuse for a purpose different from the original intent of the work, or did it repeat the work for the same intent and value?

Examples of *transformative* use include satire and parody, negative or critical commentary, positive commentary, news reporting, quoting to initiate discussion, illustration or example, and incidental use.

When unsure of whether your use might be considered fair, it is a good idea to seek permission. This can often be accomplished with an email or by identifying the handle of the content creator and starting a permission conversation on Twitter.

Opportunities for Connected Experiences, Global Connections, and Participation

School librarians are connectors. They connect their communities with content, ideas, materials, and people. Their ability to connect and synchronously interact via videoconferencing enables a multitude of powerful opportunities. Organized events such as International Dot Day and World Read Aloud Day are great starting points. Creative librarians connect authors and experts to the learning program for live classroom experiences or events, which tend to be far less costly than in-person visits. Experiences may also include live and recorded virtual field trips to museums, zoos, and cultural institutions. Live webcams can be embedded into lessons or streamed on a library screen. From poetry slams to gallery walks, to historical simulations, debates, science fairs, or biography wax museums, any class event might be enhanced with new partners. For several years, the Somewhat Virtual Book Club connected students across the country in discussions around the same book, often with surprise visits from guest authors.

With due consideration of time zones, it is possible to leverage your emerging online communities of practice to be globally connected. Never before has your world been so flat. You have opportunities to engage with global partners in inquiry relating to the shared contemporary issues represented by the United Nations' Sustainable Development Goals. Hayes Jacobs' definition of *global literacy* speaks directly to the role of school librarians as educators and information professionals. She suggests that global literacy is:

> the ability to be a fluent investigator of the world, to be able to examine different perspectives, to be able to report on and share ideas, and to take action on those ideas. Being globally literate requires learners to be able to collect meaningful information about people and places and personalize what they are learning.[5]

Immersive Reality

Virtual reality (VR) and augmented reality (AR) applications facilitate learning in a variety of ways. AR offers learners heightened versions of reality by integrating digital content into the real world and allowing participation. Both generally rely on trigger images, which when scanned on mobile devices display videos, games, simulations, and other materials and opportunities.

A growing array of VR storytelling applications now allow readers to enter a story. This is particularly powerful when used with news stories written by journalists from the *New York Times* to *CNN* to *National Geographic*. Students can travel the world, visit the moon, and go back in history. These experiences not only engage, they actually foster empathy. Immersive-reality science tools allow students to examine the human body by rotating 3-D organs and smash blocks representing elements to explore chemical reactions. For instance, Google Expeditions allow students to engage in VR field trips in the areas of history, natural history, the arts, geography, and science and technology. How about a trip to the moon in 1966, or a visit to Stonehenge, or a tour around a refugee camp, or a walk through the solar system or a tornado? Inexpensive teaching tools such as Merge Cubes, which can alternately be printed on paper and assembled, allow students using free apps on their digital devices to "hold" an ancient artifact in their hands, explore a DNA molecule, or engage in simulations such as dissecting a virtual frog. Jaime Donally's ARVRinEDU blog[6] provides excellent guidance in choosing and using immersive reality applications. Students can also use a variety of applications to create their own VR and AR.

Makerspaces

Makerspaces were discussed as part of the considerations for arranging your facility (chapter 8). You will have a variety of options as you consider the type of makerspace you may or may not want to include in your library. Your choices should connect to the learning and teaching needs you identify. Those choices might involve such low-tech opportunities as building with cardboard or LEGOs, or yarn art or upcycling fabric projects; or such higher-tech opportunities as 3-D printing, robotics, coding (perhaps introducing Hour of Code or Google's CS First program), playing with circuits, and designing computer-generated virtual reality games. See chapter 8 for Diana Rendina's "Top Ten Tips for Designing Makerspaces."

Engaging Students in Technology Leadership

Your students can be strong allies in discovering, testing, and integrating new technologies as well as in offering support to other users. Especially at the secondary level, you might gather a group of trusted, trained student volunteers to serve as a tech squad during free periods or before or after school. Some school librarians coordinate volunteer activities that resemble Best Buy's Geek Squad or Apple's Genius Bar. In addition to being ready to support others and distribute equipment, students may be very helpful in creative library projects.

Technology use is likely very natural to most of your students, including your student volunteers. You should offer them opportunities to lead and contribute. Students can curate a digital community archive and maintain the library's (actually, the school's) photo galleries. With your guidance, they can help build LibGuides or other websites, produce video tutorials and orientations, and create friendly and funny video reminders to return books at the end of the semester. Such students also support fellow students and teachers who have technology questions and help in use of loaned equipment. These activities engage students with a wide variety of talents. Volunteers can be app testers, web designers, digital photographers, videographers, and writers. Along the way, your helpers will learn much about creative digital citizenship, meeting users' needs, and collaborating to solve real-life problems. In many school libraries, students offer help designing and supporting makerspace activities. As stated earlier, their volunteer work will be training in leadership and free you to plan, advertise, schedule, and carry out digital-age instruction.

Librarians and Digital-Age Learning: Social Media and Digital Citizenship

It has never been more important for librarians to take a leadership role in digital-age instruction and ensure their influence across grade levels and content areas. In addition to using social media to share stories celebrating the learning they initiate and observe in their libraries, they model the productive use of social media platforms in creative communication and digital citizenship.

Digital literacy initiatives have become a focus of state and district efforts. While the scope of this chapter prevents going into detailed descriptions of all the possibilities for digital-age instruction, high-quality portals support this teaching and your collaborations with classroom teachers, counselors, and parents regarding this critical learning.

The areas in which librarians may lead digital-age learning across platforms include, but are by no means limited to:

- Introducing and implementing new and emerging strategies for ethical creativity and innovation

- Guiding writing across media formats—production including text, video, digital storytelling, podcasting
- Encouraging and leading student curation of reflective digital portfolios
- Supporting critical reading across multiple platforms
- Engaging in inquiry, effective searching, use and sharing of new knowledge across media platforms
- Leading news, media, and digital literacy instruction
- Negotiating truth using lateral reading strategies rather than checklists
- Avoiding filter bubbles and information echo chambers
- Understanding how algorithms influence search results and recommender systems
- Deconstructing media messages
- Constructing effective media messages
- Evaluating resources in all formats
- Respecting intellectual property and using appropriate attributions
- Encouraging the use of Creative Commons licenses to share how students' own creative work might be credited
- Promoting civic engagement and productive participation in local and global learning networks
- Empowering students to amplify their voices and work
- Managing digital footprints (especially prior to a college search)
- Respecting and understanding privacy concerns across platforms
- Encouraging kind and respectful behavior online
- Offering opportunities for coding and making and using design and computational thinking to innovatively solve authentic problems
- Modeling the selection of the best digital tools for any particular tasks
- Engaging effectively in virtual learning environments (learning management systems, virtual conference platforms, etc.)
- Understanding information privilege and recognizing that information has value and that access to information is not equitably distributed

In her book *Connected Librarians*, school librarian Nikki Robertson wrote:

> Kids need to see teachers and administrators modeling
> appropriate use of social media; they need opportunities to
> explore and practice using social media. Kids need a safe place
> to fail. The alternative is that we fail, and our students aren't
> adequately educated about social media in tangible ways.

> We send them into the real world unprepared for, and
> unprotected from, the consequences that can result from the
> misuse of social media. We doubly fail our students by denying
> them access to the amazing wealth of resources, information,
> and crucial networking that can be accessed through social
> media.[7]

Students are clearly interested in social media and their favorite platforms continually shift. A 2022 Pew Research survey[8] of 13- to 17-year-olds revealed that YouTube is the most popular platform, used by 95% of teens; followed by TikTok, used by 67%; Instagram, used by 62%; and Snapchat, used by 59%. In recent years Facebook has declined in teen popularity, dropping from 71% in 2014–2015 to use by only 32%. The report listed lesser teen use of Twitter, Twitch, WhatsApp, Reddit, and Tumblr. The research team reported that 35% of teens used at least one of these platforms or apps "almost constantly." The number of teens who say they use the Internet almost constantly has nearly doubled since 2014–2015, with Black and Hispanic teens more likely to be online than white teens. Urban teens were more likely to be constantly online than suburban and rural teens.

Discussing the opportunities for students to connect with media of all sorts, including social media, means discussing issues relating to digital citizenship. ISTE CEO Richard Culatta shared a more positive approach to digital citizenship than has been seen in many schools, one that reaches well beyond the single warning lesson designed to "inoculate" students against bad online behavior.

The skills required to thrive as a digital citizen go far beyond online safety. It includes being respectful of people with different viewpoints from our own, recognizing fact from fiction online, using technology to engage in civil action, knowing how to have the right balance of activities online and offline, and, of course, knowing how to be safe and also create safe spaces for others.[9]

A focus on "do not" mindsets and anti-cyber bullying campaigns may not be the best approach. Perhaps school librarians should teach students what it means to be good cyber friends, a practice which includes looking out for others who are not being treated respectfully online.

In a new definition of digital citizenship, ISTE, along with a wide array of respected partners (which include the National Writing Project, the National PTA, Media Education Lab, the National Constitution Center, and Google), launched the #DigCitCommit Campaign. The Five Competencies of Digital Citizenship[10] are designed to change the conversation from dos to don'ts.

In line with this more positive approach, longtime digital citizenship advocate Mike Ribble presented his now-classic "Nine Elements for Digital Citizenship":

1. Digital Access

2. Digital Commerce

3. Digital Communication and Collaboration

4. Digital Etiquette

5. Digital Fluency

6. Digital Health and Welfare

7. Digital Law

8. Digital Rights and Responsibility

9. Digital Security and Privacy[11]

For more information and a progression chart that describes Ribble's S3 Frame that describes his S3 Framework (from safe to savvy to social), see the Additional Resources. Expectations grow across the grade levels toward a more sophisticated set of skills that empowers rather than restricts young people.

The following additional resources explore how your learners can be prepared to contribute, exert a positive influence, and learn from networks while being mindful of what they share and how they use their time:

- Be Internet Awesome (Google/PearDeck Internet Safety & Citizenship Curriculum)—https://www.peardeck.com/be-internet-awesome

- Common Sense Education—https://www.commonsense.org/education

School librarians are deeply engaged in developing nuanced news, media, and digital literacy skills and dispositions with young people. Students need to deconstruct media messages, learning to recognize and understand propaganda.

One major shift in recent years has been a movement away from simple checklists or website scorecards and the artificial hoax sites which were used with students on the web 20 years ago. Binary heuristics such as demonizing Wikipedia, which plays a role in the information discovery and evaluation process, is not a solid strategy for today's information landscape. Traditional digital literacy tools and guidelines such as the Currency, Relevance, Authority, Accuracy, and Purpose (CRAAP) test simply do not work in the face of a web filled with hoaxes, deep fakes, cloaked sites, and source hackers and scammers. Staying on the site you are evaluating and reading it top to bottom, or vertically, is no longer an effective strategy. The research of the Stanford History Education Group (SHEG) reveals that professional fact checkers frequently and effectively leave the article and check its links, as well as outside sources, reading it laterally.

Evaluating on the basis of top-level domains, "About" pages, and update frequency as binary heuristics for authority are dangerous practices to promote. Believing in the inherent trustworthiness of ".orgs," noting a site's attractive design and lack of typographical errors, and celebrating the inclusion of footnotes are ineffective strategies for fact-checking.

Sometimes you just have to leave the page. All the careful reading and spotting of clues will not work when *the answer* is not on the page itself: when the page, or the image, is professionally designed to deceive. You need to use tools such as reverse image searching, triangulation, and seeking original sources.

In their curriculum for "Civic Online Reasoning," the researchers behind the Stanford History Education Group propose that students simply ask three questions prioritized by professional fact checkers when evaluating information online:

1. Who's behind the information?

2. What's the evidence?

3. What do other sources say?[12]

Additionally, students may develop the habit of using a variety of fact checkers, shared in this book's Additional Resources. They might also develop the habit of interrogating suspicious images by determining their origins and whether they have been altered or falsified. Image "authority" may be investigated using tools that allow dragging an image into a reverse Google Image Search, or using TinEye. A variety of tools and apps are emerging to identify manipulated visuals presented by deep fakes. For a list of vocabulary for news literacy, see the Additional Resources.

A full credibility/news and media literacy toolkit can be found in the Additional Resources. Here are a few favorites for engaging in digital-age learning:

- News Literacy Project (https://newslit.org)
  Engaging, standards-aligned lessons from the nonpartisan, nonprofit devoted to "helping students understand the role that credible information and free press play in their lives and in a robust democracy"

- Checkology (https://checkology.org)
  The News Literacy Project's free, engaging lessons on such subjects as news media bias, misinformation, and conspiratorial thinking

- Allsides (https://www.allsides.com)
  Balanced news coverage from all sides of the political spectrum arranged side-by-side with media bias ratings

- Civic Online Reasoning Curriculum (https://cor.stanford.edu)
  Based on the research of the Stanford History Education Group and incorporating lateral reading strategies

- Crash Course: Navigating Digital Information (https://youtu.be/L4aNmdL3Hr0)
  John Green's 10-episode video series on evaluating online information

- Crash Course: Media Literacy (https://youtu.be/sPwJ0obJya0)
  Radio show host Jay Smooth's 12-episode video course on the ability to access, analyze, evaluate, create, and act using all forms of communication

- Poynter MediaWise (https://www.poynter.org/mediawise)
  Instruction in digital media literacy and fact checking. Includes curriculum, online courses, TikTok and animated videos.

When teaching and preparing students to enter the digital literacy world, school librarians help teachers be aware of how to protect student privacy. Students must also be aware of how to protect themselves. Regulations pertaining to these matters are discussed in the next section.

Regulations Relating to Student Privacy and Safety

Among your areas of concern should be protecting student privacy and engaging students in learning about their own privacy concerns. Additional information on laws, regulations, and guidelines is shared in chapter 9.

Two federal laws apply to your efforts in selecting and using software and applications with students. The Children's Online Privacy Protection Act (COPPA)[13] places parents in control of which information is collected from their under-13-year-old children. This rule has an impact in your school or library use of commercial websites, apps, toys, digital assistants, and databases that seek to collect information without parents' consent. The Federal Trade Commission offers a helpful webpage devoted to children's privacy.[14]

Because protecting privacy and confidentiality is connected to librarians' support of intellectual freedom, you are obligated to protect users' personal data. In fact, the Library Bill of Rights declares:

> VII. All people, regardless of origin, age, background, or views, possess a right to privacy and confidentiality in their library use. Libraries should advocate for, educate about, and protect people's privacy, safeguarding all library use data, including personally identifiable information.[15]

You can find more ALA documents relating to protecting students' privacy in the Additional Resources.

The Family Educational Rights and Privacy Act (FERPA), discussed in chapter 9, protects children's education records and applies to any school that receives funding from the U.S. Department of Education.

These laws have an impact on your sharing of student circulation data. For instance, it is best to configure your OPAC to delete borrowing histories, and to share the importance of respecting student privacy with staff and volunteers. You will want to avoid recommending the use of applications that collect student data and are not COPPA-compliant. Have conversations with third-party vendors about their strategies for protecting confidentiality and privacy. These may come into play with software that monitors student reading and research habits and applications that personalize choices. Before adopting a platform, ask about what data is collected and where it is shared. Additionally, include the topic of online privacy, and such related topics as phishing, passwords, and cybersecurity, in your conversations, instruction, and programming around information literacy issues. For more information, consult the ALA-sponsored and Institute of Museums and Library Services-funded Privacy Field Guides for Libraries developed by Bonnie Tijerina, Michael Zimmer, and Erin Berman (see the Additional Resources).

Compliance with the Children's Internet Protection Act (CIPA)[16] is a requirement of E-rate funding. Schools and libraries may not receive E-rate discounts unless they certify that they have an Internet safety policy in place and that they offer protection against materials that are harmful to minors. They must also certify that they provide instruction relating to Internet safety, appropriate online behavior, and cyberbullying.

In addition to federal acts and regulations, school librarians should be aware of school- or district-level acceptable use policies (AUPs) guiding use of technology in schools, and any opt-in or opt-out policies relating to student participation in sharing media.

Models for Examining the Impact
of Technologies on Learning

As you introduce technologies, you will also need to consider how educators assess the impact of those introductions. The challenge of determining impact is that it depends on how technology is used and how its impact is measured. Two respected models address the impact of technology integration.

The Technological Pedagogical Content Knowledge (TPACK) Framework[17] describes the knowledge and practices necessary to provide the best learning experiences when incorporating technology. This Framework is the result of several researchers' efforts. The framework is illustrated by a Venn diagram with three interlocking circles representing teacher content knowledge, pedagogical knowledge, and technology knowledge. This requires that teachers take stock of their knowledge of all three areas and consider best practices as they weave these knowledges together.

The Substitution Augmentation Modification Redefinition (SAMR) model,[18] created by Reuben R. Puentadura, was designed to help teachers and librarians identify four levels of technology integration with their students. *Substitution*, for instance, is defined as the replacement of analog with digital technology (with no change in the actual work or tasks involved). Technology at the *Augmentation* level means an exchange of digital for analog, such as a teacher switching the entire class's print read-aloud with ebooks or audiobooks to their personal devices used to read and listen to individual digital stories; the devices augment the reading assignment. To reach the *Modification* level, the task is significantly redesigned. An example of this is replacing a diagram of light traveling to students with a manipulation done in an interactive computer simulation. Finally, at the *Redefinition* level, technology is used to engage learners in novel tasks. At this level, students might be assigned the task of writing a persuasive essay but encouraged to present their arguments through individually created and edited videos, a totally different response to the assignment.

Puentadura's argument is a simple one: If educators try to do exactly the same thing with technology that they did without it, they can expect the same results. Thus, for example, if a student listens to a lecture in person or sees it on a YouTube video, the amount learned is about the same. While the impact on learning is a critical consideration, teachers should not discount the value of substitution as technologies become more ubiquitous. Those applications could be labeled as *substitution*, and they may have logistical affordances beyond the impact they have on learning: for instance, their scalability, convenience, and cost-effectiveness.

Impact of Technologies on Instruction

Evidence and evaluation strategies were discussed in chapter 6. Your use of technology and the impact of your innovation strategies for integration should be documented at the local level. Many of the studies of the impact of school libraries on achievement focus on such macro measures as school-wide reading scores. While those measures are important, there are other patterns to describe and there are other stories to tell relating to impacts: learning experience by learning experience, classroom by classroom, assignment by assignment, teacher by teacher.

In your role as a technology leader, be prepared to demonstrate the ways in which the introduction and integration of technology make differences. In many cases you will be proud to show data describing use and student products that reveal improvements in work, as well as teachers' satisfaction with how technologies improve their instruction or simplify their workflow.

Digital platforms give educators more transparent and more collaborative lenses on student work and allow the ability to track growth. Using Google or Microsoft school platforms or learning management systems, you can partner with classroom teachers to watch projects grow and offer feedback, while tracking patterns of student growth. For instance, the librarian might team with a language arts colleague to see how students may have improved in their research skills over the course of a semester by using the transparent and collaborative elements of Google Docs in the teacher's Canvas shell. With the classroom teacher, you might target issues identified in early-semester writing and follow students writing persuasive essays or preparing public service announcements to examine growth relating to such skills as use of quality sources, development of a thesis, or structuring of an argument. At the end of the semester, what percentage of students met or exceeded the expectations established on the rubric?

Mindful of privacy and confidentiality, you can examine students' growth in reading and engagement with books on platforms such as Biblionasium and EPIC! as well as in your catalogs. Newer platforms such as Microsoft's Reading Progress and Reading Coach make use of artificial intelligence to offer students engaging ways to practice and improve their reading fluency while offering educators metrics on progress at the individual or classroom level.

On Curation

At this point in time, collection is not just what you buy. It's what you point to and make available. It's about the context you contribute to the content you collect. Curation is the story you tell about the resources you collect. For the librarian, whether you are working face-to-face or remotely, curation functions as your instructional voice. It is an important, visible, and tangible way to engage your community.

As you curate, you model and teach. You are inspiring your learning community to adopt a new set of tools and a new set of skills that will allow them to better organize their work flow, archive important content, create media-rich portfolios, share news, amplify events, and much more.

For curators, digital curation is a translation of traditional library practice and service. It is the school librarian's responsibility, one of many unique facets of training and experience that anticipates teaching and modeling new resources. Curation is about selection, access, organization, and equity in adding digital resources to the collection and services of the library. Librarians have always been concerned and tasked with selecting, organizing, ensuring access and equity, sense-making, adding value, instructional voice, storytelling, personalizing, and learning. School librarians curate in the lessons they create or co-create, the websites they build, the pathfinders or Guides they make available that facilitate the discovery of such resources as news, media, lessons, and the like.

During the COVID-19 pandemic, librarians upped their digital curation skills with the understanding that their work ensured equity of access to digital content for their communities. They worked to mitigate access issues relating to broadband access and restrictive password systems.

The following examples come from "Curation Situations" Wakelet, which describes the multiple ways librarians, educators, and students may choose to use curation strategies during the course of the day. (For the link to the Wakelet and a *Petting Zoo* of curation tools, see the Additional Resources.)

- *Supporting inquiry:* School librarians partner with classroom teachers to support the inquiry and workflow needs of specific learner groups for inquiry-based assessments or creative knowledge products. School librarians create topic-specific guides to support regular inquiry projects. Before building curations for any inquiry unit, check out what has already been created in the LibGuides Community.

- *Promoting reading options, highlighting titles, organizing text sets:* Pinterest boards and Wakelet and Destiny collections are fabulous vehicles for sharing new acquisitions or for digital genrefication and face-out shelving of both print and digital titles. Digital curation, using tools like Pinterest boards or Bitmoji libraries connected to online reviews, allows for the easy organization of text sets in multiple formats.

- *Presenting choice boards and learning menus:* Curate to promote student choice and menus to personalize and differentiate learning. A choice board displays options that allow students to choose from among a variety of ways to learn and communicate new knowledge.

- *Learning safaris:* Task learners with finding examples in a collaborative *safari*. Have them discover the best TED talk demonstrating a call to action, a work of art demonstrating a particular painting technique, an op-ed with a strong argument. They must offer a rationale for their choices.

- *Maintaining a mood or design board:* Redecorating your library or another part of the school? Planning a big dinner? Keeping track of clever instructional ideas? Curate them to help you keep track of your ideas visually and to have them handy when you are in need of inspiration.

- *Portfolio building and introductions:* Librarians can lead in the creation of individual, media-rich portfolios by helping faculty and students select, curate, and reflect on their work.

- *Gallery displays:* Create visual galleries of student work to promote peer feedback and present evidence of student effort. You might collect art and media with artists' statements. You might collect galleries of student memes, posters, infographics, etc. Consider using Flip video "artist statements" to add interactive AR elements to virtual or digital gallery walks.

- *Current awareness/Current events:* Keep a running collaborative collection of news for a particular discipline. Students might be responsible for posting and keeping their classmates up to date. They might also be tasked with defending their choices of important breaking news. Sharing the news live at the beginning of a class raises the level of engagement. Librarians can curate news, tweets, feeds, posts, and resources shared on social media for teachers', administrators', and students' areas of interest, perhaps in the form of a topical newsletter.[19]

Curation is prominent in the National Standards for School Librarians. The AASL Shared Foundation Curate states, "Make meaning for oneself and others by collecting, organizing, and sharing resources of personal relevance."[20] AASL offers a Toolkit called "Developing Critical Curators Seeking Diverse Perspectives." Developed by a group of 2022 ALA Emerging Leaders, this guide is based on the Shared Foundation Curate. It includes a collection of collaborative activities and web resources as well as guidance for working with learners as they practice "gathering information from diverse perspectives, evaluating and organizing their findings, and reflecting on their understanding of the information."[21]

Curation also figures prominently across ISTE's Standards, especially as it relates to promoting digital citizenship, knowledge creation, and communication. Curation is also featured in the Future Ready Librarians Framework, which identifies the school librarians' curatorial contributions, explicitly and implicitly across the Framework's seven foundational components, as a critical digital skill that librarians must collaboratively model and teach.

CURRICULUM, INSTRUCTION, AND ASSESSMENT: Curates Digital Resources Leads in the selection, integration, organization, and sharing of digital resources and tools to support transformational teaching and learning and develops the digital curation skills of others.

BUDGET AND RESOURCES: Invests Strategically in Digital Resources Leverages an understanding of school and community needs to identify and invest in digital resources such as books and ebooks to support student learning.

ROBUST INFRASTRUCTURE: Ensures Equitable Digital Access Provides and advocates for equitable access to collection tools using digital resources, programming, and services in support of the school district's strategic vision.

LITERACY: Inspires and Supports the Reading Lives of Both Students and Teachers Creates inclusive collections that acknowledge and celebrate diverse experiences and provide instructional opportunities to empower learners as effective users and creators of information and ideas.

COMMUNITY PARTNERSHIPS: Cultivates Community Partnerships Cultivates partnerships within the school and local community (including families and caregivers, nonprofit organizations, government agencies, public and higher education libraries, businesses) to promote engagement and a community of readers.

COLLABORATIVE LEADERSHIP: Leads Beyond the Library Participates in setting the school district's vision and strategic plan for digital learning and fosters a culture of collaboration and innovation to empower teachers and learners.[22]

Curation in the selection, access, organization, and equity for adding digital resources to the collection and services of the library is especially evident in the addition of subscription databases. The cost of access to databases can be a major part of any library budget.

Curation and Subscription Databases

Digital curation involves ensuring access to the databases in which districts and states have made substantial investments. These databases provide such content as newspapers, magazines, videos, ebooks, audiobooks, reference materials, and more. This high-quality curricular content would largely go wasted without the links and guides that librarians create in their own spaces and embed in the spaces of their classroom teacher partners, and often in their schools' learning management systems. The poster shown in Figure 11-1 offers rationale for students to connect with the digital content in subscription databases.

As a librarian, you will examine the databases already selected by your state or consortia and ensure that they are accessible in barrier-free ways. Some state purchases include geolocation access, which means that passwords are not needed for access within the state. With Internet Protocol (IP) authentication, your network administrator will help you ensure that students can access databases when in the library. Often you will need to design solutions for mitigating a password jumble when students access content outside the building. The free MackinVia application[23] is one solution that will allow students to access all digital content in your collection with a single login.

Collection building was discussed more thoroughly in chapter 9, but you will want to offer your students access to subscription databases that provide ebook and audiobook platforms, newspapers, magazines, reference content, media, and more. You will need to make sure the content aligns with the curriculum. As you make decisions, consider overlap. What do your state or local consortia already purchase?

You will likely need to defend subscription database purchases, offering solid arguments for the investment and actively encouraging their use by students and teachers. Move beyond by embedding them directly into instruction, assessments, learning management systems, and your own website. Before making a purchase, ask your vendor representative for trials that you can strategically share with teachers and students at the point in the semester when they might be most welcomed.

If budget allows, and when you develop a substantial digital collection of resources, you might consider a *discovery* interface. This strategy is common in university libraries and increasingly in high schools. Available as an add-on through several of the database aggregators, *discovery* allows a speedy, brand-agnostic search across all the library's digital content, including the option of including all materials in the OPAC.

Moving from curating databases, your next challenge will be curating OER. This can open a huge number of resources for your students and teachers at no cost.

Curating OER

Another digital movement to celebrate, curate, and share with your faculty is the growing bounty of OER. OER represents part of the larger open movement that includes open access, open science, open data, and open-source software. It is your responsibility to take the lead in making sense of these resources that could make a difference in teaching, learning, access, and equity in our schools. You need to ensure that your classroom teacher partners can effectively search for and integrate the content and tools they need.

The development of OER is guided by the principle that high-quality educational materials should be freely available to every student and every

Figure 11-1. Top Reasons to Use Subscription Databases.

With permission from Joyce Kasman Valenza and Brenda Boyer.

educator. True OER materials either reside in the public domain or are released under a license that allows free use, reuse, modification, and sharing with others. Creative Commons (CC) explains the 5R activities associated with OER:

- Retain: make, own, and control a copy of the resource
- Reuse: use your original, revised, or remixed copy of the resource publicly
- Revise: edit, adapt, and modify your copy of the resource
- Remix: combine your original or revised copy of the resource with other existing material to create something new
- Redistribute: share copies of your original, revised, or remixed copy of the resource with others[24]

OER includes lessons, units, primary sources, videos, interactive simulations, public-domain content, learning objects, open-access books, textbooks, assessments, worksheets, and full courses. Educators can now search a growing number of portals that contain material labeled OER. True OER resources are free to use and released in the public domain with an open license that allows no-cost use and promotes adaptation, customization, and redistribution to meet local curricular needs and to facilitate creative collaboration with colleagues. Librarians and classroom teachers and many other educators use CC licenses in their production of OER. At the university level in particular, librarians have been among the strongest advocates for OER and open access to materials for study and research.

The opportunity, especially for schools and school libraries with small or no budgets, is to leverage this free content to promote access and equity, to create new user-friendly collections, and to embed the best into instruction school-wide. Among the questions to ask are the following:

- How will you make the bounty of emerging search portals themselves discoverable?
- How will you select and curate instructional content to adapt and add local instructional value?
- How will you ensure that your valuable existing purchases will be utilized along with the free content? Will you select and add this content to your OPAC?
- How will you work with teachers to understand the Creative Commons licensing behind the resources?
- How will you build meaningful inquiry around these resources?
- As a librarian and an educator, how might you build and collaborate and contribute to OER portals?

Among the most popular of the portals are:

- OER Commons—https://www.oercommons.org
- CK12 Free Online Textbooks, Flashcards, Adaptive Practice, Real World Examples, Simulations (ck12.org)—https://www.ck12.org/teacher

- Curriki—https://www.curriki.org
- Digital Public Library of America—https://dp.la
- National Science Digital Library—https://nsdl.oercommons.org
- MERLOT—https://www.merlot.org
- OER Project (history courses for grades 6 through 10)—https://www
  .oerproject.com

The following academic OER portals may be useful for high school, independent learning, and professional development:

- OASIS (Openly Available Sources Integrated Search)—https://oasis.geneseo.edu
- Open Textbook Library—https://open.umn.edu/opentextbooks
- Pressbooks Directory—https://pressbooks.directory

A lengthy list of OER portals, and other instructional portals worth searching and curating, is shared in the Additional Resources of this book.

Curating Your Library's Virtual Presence

The COVID-19 pandemic clearly demonstrated the power of a unified virtual presence. School communities expected access to be 24/7 and ubiquitous across platforms and devices.

Librarians worked to connect schools with homes and ensure that students had access to (in many cases newly beefed-up) book collections through a variety of ebook and audiobook platforms, including Sora and connections to Libby with their public library partners, as well as the free digital content they added to their OPACs. Librarians not only shared links to their research databases on their own virtual libraries, they also embedded those links at the points of need in the learning management systems of classroom teachers.

During the pandemic, school librarians discovered that too many library websites were more brochure than *destination*. As a new librarian, you will want your virtual library to reach well beyond a simple website listing hours, librarians' names, the catalog, and their favorite links. You will want it to be at the center of digital instruction, learning, and literacy. You will want to become a vibrant component of your school's virtual culture. You will want students to return to your spaces across all their devices. You will also want your instructional voice and the resources you share to be embedded throughout the school.

Having a rich digital presence is no longer optional. It is essential to translate practice in order to communicate with school communities and to support and inspire learning. It is also tangible, visible evidence of your practice and your impact, especially in unstable times. You can follow the plan found in the *Canadian School Libraries Journal*. Anita Brooks Kirkland issued a call to action to present library web spaces as virtual learning commons:

> We have almost universally moved beyond understanding the physical space of the library as an information warehouse—a place where we go to find information and then leave. We understand the physical space of the library as a learning hub,

and so we must design virtual spaces that, yes, facilitate access to resources, but also facilitate access to learning experiences and teaching expertise. The virtual space is flexible, far-reaching and dynamic. It extends the reach of the library into classrooms, students' homes, and extended communities. It complements and enhances learning in the physical space of the library and the school. The virtual library space has never been more essential, and now is the time to leverage the pandemic tipping point to make it a universal part of the library learning commons.[25]

Sometimes it is truly worthwhile to invest money in a product that is designed to do the intended job. Although free products such as Google Sites make fine generic websites, LibGuides offers affordances that address library-specific needs, such as embedding catalog boxes and search tools and allowing important content to be conveniently shared across your network of Guides. Consider that your dentist uses dedicated professional software designed for their practice. Professionals outside of education rarely rely on applications that have been forced to address needs that those applications were never designed for. However, others have done this quite successfully by just beginning the process.

Over the course of 20 years, one of this book's authors maintained a virtual library, migrating it from an HTML website built from scratch (based on a hyperlink image map designed by her daughter in 1996) to a network of hundreds of Wikispace wikis with a representation of her front doors, and then to an even more complicated network of daisy-chained LibGuides (Figure 11-2).

Figure 11-2. Springfield Township High School Virtual Library (2006).

With permission from Joyce Valenza.

These personalized Guides welcomed multiple interactive embedded platforms as they emerged. Their development engaged the talents of a number of generous high school students. The website in turn was linked to teachers' pages and across the school's learning management system.

From the data collected, it was obvious that the interfaces were heavily used at all hours of the day on all days of the week. Students reported that they related to the familiar metaphor presented by each representation, they knew where everything was, and they knew it was designed for them.

The important thing about your virtual presence is getting started. Control of your site is critical. Ideally, you choose your own platform and maintain your own site. Avoid relying on a technology director to add links to your site. The goal is to give the school or district the link to the site you yourself maintain. You can choose among a variety of platforms:

- LibGuides: the industry standard, which is designed for library content, reasonably priced for districts, and supported by a generous sharing community. http://community.libguides.com

- Google Sites: free and flexible; an especially good choice if your school is already invested in Google For Education and Google Classroom.

- Google Slides: frequently used with Bitmoji scenes.

- Buncee: also frequently used with Bitmoji library scenes.

- Blogging platforms such as WordPress.

- Free web-building tools such as Wix and Weebly.

- Your OPAC, using its standard homepage as a landing page to present the full range of virtual library resources that may extend beyond catalog content.

Your digital front door should be attractive and it should allow you to:

- Share and scale your resources

- Ensure the return on investment (ROI) for your purchases.

- Leverage a growing number of OER.

- Promote collaborative efforts and highlight the work of your classroom teacher partners.

- Share the library as part of the school culture through image galleries, video channels, and social media feeds.

- Ensure that learners have immediate access to the quality resources your learning community values.

- Promote books in all their delightful varieties.

- Share resources with teachers and archive everyone's professional development experiences.

- Create dashboards of apps to support a variety of creative tasks.

- Present your instructional voice and represent yourself as an educator and information professional across the school and the community and across devices.

As a second "front door" for your library and the representation of your virtual instructional presence, your digital space can become a center for engagement. Whichever application you select for your landing page, you should be able to link to or embed additional curations on a variety of platforms that accommodate a variety of media. Appendix I offers advice on how to make your library website a true destination for your stakeholders, as well as a support for your own personal knowledge management.

Some wide-scale efforts offer models for curating your library's virtual presence. For instance, Rhode Island's RILINK offers subscriptions to the LibGuides platform for school libraries across the state and presents a variety of indexes to a vast array of content curated to support learning statewide. During the pandemic, Rutgers library and information science students and volunteer practitioners in New Jersey created a large network of LibGuides to address the needs of their multiple stakeholders. Links to these efforts can be found in the Additional Resources.

David Loertscher, whose learning commons model you read about in chapter 8, suggests the virtual learning commons (VLC) as an example of a collaborative learning environment. A VLC would appear as a website or series of websites in which teachers, other adults, and students are all learners, all interacting, contributing, solving problems, creating, communicating, and learning together through the entire school, community, country, and across the globe. Designed by graduate students at San Jose State University, this Virtual Library Guide was launched during the pandemic when few librarians could open the physical doors of their facilities.

The New York City School Library System offers its Connect, Create, Lead LibGuide for school librarians across the city schools. Useful well beyond New York City, this portal, with its many pull-down menus, offers a "Guidebook" for collection development, program administration, planning facilities, and more. It links to the New York State School Library Program Rubric and presents opportunities for professional learning. Its impressive instructional resources include alignments, lesson plans, and a rich array of assessments built around the New York State Information Fluency Continuum and Stripling's Model of Inquiry.

After creating your website and its content, the next step is to confirm its accessibility. Steps to ensure digital accessibility are discussed in the next section.

Website Accessibility Matters

Physical accessibility issues were described in chapter 8. Website accessibility must be considered as well. Students with vision issues must be able to use screen readers and may require clear and stark contrast between text and background and labeled images, maps, charts, or the provision of alternate text (alt-text). Information cues conveyed by color alone may be missed by students who are color-blind. Deaf or hard-of-hearing students will require captioning of media or transcriptions, and people whose disabilities affect their ability to grasp and use a mouse or trackpad may use voice recognition software to control their computers and other devices with verbal commands. Websites themselves should comply with accessibility codes and laws.

School librarians know that none of this matters to members of your community for whom web access itself is a barrier. Working with the technology team in your school and district, you must identify gaps relating to wifi access and hardware availability and close them. This may require working with others who are responsible for technology in the school and district.

Other Technology Staff and Possible Turf Issues

While you plan to be a technology leader, you may not be the only one who sees this as their responsibility. You will likely meet district-level technology directors and network administrators. You may have technology integrators and coaches at the district and building levels and also, perhaps, at various grade levels. In addition, you may find that some schools have technology committees. You will also discover many de facto technology leaders among the classroom teachers in your building. Build alliances. Join committees. Share your best discoveries shamelessly and vigorously. There is enough room for everyone to contribute, reflect, and share as everyone grows. Learning will be transformed.

Your role is different from the roles of those colleagues. From your vantage point, with your expanding and broad knowledge of curriculum across grade levels and content areas, and your growing responsibility for developing instruction with classroom teachers, you are central to integrating technology into the curriculum. Your expertise in discovering and selecting resources creates great opportunities for integrating technologies into inquiry projects across grade levels and curricula. You will make a big difference as a scout for those teachers who will benefit from and those who most enjoy using emerging technologies in their instruction and their projects. You will be collecting the very best instructional portals, digital content, and apps to meet and exceed busy educators' needs.

You will be working on ensuring that digital content is discovered, as well as ethically and creatively used, by curating and collaborating on lesson and unit plans and by modeling effective strategies for information workflow and communication. Do not wait to ask. Once you know of a major upcoming project, be brave enough to suggest ideas or make little unsolicited digital products. You will be connecting the entire learning community with access to books and media across platforms and formats. You may have the only makerspace in town where digital tinkering and exploration are encouraged.

Getting a Seat and Making a Difference at the Tech Table

As you begin your job, plan to ask for a meeting with the director of technology to discuss your vision and their vision for the library. Give yourself a little time to assess the situation and develop your vision before scheduling this meeting. You will do some groundwork by locating existing acceptable-use and opt-in/opt-out policies for media sharing. Ask students and teachers about what the 1:1 program looks like and how and when technology is used. Ask about favorite projects that incorporate digital tools. Ask about the quality of wifi in the schools. See if a technology survey has been conducted to assess access in students' homes. The COVID-19 pandemic may have inspired such inquiry, and if so the results will offer useful data regarding equity concerns. Do not forget to assess issues your fellow educators may have regarding access.

Most importantly, you will want to be an advocate for learners and for teaching and learning. You will likely come into contact with technology or network administrators who are reluctant to adopt or approve promising new platforms until you can demonstrate their value. When it matters, do not stop at "no." Getting to "yes" is an important skill.

To demonstrate your expertise and be a leader, you will want to volunteer for any important technology committees at both the school and district levels. You need—no, you *deserve*—a seat at those tables. As Shirley Chisholm advises, "If they don't give you a seat at the table, bring a folding chair." And once you are seated, remember to lean in.

Your work will connect you with district network administrators. Some in this position are educators as well. Though this is less frequently the case these days, some may come strictly from the business community, where they may have developed a mindset quite different from your own. It is possible that their previous business experience was in a highly controlled environment where suggestions and change were not welcomed.

In many cases, integrating free and inexpensive COPPA-compliant applications will not require permission, especially if you are at the high school level. If you are in a position where you are worried about getting permission to use new applications or introduce new technologies from the technology director or a network administrator, a few questions should help. In a very aptly titled 2014 blog post, "Somebody, somewhere, is doing the same thing you say you can't do," school administrator, author, and educational consultant George Couros identified "Four Guiding Questions for Your Instructional Technology (IT) Department" that you should be able to clearly answer and share as you approach them with an important suggestion. Those questions are:

1. What is best for students?

2. How does this improve learning?

3. If we were to do _____, what is the balance of risk vs. reward?

4. Is this serving the few or the majority?[26]

These questions ensure that you approach innovation with your mission and vision in mind and a sense that your requests are absolutely justified. In addition, connecting your requests to the National School Library Standards and other state and national documents will justify your proposals-for-adoption requests.

Once you have met those others assigned professionally to technology and other willing technology adopters in your district, you are ready to find your compatible colleagues.

Finding Your People

Congratulations! You are not only entering a school learning community, you are entering a profession that shares shamelessly and generously over state, national, and global networks. Yes, you will absolutely be discussing technology online, on social media, and (of course) in your building and district, with other librarians. These conversations are important, but these people are not your only people. Professional development is discussed further in chapter 12, but this one emphasizes the critical importance of your own development as a contributing member of online communities of practice.

As you build your networks, be careful not to become limited by echo chambers, listening to the very same voices year after year. Like gardens, networks require cultivation. Your network will include fellow school librarians, and it will also include authors, technology coaches, professors, classroom teachers, subject experts, administrators, edtech and app developers, and more. The conversations are rich and often lead to new publications, promising digital tools, blog posts sharing practical do-it-tomorrow ideas, research, upcoming webinars and conferences, and so much more.

Your ever-growing expertise in exploring how new and emerging technologies enhance learning and instruction will position you as a valuable member of the team and play a critical role in moving your school forward. You will inspire students to create and engage with your teacher-partners as you collaborate in taking calculated risks for growth. Your expertise in selecting applications and offering knowledge relating to such topics as intellectual property and remix ethics will prove invaluable.

You will need to document your successes with such outcomes as creative student projects, and reflect on and grow from any less-than-exceptional efforts. You will want to share these outcomes with your administrators. Success tends to lead to more success. When you can share improvements in learning and student engagement, you are likely to engage your administrators in supporting new purchases or endorsing the adoptions you recommend.

The school librarian is in a position to offer solutions to narrow the homework gap, ensure digital equity to provide access to information for all. It all comes down to providing students with the tools they need when they need them, especially when those students come from homes with limited access to hardware and wifi.

Keeping up with promising emerging technologies is an essential part of the job. How to remain current and lead your classroom-teacher partners in keeping up to date is the focus of chapter 12.

Key Takeaways

- As the school librarian, you are a technology leader.

- Your digital, instructional presence is a critical part of your impact on the learning community.

- Your enthusiasm for use of technology in learning will spread across your school and address serious equity issues.

Challenges to Promote Growth

1. Choose an exciting application from AASL's Best Digital Tools for Teaching and Learning from a year of your choice. List the affordances and constraints of the tool. Consider with whom you might share it and describe its potential for enhancing efforts in addressing the Shared Foundations.

2. Using a curation tool such as Wakelet or Pearltrees or Padlet, engage in a class-wide library "website safari" sharing your discoveries. Why did you select those particular library websites? In which categories are your choices strongest? What are they missing? How might you edit your favorite example of effective practice to meet the needs of students and teachers with whom you would like to work? Create an outline (or a wireframe) for the virtual library of your dreams.

Notes

1. AASL. (n.d.). "Standards Crosswalks." https://standards.aasl.org/project/crosswalks

2. AASL. (2020). "Second Snapshot of School Librarian Roles During School Closures." *Knowledge Quest* (May 5). https://knowledgequest.aasl.org/second-snapshot-of-school-librarian-roles-during-school-closures

3. AASL. (2020, July 13). "School Librarian Role in Pandemic Learning Conditions." http://www.ala.org/aasl/sites/ala.org.aasl/files/content/advocacy/SchoolLibrarianRolePandemicChart_200713.pdf

4. American Association of School Librarians. (2018). "AASL Standards Framework for Learners." https://standards.aasl.org/wp-content/uploads/2017/11/AASL-Standards-Framework-for-Learners-pamphlet.pdf

5. Heidi Hayes Jacobs. (2014). "Mastering Global Literacy." *The Brainwaves Video Anthology* (March 3). https://youtu.be/S3Hhd8K6KM4

6. Augmented, Virtual + Mixed Reality: Immersive Technology in Education. (n.d.). https://www.arvrinedu.com

7. Nikki D. Robertson. (2017). *Connected Librarians: Tap Social Media to Enhance Professional Development and Student Learning.* Eugene, OR: International Society for Technology in Education, p. 35.

8. Emily A. Vogels, Risa Gelles-Watnick, and Navid Massarat. (2022). "Teens, Social Media and Technology 2022." *Pew Research* (10 Aug.). https://www.pewresearch.org/internet/2022/08/10/teens-social-media-and-technology-2022

9. Richard Culatta. (n.d.). "Make Digital Citizenship About the Do's, Not the Don'ts." ISTE. https://youtu.be/tZeNr1q5QTU

10. Jerry Fingal. (2021, October 12). "The 5 Competencies of Digital Citizenship." ISTE. https://www.iste.org/explore/5-competencies-digital-citizenship

11. Mike Ribble. (2017). "Digital Citizenship Progression Chart." *Digital Citizenship.* https://www.digitalcitizenship.net/dc-progression-chart.html

12. Stanford History Education Group. (n.d.). "Civic Online Reasoning [COR curriculum]." https://cor.stanford.edu/curriculum

13. Federal Trade Commission. (n.d.). "Children's Online Privacy Protection Act." https://www.ftc.gov/legal-library/browse/statutes/childrens-online-privacy-protection-act

14. Federal Trade Commission. (n.d.). "Children's Privacy." https://www.ftc.gov/business-guidance/privacy-security/childrens-privacy

15. American Library Association. (1939/2019). "Library Bill of Rights." https://www.ala.org/advocacy/intfreedom/librarybill

16. Federal Communications Commission. (2019, December 30). "Children's Internet Protection Act (CIPA)." https://www.fcc.gov/consumers/guides/childrens-internet-protection-act

17. Punya Mishra and Matthew J. Koehler. (2006). "Technological Pedagogical Content Knowledge: A Framework for Teacher Knowledge." *Teachers College Record* 108, no. 6: 1017–1054; L. S. Shulman. (1987). "Knowledge and Teaching: Foundations of the New Reform." *Harvard Educational Review* 57, no. 1: 1–22.

18. Ruben R. Puentadura. (2014). "SAMR: An Applied Introduction." http://www.hippasus.com/rrpweblog/archives/2014/01/31/SAMRAnAppliedIntroduction.pdf

19. Joyce Valenza. (n.d. "Curation Situations." https://tinyurl.com /curationtaxonomy

20. AASL. (n.d.). "Shared Foundation: Curate." https://standards.aasl.org/curate

21. AASL. (n.d.). "Developing Critical Curators Seeking Diverse Perspectives." https://standards.aasl.org/project/curators

22. All4Ed. (n.d.). "Future Ready Librarians® Framework." https://all4ed.org /publication/future-ready-librarians-framework

23. MackinVIA. (n.d.). https://mackinvia.com

24. Creative Commons. (n.d.). "Open Education." https://creativecommons.org /about/program-areas/education-oer

25. Anita Brooks Kirkland. (2020). "The Virtual Library Learning Commons: Leveraging the Pandemic Tipping Point for Lasting Change." *Canadian School Libraries Journal* (June 2). https://journal.canadianschoollibraries.ca/the-virtual -library-learning-commons-leveraging-the-pandemic-tipping-point-for-lasting-change

26. George Couros. (2016). "Somebody, Somewhere, Is Doing the Same Thing You Say You Can't Do" [blog entry]. *The Principal of Change* (August 2). http:// georgecouros.ca/blog/archives/6580

12
Professional Development

If you want one year of prosperity, grow grain. If you want 10 years of prosperity, grow trees. If you want 100 years of prosperity, grow people.
—Chinese proverb

I alone cannot change the world, but I can cast a stone across the waters to create many ripples.
—Mother Teresa

If, like many others, you are concerned social media is making people and cultures shallow, I propose we teach more people how to swim and together explore the deeper end of the pool.
—Howard Rheingold

Education is what people do to you. Learning is what you do to yourself. Focus on being connected, always learning, fully aware and super present.
—Joichi Ito

Essential Questions

- Why and in what ways should school librarians engage in professional growth following their initial library and information science preparation?

- What are the potential roles of the school librarian in school-wide professional development?

The quotes that open this chapter represent the scope of this chapter's purpose: your commitment to supporting and modeling a growth mindset for those you serve, your dedication to working with fellow educators to continually make ripples, and your interest in using the tools of the time to question and explore beyond the surface. The final quote, by Joichi Ito, entrepreneur and former professor at the Massachusetts Institute of Technology Media

Lab, reflects our ability and responsibility to learn and grow beyond formal schooling.

In chapter 11, the school librarian's role as a scout and as a professional responsible for introducing and integrating new technologies for learning was presented. You will use your own connections to connect others and promote their growth as well as your own.

So, how specifically will you keep up, and how will you lead?

In some districts, professional development is a requirement. You will be encouraged to attend a certain number of professional development sessions or expected to earn a certain number of graduate credits within a prescribed amount of time to sustain a credential. This extrinsic motivation is embedded into school districts to ensure professional growth, just as lawyers must regularly enroll in continuing legal education and doctors must enroll in continuing medical education. While they may help you better understand the needs of your classroom teacher partners, you may discover that not every school- or district-wide professional in-service or staff development day truly meets your needs for growth. As a professional, you are responsible for your own professional growth.

With an information landscape that continually shifts, and platforms that regularly emerge, beyond the extrinsic requirements and demands, the school librarian should be the educator who has an intrinsic motivation to stay fresh and to infuse newly discovered ideas into practice. Innovative practice requires exposure to new ideas. If you maintain an innovator's mindset as well as a disposition to inquire, you will ask questions about your practice and press forward in the discovery of new strategies to improve teaching and learning.

This chapter explores a wide variety of ways to stay alert to potential changes in the education landscape that can influence local teaching and learning. The value of developing a personal learning network as part of a virtual community of practice will be discussed, and the ways educators share in school professional learning communities will be examined. A variety of free or low-cost online options for professional learning (both formal and informal) will be presented. Finally, your role in leading professional learning and learning in the larger school community will be described.

Personal Learning Networks (PLNs)

In the old days school librarians felt isolated. Unlike our public or academic colleagues, school librarians are often the only one of their kind in their buildings. There is no longer any excuse to feel alone. School librarians have been among the very first to connect online and via social media. Launched in 1992, the Library Media Network (LM_NET) (http://www.lm-net.info) is the world's largest listserv for school librarians and serves nearly 12,000 members globally. It is still an active discussion group and offers a helpful searchable archive.

Relying on subject headings, listservs aggregate conversations into one feed. Social media allows school librarians to choose which accounts and which hashtags to follow across a wide variety of platforms. Those choices they make build their networks. They choose how wide their networks reach, who influences their learning, and whom they choose to influence. Wherever you decide to build your network, you will be selecting people as well as the platform.

In *Personal Learning Networks: Professional Development for the Isolated School Librarian*, Mary Ann Harlan describes a PLN as "the people with whom you surround yourself, the tools you use, and the resources you rely on to introduce yourself to new ideas and best practices. It is a network that encourages learning and personal growth."[1]

Why personal? A PLN is personal because you get to shape it. Even within the same relatively narrow field (i.e., school librarianship), individuals' interests vary. The strength of our networks depends on their diversity and their reach. You will want to avoid a network that becomes an echo chamber. Echo chambers limit new ideas and suppress divergent opinions. PLNs develop over time. As you build yours, you will be exploring continually emerging relationships and honing your network for relevance and new trends and interests.

You may begin by picking a school librarian you admire. See who they follow. See who follows them and follow those who interest you. Of course, you will have many school librarian colleagues in your network, but that is just the beginning.

For many school librarians, the network reaches beyond the school library world. Follow your favorite professional associations and those publications that most interest you. One excellent professional development innovation has been the generosity of those attending conferences. Using such hashtags as #NotAtISTE or #NotatALA, attendees share events for those who could not travel or for whom travel costs are prohibitive by curating links to presentations, videos, and resources shared at events. Simply following the official hashtags of a conference at home will lead you to live updates, resources shared by those using social media to globally amplify the reach of an event.

Keep an eye out for authors, publishers, reviewers, educators, newsletters, edtech experts, administrators, and academics who regularly share goodies. These goodies can take the form of relevant research, new publications, webinars, events, news, display ideas, author visit opportunities, innovative scheduling strategies, emerging instructional portals, new databases, collaborative global opportunities, or simple ideas to implement in your library tomorrow. Remember, you are not only connecting with individual authors: you are connecting with the entire networks of any individual you add to your own network. As illustrated in Figure 12-1, pivotal nodes in your network function as connectors to other networks, feeding fresh ideas to you and your PLN in turn.

Your network is for professional development and it is also for building relationships, maintaining current awareness, and discovering opportunities. Your network need not be local. Reach beyond your state. Connect globally. For instance, participating on Twitter will likely alert you to the Future Ready Librarians Facebook Group events, or a free *School Library Journal* webinar, or an author interested in doing free virtual visits, or a new primary source resource from the Library of Congress, or a librarian in Australia looking to connect for a collaborative inquiry project. As you make these discoveries, you will want to share them with your school community. Your discoveries will inform and potentially transform the practice of the classroom teachers and administrators in your own community. You may also contribute to helping them develop their own networks. Your network can extend across a variety of social media platforms including blogs, Twitter, Facebook, Instagram, TikTok, Pinterest, Zoom, Clubhouse, and more.

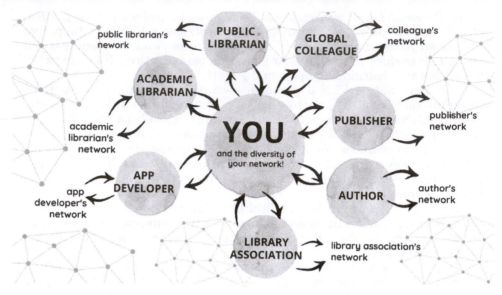

Figure 12-1. Building Your Network.

Used by permission from Joyce Valenza.

Blogs

A *blog* is a regularly updated website often focused on a particular topic. School librarians were among the earliest members of education and edtech blogger communities. Blogs are created by individuals or may be maintained by groups, associations, or publications. Some are content specific, whereas others offer regular updates or current awareness on news in education and education technology.

School Library Journal offers access to a network of bloggers[2] across a wide range of youth librarianship interests. Among the popular blogs you will find in the *SLJ* network are *Teen Librarian Toolkit*, Betsy Bird's *A Fuse 8 Production*, and the *Heavy Metal Mock Newbery* blog.

The American Association of School Librarians' (AASL's) *Knowledge Quest* blogs are written by a network of bloggers who represent practitioners, academics, authors, and leaders. Posts are organized by broad topics: Advocacy/Leadership; Collection Development; Community/Teacher Collaboration; Equity, Diversity and Inclusion; Intellectual Freedom; Makerspaces/Learning Commons; National School Library Standards; Professional Development; STEM/STEAM; Student Engagement/Teaching Models; and Technology.

The blogs you regularly read become elements of your PLN. Consider their variety and reach as well. You will likely want to include the blogs of authors, publishers, database vendors, classroom teachers, academics, edtech experts, and others in your network.

While you may often visit these or the many other individual blogs that speak to you, blogs and traditional columns and other regularly published content have RSS feeds that alert users to updates and can be embedded or subscribed to for a constant flow of resources and professional ideas. RSS embed code can be added to your own blogs or websites. Tools such as Feed Reader[3] will allow you to scan updates from all your favorite blogs in one visit. In other words, you will *push* rather than *pull* content.

Reading the blogs of other professionals who speak your language is a solid and substantial form of professional development. However, writing your own blog is not only an excellent way to share your knowledge with others and contribute to professional knowledge and growth, it is also a way to reflect on and curate your own practice. The journal you create becomes evidence of your efforts and your role in change and allows you to share tangible evidence of your learning and experiences with others. If you are proud of what you present, you can amplify your discoveries on social media. You will find a playlist of bloggers and other social media contributors in the Additional Resources.

Podcasts

The podcast arena is enjoying a resurgence. Podcasts can be discovered on a variety of podcast indexes, and some are embedded in blogs. Among the greatest benefits of podcast learning is that the format is accessible across devices and is multitasker-friendly. Podcasts can be listened to hands-free, during a commute or while making dinner. You can boost the speed a bit to get even more listening punch for your time. Again, you have opportunities to build a diverse network of *listens*. For instance, you might include Travis Jonken's *The Yarn*, a behind-the-scenes peek at children's literature, or Amy Hermon's *School Librarians United* interviewing practitioners about issues and challenges in the field, or Shannon McClintock Miller's *Leading from the Library Podcast* for Future Ready Schools, or *American Libraries' Dewey Decibel Podcast*. You might choose to reach beyond the library for practical pedagogical tips from the *10 Minute Teacher Podcast* with Cool Cat Teacher Vicki Davis or *The Cult of Pedagogy Podcast* with Jennifer Gonzalez. (Some podcasters offer certificates of attendance for their broadcasts.)

Twitter

A large number of librarians who were very early adopters use Twitter for professional connections and support. Launched in 2006, Twitter is a microblogging and social media platform. As of the time of this writing, Twitter is undergoing a shift in ownership and potentially a shift in culture. Nevertheless, it has been critical in solidifying networks across the worlds of librarianship and educational technology.

Hashtags make the platform rich for discovery. It is fine to test the waters. In fact, you do not need to join most networks to search them. On Twitter, begin with a few searches using http://search.twitter.com. You may start your explorations by searching or following #tlchat, #istelib, or #futurereadylibs. Scan the posts of some persons you admire. Search the feeds of a few promising hashtags. You may choose to use hashtags to search a focused area of interest: for instance, #graphicnovels or #ReadGraphic or #newcomicwednesday. You will find that common hashtags work across many of the social media networks. You will discover hashtags well worth sharing with your classroom teacher colleagues to support their professional interests. For instance, your English Language Learner colleagues would likely want to follow such hashtags as #ELT, #TESOL, #TEFL, #ESL, #learnEnglish, and #CLIL.

As you build your own PLN on Twitter, you will discover that related professions have strong networks as well. School administrators' networks engage leaders in sharing with each other and point to relevant news, trends, and regulations that affect the world of education and help them make decisions. If your administrators are not yet connected, you might be able to funnel this news to them or help them build their own networks.

One excellent professional development innovation has been the generosity of those attending live events, webinars, and conferences. Using event hashtags, attendees share with those who could not travel or for whom travel costs are prohibitive by curating links to presentations, videos, and resources shared at events. Simply following the official hashtags of a live event at home will lead you to updates, resources shared by those using social media to globally amplify the reach of an event. Should Twitter become an important part of your network, a tool such as TweetDeck will help you organize your feeds into a customizable dashboard for easy scanning. While Twitter has been professionally important for school librarians, it is important to be nimble. Librarians need to be and build networks where their colleagues and communities live, play, and work. This may require occasional platform migrations.

Facebook

School librarians and other educators have a significant presence on Facebook. You can follow colleagues, associations, publishers, and vendors for news, events, and occasional giveaways. You may want to follow such Facebook pages as

- *School Library Journal*
- HarperKids Books
- American Library Association
- Smithsonian
- NYPL

or you may want to join professionally relevant Facebook Groups. A large part of the professional action happens in Facebook Groups. If a group is not public, you will need to ask to join it by answering a few questions demonstrating your professional connection to the particular group. Among the groups you might choose are:

- School Librarians
- Bitmoji Craze for Educators
- Future Ready Librarians
- Learning Librarians
- Elementary Library Exchange
- Fellowship of High School Librarians
- Hyperdocs
- Nerdy Book Club

YouTube

YouTube is another excellent resource for professional development resources. For instance, many school library database vendors present full suites of tutorials on the platform. If you are new to the Destiny Catalog,

Follett Learning offers training videos as well as author interviews and first-chapter reads.

Librarians use YouTube as both consumers and producers. You can organize the tutorials you make and those you curate into embeddable learning playlists for students and colleagues. You will find collections of book trailers, author talks, read-alouds, storytimes, finger plays, and tutorials of all sorts made by other librarians, all of which you might embed to share with your own community.

Visual Social Media Curation Platforms

Pinterest

Visual networks offer inspiration. Launched in 2010 as an image-sharing and social media platform, users on Pinterest create pinboards to highlight photographs, visuals, and GIFs. Pinterest continues to be a gold mine for visual library inspiration, ranging from display ideas, to book collections, to anchor charts, to design and remodeling ideas, to posters and infographics.

Instagram

Launched in 2010, Instagram is a social media application focused on sharing images and short-form videos. Librarians frequently use Instagram to share new books and displays, to promote and celebrate events, and to enhance their library's brand. Hashtag trends such as #bookface or #Book-FaceFriday create widespread fun and engagement. For inspiration, check out #librariansofinstagram, #librarylife, #library, and #bookstagram, or follow favorite publishers or libraries such as NYPL[4] or Library of Congress.[5]

TikTok

While its future is controversial because of potential global security risks, TikTok is a social media app that allows creators to share music- or media-based video shorts up to three minutes long. Although used by librarians, the heaviest TikTok users are most often teens and twenty-somethings. Dance videos featuring popular music are common. Like other social media apps, hashtags allow users to discover content, and algorithms push content to you based on your likes and previous selections. The #BookTok community offers reviews, recommendations, and book talks. Librarians also use TikTok to connect with their communities for brief tours, to creatively market services and resources, and to simply engage. Test the waters by checking out #LibraryTikTok, #LibrariansofTikTok, and #schoollibrarian.

Wakelet

Founded in 2014, the Wakelet curation platform is currently used by millions as a tool for attractively curating content, creating digital portfolios, storytelling, newsletters, and more. Librarians were early adopters and collaborators. The platform can be searched by keyword and related collections are automatically suggested. By following other Wakelet creators and through regular Wakelet events and webinars, librarians can share ideas and strategies.

Webinars

Webinars are seminars, meetings, or workshops that are presented online. Some are presented free of charge and others charge a registration fee. The COVID-19 pandemic changed the game and eased availability for professional learning, resulting in an abundance of easily accessible webinars.

You can discover webinar offerings through email announcements and social media alerts. Among the entities offering webinars are government agencies, departments of education, universities, libraries, publications, organizations and associations, application developers, vendors, and publishers. Personnel in state libraries and state departments of education may have contracted for development, and the webinars are announced to librarians within the state. Some webinar experiences provide professional development credits and offer certificates of attendance to meet school district requirements.

Workshops and Institutes

Workshops are hosted by a variety of individuals, groups, and associations. In many cases, these are now provided as hybrid or webinar experiences. When a new process is initiated in a state, the department of education may bring school librarians and other educators together to learn about the initiative. When states purchase new databases for use by all libraries in the state, attending a workshop to learn about the content and interface becomes essential for all librarians, who will then share what they learn with teachers and students at their schools. All-day workshops may be a part of a state association conference, or they may be offered by a regional state office or a regional group of librarians. Such workshops are usually offered at no cost beyond travel to the site, and present quick and easy ways to get acquainted with and network with your colleagues.

Institutes are funded by agencies such as the state department of education, museums, universities, or national agencies or associations. For instance, the Library of Congress, the National Endowment for the Arts, the U.S. Holocaust Memorial Museum, and the Smithsonian offer institutes for educators. You will discover that many of these are conveniently offered in the summer. Participants are usually asked to submit applications. These meetings are usually free for those selected to participate.

Another place to gather information is through membership in professional associations. These may be both library and education associations, and they may be local, statewide, national, and even international.

Your Local School District

Professional Learning Communities (PLCs)

The professional learning community or PLC is a building-based, professional development strategy designed to build a culture of collaboration devoted to improving learning. Teachers themselves identify, reflect on, plan, and assess solutions to local problems. This work can lead to change through the action research described in chapter 6.

For instance, a PLC addressing student writing might include the seventh-grade team, the English Language Arts (ELA) chair, and the librarian. This team would engage in collaboratively examining student work to evaluate the effects and effectiveness of the assessment, description, writing prompts, and rubrics on student success.

Educators are under exceptional pressure as schools and families recover from the impact of a long-lasting pandemic and face the challenges of inflation, political division, and social crises. School staff must address the needs of increasingly diverse populations. The everyday challenges of educating students are further complicated by the needs of various at-risk student populations: students with learning challenges, economically disadvantaged families, and an increasing number of English language learners. Whether the solutions are small or grand, educators may welcome the use of PLCs as a strategy for school improvement.

Librarians can be major contributors in the creation and supportive shared leadership of PLC efforts. They understand the values and vision of the school; they know all the teachers and how they teach, all the students and how they learn, and all curricula across grade levels. Librarians lead in developing supportive conditions in which to allow change to happen and they can dramatically support and enhance the work of PLCs by sharing relevant current research, professional journals, blogs, and social media. The school librarian may initiate the creation of PLCs to address a specific issue such as academic integrity and the effectiveness of project rubrics mentioned earlier. Librarians remind teachers of their part in collaborative teaching teams, sharing the development of unit plans, proposing experiences that could cross both grade levels and content areas.

Because school librarians represent no single grade level or subject area, they are able to take leadership roles in PLCs, guiding them to help consolidate the collective creativity of teachers and providing an active role within subgroups in the school. Librarians can organize teachers into collaborative efforts to create lessons that use as many different teachers as possible in implementing the curriculum. When the principal is busy with other matters, librarians are uniquely qualified to lead this effort as their part of the PLC.

Librarians might also introduce *protocols*, or structured processes, which are designed to foster professional dialogue and collaborative problem solving. These can be extremely valuable in facilitating productive meetings. A variety of respected web portals share protocols that are useful in leading local conversations around school improvement. Examples include the National School Reform Faculty Protocols, School Reform Initiative Protocols, and Harvard Project Zero Thinking Routine Toolbox. Protocols are also useful for leading classroom conversations. You will find links to these portals in the Additional Resources.

Planning Professional Development

School librarians plan professional development for two primary audiences: teachers and administrators. They may also plan adult learning experiences beyond the school for parent groups, often through a PTA or PTO.

Because of the time challenges they face, classroom teachers can be a difficult audience. It is important that you respect their voluntary investment of time and address their real needs in your sessions. Begin the process by making sure teachers are involved in determining the needs to be addressed and planning the activities. Evaluating what happens in the workshop informs and improves future efforts.

The second audience is your school administrative team, who need to know about any new educational regulations, movements, theories, and strategies. Keeping these educators on the cutting edge of innovation and leadership in teaching and learning builds your social capital and increases your value as a member of the team. By addressing local professional development needs, you take a step forward in partnering in one of your administrators' areas of concern.

In a collaborative environment, the school librarian will not feel totally responsible for professional development. In some schools a professional development team works with school administrators to identify needs and plan learning experiences. These learning experiences should grow out of problems perceived as significant to teachers or administrators. A needs assessment—even one as brief as an informal, anonymous survey or a casual conversation across the faculty—can help, because few teachers and even fewer administrators are eager to admit gaps in skills or knowledge. This may especially be the case with new and emerging technologies, which present opportunities for the librarian to discover and introduce the tools that will have the most impact and be most valued.

When funding is available, an outside consultant may be an excellent jolt of fresh air, even when the school librarian or another person on the school staff is competent to conduct the training. The aura and experience of a consultant may be valuable in moving your faculty forward on adoption of a new technology, curriculum, initiative, or platform. An outside presenter can help strengthen the case without appearing to be self-serving. Once a topic is chosen, one needs to begin the actual plan.

Keeping the school community aware of educational innovation is an ongoing process, not the work of a yearly presentation. This awareness can be fostered at several levels. Attractive interactive hyperlinked newsletters can be effective. Share your new discoveries in library blog posts. Target emails to specific administrators, teachers, coaches, grade levels, or content-area chairs. Go low-tech and place copies of articles in mailboxes. Ask your principal about doing regular quick presentations at faculty meetings.

Think about opening a faculty meeting with a brief introduction to a new app with an early-adopter classroom teacher partner. If your principal regularly includes a "media minute" in faculty meeting agendas, you might use this time to introduce new resources or technology tools. This type of update is easy to sustain because of the frequency with which you will likely discover new resources, new trends, and new technologies. Given more than a minute, these presentations should be engaging, participatory, and brief, offering a preview designed to draw those interested into a full session and perhaps into the library for integration with an assignment.

You might also organize an informal lunch-and-learn session, where teachers are invited to simply bring their food and drop in for a variety of technology "petting zoo" lunches. These sessions and their resources can be archived on the library website for future reference as tutorials. Again, these sessions work most effectively when early adopters collaborate by sharing examples of their use and when educators have opportunities to engage in make-and-take experiences that address immediate classroom needs.

When you have the opportunity to present professional development experiences, value the limited time of your colleagues. Plan carefully. Prepare measurable, observable learning objectives. Plan engaging interactivities. Get feedback to assess the success of your events and inform your plans for the future. Whenever possible, try to spotlight the creative efforts of your teacher partners that result from the learning.

At a higher level (generally when the librarian is a member of the professional development team), the librarian may be asked to collaborate in planning specific training days for teaching staff and to recommend presenters and consultants. Optimally, you will want to offer teachers choices. Potential presenters may be teachers within the district who have achieved success with a new strategy, faculty from schools of education in nearby colleges, or technology experts with new platforms worth integrating.

Not all experts at a task are necessarily good presenters. In fact, some may be utter duds. If the librarian has not attended a session with a particular speaker, confirming the quality of the presentation is critical. Seek the advice of your colleagues from other schools and districts: ask about the presenter's depth of knowledge and their ability to engage and maintain the interest of the intended audience. You might use tools such as LinkedIn and educator blogs for this research. Look for YouTube videos, TED Talks, slide decks from webinars and conferences, and the published writings of potential speakers to get a sense of their fit for your needs, their personality, and the strategies they use to engage audiences and convey their message.

When going beyond the school district, a stipend may be necessary for the speaker. Honoraria, travel, and a per diem for housing may be necessary if the speaker comes from a distance. High-profile speakers may require additional funding support from the district. It is often valuable to investigate cooperative ventures and share costs with nearby school districts.

Although a session is often more powerful if the presenter appears in person, interactive online presentations or webinars have become commonplace and almost seamless. During the pandemic, Zoom presentations followed by question-and-answer sessions made experts far more accessible, especially if these sessions were recorded for future reference. This cost-effective practice will likely continue as a professional development option; the librarian can play a role in organizing these as well as author and expert sessions for students.

When a training session is arranged during regularly scheduled inservice days or shorter sessions at a teachers' meeting, you will want the trainer to allow participants time for ample practice with the new skills and/or tools. Nothing is as frustrating as a presenter *explaining* the use of a technology or database or ebook platform to a large audience, and expecting those instructions to stick if no relevant and personally meaningful practice is involved. Hands-on, meaningful experiences are critical for all learners.

As mentioned earlier in this section, evaluation of the training session helps assess participants' engagement and learning and helps determine future needs. Attention should be paid to this feedback before planning additional sessions and determining whether an outside consultant should be invited back. Whatever is planned, the program must be considered with regard to its effect on the instructional program of the school. Through their effective professional development efforts, school librarians have an opportunity to reach a wider group of teachers, resulting in the expansion of services into more classrooms.

Parents, caregivers, grandparents, and other community members are a critical stakeholder group who also have needs as adult learners, especially as they support their students' learning success. Although parents are not literally involved in professional development, you can build strong advocates by volunteering to present at meetings. For instance, share essentials to support student academic inquiry, protect digital privacy and digital citizenship, and help with inquiry projects at home. You can also present strategies to mitigate language issues faced by parents new to your community. These adults should be kept up to date about potential changes within the school, as well as innovations and changes in the curriculum. Relationships should be established with these critical allies well before any emergency issues arise. Librarians can establish connections to share how assignments, research databases, helpful apps, ebooks, and more may be accessed through the school or library websites. Parent-teacher meetings, open school nights, and award events are excellent times to connect with parents, especially if these events are actually held in the library. Using students to help demonstrate what's going on in the school is always an excellent way to draw an audience to the school. It would also be an effective way to get the community to view a podcast or video about changes happening in the school. If the event is at the school, always make sure the media and/or a local politician is invited to attend. Sending notices to the media about where they can view the program may interest them in writing an article.

Professional Associations

This discussion begins with educational associations. The first two associations may have mandatory membership when the school district comes under a union contract. These are discussed not only for their role as a professional development opportunity, but as a place for librarians to work to change perceptions of their role in the school.

Education Associations and Events

Among the variety of education associations for school librarians, at the national level, educators choose to join either the National Education Association (NEA) (www.nea.org) or the American Federation of Teachers (AFT) (www.aft.org). Conferences of these associations provide speakers and sessions with new information, but they also have another purpose. Both of these national associations have state and local affiliates. School librarians may teach under contract to a local affiliate of NEA or AFT that acts as the bargaining unit. Although affiliation may not be mandatory in a local school district, it is usually an uncomfortable situation for a librarian to refuse to join fellow teachers in negotiating contracts for their units. Resentment directed at the school librarian who does not join may extend to resentment toward the library program.

When the school district has a local bargaining unit, membership in both state and national associations is required and automatic. Also, the teacher and librarian cannot join only the national association, but must join their local and state associations as well. These teachers' associations offer librarians the opportunity to attend local and state meetings and possibly become delegates to the association meetings.

Librarians who belong to their education association should work within that association to improve perceptions of the library program. When teachers, especially at the elementary level, consider the library their contractual free period, librarians may need to engage in efforts to "sell" the value of instructional partnerships. Simple solutions such as inviting two classes at once for book exchange, free reading, and book talks might open periods to work on collaborative units during class time.

If possible, a librarian should be a member of the contract unit's negotiating team to demonstrate the need for staffing the library as part of the bargaining team's negotiations. When librarians neglect this important opportunity, they risk being moved into a special category, apart from the regular teaching staff. When this happens, additional time may be assigned to the school librarian's role. For example, in one state, it was ruled that because librarians did not have student work to take home to grade, they were expected to report to school 30 minutes earlier and stay 30 minutes later than classroom teachers. School librarians need to be seen as collaborative teachers who are involved in the planning and teaching of units of instruction and the assessment of student work that is based on collaborative instructional design. When a librarian is on the negotiating team, that is much easier to convey.

The International Society for Technology in Education (ISTE) (http://www.iste.org) provides leadership and service to improve teaching and learning by advancing the effective use of technology in K–12 education and teacher education. It boasts a worldwide membership of leaders and potential leaders in educational technology. ISTE schedules a major conference that traditionally runs in June around the same time as the American Library Association (ALA) annual meeting. Many school librarians are active ISTE members and conference goers and thus are often forced to choose between the two events. The ISTE educational technology event is one of the biggest such events in the world. School librarians participate in one of the largest *playgrounds* of the conference. Many ISTE presenters come from the school library ranks. Attending ISTE is an excellent way to discover new products, promising trends, and how other educators are effectively integrating technology in schools.

The SXSW EDU Conference and Festival (https://www.sxswedu) is an exceptionally exciting event hosted in Austin, Texas, before the SXSW conference begins. The annual event targets all educational stakeholders, celebrates educators as rock stars, and fosters "innovation and learning within the education industry." Additional major edtech conferences include the Future of Education Technology Conference (FETC) (http://fetc.org) and Computer Using Educators (CUE) (https://cue.org).

Library Associations and Networks

School librarians who wish to meet others working in school libraries may be able to participate in a local association, which is usually an informal group. Membership is inexpensive and participation time minimal, except perhaps for the officers. If you are in a pre-service program, a special student membership rate is often available.

Participation in your state association provides an excellent opportunity to build leadership skills, even when you are still a library and information science student. At the state level, it is often easy to become active in committee work and present at the annual meeting. In fact, in larger states, these conferences often include regional meetings where you can network with leaders who are located in your neighborhoods. Your instructors and professors may be able to help you—and in fact may strongly encourage you—to connect.

The American Library Association (https://www.ala.org) represents all types of librarians, information professionals, and trustees of public libraries. The American Association of School Librarians (https://www.aasl.org) is a division of ALA, and members of AASL receive the benefits of ALA membership, including a lobbying effort in Washington, DC. AASL maintains a directory of state and regional associations.[6] An ALA annual meeting is held each year and a midwinter event, now called LibLearnX, is offered to emphasize active and applied learning and networking opportunities for library professionals.

ALA Annual offers not only meetings of executive boards of divisions and their committees but also speakers, preconference workshops, exciting meal functions such as the Newbery/Caldecott dinner, the Coretta Scott King Breakfast, and a vast array of exhibits. A number of library-affiliated groups gather at the same time, including membership in the Black Caucus of the ALA, the American Indian Library Association, the Asian/Pacific American Librarians Association, the Chinese-American Library Association, and the membership meeting for Beta Phi Mu, the International Library Science Honor Society. You may also be invited to a variety of vendor and publisher receptions. Like most conferences, ALA offers a conference app which is helpful for planning your time in advance. In addition to sessions planned by AASL, you may also want to consider sessions offered by the Young Adult Library Services Association (YALSA) (https://www.ala.org/yalsa) and the Association for Library Service to Children (ASLC) (https://www.ala.org/alsc), among others.

In addition to the national conference of ALA, AASL hosts its own national conference every second year. This conference will connect you with your people. Planned by AASL members, all programming is directly related to school library services. Rather than plunging into a much larger ALA event, many AASL members see this conference as the best way to connect and learn at a national level. This conference also provides an opportunity for practitioners and researchers to present information on their program and research results. Exhibits and presentations are directly related to school libraries.

AASL is governed by a board of directors made up of the past president, the president, the president-elect, the secretary-treasurer, the division councilor, the Chapter Assembly representative, and three directors-at-large. Each state chapter sends representatives to serve on the Chapter Assembly.

A wide variety of committees exists for AASL members. These include the AASL Budget and Finance Committee, National Conference Committee, Awards Committee, Joint Committee on School/Public Library Cooperation (with AASL, ALSC, and YALSA), Leadership Development, Professional Learning, Standards, Best Digital Tools for Teaching and Learning. See the full current list of AASL committees at https://www.ala.org/aasl/about/coms.

The AASL Editorial Advisory Committee reviews the publication of the association journal, *Knowledge Quest*, which is published bi-monthly. Their research journal, *School Library Research*,[7] is available online. AASL also has an Advisory Group: Publications, The Editorial Boards for *Knowledge Quest*, *School Library Research*, and Social Media. When necessary, task forces are appointed by the AASL president and one member of AASL is appointed to each of the ALA Working Groups.

AASL frequently hosts Town Halls around current issues which are archived for members. The AASL Learning Library (ALL) functions as a repository of webcasts, podcasts, and other digital resources from AASL, including content from *Knowledge Quest*, *School Library Research*, and selected conference sessions.

Though not an association, the Future Ready Librarians Network (https://all4ed.org/future-ready-librarians-hub), operating as part of the national nonprofit advocacy group All4Ed, offers a Framework, built on the research-based gears of the larger Future Ready Schools Framework. The network hosts regular webinars, summits, and chats as well as a podcast.

In addition, school librarians frequently engage in the conferences and read the journals of national education associations beyond the scope of the library profession. School librarians with interests in specific subject areas may join the relevant associations to help keep the library visible to other educators. Among them are subject-area associations such as the National Council of Teachers of English (NCTE) (http://ncte.org), the International Literacy Association (formerly the International Reading Association; http://www.literacyworldwide.org), and the National Council for the Social Studies (NCSS; http://www.ncss.org).

Related organizations include the Association for Supervision and Curriculum Development (ASCD) (http://www.ascd.org). Choosing to become active in ASCD brings librarians into direct contact with superintendents, principals, and curriculum directors in school districts. Its mission statement states that ASCD is a diverse, international community of educators, forging covenants in teaching and learning for the success of all learners. The Association for Educational Communications and Technology (AECT) (https://www.aect.org), with its state and international affiliates, is a relevant choice for all educators interested in instructional design and technology integration.

International Associations

For school librarians who enjoy meeting their counterparts from other nations, two organizations are available. The International Association of School Librarianship (IASL) (https://iasl-online.org) is open to school librarians from all over the world. A graduated dues schedule allows persons from developing nations to join for a reduced fee, and members are encouraged to adopt a member from a less wealthy nation. Two scholarships are available for someone from this category to attend the annual meeting.

Members can present papers at IASL conferences and hear speakers with national and international viewpoints on education and school librarianship. Many of the social events include visits to school libraries and homes of school librarians in other countries as well as historical sites. Preconference and post-conference tours and educational experiences add to the value of membership in this association.

The governance structure of IASL includes an executive board with a president, three vice presidents, and a financial officer. The board of directors includes the executive board and six directors who represent their regions of the world. The executive secretary serves *ex officio* on both boards. IASL members receive the online research journal, *School Libraries Worldwide*, an online newsletter, an up-to-date website, and an active email list.

The School Library Section of the International Federation of Library Associations and Institutions (IFLA) (http://www.ifla.org) also provides a forum for school librarians worldwide. Because IFLA is primarily an association made up of associations (e.g., ALA and Special Libraries Association) and major research libraries (New York Public Library, Harvard University Library), fewer individuals join as personal members. Instead, they participate as voting representatives of their professional associations.

Both of these associations allow school librarians from the United States to meet and discuss library programs with professionals from around the globe. Participation in these international groups could provide opportunities for school libraries to engage in global collaborative programming and instruction. Because both associations often meet outside the United States, active membership means the librarian will travel to an international location and develop new perspectives on libraries and education issues around the world.

Certainly, more associations exist than most school librarians can hope to join. Nevertheless, choosing as many as possible and participating actively is essential to the effectiveness of the school librarian and the profession. Membership in an association exposes librarians to trends in education and librarianship and enables them to join forces with peers to influence and advocate for the continuing expansion of school library programs at local, state, and national levels on behalf of the learners we all serve.

While it is an exciting learning experience to attend a local, national, or international conference, it will not be long before you have knowledge and experiences worthy of sharing. Be alert to calls for proposals and do not be afraid to contribute by presenting what you have learned. More resources and associations and their conferences are listed in the Additional Resources.

Certifications as Professional Development Opportunities

Informal learning activities are now widely available for yourself and your community in the form of microcredentials or nondegree opportunities that acknowledge competencies. These opportunities, which are more granular than a formal degree, are valuable to discover for your own development and to share with your stakeholders. They are often free or very affordable. These activities often lead to digital badging and certificates acknowledging achievements that not only recognize growing knowledge and skills, but are also shareable on digital and traditional portfolios.

A recent trend relating to technology competencies is the involvement of software companies and platforms in professional development and the engagement of educational professionals as ambassadors for these platforms. Among the platforms widely adopted by librarians is Wakelet, a collaborative tool used for curation, portfolios, presentations, archiving conferences, and much more. The annual Wakelet Community Week, which involves an international community of educators and librarians, celebrates the multiple ways this tool can be used in education and demonstrates the power of the tool to archive all the media sharing of the event. Wakelet also offers an Student Ambassador program[8] that engages learners in valuable and relevant digital curation activities. You will find a wide variety of other informal learning opportunities for students, many of which offer microcredentials or badges. Other microcredential or informal learning programs for students are listed in the Additional Resources.

Many of these platforms encourage users to expand and push creative use and to use their tools to grow in their professional practice. Major vendors and developers offer professional development experiences and opportunities to earn certificates. Most of these opportunities are now offered online.

Among the professional development options available are certifications and badges. Educators have the opportunity to earn endorsements from a variety of digital tools and companies. Examples of certification opportunities include, but are not limited to:

- Google for Education
- Microsoft Innovative Educator

- Adobe Creative Educator
- Canvas Certified Educator
- Discovery Educator
- Wakelet Ambassador
- Flip
- Nearpod Certified Educator
- Common Sense Media Educator
- ISTE: vendor-neutral, internationally recognized credential for educators who have demonstrated mastery of the Educators section of the ISTE Standards.

Journals to Know

A number of journals are available to spur your growth as a professional school librarian. Some are paid subscriptions, some are available as part of your membership in organizations, and some (or parts of some) are freely available online. As you become more comfortable in your practice, consider going beyond simply reading to contributing. Lists of journals of interest to school librarians and other educators are shared in Appendix E and the Additional Resources.

Leading Professional Learning

School librarians have no excuse to feel alone as a single librarian in their building. You will find many ways to connect beyond your building. As a professional who models a growth mindset, you will plan your professional development and encourage professional development among all those in your learning community. It is never too early to explore opportunities and join professional learning networks.

This chapter explored the school librarian's leadership role in the organization and provision of professional development for teachers and administrators. It suggested strategies for keeping personally up-to-date as a forward-thinking professional and innovative educator. The next chapter, chapter 13, addresses advocacy and the many ways to share the role of the school librarian with the school, the school district, the local community, the state, and the nation.

Key Takeaways

- As a school librarian, you may be alone in your building, but you have a global community of colleagues to support you.
- Whether independently or as a member of a school professional development team, as a school librarian you can make an impact on school- and district-wide professional learning.

Challenges to Promote Growth

1. If you are already working or in a field experience, consider in which ways your current school supports professional growth. Reflect on whether the environment supports or rewards risk-taking, innovation, and an inquiry mindset. Which professional development needs are met? Which needs might be better met?

2. Pick an application, database, or creative inquiry activity you think would be new to most teachers and design a professional development session to teach it. Be sure to indicate the materials/equipment needed and outline how you would engagingly introduce the session, actively involve your adult learners, and assess their learning and future needs.

3. If you already have a personal learning network, share a sentence or two about how the most important contributors regularly add to your knowledge. If you do not have a PLN, create a wishlist of 10 people, associations, or publications you would most like to include.

4. Review the AASL committees found on the AASL website. Draft a letter to the current president-elect of AASL who will make new appointments and volunteer to serve on the committee of your choice. Be sure to state your qualifications for this committee as well as your desire to serve.

5. If you were to ask your school or school district to help fund your attendance at the local state school library conference, how would you ask? Which events would you most want to attend and how would you justify your attendance if asked to?

6. Scan some of the Finding Your People blogs on School Library HQ and scan relevant social media hashtags for announcements of webinars and other learning events. List at least five events you might attend over the course of the next couple of months.

7. Imagine your first professional presentation. Find a call for proposals for a state or national event and design a presentation on a topic about which you feel passionate and with which you have some experience.

8. Imagine your first post in an existing professional group blog or your first article in a publication. Where would you publish and what would you write about?

9. Choose a recent print or online periodical listed in Appendix E. If there is a "Letters to the Editor" feature, or if online articles or blog posts accept readers' comments, examine them. Choose a print or online article or a significant blog post that interests you. Draft and submit a "Letter to the Editor" or a substantive comment.

Notes

1. Mary Ann Harlan. (2009). *Personal Learning Networks: Professional Development for the Isolated School Librarian*. Westport, CT: Libraries Unlimited, p. 1.
2. *School Library Journal*. (n.d.). SLJ Blogs. https://www.slj.com/section/blogs
3. FeedReader. https://www.feedreader.com
4. The New York Public Library Instagram. https://www.instagram.com/nypl
5. Library of Congress Instagram. https://www.instagram.com/librarycongress
6. AASL Chapter Directory. https://www.ala.org/aasl/about/chapters/directory
7. AASL. *School Library Research*. https://www.ala.org/aasl/pubs/slr
8. Wakelet Student Ambassadors. https://community.wakelet.com/studentambassadors

13
Advocacy

Advocacy as disruption? Yes! What if we revolutionize the way we fund and equip our libraries in order to confront head-on the inequities that we often decry on our protest posters and in our institutional committees? What if our lowest-income neighborhoods become home to our most well-funded and well-staffed school libraries? . . . What if we connect the dots between library and community disinvestment and position our advocacy efforts to counter them both? I believe we can. What's more, I believe we must.
—Tracie D. Hall, American Library Association Executive Director

Essential Questions

- Why should school librarians pursue advocacy within the school and broader community?

- How can they enlist others to become advocates for student access to a quality library?

- What steps can librarians take to become advocates for students and school libraries with elected officials?

Advocacy is interpreted in many ways in this chapter. Deborah Levitov explains that advocacy is "a gray area for school libraries. It is frequently associated with attributes equivalent to public relations and marketing" and thus may be interpreted as "self-serving and motivated by job security."[1] It is essential that school librarians' advocacy efforts are not about the library itself, but about who they serve: the students, the teachers, and the broader community. Advocacy is about solving other people's problems.

The American Association of School Librarians' (AASL's) Advocacy Committee developed definitions for *advocacy* along with *public relations* and *marketing*. AASL defines *advocacy* as an "on-going process of building partnerships so that others will act for and with you, turning passive support into educated action for the library program."[2] In the previous edition of this text, advocacy was modeled on the methods used by businesses to market their products to potential clients. This is a more transactional approach to advocacy. As businesses and social media have evolved in our changing global environment, businesses are now focused more on engaging with potential clients. This engagement encourages a give-and-take approach to marketing. AASL also points out that public relations and marketing are different processes, and explains the difference. Public relations (PR) is a one-way communication mode to get the school librarian's message across. When engaging in PR, school librarians are notifying stakeholders who they are and what they can do. It typically involves the 5Ws and an H—Who, What, When, Where, Why, and How. Marketing is a more strategic process that includes goal setting, needs assessment, and planning to meet those needs. It is a more engaged approach to advocacy. Both PR and marketing are important advocacy tools. Advocacy itself is an ongoing process based on relationship building. It should be intentional and focused.

Each school librarian enters the profession with a perception of the role based on observations of other school librarians, and they join a teaching staff and administration who have their own perceptions of that role. Finding out what these perceptions are is very important because the answers will indicate how to begin the task of planning the year's program. School librarians must make sure their programs are recognized as vital in and to the education of students. This chapter begins with ways to change perceptions some may have of the library and its role in education. It covers ways for you to make the goals and objectives clear to a wide variety of audiences within your school, your district, and your community, and an even wider audience to support access for all in your state and your nation.

Changing Perceptions Through Public Relations

The importance of the school library program seems immediately apparent and obvious to librarians. Unfortunately, this is not an automatic reaction for all users or potential users: students, teachers, administrators, parents, or the community at large. These groups may base their perceptions on their own personal experiences, which could have been formed in previous situations (perhaps long ago) where no library existed, or it was poorly stocked and seldom open, or the librarian was not friendly. Or they may see the library as an important part of the school community because of their previous experiences. Changing negative perceptions and establishing the library as essential is an important part of our advocacy efforts so that the library and you, in your role as the school librarian, can effectively and creatively provide services to our communities.

What happens when perceptions are inaccurate? School administrators, principals, and superintendents who do not know the potential impact of a quality library program and certified school librarian may see the library budget and your position as expendable when faced with difficult decisions. This perception can spread when administrators get together to discuss potential savings in difficult budget times. However, if you have demonstrated to your administration that the students in their school have enriching, meaningful, and transformative experiences through the library, your administrator will speak up about the necessity of retaining and even strengthening support for the library. The first step is to work to enhance or change perceptions of the library and its purpose and how the librarian makes this happen. As you implement your efforts, record what you are doing and its effect, as suggested in chapter 6. Many of the results will become a part of your monthly report or newsletter to your community: principal, teachers, students, and parents. Begin with your students.

Some students start school with memories of visiting a public library for story times and choosing books from a children's room; other students have never been to a library. When they first enter their school library, they should feel that this is *their* library. They can visit this library without barriers and know that everything there is *theirs*. This begins when they open the door. Is that first impression welcoming? Do they think the library belongs to the librarian, or does it belong to them? Is the library a place for books as well as a place of activity and energy? If their library does not seem to welcome students, ask them what would help change that image. Those students will tell their parents about the friendly library and helpful librarian and staff. Teach them that *the library belongs to them*. Use available spaces to display student work and encourage students to invite their parents to the library to see their work on display. Suggest that they invite their parents to stop in to the library if they are visiting the school for any reason.

As mentioned several times before, think carefully about any potential negative messages that you might be conveying. What does your signage say? Is it all about the "don'ts" instead of the "dos"? Fines and limitations of any sort are not effective ways to advocate with your students. It is essential that your kindergarteners be able to take as many books home as they might need to build a love of reading. Charging students for overdue items does not teach responsibility and is discouraged by ALA. It penalizes students who may not use the library for fear they might forget the item and cannot afford to pay any fines. Students who see the library as their own will understand that returning materials is a way to assist fellow students and is part of their civic responsibility. Losing a few books each year is a small price to pay in exchange for developing positive relationships with students and encouraging them to read. You would rather lose a book than a reader.

Ask students at the beginning of the year if they would like to check books out for a longer time, with the understanding that they will return them if someone else requests them; this teaches responsibility not only for care of the item but also their responsibility to their classmates. Encourage students to suggest books they would like to read. Consider creating an easily accessible online form for students to submit requests. If budgets allow or through grant funding, take students to the local bookstore to select books. They should be able to use your online public access catalog (OPAC) on their mobile devices to see if the library already has a copy. Alternatively, create digital lists from which children can shop to add to the collection. Be the go-to person when information is needed for a project or when a small group needs to meet. Be the tech expert when students want to film a commercial using the green screen. If they tell their fellow students about the success they had getting support from the librarian and using resources from the library, either on the shelf or online, the numbers who come to do both will grow.

Teachers may not be aware of the resources and services that the librarian can provide to enhance their instructional practice. When teachers recognize the potential success that comes from collaborating with the librarian to improve student learning, they become advocates. Working with one teacher at a time, the librarian demonstrates the value of a program that offers the resources to have a significant impact on student learning. When school librarians plan and help conduct staff development, teachers learn about new resources and trends in education. Because of your big-picture perspective, you have the opportunity to share new tools and strategies that will enhance student learning. Developing lasting partnerships with teachers moves beyond the one-time assist and toward an integrated co-teaching landscape, one your partners will fight to preserve.

Other activities discussed in this chapter will also help you reach the wider community. Building relationships with the community not only informs them about what you and the library can provide, but also develops advocates for the school library as an essential part of education. Community members may also be available to volunteer in the school, or they may bring expertise to a subject or topic that would increase the students' understanding.

Another group within the community includes librarians in academic and public libraries. These professionals can be allies when you face intellectual freedom challenges, in sharing resources, in their willingness to invite students to their libraries for any number of reasons, and for their support in explaining the role of libraries in the lives of students before and after basic education.

Marketing

Marketing is used by businesses for models to build a public relations program. According to Philip Kotler, *marketing* is the "purposeful coalescence of people, materials and facilities seeking to accomplish some purpose."[3] Though dated, the definition remains accurate. Translate this into the purposeful coalescence of teachers and librarians seeking to prepare students for adult society. The librarian, the library staff, and the advisory committee plan both the services and how to promote those services by partnering with teachers so that students move to the next level well prepared. Teachers, in turn, join with the librarian and staff to determine needs, develop services and resources, and then promote those available resources and information to students. These efforts market the library's positive image so as to gain budget support for increasing services to administrators, parents, and the community . . . and the cycle continues. The success of such a marketing campaign is confirmed when teachers begin co-teaching with the librarian and when joint curriculum planning is commonplace.

Marketing requires paying attention to the ambiance of the library, both physically and virtually, so it is attractive to both teachers and students. Teachers and students are asked what is needed to make the library, its website, and its social media presence more welcoming, interesting, inclusive, and attractive. Social media discussions and postings should be kept up to date, and good signage in the library will allow users to locate things easily.

The librarian must consider three facets of marketing: public relations, dissemination of information, and development of services to meet needs based on needs assessment. The first, a public relations program for the library, is centered on the person in charge and how that person and the staff are perceived.

A basic problem for marketing concerns personnel, and this problem is not unique to education or libraries. School library staff—both personally and through the programs and information services they offer—must project a positive, energetic, and helpful image to all the students and adults in the building, from kindergarten through high school, including custodians, clerical staff, cafeteria workers, bus drivers, teachers, administrators, and parents. You represent the library world to the stakeholders you serve, particularly if those stakeholders make little or no use of any other information agency. How you act is the model for the community showing how all librarians (school, public, and academic) will act, and this is a large legacy to hand down to students before they enter adulthood.

One aspect of public relations is to demonstrate the value of the library and its services. This includes providing access to information for all users and helping them learn how to find, assess, and use information independently. In the age of virtual information, you will make sure your student users understand how to find that information, assess the value of that information, and apply that information to meet their needs. Your library should be a place that supports student creativity, communication, critical thinking, and exploration. To make this happen, you will need to include information on educational trends, new teaching methodologies, and applications of newer technologies that are of potential interest to teachers and administrators. Post events, new services, and activities on the communication avenues that your patrons are using. Be active on the social media that students are using, such as SnapChat, TikTok, and Instagram. If parents are using Facebook, maintain a Facebook page to get the word out to the community.

The process of developing services based on needs assessment is another facet of the marketing process. Obviously, the services you offer should reflect services that users deem necessary. You must consult both teachers and students to determine what services they need. Solicit input from your advisory committee and all of your stakeholders to identify needs in your school and then engage in developing services to meet those needs. This will help bring users to the library to use the services—another component of the marketing process. When you initiate partnerships with teachers around instruction and participate in implementation and assessment, you will find teachers more eager to work with you. Leading the involvement of as many teachers as possible in this process, particularly including those who might not previously have been library users, will expand collaboration exponentially.

When students are welcomed in the library and see it as a space that supports not just their academic success but also their personal interests, they will come and return often. Encouraging them to use the library and its resources for working with their classmates, exploring potential hobbies, discovering new tech tools, and developing their individual interests will lead to a bustling and exciting place that students want to visit regularly.

What to Market

"Marketing in the firm begins and ends with the customers."[4] To determine what to market, an organization chooses which of its desirable assets it wishes to place for "trade." Your Advisory Committee begins the process of helping determine which assets are most important to your customers: school library users. The primary commodity for most library programs is its services and its access to information for all. The secondary commodities are the resources available either in-house or online. Plans should be developed to market the following:

1. Those services that have been determined to be priorities by the majority of users. These are the services that must be provided because they are the most often requested.

2. New services to be offered because one or more teachers or students have requested them; the need exists as pointed out in the research or through observation. Once new services are selected to be offered, it is important that teachers and students learn of their existence and that training in their use be provided when necessary.

3. Services that are provided but are not requested because teachers or students are not aware of them should be assessed for importance. Advertising these services should draw or develop a pool of potential users; if not, they should be discontinued or removed.

4. New materials, digital resources, and equipment added to the collection and their availability both within the school and outside the school building.

5. Special collections made available for teachers and students.

6. Activities being held in the library that would be important to parents as well as teachers and students, such as speakers, visiting (both in person and virtual) authors and illustrators, and visiting city and state government officials, among others.

Once you have chosen which services to market, you must decide what methods will be most effective to carry out the marketing process.

How to Market

A marketing program is ongoing. Data should be available to respond to inquiries from parents, community members, teachers, and administrators. To be prepared to market your program, you need to gather general information so that you can quickly share it as needed. General information on the library program should include statistics about the physical library: its size, amount of seating, numbers of volumes, media and databases, budget, amount of use by class and individuals, and types of uses (e.g., storytelling, viewing, research, online searching). Output measures such as usage of databases, numbers of collaborative units, or topics (by name) should be included, as well as interesting input measures such as the number of new resources purchased each year and the average cost of each, from books through databases and hardware. You will want to gather photos of your library and have examples of successful programs and activities to use in your marketing materials.

The evidence of the value of the school library in the lives of students and teachers must be constant and well documented from the first day of school throughout the school year. School librarians seem to be asking each other constantly about ways to show this value; in fact, this was a question answered by Connie Williams in an email to members of the CA School libraries listserv:

> I absolutely agree with those who said to give them data. What saved our elementary libraries last year was the listing they did of the successful programs they put on—including numbers of students who attended/participated, and the data of times/classes/books used/student numbers, etc. Their positions had been put on the chopping block because "who needs libraries that are closed during a pandemic?" But when they showed how they jumped in with story times, book access through curbside,

etc., the Board was blown away by how much gets accomplished in the library (even when "closed"). Make sure they know that the library is never really closed.

Show how much you have already impacted student access (there's that data again), AND then show what you've got planned (purchase orders and all), and how many students will receive the benefit of these materials AND how important it is for teachers to have access to these materials for their classes. Show what will go away. Ask them to check in with where that money goes if not to the library—then show why and how the library provides the better bang for the buck; not only reaching all students and teachers but reaching across all content areas as well as personal growth and perspective.

Show any and all of the results of your activities. Share what you did to ensure access during COVID stay-at-home, and how your library materials and programming will better impact now that we're back; AND your students need the financial support directed to the library so that all have access to all the materials.

Get teachers and parents and even some students to attend the meeting.

Since you asked: here's my go-to "pithy" statement to School Boards that I've used through the years, gathered from the wisdom of our colleagues:

Anything less than an open, online, and in-person school library greatly diminishes the effectiveness of the total educational program, devalues your investment in library materials, and short-changes your students as they prepare for life in an information society. Defunding your school library will diminish what is for many students the only access to reading materials they have. I recognize the fact that many programs will be asking for your continued support. However, the library program is the only one that positively impacts all the students at each school site. Please support our students by supporting our library.[5]

Who should do the planning for your marketing efforts? In a single-person library, the planning may incorporate ideas from the advisory committee. It will quickly expand to include administrators, teachers, students, parents, and finally members of the community who will have suggestions for how they can participate. It ends with your marketing plan.

As stated earlier, a marketing plan follows the strategic planning process. In fact, marketing may be a goal in your strategic plan. Objectives are developed, the current situation is described, and the expected progress is outlined. Alternative strategies are written for achieving the objectives, with reasons given for each strategy. Specific actions are then listed and any needed budget proposed. Staff members are assigned to specific implementation tasks. Finally, evaluation of each step is indicated, with a timeline showing how often to review.

PR or Promotion Ideas

An important point to remember in developing a marketing plan is that promotion itself is a form of communication. Kotler lists several promotion tools, which have been modified for the school library program setting.[6] An important aspect of your marketing and public relations strategy is to develop branding for your library and its services. *Branding* is the consistent image and message you want to convey to your stakeholders. When considering the branding for your library, what name will you give it? Is it the learning hub, the media center, the library, the learning commons, or something else? Use that name consistently. Use Canva or another free graphic design online program to design a logo for your library. Students might be asked to help choose a theme for the year and to suggest ways to follow through with an ongoing plan to keep the library in the center of attention at the school.

Once you have developed a brand, logo, or theme, use it consistently across all of your messaging. Develop graphic templates for slides, different social media platforms, your virtual newsletter, and other means of communication. More important than the color and the logo that you develop is the hashtag or hashtags you use to identify your brand and your services. Hashtags are searchable and can be used to amplify your message. Consider using #?MSReads for motivating your middle school reading culture. Your hashtags also connect with larger movements in the education world. For example, using #myschoollibrary (whatever your hashtag is) and #spinepoetry will connect your school community and activities with those beyond your school and district. Explore potential hashtags for events:

- Dot Day—#DotDay
- National Library Month—#NLM, #nationallibrarymonth
- Banned Books Week—#bannedbooksweek
- World Read Aloud Day—#wrad, #worldreadaloudday

More ideas for developing your library brand are available in the Additional Resources.

Social media is an effective way to connect with your stakeholders. It is important to know that different stakeholders use different platforms for different purposes. Check your district's social media policies before creating official library accounts on social media platforms. Make sure you follow those guidelines in creating your content. You will also want to remember that there are age restrictions on some of the sites. Many of these platforms can provide you with analytics to determine the reach of and interaction with your posts. Remember also to make use of handles, hashtags, and your consistent branding. Additionally, you will find ways to keep up and connect with the many authors, artists, publishers, developers, leading educators, organizations, and associations who maintain their presences across the wide variety of social media platforms.

Social Media Tools for Marketing

While platforms come and go, they share a variety of similar strategies for connecting with stakeholders and amplifying messages.

- **Facebook** can be used to create posts, pages, groups, and events. Libraries use it to publicize, organize, and amplify events and activities. You can use it to link to important articles and studies. Consider using hashtags to communicate with parent advocates or creating a group for your book club.

- **Twitter** allows some of the same functionality as Facebook, but there are no groups. Like Facebook quotes, tweets can include links, photos, and media. Twitter will allow you to spread and amplify your campaign using hashtags and handles. You can send multiple tweets in a thread, connect with others using hashtags, and expand your network to include people outside of your community and the school library world. By simply using an @ sign (or a handle) for a celebrity, author, association, or politician, you can expand the reach of your message beyond your local community. You might create a "bank" of Twitter hashtags and handles in promoting a specific message. Your bank might include local politicians, public librarians, and other ally groups to draw attention to other events or campaigns. Twitter Lists allows you to organize your feeds, and follow groups of handles as well as lists created by others. The Tweetdeck Twitter client creates a dashboard of columns to strategically display and organize your own timelines as well as lists, hashtags, direct messages, mentions, and tweets of single users.
- **Instagram** was initially launched as a photo-sharing application. It now allows for the posting of stories. Although used by all ages, Instagram is probably more effective for and is used more heavily than other platforms by younger audiences. Stories have a shorter lifespan and are available for a limited time. Because Instagram is a visual platform, you can use it to provide pictures of new book arrivals and events. Check out hashtags such as #bookstagram, #librariansofinstagram.
- **TikTok** users post short videos (three minutes or less), often with captions and hashtags. Viewers can respond with likes and duets. TikTok is often used to present short instructions or tutorials. Young people appear to be using TikTok as an information source. TikTok videos often include emojis and stickers and can be presented live. Filters and other special effects are popular. TikTok themes often include challenges identified by hashtags. Check out some relevant hashtags such as #booktok, #librariansoftiktok.
- **YouTube** shares video content of any length, allowing for the posting of videos longer than those hosted on other applications. You can create channels and playlists where you organize your videos and those created by others. Similar to other platforms, you can follow other YouTubers. YouTube is a very effective platform for capturing what is happening in your library in either short or long form. You can use it to organize and archive your videos into channels and playlists and you can link or embed YouTube videos or playlists on your websites.

Build social capital by amplifying the message of individuals, organizations, and other allies that share your vision and mission. Browsing and "liking" posts and videos by other librarians and educators supports idea generation. Connect with memes and trends to amplify your message. Many of these platforms support analytics such as likes, retweets or shares, reactions, or reach/views. Use the analytics to hone your message and reach your targeted audiences.

Space and time advertising could take the form of an article for the school newspaper. If the school publishes a literary newsletter or magazine with articles by students, the library could sponsor a well-written book review or other media review. A library column with critiques of films in local theaters could be patterned after the entertainment column in the local newspaper. These should all be written by students, some of whom may also work in the library as assistants. You could host a blog with book reviews contributed by teachers and students or a personal blog of favorite new titles. If your OPAC allows it, you could encourage students to post reviews of books within the catalog itself.

Loudspeaker or broadcast advertising of the library could be offered through school intercoms. If your library produces a daily or weekly news broadcast for the school, take advantage of that opportunity to include students in promoting the library and its resources. If you have daily announcements through an intercom system, include information about the library in those announcements. Publicize happenings in the library that will attract students and teachers to the library to meet guest speakers, participate in author visits, see newly arrived books, or submit an entry for the current contest.

The equivalent of *mailings*, another method of marketing, could be achieved by putting information in teachers' boxes, distributing notices during students' homeroom period, and/or posting on websites or social media. Make your message clever and attractive so it will be read and remembered and associated with the library. Take full advantage of the ease of design and distribution of digital newsletters that can be created and distributed electronically through means such as Smore. A bonus for this approach are the analytics that will help you assess both reach and engagement.

The *sales presentation* or formal pitch might include the presentation of new materials at a teachers' meeting, or a book talk in a classroom, or introduction of an app at a professional development session. The presentation should be relaxed and include a "reward" at the close. For instance, students may get excited to check out the books presented. The app you present addresses a teacher's problem. Demonstrations should provide new information and truly pique your audience's interest. Ask your principal for a minute of time during each faculty meeting so that you can highlight a new resource or activity in your library.

Contests are another successful strategy when they spark the competitive spirit of the intended audience. This can happen through an interactive bulletin, for instance, presenting trivia around a curriculum area. Big events such as Battle of the Books or the science fair not only engage participants, but also can be fun for the entire school—and they are even better when they are associated with the library! Providing games or puzzles in the library can offer students time to relax. Ask students (or teachers) to share a baby picture and then have a contest to see who can identify the most; this can draw students into the library. Market your newly expanded graphic novel and comics collection by running a contest for students that asks them to identify superheroes from a large poster that includes more than 100 different superhero images. Prizes for contest winners need not be physical or tangible things (that must be purchased); a reward could consist of honoring winners in a READ-style poster similar to those sold by the American Library Association (ALA). (Templates for creating READ posters are available from ALA.) You could also create your own home-grown versions using poster design tools: put in student pictures with their favorite book on display, and then send the poster home with the student. It is a clever way to feature teachers and the principal sharing their favorite books.

Another marketing device is the *point-of-sale display,* often used in grocery stores to feature a certain product. A poster and a stack of books near the circulation desk encourage students to borrow something to read. Displays of new books at the entrance of the library, just as at the entrance of a bookstore, encourage checkout. Displays elsewhere in the library might show books that have been made into movies or a genre grouping to attract readers.

Sales literature could take the form of bookmarks or shelf talkers generated to show users what is available around a theme. Other forms of sales literature are flyers to describe a workshop or a guest speaker and an exhibition book about a special exhibit that a student or teacher might place in the library.

Take advantage of your OPAC's ability to create topical material lists. Create bookmarks with lists and include a Quick Response (QR) code that brings students back to your website. In fact, QR codes embedded all over your library can lead students to surprising videos or series lists.

Another marketing device, the *brochure* (probably digital), can provide a quick overview of a particular service. Digital brochures can be shared via email, downloaded, printed, and shared broadly. The brochure may describe one book, a school, or a community event or an author visit or a book fair. You could create a brochure in the form of a menu as though you were providing small plates or entrees—small services or larger collaborations.

Another marketing tool is the *formal presentation* made by the librarian to groups both inside and outside the school. An enthusiastic, carefully orchestrated talk with interesting visuals can draw far more positive attention to the library than many of the methods discussed earlier. Such a presentation, followed by a lively question-and-answer period, can do much to change any negative images of library professionals and library programs and help to build a positive image of the school library in the community. Suggestions for preparing presentations are given in the next section.

You will likely want to present about school libraries to service organizations. These include your area's Lion's club, Kiwanis, Rotary, gardening groups, and others. These groups meet regularly, and the person in charge of programs is always looking for new speakers. Offering to show what students experience in a modern, inclusive library could allow you to provide a pleasant after-lunch speech. Often, these organizations will make a small donation to purchase something for the library. Also, the school's parent-teacher association and a local school foundation may respond after you present a program to them. All of these increase the positive perception of the school library by the community. Such programs are not that difficult to prepare, and the social capital you build may create long-term relationships.

Preparing Presentations

Much has been written on effective speaking and presentations. As the librarian, you are a communications and technology specialist. It is important that you demonstrate effective strategies to engage your audience. Many examples of librarians' speeches and keynotes are available on YouTube or through the websites of those you follow. Look to them for inspiration. You are looking not just at the structure of their content but also at their affect, use of rhetorical devices, body language, modulation of voice tone, and engagement with the audience. Here are some tips:

- Value the time of your audience. Stick to the time limit!

- Identify your own message. What do you want your audience to take with them?

- Plan a strategic grabber. It could be a short anecdote, a quote, or a fun fact.

- Show rather than tell. Use powerful images, locally relevant when possible. Avoid clip art and lots of text.

- Seek opportunities to showcase examples of student work, photographs of students using materials or space, and student video testimonials.

- Plan the structure of your speech, especially if you are presenting an argument.

- Practice your presentation. You should be comfortable enough to talk directly with your audience and not read a speech.

- Use compelling evidence or examples. For example, if you are describing the age of your collection, do not overwhelm your audience with too much data; instead, share the cover of the oldest book in your collection or an example of the age of a subcollection or topic.

- Be aspirational. Avoid complaining or bad-mouthing anyone.

- Consider interactivity. Depending on the type of presentation and time constraints, include the audience.

- Close powerfully. Make the last few words that you use resonate with your audience.

- Leave time for questions.

- Evaluate your presentation. Was your message effectively conveyed?

School librarians have only a few opportunities in front of school boards. When you have such an opportunity, do not take these few minutes lightly. Your speech represents you as a professional and will make a difference in how you are perceived as a leader.

Advocacy to Activism

Readers of Deborah Levitov's *Activism and the School Librarian: Tools for Advocacy and Survival* are introduced to the theoretical foundation for activism; ways to move from advocacy to activism; and how to create a culture of advocacy in terms of working with parents, community groups, and local businesses. The process involves understanding exemplary practice, which is discussed throughout this text. School librarians who work to gain support for their libraries and their positions "have to be willing to embrace the future and make changes that will transform and reinvent positions and programs, making them learner centered and essential for education in this century."[7]

While some might argue that this is indeed self-serving and aimed at saving one's job, in reality it is saving our democracy. Today's students must not only learn to read, write, and do arithmetic, they must also have access to information, learn how to find information, and be able to assess that information to determine true from false, facts from biased opinion, and real from another person's declaration of reality. To do this, the librarian establishes a "Culture of Advocacy" as stated in the following points, which have been chosen from Kaaland's steps.

- Advocacy must be about student learning.

- Advocacy must be altruistically motivated.

- Advocacy must be ongoing.

- Advocacy must be positive.

- Advocates must be vocal and articulate.

- Advocates must do homework.

- Advocates must anticipate change.

- Advocacy is about access for all.[8]

All of these are very important, but the last one—"access for all"—is the critical need to sustain a democracy. When demagogues can keep information from people or can convince the population that what is being said to them is the truth when in fact it is questionable, it will be up to you and other school librarians who have a captive audience for their libraries to ensure that students have access to information and can critically evaluate the truth. These students are brought into the library or assigned projects by teachers on a regular basis for 12 or more years of their life, placing school librarians in the best position to develop informed citizens. Librarians who are active in the political process make sure their students have access to information and learn.

Top Ten Tips for Effective School Library Advocacy

1. *Know your influencers*
   Identify those who can help secure staffing, budget, & resources for the library. Match what they care about with library objectives. Include PTA leaders, school board.
2. *Know What to Say*
   Develop targeted messaging that resonates with the stakeholder you are addressing.
3. *Know & Share the Library's Value*
   Collect research, evidence, & stories and share them. Use social media, communicate with local media outlets.
4. *Build a Team/Build a Network*
   Foster advocates within the school and in the community. Organize and share with district or regional school librarians.
5. *Implement a Strategic Plan*
   With your team, create targeted, doable actions, assign activities, & evaluate successes.
6. *Integrate the Library with the School*
   Contribute to school priorities and agendas; join committees. The library is NOT a silo.
7. *Collaborate with Teachers*
   Be a team member; provide PD [professional development]; curate resources to match curriculum; offer to teach and evaluate student work.
8. *Stay Informed about Education & Library Legislation*
   Connect with legislators on relevant bills and concerns. Participate in professional organizations.
9. *Be a Resource to the Principal & Other Administrators*
   Know their priorities; show how the library can be a solution.
10. *Show Them the Money!*
    Engage in grant writing, fund raising, and apply for recognition awards.

By Debra E. Kachel, Affiliate Faculty, Antioch University Seattle, School Library Endorsement Program, Project Director, SLIDE: The School Librarian Investigation—Decline or Evolution? www.libslide.org

School Librarians and the Political Process

School librarians should be aware of the need to become effective in the political process. It is not an assignment for someone else. Librarians must recognize that they may be the only "someone else." Ann Dutton Ewbank's book *Political Advocacy for School Librarians: Leveraging Your Influence*[9] provides excellent guidance on developing your skills in advocacy at local, state, and national levels. She explains that political advocacy should be:

1. Ongoing—Embedded in your daily activities

2. Relational—Built on relationships you develop and maintain

3. Mobilizing—Based on a team effort

4. Action-Oriented—Aimed a taking targeted action or monitoring potential issues

5. Vision-Driven—Focused around your mission and vision

6. Influences Policy—Sustained effort affects policy development

Your advocacy should begin at the local level in your own school building and community.

Lobbying at Home

That school librarians are a public asset is a fact that was discussed at the beginning of this chapter. Perceptions of others often need revision. This is discussed throughout this book but bears being repeated here.

Lobbying begins at the local school building when the librarian promotes the values and the needs of the library program to students, parents, teachers, community, and (most of all) the principal in order to affect budgeting and strategic long-range planning. Stakeholders must understand the impact of the school library program on students from the first day of each school year and throughout the year. This starts with the teachers, who must understand the many ways to collaborate, co-teach, conduct guided inquiry sessions (among others), and allow the school librarian to share the latest technical advances to teach.

One way to look at this was explained by Judy Moreillon to an audience at a state conference. Some teachers feel even more isolated than the librarian. New teachers have all those students and all those parents who expect their children to learn, and they may have very little help from another teacher unless the district places mentors with new teachers. Even then, the mentor may not be available as often as the teacher feels the need for help. Working with new teachers makes their classes more rewarding and helps provide better learning for their students. Supporting new teachers is an excellent way for the school librarian to build partnerships.

You should work with teachers so that they see what an outstanding library program can be and what is needed to create an inclusive, student-centered library. This means working with all the teachers in the building to provide the best education possible. You, as leader and instructional partner, introduce this concept from your first day in your school. Support is built through demonstrations of teachers and librarians working together to build units of instruction, co-teaching, and evaluation of each unit and each student's response to the unit, noting what is most effective and what changes could be implemented to make the unit even stronger the next time it is taught.

Demonstrate the creative, thoughtful ways you can extend the curriculum through co-teaching and partnering with classroom teachers. Participate in teacher professional development, department and grade-level meetings. Work with groups of teachers to develop innovative and student-centered learning. Sharing the effect of these multi-teacher experiences with students will grow, sometimes slowly but often rapidly as students become more active in their own learning process. This will make advocates of teachers who recognize the difference in how students expand their learning.

High school teachers can encourage students to begin their role in democracy by encouraging them to register to vote.

> Participating in a democracy requires being a good citizen and helping elect candidates for office at all levels. . . . Every 18-year-old should register to vote. You can encourage teachers who teach seniors to mention this in classes or even go into classes with voter registrations in hand, mentioning that right after class you will be there ready and willing to help them fill out that form. Helping their children register to vote and celebrating afterward could be a birthday gift for parents to give their children. The library should have the information about the locations to go register to vote or have forms on hand and post this information all year.[10]

The first person with whom to share these positive effects (which of course will have been carefully documented) are the school's administrators.

The support of teachers, students, and parents has great potential to make an impact on the perception of principals and confirm that the library is an integral part of each child's education. Present examples of successful learning, innovative projects, engaged collaboration with teachers, and exciting activities going on in the library (from a graphic book corner, to a wider area for makerspaces, to a presentation from a member of the community to support a unit of instruction). All these demonstrate that the school has an outstanding school library program.

Any principal with a model school library program can convince superintendents, school boards, and administrators in other districts of what a quality library in a school requires. The school librarian may do this by helping the principal to separate and even begin to implement the best from all the new developments being proposed by other principals and superintendents.

The school librarian who works closely with the principal and other administrative staff to keep them informed about the learning successes in the school and the library will remain essential to the school when budgets are reduced or when a different resource allocation process is put into place. This PR effort is not a once-a-year effort; it is ongoing and requires constant, well-presented activities and publicity about their results in a manner that makes the principal want to see and learn what is happening in the school library. Identify what your administrator worries about and then work with them to solve that issue. Principals will appreciate problem-solvers. Confirmation of the success of your PR campaign may take the form of the library becoming the go-to place for the principals when they want to impress visitors with their school.

Mini Presentation: The Elevator Speech

One effective way to build support and be prepared at a moment's notice to advocate for your students and library is to develop an *elevator pitch*. An elevator speech or pitch is a short, highly focused way of sharing your message to persuade a specific stakeholder. The reason it is called an elevator pitch or speech is because it should last about the length of an elevator ride: no more than one or at most two minutes. The length would be about 200 to 250 words. You should always begin your speech by greeting the person by name and establishing a connection. Appendix D provides a template created by Deb Kachel for creating your own elevator speech. This template sets out five steps for developing your speech:

1. Introduce yourself so the stakeholder knows who you are.
2. Create a "hook" by introducing something the stakeholder would be interested in.
3. State your position, demonstrating how what you are pitching could affect students.
4. Provide supporting points or proof based on data or research.
5. Share your position, and invite the stakeholder to participate or further the discussion, and "ask" for what you are pitching.

Each elevator speech or pitch should be developed to address specific issues; it should not be a general statement about "Libraries are great! Save our jobs." Instead, keep your focus on students, student learning, and what you need to provide all students with a quality educational experience. Be professional. As part of your introduction at the start of your speech, hand the person your business card. If not provided by your school, design and purchase your own business cards using your library branding.

Here is a transcript of a video recorded by one of the authors as a model for her LIS students:

> Hello, Mrs. Alvarez. It's great to see you and Joyce from the high school library. I have your daughter Ana in 11th-grade English. She's come in so many times and I know she loves to read. Since I'm seeing you here at the supermarket, I wanted to tell you about the project we just completed on reinterpreting a soliloquy from Shakespeare's *Hamlet* this week.
>
> Ana did a fabulous job choosing the most evocative Creative Commons images, really reinterpreting the piece based on her research. I am just so excited about her project. I've got a portfolio of all the students' work on the library website and I would love for you to visit it. I know you come in for PTA meetings, so I know you know this, but we're so excited about giving our students an opportunity to think, create, share, and grow.
>
> How about taking a look at Ana's work and then let's get together and think about sharing some of our students' work at the next PTA meeting? I'm looking forward to hearing back from you. Here's my card. It gives you the library's website address and my own email address. Let's talk soon.

Reaching School Boards, Parents, and the Community

Ask for regular time at a school board meeting for students to show the result of their special projects. These presentations make for an engaging event and generate positive results. Parents will be bringing their children to the board meetings and staying to see a school board in action. This is the time to report on the progress of any proposal that required board approval. Such presentations should happen during the project, not just at the end; the event could be a show-and-tell held at your school. Most principals would like to show off their school to the superintendent and school board when they know that these are well-planned events that will make the teachers and principal look good.

It is essential that you create opportunities to interact with and support parents. They are essential in the care and welfare of their children and are interested in what happens to their children during those daily hours in school. They are directly involved in what goes on in classrooms and in the arenas where their children participate in sports activities. They will need to have the importance of the library both explained and demonstrated to them as often as possible. Encourage students to bring their parents to the library to learn about its role in their education; involving parents in the library program may result in their volunteering to help. Help can take many forms, from overseeing activities in the library, to storytelling to small groups or classrooms, to providing content as a visiting expert.

You should participate in your school's open houses or parent orientation events. If this is not a standard procedure in the district, your making coffee, tea, and cookies available in the library will be welcomed as parents move from visiting one teacher to another in the upper grades or from a conference with their student's teacher. If you concurrently have students demonstrating some of their activities in the library, parents will see and hear what is going on in that room.

Parents are the greatest potential support for the library program. They can become advocates for student access to a quality school library program. For more information about how parents can advocate for your library, visit AASL's Parent Advocacy Toolkit (a link is included in the Additional Resources).

The more members of the community who are directly involved with a school, the more likely it is that issues like bonds for more school funding will pass. Members of the community have much to offer when their skills are identified and they are invited to help. This goes beyond the police officer who comes to the school to help with child safety, although this is very important. High school students need to learn about different occupations in the community. The auto mechanic, the small business person, the plumber, the electrician, local artists and musicians, the construction worker: these and many others can all provide information for students who are not planning to go to a higher education institution. Don't forget veterans in your community. Any member of the community who can help students when they are creating in the makerspace area is golden. Invite those with expertise in the topics taught in your school to share their knowledge with students.

Your advocacy must also go beyond the local community to the legislative decision makers who are elected to state and national offices. The next section discusses these important connections.

State and National Legislative Lobbying

Kaaland and Kachel propose that "school library *legislative* advocacy begins with the development of a relationship between school library advocates—librarians and beyond—and legislative decision makers."[11] The novice lobbyist may go to the ALA's Public Policy and Advocacy webpage[12] to find not only the names of federal and state legislators, but also information on current issues. Some background research on your legislators will be helpful. Know their educational background and their work history. Learning their hometowns enhances your opportunities to meet them in a more social situation as well as in their legislative offices. Their political party is also important, especially if you are a registered member of that party or another. The Young Adult Library Services Association (YALSA) has a detailed *Legislative Advocacy Guide for Members & Supporters*[13] which can guide you through the process of communicating and meeting with legislators at both the state and national levels. Other suggestions are made by George Miller and John Lawrence[14] (see Appendix F). The following is a list of suggestions summarized from their article:

- Consult the legislative calendar to determine when legislators will be in their home districts.
- Call the local office of the legislators to schedule a time to meet or for a visit to your school library.
- Establish that you are a constituent.
- Explain the reason for your visit or legislation for which you are providing input.
- Provide accurate and up-to-date information.
- Be very specific about what action you want the legislator to take.
- Take pictures with your legislator and share it with the media.
- After your meeting, send a thank-you note and continue to follow up about the issue.

School librarians should be willing to lobby. *Lobbying* is the process of making opinions heard and getting ideas to decision makers. It involves collecting appropriate information and using that information for advocacy. Ultimately, lobbying can result in influencing legislation, but librarians need not begin their lobbying efforts by trying to change federal laws. It is much easier and more effective to begin at home, in the offices of your state representatives, where you need to talk about what is going on in your state that affects schools and funding for school libraries. Work with a small group of teachers and librarians to try out methods before planning an actual visit to a political official. When you include parents and students in the visit to your official, you help teach the political process.

Securing the consideration of state-level funding agencies and legislators requires a more sophisticated organization to implement your efforts. At this level, more groups are demanding attention from these agencies and individuals, and your message can easily be lost or ignored. For this reason, novice lobbyists need to remember that legislators at any level are still elected officials. They serve at the pleasure of their constituents, and as voters, school librarians and other members of the school staff and the parents of students are their constituents.

Another thing to remember is that these officials work for their constituents and were elected by their votes. They are interested in helping make things better for those voters. They are elected officials in a democratic society that they and all other citizens wish to remain democratic. To support this, citizens must be informed voters—and, as the leaders who developed the U.S. education system believed, this depends on teaching students to read. In our present information society, this also means that citizens must be information literate, having had open access to and learned to test the validity of information as part of the education process. That access comes in through the library. Elected officials need to be kept aware of the central role of the school library as the information center in the education of youth.

Using the information from the Legislative Action Center or the previously mentioned article by Miller and Lawrence, you can regularly send messages to elected officials, requesting their action. Office staff will tell you that congressional offices are interested in hearing from constituents, in part because they often do not understand the issues involved in specific pieces of legislation. Sometimes legislators receive no comments from any constituents concerning certain legislation. In some cases, opponents of legislation affecting education may send a few persons to state a case against a bill, and the legislator acts in their favor because no one from the education community has offered another viewpoint. Meeting the legislator with other interested constituents greatly supports your message.

Writing an email message takes only a little time and is of great help in expediting communication with a legislator. Because of security procedures, sending a physical letter to Washington may take longer than you want. Instead, locate the legislator's local office and send or deliver the letter there.

However you are sending your message, follow YALSA's tips for communicating in writing with elected officials:

1. Address the official as "The Honorable [FirstName LastName]."
2. Always identify yourself.
3. Be concise, specific, and support your views with facts when possible.
4. Be polite and respectful.
5. Stay on message and keep to your main points.
6. Always be sure to thank officials for their time.[15]

State and national associations keep their members informed of issues that should be addressed and urge support as soon as these messages arrive in your email—another reason for joining your state associations. These associations often support Legislative Days, when members of the association go to the state capitol to call on legislators; this can be effective. Although school librarians often cannot be away from school on these days, that does not mean they cannot be effective lobbyists. Indeed, Miller and Lawrence suggest that it is more effective to meet legislators at their local offices. The local offices of state legislators and members of Congress can be easily determined by exploring their official websites. Make sure you schedule an appointment, and do not be disappointed if you meet with legislative staff instead of the legislators themselves. Staffers are often more knowledgeable about specific issues and can be effective conduits for your message.

A legislator most often hears from constituents when they want something. However, it is desirable to establish communication with legislators and their office staff before a need or crisis arises. This can smooth the way for a visit in time of need. Again, remember that legislators need information from their constituents to better understand issues. As a reliable information provider, you can convince your legislator that school librarians are friends of lawmakers, there to help them understand the educational needs of students.

Sometimes the librarian must move to block proposed legislation. Professional associations usually have a legislative network in place to notify members when it is necessary to visit legislators, write letters, or make telephone calls against, as well as for, a bill. When a call comes, it is important to act quickly. Consult ALA's State Legislative Toolkit[16] for more ideas on working with legislators. For the librarian who becomes involved in local, state, and national politics, there are some simple rules:

1. Give legislators carefully researched and correct information. Telling a state legislator that the average per-pupil expenditure for materials in a state is very low, only to have incorrect information contradicted, will be embarrassing to everyone—perhaps critically so to the legislator.

2. Follow legislation of interest to school librarians from introduction through signature. Carefully choose legislators to support the issue. Learn to gather support from news media—local newspapers and television—as well as lawmakers.

3. Learn to write letters to lawmakers, and then write them. The image of library programs must be a positive one, and lobbying will help create a positive image of school librarians and their programs.

Additional support for your lobbying efforts can be found through EveryLibrary. EveryLibrary is the United States' first and only political action committee dedicated to preserving and promoting libraries. The EveryLibrary Institute is the companion organization to EveryLibrary, which is dedicated to research, charitable work, and promotion of the role of libraries in the community. The Institute provides many resources, including advocacy tools and training. Additionally, EveryLibrary provides targeted support for school libraries through the SaveSchoolLibrarians.org initiative.

To ensure the continued improvement of information services for students and teachers in schools, school librarians must advocate every day for their meaningful programs, demonstrating to students, teachers, administrators, and parents that they and the services in library programs make a difference in the lives of children. School librarians also must keep reminding their community members how important information resources in schools are for the education of future taxpayers. Finally, state and national government officials must be made aware of the danger of cutting funds to school libraries. Such actions will negatively impact students' equitable access to information, academic achievement, and potential as well as their preparation for informed civic participation.

This is a formidable assignment, but one that must be undertaken. It is not the responsibility of one school librarian but of all school librarians. It is always easier to work with someone else who can then enlist other supporters. Start in your own town to build a group. Your local state school library association will have an active legislative group to join. If school librarians wish to make a difference in students' academic achievement, they must ensure that attention is paid to the continuation of strong school library programs, because those programs are essential to student learning. As Lance and others have pointed out in many states:

- The size of a library media center's staff and collection is the best school predictor of academic achievement.

- The instructional role of the librarian shapes the collection and, in turn, academic achievement.

- Library expenditures affect library media center staff and collection size and, in turn, academic achievement.[17]

A final reminder to offer those who control the purse strings is that the school librarian and the school library provide equal access to information to support the education of *all* the students in their school. The recent SLIDE study[18] demonstrates that equity is an essential issue in access to school librarians. The study has found that the loss of librarians is not universal. Districts with students living in poverty, more minority students, and more English language learners are more likely to lack access to a school librarian. Without this protection of access to information, students will not have the foundation for effective citizenship in a democracy.

School Librarians as Politicians and Elected Officials

One way a school librarian could have a greater impact on decision making is as an elected official. The most direct application of authority is the school board. School boards may be appointed, but they are most often elected. It would be unlikely for school librarians to be eligible to run for school board in their own school district, but they might live in the town next to where they teach. Certainly, election to the school board provides a strong voice in the management of a school district.

Being active in a political party can also provide a voice for the platform of many who are running for office. One state was able to secure funding when two school librarians were active in their political parties: one was county chair of the Democratic Party and another was county chair of the Republican Party.

School Librarians: Advocating in the Global Community

Many school librarians in the United States are aware of the need to participate in the global community and to support school libraries throughout the world. This has great benefits for the students in their schools. The world is shrinking with the expansion of access to communication and movement of resources from one country to another. Language is a lesser barrier as websites and apps improve their instant translation services. Students in schools today need to know how to interact with their peers in other nations. Take advantage of opportunities to partner with a school librarian in another country and facilitate a virtual meeting of students so they can learn from each other. They are likely to find that they have much in common.

School librarians need to be models of interaction with others throughout the world. Attending annual conferences of the International Association of School Librarianship (IASL) and the International Federation of Library Associations and Institutions (IFLA) provides an opportunity to meet school librarians from other nations. School librarians in the United States should become aware of the problems and successes of school libraries in other parts of the world and should begin to help plan solutions to problems and implement their successes.

Both IASL and IFLA are described in chapter 12. They both have special interest groups (SIGs) where members can interact with and learn from each other.

School librarians provide access to information, opening the world of information to students, teachers, administrators, and the community. They can and do make a difference in the lives of students every day of every school year. They will continue to do so as long as they keep their community aware.

Collecting the Evidence

Prior to engaging in advocacy or change of any sort, be sure to gather baseline data so that you can examine the impact of your efforts. Moving forward, collect and record data. For instance, compare the number of graphic novels circulated after you complete your student contest identifying superheroes in the poster to the circulation from the previous semester. Knowing what was successful allows you to repeat that effort, perhaps with a slight modification at another time. Any plan that was less successful should be analyzed to determine its failures and decide how and even if it should be revised. This analysis requires input from your Advisory Committee and other librarians who might help with determining how to improve.

The successes make very good information for sharing with your stakeholders, and it is a part of your semester or annual report to your principal. Make sure to use stories, testimonials, photos, and student work to illustrate your successes. Your camera is very important. Enlist students as photographers to regularly document their work and library events and activities. Work with students and parents to develop ways to share your successes through social media, newsletters, and articles to the local newspaper.

Marketing and advocacy may not seem like something that should be in the job description of the school librarian, but they are both essential to ensuring continued service to learning and the community. Chapter 14 discusses playing with and innovating your library's future.

Key Takeaways

- Advocacy is an ongoing, essential process grounded in building relationships with students, parents, teachers, administrators, the community, and political leaders.

- Developing and delivering your message should be centered around the impact of the library on students and their learning and well-being.

Challenges to Promote Growth

1. Using the template in Appendix D, write your elevator speech and then practice it with another school librarian or classmate. Create it in a tool such as Flip that will allow you to share with your classmates and engage in peer review.
2. Develop an outline for a presentation to a school board meeting about your school library. What student learning can you highlight? What data can you share?
3. Describe a presentation you would make to a service organization, including what visuals you would share with them.
4. Explore examples of advocacy campaigns on our playlist (see the Additional Resources). Choose one that you think is a good model that would suit your community's needs and interests.
5. Using a tool such as Canva, develop branding for your library program. What types of available templates could you use and how would you use them?
6. Develop a social media plan to address any of the following stakeholder groups: parents, teachers, students, administrators, others. Which platforms would you use with each group?
7. Investigate the latest legislation in your state that would affect school library services, and write a letter supporting the position that would most help improve these services.
8. Gather evidence of the recent activities, special events, or accomplishments in your library and plan how to present this evidence to a local political leader. Contact a local political leader and request an appointment or plan an activity to invite your state or national legislator to your school library. Invite your local media to cover the visit.
9. Plan a visit to a state legislator or member of Congress; explain who you would take along with you and why you chose this person and not someone else. When might you include students and their parents in this visit? What would you want them to share? How would you prepare them for the visit? What would you ask them to be prepared to discuss?

Notes

1. Deborah D. Levitov, ed. (2012). *Activism and the School Librarian: Tools for Advocacy and Survival*. Santa Barbara, CA: Libraries Unlimited, p. xi.

2. AASL. "What Is Advocacy?" https://www.ala.org/aasl/advocacy/definitions

3. Philip Kotler. (1975). *Marketing for Nonprofit Organizations*. Englewood Cliffs, NJ: Prentice Hall.

4. *Ibid.*, 6.

5. Connie Williams. (2021, August 26). Message to calibk12@googlegroups.com

6. Kotler, *supra* n. 8.

7. Levitov, *supra* n. 1, xii.

8. Christie Kaaland and Debra E. Kachel. "School Library Legislative Advocacy Defined." In Deborah D. Levitov, ed. (2012). *Activism and the School Librarian: Tools for Advocacy and Survival*, 40–45. Santa Barbara, CA: Libraries Unlimited.

9. Ann Dutton Ewbank. (2019). *Political Advocacy for School Librarians: Leveraging Your Influence*. Santa Barbara, CA: Libraries Unlimited, pp. 13–14.

10. Blanche Woolls and Connie Hammer Williams. (2019). *Teaching Life Skills in the School Library: Career, Finance and Civic Engagement in a Changing World*. Santa Barbara, CA: Libraries Unlimited, p. 151.

11. Christie Kaaland and Debra E. Kachel. (2012). "School Library Legislative Advocacy Defined." In Deborah D. Levitov, ed., *Activism and the School Librarian: Tools for Advocacy and Survival.* Santa Barbara, CA: Libraries Unlimited, p. 57.

12. https://www.ala.org/advocacy/advocacy-public-policy

13. YALSA. (n.d.). "Advocacy." https://www.ala.org/yalsa/advocacy

14. George Miller and John Lawrence. (2017). "How to Make Your Voice Heard in Washington." *Los Angeles Times,* February 15, p. A13.

15. YALSA. (n.d.). "Communicating with Elected Officials." In *A Legislative Advocacy Guide for Members & Supporters,* p. 3. https://www.ala.org/yalsa/sites/ala.org.yalsa/files/content/LegAdvocacyGuide.pdf

16. ALA. (n.d.). State Legislative Toolkit. https://www.ala.org/advocacy/state-legislative-toolkit

17. Keith Curry Lance and David Loertscher. (2002). *Powering Achievement: School Library Media Programs Make a Difference: The Evidence,* 2nd ed. San Jose, CA: Hi Willow Research and Publishing.

18. Keith Curry Lance and Debra E. Kachel. (2021, July). "Perspectives on School Librarian Employment in the United States, 2009–10 to 2018–19." *SLIDE: The School Librarian Investigation—Decline or Evolution?* https://libslide.org/publications/perspectives

Part IV
Looking Forward

14
The Future

Never doubt that a small group of thoughtful, committed citizens can change the world. Indeed, it is the only thing that ever has.
—Margaret Mead

Urgent optimism is the desire to act immediately to tackle an obstacle, combined with the belief that we have a reasonable hope of success.
—Jane McGonigal

You have to act as if it were possible to radically transform the world. And you have to do it all the time.
—Angela Davis

Never look down to test the ground before taking your next step. Only he who keeps his eye on the far horizon will surely find the right road.
—Dag Hammarskjöld

Essential Questions

- What might the future of school libraries look like?
- How do innovations happen in organizations like schools?
- In what new ways might school librarians lead learning communities?

According to its mission, the American Association of School Librarians (AASL) empowers leaders to transform teaching and learning.[1] This chapter focuses on the words *leaders* and *transform*. School librarians can transform cultures and creatively move communities forward. They can hit the start button to make magic happen. To accomplish an explicitly transformational mission, librarians must reinterpret and lead as information and communication landscapes change, seek problems worthy of solving, and see their spaces and their programs and their schools as growing organisms. School librarians engage with the future by monitoring trends for the stickiest of ideas. They listen to and understand the needs of their communities; they connect those needs to professional values and they plant relevant new ideas in fertile soil. They also connect other dots, scanning the environment inside and outside of libraryland, inside and outside of K–12, for inspiration. They do not embrace change solely for the sake of change. They consistently make connections to their core values and common beliefs—what Simon Sinek, in his golden circle model of leadership, refers to as *their whys*—their cause, vision, and purpose.[2]

This edition was written at a particularly challenging time. The world's population is either emerging from a global pandemic, or they are learning to live with and mitigate a virus that will perhaps become endemic. It feels certain that COVID will be here for some time. Habits and practices developed during pandemic times affected the way people worked and the way they learned, perhaps accelerating hybrid and remote strategies and having as-yet-undocumented impacts on social and emotional health. Documentation about school libraries and librarians has not been good news.

The school library profession faces a 20-year reduction in the numbers of school librarians, as noted by Lance and Kachel's SLIDE study.[3] Librarians find themselves at the center of a cultural storm where large organized groups are questioning both materials that address issues of race, gender identity, and politics and the librarian's professionalism. The nation faces serious political divides and economic crises. The citizens in countries throughout the world face threats to democracy, human rights, and their very existence as well as a climate crisis. It is a time to question the facts one sees, reads, and hears.

The pandemic brought to light what the World Health Organization labeled an *infodemic*: "a tsunami of information—some accurate, some not" which can spread at a viral rate.[4] The infodemic is compounded by the spread of political and war propaganda. The emergence from pandemic learning conditions brought to the front the social and emotional needs of children. In the midst of these storms, and perhaps because of them, school librarians and school libraries have never been more needed, and this means that opportunities abound.

Future Ready Schools and Future Ready Librarians' "Let's Talk" document posits that the recent storms, particularly the pandemic, present opportunities for rethinking practice and rethinking the place called *school*.

> The exceptionality of the current situation is an opportunity to be reflective of our own practices, beliefs, and assumptions. While you acknowledge that the stress and uncertainty may cause you or others around you to act in different ways than before the pandemic, it is also important to be observant without judgment or prejudice. Take the time to be thoughtful about what you are doing, what you are learning, and what you are wondering about. These insights can help inform how you plan for your own professional future and ensure that you are part of the important work of restoring and/or reimagining school for your students, teachers, and community.[5]

Although this book is entitled *The School Library Manager,* and is heavily focused on day-to-day management strategies, it is hoped that the ideas that are shared relating to what it takes to manage will give you the confidence to reflect on possibilities and lead you to *lead*—to hit the start button, to analyze the situation and take action. You are challenged to face the obstacles of today and to seize opportunities to design better tomorrows for all those you serve. Ultimately you work for the students.

Remember those questions you were asked in the beginning?

What are my *whys*? (My purpose, cause, beliefs, core values)

What if I/we could?

Why shouldn't I?

Remember the growth mindset discussed in chapter 6? Remember the library innovator mindset illustrated in Appendix A? In her neuroscience research, Carol Dweck[6] describes the importance of recognizing the "power of yet" over the "tyranny of now," and advises that you are not chained to your current abilities. Dweck notes that new teachers themselves cannot expect to be perfect right away (or ever!) or have everything go smoothly immediately. Instead, they need to give themselves grace as they learn from their missteps and the opportunities to take risks as they grow.

Change can begin in the library. You can lead from the center. Remember that your ideas cannot develop in a vacuum. You are not alone. You will be in a position where you can make a difference in the lives of young people. You can help teachers teach and help learners learn. You can be a member of a team that initiates change. Reflect on the School Librarian Innovator's Mindset poster in Appendix A.

It is important to recognize that adoption of innovations does not happen simultaneously among the members of a community. A classic model of how change occurs in an institution was developed by E. M. Rogers in 1962. In his Diffusion of Innovation (DOI) Theory,[7] Rogers explained how ideas or initiatives gain momentum: how they diffuse or spread, and are adopted by a social system. Adopters bring a variety of personalities and timelines to this process. As you introduce change, you need to be aware that you will meet the following people, identified by who will require different strategies for their adoption of change:

1. **Innovators** (2.5% of population) are the first to try an innovation. They are eager to take risks and will be willing and early partners in change.

2. **Early Adopters** (13.5% of population) are opinion leaders who embrace opportunities for change and are comfortable adopting new ideas. Though they may not need convincing, these partners may need introductions and training to get confidently onboard.

3. **Early Majority** (34% of population) are seldom opinion leaders. They tend to adopt new ideas before the average person, but only after seeing evidence of the innovation's effectiveness.

4. **Late Majority** (34% of population) are skeptical of change, and will adopt an innovation only after it has been tried by the majority.

5. **Laggards or resisters** (16% of population) are conservative and possess no opinion leadership. Bound by tradition, they are highly skeptical of change. They will be the most challenging group and may require convincing from the other adopter groups and administrators to get on board.[8]

Rogers suggests that within an organization, two critical and respected roles spread the word about innovation and are useful as you consider your positions in the learning community. *Opinion leaders* have informal influence on their community's behavior and perhaps some status outside the community. They possess technological competence and social accessibility and are known to conform to the community's norms. *Change agents* bring innovations to the community and function as mediators between those innovations and the community. They help to promote change, build community rapport, create awareness and knowledge, identify needs, and empathize with those who may need assistance. Librarians can work with those people and librarians can be those people.

The characteristics of those two influential roles, described in Rogers' classic model, might be reframed as you imagine the dispositions needed to promote the diffusion of future innovation. In her book *Imaginable*, game designer, researcher, and futurist Jane McGonigal describes the notion of playing with possible futures and introduces the concept of *urgent optimism*. She describes three psychological strengths for thinking like an urgent optimist:

1. *Mental flexibility* allows you to seek signals of change, the weird stuff you observe that may not have happened before. You can increase this skill, and get unstuck by imagining scenarios others would describe as unimaginable or unthinkable in order to overcome a normalcy bias.

2. *Realistic hope* is based on a balanced mindset with awareness of risks and threats to prepare for, as well as the new technologies, social movements, policy ideas, solutions, and other positives that could help mitigate the risks to build a better future, one we are excited about living in. McGonigal suggests regularly checking in with Google Trends to keep up with such trends across various areas of interest.

3. *Future power* involves taking intentional actions with a feeling of agency and may begin with creating lists of things you can do today to prepare for potential risks and threats and actions to prepare you for opportunities that might present themselves in future worlds.[9]

The world of the school librarian need not return to "normal." This is an exciting time for practitioner inquiry and collaborative leadership. How might you audit your current practices, consider innovations, and build new relationships? Keeping true to your common beliefs and core values, what tired ideas are actually weeds you might pull? Fines are not necessary; reference books can circulate; children can borrow as many books as they want on any reading level. Which roots are essential for you to cultivate?

Connecting the Dots

You will want to look outside for trends. Scanning the environment inside and outside of libraryland, within and outside of K–12, for inspiration, innovators discover and connect dots. Scan the horizon. Innovative leaders know their *whys* and they monitor trends. They do not embrace change solely for the sake of change. They listen to and understand the needs of their communities; they connect those needs to their whys and their professional values and they plant relevant new ideas in fertile soil.

As suggested in Walter Isaacson's book *The Innovators*,[10] innovators exploit the critical confluence of timing, technology, and team. And, in true library spirit, they share, presenting their practice transparently to inspire others. Innovators plan beyond the day or week. They are playful, curious risk takers who seek and discover new paths and imaginative solutions.

Where do you look for those aforementioned dots? The dots are everywhere, but you can start your search in a few of the following. You will want to regularly scan practitioner journals, educational research, new applications, social media, and the news. Google Trends was mentioned earlier as a tool that presents a global, widespread lens. ALA's Center for the Future of Libraries[11] offers a newsletter as well as a "trend collection" that will help you identify change especially relevant to libraries. You will also want to keep up with ALA's annually published *State of America's Libraries* report and the regularly published *IFLA Trend Report*.[12] Although it focuses on higher education, EDUCAUSE hosts the collection of Horizon Reports. Developed by expert panels, these reports profile "key trends and emerging technologies and practices shaping the future of higher education, and envisions a number of scenarios and implications for that future."[13] You might also regularly scan the themes presented and archived in the American Library Association's *Library Technology Reports*.[14]

Connecting the Chapters of This Book to Change

You are invited to play with futures as they relate to the chapters and themes in this book. As you look at your library's future, what questions might you ask about the various elements of your program? How might you engage your learning community in this visioning? How might you apply urgent optimism and a radical lens, as well as evidence by, for, and from practice to infuse innovations by addressing the following facets?

Collection/Reading: Beyond books, what will your future collection contain or point to? How will you continue to make your collection more discoverable? How will you ensure that your collection meets the needs of your community? How will you leverage the bounty of open educational resources (OER) and other freely available content to ensure equity and currency of teaching materials? How will you ensure that your community has a collection that reflects its interests? On which platforms will your future students prefer to read? What might the reading experience look like in the future? How will you evaluate and grow your collection to ensure its diversity and inclusivity? How will you address potential challenges? Who are your allies? How might you build schoolwide cultures of reading and literacy?

Teaching and Learning: In which ways might technologies such as artificial intelligence (AI) affect and enhance learning analytics, support, and assessment? Might AI data better and more efficiently inform you of learning needs and improve personalization? How will we negotiate and celebrate new AI writing tools like Chat GPT while maintaining cultures of academic honesty? How will you leverage the availability of informal learning and microcredentialing opportunities? How might you encourage both lifewide and lifelong learning? How will you inform your professional community? Who are your future collaborators in learning? What types of global experiences might you initiate to help students recognize their place in the world as global citizens? Might the United Nations' Sustainable Development Goals[15] inspire your instructional planning? How will you continue to ensure that you create instruction that is culturally connected, relevant, and responsive? How will you encourage resilience, build curiosity, and foster a growth mindset in school-wide teaching and learning?

Inquiry-Based Learning: How will you use your growing knowledge of the curriculum to model the importance and the lifelong relevance of inquiry in learning for your teachers, administrators, and learners? Across grades and content areas and the adult community, how will you inspire a culture of inquiry? How might you encourage a shift away from modes of assessment that are deficit-based and decontextualized to assessment based on personally meaningful and creative problem-solving?

Staff: What opportunities might you identify to leverage the talents of the adults and young people in your community and beyond? Might your parent volunteers meet and support their school library remotely? Beyond the traditional activities of shelving and straightening, how might you appreciate and engage your community in enhancing your library program?

Schedule: If you work within a fixed schedule, how might you revise that schedule to ensure not only that teachers have their prep periods, but also that learners have opportunities to visit with their teachers to engage in curriculum-relevant inquiry projects? If you are in an elementary school with a fixed schedule, how might you build support for moving to a responsive schedule to better integrate emerging literacy skills with classroom learning? What strategies can you use to provide equitable opportunities to develop digital literacy skills for students whose teachers are not currently library users?

Facilities: What trends from the world outside school libraries and libraries other than school libraries will affect your learner-centered library space? Which emerging technologies will find room in your space? What types of flexible, barrier-free, welcoming spaces can you imagine? How will you create that enchanting "third space" for your students? How might you model practices of sustainability?

Technology: How will you actively keep up with emerging strategies to connect, communicate with, and inspire learning and literacy in your communities while protecting privacy and confidentiality and inspiring safe, ethical, and productive activities? How might you partner with classroom teachers to build engaging digital spaces that meet students' curricular needs? How might you engage learners in technology opportunities that reach beyond the curriculum and address learners' lifewide interests? In which ways might immersive reality opportunities and artificial intelligence enhance existing curricula? How will learning opportunities extend beyond your library walls? What types of global opportunities will you introduce that might inspire global citizenship? What strategies will you adopt to keep up with shifts in the edtech landscape?

Access and Equity: How will you ensure that all students have intellectual and barrier-free physical access to accurate, age-relevant information that they can read, understand, and trust? How will you remove barriers related to language, culture, and abilities? How might you mitigate issues relating to technology access at school and at home? How will you protect student privacy in a future with increasing surveillance? How will you engage with those who wish to limit access to content by removing materials from your collection? What will you do to create and nurture advocates for intellectual freedom in the community? How can the library support instruction that is personalized and differentiated? How will you advocate for student access to the future resources and tools that they need to think, create, share, and grow?

Professional Development: What strategies will you use or introduce to keep yourself and your learning community aware of the most promising trends in technology? What impacts might the increasing number of available microcredentials and informal learning opportunities have on your stakeholders' opportunities for participation, learning, and growing portfolios? How will you build a personal learning network that continually refreshes your learning and presents exciting discoveries to feed you and your community?

Planning: How will you engage your community in envisioning a learner-centered plan for school improvement? How will you anticipate and identify the needs of your learners and incorporate them into your library's strategic planning? What role will data and evidence play in your planning? What critical goals will your three- or five-year plan establish?

Advocacy / Support: What activities will you plan to show the students, teachers, administrators, school board, and community the values of having a school library and school librarian in your school? How can you support your school community and build their support for access to a library that embraces diversity and innovation?

The Future Is Yours and The Future Is You

What will school libraries look like in the future? What will school librarians look like? It is up to you. It will be about how you represent our profession and how you affect teaching and learning. As you grow in your position and build the respect of your colleagues, you will grow into leadership. Lead with kindness, curiosity, and empathy.

Remember that you are not alone. As part of a network of professionals who connect with professionals across a range of fields and interests globally, you will make exciting discoveries. With the needs of your community in mind, you will decide what makes sense to introduce and implement. Librarians are most successful when they exert influence and leadership in their schools; when they function as instructional partners, sharing their discoveries, skills, and creativity to enhance learning activities and engage learners, crafting better ways to teach and better ways to prepare students for their lives beyond school and after they have left school.

Build relationships first. Discover the significant common ground you share with your stakeholders. You cannot work alone. Your local network and support system develop from the friendships you nurture—with your teacher colleagues, of course, but also with your administrators, counselors, custodians, aides, secretaries, carpenters, and the parents you support. Be there for them and they will be there for you and build the future with you.

Use your position powerfully. Make an impact on the lives of the young people you serve and the teachers and administrators with whom you partner and whose practices you can inform, enhance, and inspire. As Sharon Coatney shared in the preface for this book:

> As expert teachers and information specialists, you and they
> can have a phenomenal impact on student learning. School

librarians are lifelong learners. It is my greatest hope that they will see the need to broaden their effect. Publish. Speak. Travel. Visit. Consult. You have unusual experience and a stance—a very broad unique look at schools and student learning—that needs to be heard and shared.

Some Advice from Your Authors

Best practice today has a limited shelf life. All textbooks become dated soon after they are published. In a continually shifting information landscape, a that's-the-way-we've-always-done-it (TTWWADI) response simply provokes defiance. While your work has the potential to make a deeply meaningful and long-lasting impact on learners, it is not static, and it is *not* brain surgery. While you work with solid understanding of the needs of your communities, keeping professional values and evidence in mind, no patient will die if you take responsible risks, try something new, and unleash your personal passions and talents and your best efforts, even if they do not immediately or completely work. If you want to grow innovative learners, you need to model a growth mindset, an inquiry disposition, innovative practice, and a sense of urgent optimism.

There is really no box. As you explored this text you discovered opportunity. Hopefully, wherever you land in that first professional position, you will feel empowered to make a difference. You do not need to be a rock star. Here is what you *do* need to do: You need to learn about your community. Identify problems or gaps. As you observe, consider your potential role in addressing those gaps. With knowledge of your practice, core values, and a sense of the national standards, establish a baseline and make a plan. If you are going to dream and plan, you might as well dream big and dream differently.

Above all, it is important to continue to learn and grow. You have no excuse for feeling alone. You will find a bounty of blogs and webinars, and conferences, and hashtags to connect you to smart and giving colleagues. Come away from this text with a sense of hope and enthusiasm and perhaps a bit of a jolt. Come away with the confidence to push the start button on thoughtful, meaningful change and innovation. We hope this text has confirmed your career choice.

When your passion drives you, people around you will notice and want to be around you. You will become an agent of change.

To add another quote to this quote-filled chapter, as Oscar Wilde said in *Lady Windermere's Fan*, "We are all in the gutter, but some of us are looking at the stars."

Please decide to look up! Be aspirational. Look at the sky or the ceiling, rather than the floor, of your practice.

Just one more quote comes from author/journalist Ta-Nehisi Coates, from *Between the World and Me*. In Coates' description of his university experience, he reminds us that for some students, the library may be the most liberating space they find in their schools:

The pursuit of knowing was freedom to me, the right to declare your own curiosities and follow them through all manner of books. I was made for the library, not the classroom.

The classroom was a jail of other people's interests. The library
was open, unending, free. Slowly, I was discovering myself.[16]

Empathize. Please try to put yourself in the shoes of your students, your
classroom teacher partners, your administrators, the parents who count on
you to inspire their children. What keeps them up at night? Remember:
Advocacy is solving other people's problems.

Continually reflect on your practice. Especially now, be playful with
your current situation and with the future. Always consider how you
can best inspire learning. Weigh risk against rewards and consider your
decisions in terms of your core values. You are the hope for the profession. Please continue to create, invent, and enchant those around you.
Share your contributions. Go out there and innovate. Show them what
a school librarian really looks like. Demonstrate your growing ability
to build literacy and collaboratively lead teaching and learning across
school culture.

Be guided by your heart. Whenever you make decisions, make them in
the best interest of the young people you serve, teach, and inspire.

Key Takeaways

- Cultural change can begin with the librarian if the librarian takes
  a leadership role.

- Be a leader who thinks flexibly and, with a sense of urgent optimism, sees opportunities rather than obstacles to build libraries
  with the brightest futures.

Challenges to Promote Growth

1. In what ways does your own vision for the future connect with the school
   or district mission or vision statements or profile-of-a-graduate description? Create a document copying those documents and design vision and
   mission statements and three goals that connect your vision of the future
   to the larger organization's vision.
2. Reflect on your strengths as a leader to engage members of your
   community in developing a shared vision for the change process. How
   might you apply McGonigal's three psychological strengths as an urgent
   optimist?
3. Activist and scholar Angela Davis reminds us that the word *radical* "simply
   means grasping things at the root."[17] What if you looked at your school
   library's future through a radical lens and examined roots to see how its
   elements might grow differently? Inspired by an activity introduced by
   educators Will Richardson and Homa Tavanger in their 2020 BIG Questions Institute webinar, "Imagining Radical Acts of Education," try applying the radical lens of your choice to one aspect of school library practice.
   Examine Table 14-1. Feel free to recreate or edit it with your own radical types of thinking or your own elements of your practice or program.
   Alternatively, you might collaboratively use BQI's Radical Random Acts

Generator for Education (RRAGE) cards (https://bigquestions.institute /rrage) to inspire conversations about looking differently at libraries and schools.

Table 14-1. Planning for Radical Change

Planning for Radical Change	Radical Empathy	Radical Inclusion/ Belonging	Radical Creativity/ Imagination	Radical Hope/ Optimism	Radical Justice	Radical Joy
Teaching & learning						
Opening/ Orientation						
Inquiry						
Assessment & evaluation						
Collection						
Library spaces						
Budgeting						
Staffing						
Scheduling						
Advocacy						
Professional development						
Technology						
Relationships with classroom teacher partners						
Relationships with administrators						
Relations with parents/ caregivers/ grandparents						
Relations with the larger community						

Adapted with permission from Will Richardson and Homa Tavanger. (2020). "Imagining Radical Acts of Education." BIG Questions Institute. https://bigquestions .institute/free-radical

Notes

1. ALA News and Press Center. (2014, July 15). "AASL Transforms Learning with New Mission Statement and Strategic Plan." *ALAnews*. https://www.ala.org/news/press-releases/2014/07/aasl-transforms-learning-new-mission-statement-and-strategic-plan

2. Simon Sinek. (2009). *Start with Why: How Great Leaders Inspire Everyone to Take Action*. New York: Penguin.

3. Keith Curry Lance and Debra E. Kachel. (2021, July). "Perspectives on School Librarian Employment in the United States, 2009–10 to 2018–19." *SLIDE: The School Librarian Investigation—Decline or Evolution?* https://libslide.org/publications/perspectives

4. World Health Organization. (2021, October 19). "Infodemic Management: An Overview of Infodemic Management During COVID-19, January 2020–May 2021," p. iv. https://www.who.int/publications/i/item/9789240035966

5. Future Ready Schools and Future Ready Librarians. (2020). "Let's Talk: A Conversation Starter for Future Ready Librarians® Building Collaborative Relationships," p. 15. https://futureready.org/wp-content/uploads/2020/06/Let%E2%80%99s-Talk-A-Conversation-Starter-for-Future-Ready-Librarians%C2%AE-Building-Collaborative-Relationships_6.3.20.pdf

6. Carol Susan Dweck. (2008). *Mindset: The New Psychology of Success*. Random House Digital.

7. Everett M. Rogers. (1995). *Diffusion of Innovations,* 4th ed. New York: Free Press.

8. *Ibid.*

9. Jane McGonigal. (2022). *Imaginable*. New York: Spiegel & Grau.

10. Walter Isaacson. (2014). *The Innovators: How a Group of Inventors, Hackers, Geniuses and Geeks Created the Digital Revolution*. New York: Simon and Schuster.

11. ALA Center for the Future of Libraries. (n.d.). Home page. https://www.ala.org/tools/future

12. IFLA. (n.d.). Trend Report. https://trends.ifla.org

13. EDUCAUSE. (2022, July 18). *EDUCAUSE Horizon Reports*. https://library.educause.edu/resources/2021/2/horizon-reports

14. ALA TechSource. *Library Technology Reports*. https://journals.ala.org/index.php/ltr

15. United Nations, Department of Economic and Social Affairs. (n.d.). Do You Know All 17 SDGs [Sustainable Development Goals]? https://sdgs.un.org/goals

16. Ta-Nehisi Coates. (2015). *Between the World and Me*. New York: Random House, p. 48.

17. Angela Yvonne Davis. (1990). *Women, Culture & Politics*. New York: Vintage, p. 14.

Additional Resources

AASL. Advocacy Toolkit. http://www.ala.org/aasl/sites/ala.org.aasl/files
/content/aaslissues/toolkits/AASLAdvocacyToolkit_180209.pdf

AASL. Best Digital Tools for Teaching and Learning.
https://www.ala.org/aasl/awards/best

AASL. Developing Critical Curators Seeking Diverse Perspectives
Activity Guide.
https://www.ala.org/aasl/sites/ala.org.aasl/files/content/advocacy
/tools/docs/CriticalCurators_ActivityGuide_220714.pdf

AASL. *Knowledge Quest* Blog Topics.
https://knowledgequest.aasl.org/category/blogs

AASL. *National School Library Standards*. https://standards.aasl.org

AASL. *National School Library Standards Crosswalk with Code
with Google's CS First Curriculum*. https://standards.aasl.org/wp
-content/uploads/2019/11/aasl-standards-crosswalk-cs-first.pdf

AASL. *National School Library Standards Crosswalk with Future
Ready Librarians* (2018).
https://standards.aasl.org/wp-content/uploads/2018/08/180828-aasl
-standards-crosswalk-future-ready.pdf

AASL. *National School Library Standards Crosswalk with ISTE Standards for Students and Educators* (2018).
https://standards.aasl.org/wp-content/uploads/2018/08/180828-aasl
-standards-crosswalk-iste.pdf

AASL. Open Educational Resources Toolkit.
https://www.ala.org/aasl/sites/ala.org.aasl/files/content/advocacy
/tools/docs/OER%20Toolkit_191105.pdf

AASL. Position Statement: The School Librarian's Role in Reading.
https://www.ala.org/aasl/sites/ala.org.aasl/files/content/advocacy
/statements/docs/AASL_Position_Statement_RoleinReading_2020
-01-25.pdf

AASL. Position Statement on School Library Scheduling.
https://www.ala.org/aasl/sites/ala.org.aasl/files/content/advocacy
/statements/docs/AASL_Scheduling_Position_Statement.pdf

AASL. Position Statements.
https://www.ala.org/aasl/advocacy/resources/statements

AASL. School Librarian Interview Question Matrix. https://standards
.aasl.org/wp-content/uploads/2020/04/SL-Interview-Matrix.pdf

AASL. School Librarian Job Description. http://standards.aasl.org/wp
-content/uploads/2020/04/SL-Job-Description_3-30-2020.pdf

AASL. School Librarian's Role in Reading Toolkit. https://www.ala.org
/aasl/advocacy/tools/toolkits/role-reading

AASL. School Library Evaluation Checklist.
https://standards.aasl.org/wp-content/uploads/2018/10/180921-aasl
-standards-evaluation-checklist-color.pdf

AASL. Standards Crosswalks. https://standards.aasl.org/project/crosswalks

AASL. Standards Crosswalks. https://aasl.ala.org/standards/crosswalks

AASL. Toolkits. https://www.ala.org/aasl/advocacy/tools/toolkits

AASL. Toolkit for Promoting School Library Programs.
http://www.ala.org/aasl/sites/ala.org.aasl/files/content/aaslissues
/toolkits/promo/AASL_Toolkit_Promoting_SLP_033016.pdf

ALA. Center for the Future of Libraries.
https://www.ala.org/tools/future

ALA. Library Privacy Checklist for Students in K-12 Schools, Revised
Jan. 14, 2021.
https://www.ala.org/advocacy/privacy/checklists/students

ALA. Library Privacy Guidelines for Students in K-12 Schools.
https://www.ala.org/advocacy/privacy/guidelines/students

ALA. Library Technology Reports. https://journals.ala.org/index.php/ltr

ALA. Privacy: Students & Minors.
https://www.ala.org/advocacy/privacy/students

ALA. Privacy Field Guides for Libraries. http://libraryprivacyguides.org

ALA. Public Library & School Library Collaboration Toolkit.
https://www.ala.org/alsc/publications-resources/professional-tools
/school-public-library-partnerships

ALA. Resolution on Monetary Library Fines as a Form of Social Inequity (January 28, 2019).
https://www.ala.org/aboutala/sites/ala.org.aboutala/files/content
/Resolution%20on%20Monetary%20Library%20Fines%20as%20a%
20Form%20of%20Social%20Inequity-FINAL.pdf

ALA. Resource Guides. https://libguides.ala.org/home

ALA. Resource Guides: Sustainability and Libraries: ALA and Sustainability. https://libguides.ala.org/SustainableLibraries

ALA. State Privacy Laws Regarding Library Records.
https://www.ala.org/advocacy/privacy/statelaws

ALA. State of America's Libraries (published annually; URL varies).

ALA LibGuides. Building Libraries & Library Additions: School Libraries. https://libguides.ala.org/library-construction/school-libraries

Alive Library!
https://sites.google.com/view/alivesuperschoollibraries/home

Alman, Susan W., ed. *School Librarianship: Past, Present, and Future* (Lanham, MD: Rowman & Littlefield, 2017).

Americans with Disabilities Act. https://www.ada.gov

Augmented, Virtual + Mixed Reality. Practical ARVRinEDU® for the Classroom. https://www.arvrinedu.com

Baltimore Library Project. https://www.baltimorelibraryproject.org

Big6 and Super3. https://thebig6.org

Brown, Stacy. *The School Librarian's Technology Playbook: Innovative Strategies to Inspire Teachers and Learners* (Santa Barbara, CA: Libraries Unlimited, 2020).

CC0 Image Portals playlist. https://tinyurl.com/CC0Portals

Choice Boards playlist. http://tinyurl.com/ChoiceBoardsPlaylist

Common Sense Education. https://www.commonsense.org/education

Craver, Kathleen W. *School Libraries in a Time of Change: How to Survive and Thrive* (Santa Barbara, CA: Libraries Unlimited, 2019).

Creative Commons. http://creativecommons.org

Creative Commons License Chooser.
https://creativecommons.org/choose

Credibility Toolkit playlist (Media and News Literacy Instruction and Fact Checkers). https://tinyurl.com/credibilitytoolkit

Crossman, Bridget. *Community Partnerships with School Libraries: Creating Innovative Learning Experiences* (Santa Barbara, CA: Libraries Unlimited, 2019).

Curts, Eric. Google Tools to Support All Learners.
https://docs.google.com/document/d/1hvT8nb0fpl6VwQ6i0wSsWIV vaTomI7MqPdgq-wjdv3Y/edit

Danielson Framework for Teaching Evaluation.
https://danielsongroup.org/framework

Databases: A State-by-State Look. https://tinyurl.com/databasesstates

Dawkins, April M., ed. *Intellectual Freedom Issues in School Libraries* (Santa Barbara, CA: Libraries Unlimited, 2020).

Dawkins, April M., and Emily Eidson. 2021. "A Content Analysis of District School Library Selection Policies in the United States." *School Library Research* 24.
www.ala.org/aasl/slr/volume24/dawkins-eidson

Defending Intellectual Freedom in School Libraries Wakelet.
https://tinyurl.com/DefendingIntellectualFreedom

Digital Design Tools playlist. https://tinyurl.com/DesignToolsPlaylist

EdTech Bloggers. https://tinyurl.com/edtechbloggers

Empire State Information Fluency Continuum [based on Barbara Stripling's model]. https://slsa-nys.libguides.com/ifc

Evaluation/Evidence-Based Practice playlist. http://tinyurl.com/evaluationEBP

Everhart, Nancy. *Evaluating the School Library: Analysis, Techniques, and Research Practices, 2d Edition* (Santa Barbara, CA: Libraries Unlimited, 2020).

Ewbank, Ann Dutton. *Political Advocacy for School Librarians: Leveraging Your Influence* (Santa Barbara, CA: Libraries Unlimited, 2019).

Exit Tickets/Backchannel playlist. https://tinyurl.com/ExitTicketsBackChannel

Facilities/Spaces playlist. http://tinyurl.com/facilitiesspaces

Fleming, Brittany, Julie Jamieson, and Jennifer Roth. *Copyright and Creativity.* https://copyrightandcreativity.org

Foote, Carolyn. Library Design. *Not So Distant Future.* https://futura.edublogs.org/library-design

Future Ready Librarians® Hub. https://all4ed.org/future-ready-librarians-hub

Future Ready Schools® Librarian Self-Reflection Tool. https://futureready.org/the-future-ready-schools-librarian-self-reflection-tool

Future Thinking playlist. https://tinyurl.com/SLFutureThinking

Georgia Library Media Association. The School Librarian Evaluation Instrument (SLE). https://www.glma-inc.org/slei

Getting Ready for Action playlist. https://tinyurl.com/gettingreadyforaction

Google Trends. https://trends.google.com/trends

Guidance on Web Accessibility and the ADA. https://beta.ada.gov/resources/web-guidance

Guided Inquiry Design. https://guidedinquirydesign.com

Harada, Violet H., and Sharon Coatney. *Radical Collaborations for Learning: School Librarians as Change Agents* (Santa Barbara, CA: Libraries Unlimited, 2020).

Harvard Project Zero's Thinking Routine Toolbox. http://www.pz.harvard.edu/thinking-routines

Harvey, Carl A., II, and Audrey P. Church, eds. *School Library Management,* 8th ed. (Santa Barbara, CA: Libraries Unlimited, 2022).

Horizon Reports (EDUCAUSE). https://library.educause.edu/resources/2021/2/horizon-reports

Hough, Brenda. *Crash Course in Time Management for Library Staff* (Santa Barbara, CA: Libraries Unlimited, 2018).

How the Tuning Protocol Works (ASCD).
https://www.ascd.org/el/articles/how-the-tuning-protocol-works

IFLA Trend Report (published annually). https://trends.ifla.org

Inclusive Collections and Diversity Audits playlist.
https://schoollibrarynj.libguides.com/Librarians/collection

ISTE, Follett, Future Ready Librarians. Crosswalk: Future Ready Librarians Framework and ISTE Standards for Educator (September 2018). https://iste-standards-e_frl-crosswalk_6-2018_v7-2.pdf

Knowledge Quest Blog Topics.
https://knowledgequest.aasl.org/category/blogs

Let's Talk! Conversation and Activities Protocols for Teaching and Learning Wakelet. https://tinyurl.com/LetsTalkProtocols

Loertscher, David V. *Create by Design* (Provo, UT: Commons Press, 2022). davidloertscherlibrary.org

Loertscher, David V., ed. *The Library Learning Commons: Start a Revolution* (Papers of the Treasure Mountain Research Retreat #22). (Salt Lake City, UT: Learning Commons Press, 2015).

Loertscher, David V., and Fran Komper. *The LIIIITes Model.* (Salt Lake City, UT: Learning Commons Press, 2018).
https://sites.google.com/view/liiiitesmodel/home

Loertscher, David V., and SJSU INFO 266 Students. Virtual Library Guide. https://sites.google.com/view/virtual-library-guide/home

Loertscher, David V., with Ross Todd. *We Build Achievement: Micro Documentation Measures for Teacher Librarians* (Salt Lake City, UT: Learning Commons Press, 2018).

Loertscher, David V., and Blanche Woolls. *Symposium of the Greats: Wisdom from the Past & a Glimpse into the Future of School Libraries.* (Salt Lake City, UT: Learning Commons Press, 2019).

Managing the Collection/Genrefication playlist.
https://tinyurl.com/SLCollectionPlaylist

Mardis, Marcia A., and Dianne Oberg, eds. *Social Justice and Cultural Competency: Essential Readings for School Librarians* (Santa Barbara, CA: Libraries Unlimited, 2019).

Markgren, Susanne, and Linda Miles. *How to Thrive as a Library Professional: Achieving Success and Satisfaction* (Santa Barbara, CA: Libraries Unlimited, 2019).

Mike Ribble's Nine Elements of Digital Citizenship.
https://www.digitalcitizenship.net/nine-elements.html

Miller, Shannon McClintock, and William Bas. *Leading from the Library: Help Your School Community Thrive in the Digital Age* (Portland, OR: ISTE, 2019).

Mindset for School Library Innovators (poster).
https://tinyurl.com/slmindset

Moorefield-Lang, Heather, ed. *School Library Makerspaces in Action* (Santa Barbara, CA: Libraries Unlimited, 2018).

Moreillon, Judi. *Maximizing School Librarian Leadership: Building Connections for Learning and Advocacy* (Chicago: ALA Editions, 2018).

Moreillon, Judi, ed. *Core Values in School Librarianship: Responding with Commitment and Courage* (Santa Barbara, CA: Libraries Unlimited, 2021).

National Board for Professional Teaching Practice: Library Media Standards. https://www.nbpts.org/wp-content/uploads/2021/09/ECYA-LM.pdf

National School Library of the Year Award and Rubric. https://www.ala.org/aasl/awards/nsly

National School Reform Faculty. NSRF Protocols and Activities . . . from A to Z. https://nsrfharmony.org/protocols

New York City School Library System: Robin Hood Project. https://nycdoe.libguides.com/RH

New York City School Library System: Connect, Create, Lead. https://nycdoe.libguides.com/home

New York State Education Department. NYSED School Library Program Rubric. http://www.nysed.gov/curriculum-instruction/nysed-school-library-program-rubric

News Literacy Vocabulary. http://tinyurl.com/newslitvocab

OER Portals playlist. https://tinyurl.com/OERPortals

Professional Growth & Job Search playlist. https://tinyurl.com/jobsearchprofessionalgrowth

Rendina, Diana. *Reimagining Library Spaces: Transform Your Space on Any Budget* (Portland, OR: ISTE, 2017).

Renovated Learning Blog (Diana Rendina). http://www.renovatedlearning.com/blog

Revised Bloom's Taxonomy (Iowa State). https://www.celt.iastate.edu/instructional-strategies/effective-teaching-practices/revised-blooms-taxonomy

Rhode Island's RILINK. https://guides.rilink.org/home

Riedling, Ann Marlow, and Cynthia Houston. *Reference Skills for the School Librarian: Tools and Tips,* 2d ed. (Santa Barbara, CA: Libraries Unlimited, 2019).

Rohrback, Carol, and Joyce Kasman Valenza. "Changing School Culture at Springfield Township High School: A Research Integrity Policy that Works." In Ann Lathrop, Kathleen E. Foss, and Kathleen Foss, *Guiding Students from Cheating and Plagiarism to Honesty and Integrity: Strategies for Change*, 122–134 (Santa Barbara, CA: Libraries Unlimited, 2005).

San Jose State University LIS Wiki List of Scholarly LIS Journals. https://ischoolwikis.sjsu.edu/lispublications/wiki/lis-scholarly-journals

Saponaro, Margaret Zarnosky, and G. Edward Evans. *Collection Management Basics* 7th ed. (Santa Barbara, CA: Libraries Unlimited, 2019).

School Library NJ: Home. https://schoollibrarynj.libguides.com/home

School Library HQ: Librarian Resources.
https://schoollibrarynj.libguides.com/Librarians/home

School Reform Initiative Protocols.
https://www.schoolreforminitiative.org/protocols

Stephens, Wendy. *Mindful School Libraries: Creating and Sustaining Nurturing Spaces and Programs* (Santa Barbara, CA: Libraries Unlimited, 2021).

Student Privacy and Safety playlist. https://tinyurl.com/PrivacyPlaylist

Thomas, Nancy Pickering, Sherry R. Crow, Judy A. Henning, and Jean Donham. *Information Literacy and Information Skills Instruction: New Directions for School Libraries* (Santa Barbara, CA: Libraries Unlimited, 2020).

Top Reasons to Use Subscription Databases (Joyce Valenza and Brenda Boyer). https://tinyurl.com/topdatabasereasons

Treasure Mountain Canada. TMC7 2022: Post Pandemic Library Learning Commons—From Crisis to Invention.
https://tmc.canadianschoollibraries.ca/tmc7-2022

Valenza, Joyce. 50 (or so) Ways to Ditch Your Paper or Book Report and Tell Your Story. https://tinyurl.com/50WaysPaper

Valenza, Joyce. Anchor Charts Away. Neverending Search. *School Library Journal* (10 Dec. 2014). https://blogs.slj.com/neverending search/2014/10/12/anchor-charts-away

Valenza, Joyce. Curation Situations.
https://tinyurl.com/curationtaxonomy

Valenza, Joyce. Library as Domestic Metaphor. Neverending Search. *School Library Journal.* https://blogs.slj.com/neverendingsearch /2008/08/25/library-as-domestic-metaphor

Virtual Library Guide.
https://sites.google.com/view/virtual-library-guide/home

Weisburg, Hilda K. *The Art of Communication: A Librarian's Guide for Successful Leadership, Collaboration, and Advocacy* (Santa Barbara, CA: Libraries Unlimited, 2022).

Wiegand, Wayne E. *American Public School Librarianship: A History* (Baltimore, MD: Johns Hopkins University Press, 2021).

Woolls, Blanche. "School Library Management Then to Now." *School Library Connection* (August–September 2018).

Woolls, Blanche, and Connie Hamner Williams. *Teaching Life Skills in the School Library: Career, Finance, and Civic Engagement in a Changing World* (Santa Barbara, CA: Libraries Unlimited, 2019).

Appendix A:
Mindset for School Library Innovators

Some questions for transforming teaching & learning:*

What are my "whys"?**

What if I could?

Why shouldn't I?

Characteristics of a Transformative Leader

Models & Remixes, Standards & Values

- Defends intellectual freedom and privacy
- Champions access/equity across platforms
- Promotes traditional & emerging literacies
- Empowers learners to think, create, share & grow* across media & platforms
- Translates all elements of practice for changing times

Connects

- Scans environment for trends in and outside of library and education
- Connects globally with professionals, classroom authors, experts

*AASL Mission & Guidelines (inspired by George Couros, Simon Sinek, and Carol Dweck)
**Your purpose, cause, beliefs, values

- Networks, bridges communities, builds relationships
- Listens to community needs. Sees whole child needs. Is culturally responsive
- Curates discoverable, accessible, diverse collections across formats

Risks, Learns, Shares

- Models playful approach. It's okay to sandbox, to be beta!
- Takes responsible risks; sees opportunity, not obstacles!
- Values both formal & informal learning
- Creates, shares, contributes. Practices transparently!
- Recognizes power of student participation & agency

Plans, Reflects

- Acts & thinks empathetically. What is it like for the learner, teacher, admin, parent?
- Finds & solves problems. Models inquiry & design thinking
- Plans beyond the day or week or month
- Uses evidence to inform and grow practice
- Learns from successes & missteps

Cultivates a growth mindset.

For an illustrated version of the Mindset for School Library Innovators, see https://tinyurl.com/slmindset

Appendix B:
Interview Questions
for School Librarians

The questions included here are typical and common, and some form of each is almost always asked in an interview. Using these as a guide should help prepare the interviewee to field most variations. For more interview questions, live links, and employment advice, see https://schoollibrarynj .libguides.com/Librarians/EmploymentJobBoards.

Note:

Interview season generally begins in March, but keep an eye open for unplanned leaves and unexpected openings. The interview process may have multiple levels—e.g., virtual screening, head of library services, school-based panel, sample lesson, writing sample, meeting with the superintendent— and involve multiple contacts.

Personal/Teaching Style

Tell us a little about yourself (classroom teaching and library experience, background, vision). Leverage this open-ended invitation to potentially share your three bullet points and express a bit about who you are and what you care about. Use this as an opportunity to share your voice. Don't simply list the items on your résumé. Open with a brief story if you can.

Why did you decide to become a school librarian?

What do you know about our school program/community? (In other words, did you do your homework and connect a few dots?)

How do you envision the role of the library in school culture?

If I were to visit your last school, how would the students describe you?

How would the classroom teachers with whom you worked/co-workers describe you?

Why did you become a librarian? [Or . . .] What do you love about being a librarian?

Describe a situation in which you felt challenged.

What are you currently reading? [It's a nice touch to carry a book with you.]

How do you promote equity, diversity, and inclusion in our library?

How do you support diverse learners?

How do you support social and emotional learning?

In what ways will your instruction and your collection be culturally responsive?

How will you ensure both intellectual and physical access to library resources?

Describe the type of environment you would like to create in our library. How will you ensure that all students and teachers feel welcome?

Instruction/Learning

What kind of atmosphere/learning culture would you like to create in your (our) library?

Describe your classroom management style.

What strategies do you typically use to engage learners?

Please describe a project or program that you implemented about which you feel proud.

Describe a push-in lesson and a pull-out lesson. What standards would be addressed?

What are your top three instructional priorities relating to information/ media literacy for elementary/middle/high school students?

Can you describe a program or lesson you tried that failed? How did you use the experience to grow or fail forward?

How would you partner with our [language arts/social studies/science/ first-grade/ninth-grade, etc.] program/classroom teachers?

How would you work to integrate information skills and emerging literacies into the various grade levels or content areas?

How will you ensure that all learners are supported?

How would you encourage collaboration/partnership with more reluctant classroom teachers?

What type of schedule do you prefer? How does fixed/flexible/block scheduling affect student learning in the library?

Describe the process you (would) use to select materials and resources, and in the larger sense develop a library collection.

How would you handle discipline issues in the library?

How will your library program improve student achievement?

How will you encourage a school-wide culture of inquiry? Is there an inquiry model you prefer?

Please describe one of your most successful collaborative lessons or instructional units.

Do you have (and can you share) a teaching portfolio?

How familiar are you with the CCSS, ISTE, NGSS, etc. standards or the Future Ready Schools framework?

Why is it important for school librarians to align library learning with classroom standards?

Are you familiar with any of the following—responsive classroom, OPAL, Genesis?

Do you consider yourself a Future Ready Librarian? In what ways do you address the Future Ready "gears"?

How would you support teacher learning?

What is your understanding of the school librarian's role in professional development?

Philosophy/Professionalism/Administration

What do you consider the most important role(s) of the teacher-librarian?

What are the most important aspects of your library program?

How do you ensure that you grow as a professional?

Do you have a PLN? How do you use your PLN?

What component/piece of your portfolio would you most like people/us to see?

How would you define *literacy*?

How will you foster professional learning in our school?

What would your budget priorities be for our school library?

Given the opportunity to conduct a staff development session, what would you like to present?

How would you work with our staff to ensure that information skills/transliteracy are integrated into teaching or learning programs in classrooms?

How would you handle issues relating to plagiarism/intellectual property? Challenged materials?

How much do you know about the Creative Commons movement?

How active are you in professional organizations?

Which conferences do you regularly attend?

Have you written any grants? Tell us about them.

In what ways will you lead our school? How will you lead beyond the library?

Describe an exemplary school library in detail as if there were no limitations on budget or facility.

What would someone see and hear when they walked into the library?

Technology/Maker Culture

How do you integrate technology into instruction?

What are some of your favorite subscription databases for high school/elementary/middle school students?

What are some of your favorite online programs or apps?

How would you help apprehensive staff members overcome their reluctance about integrating information and communication technology into instruction?

What examples can you give of incorporating information technologies in your lessons?

How would you rate your searching abilities?

What are your favorite search tools? Databases? Online resources?

What experience have you had with circulation or catalog systems?

What is the technology skill or application you have most recently developed or mastered?

Do you have a website? Blog? Any wikis? LibGuides? Curation efforts?

What experience have you had in curation?

What strategies do you use to keep up with rapid changes in information technology?

Have you ever led an iPad, Chromebook, or 1:1 rollout?

What experience do you have with maker culture?

How would you curate digital resources, tools, and apps for the big and small screens?

What experience do you have with flipping, remote, or hybrid instruction?

How will you build a culture of digital citizenship/leadership?

How would you integrate OER into our program?

What role do you see for social media in your program?

Literature/Reading Promotion

What was the best YA/children's book you read this year?

What is your favorite YA/children's book and how would you book-talk it to students?

Describe the process you would use to select materials and resources to develop a high school/middle school/elementary school library collection.

How would you encourage independent reading among our students?

How would you ensure that our library collection is culturally responsive, diverse, and inclusive?

Have you ever faced a book or materials challenge? How did or how would you respond to a challenge?

What review journals/blogs do you rely on to help you select materials?

How would you encourage independent reading among our students?

Do you support the use of any reading promotion initiatives or commercial reading programs with students? [e.g., Accelerated Reader, Battle of the Books, Read Across America, Teen Read Week]

What are your favorite ebook or audiobook databases or book-related websites?

How would you use our library website to promote reading?

Can you do a quick book talk for a favorite children's/YA book?

How would you help build a school-wide reading culture?

Relations with Community and Staff

How do/would you communicate with parents and how often?

What would you do if a parent challenged a book in your collection?

How might you involve the broader community in your program?

What (local) authors would you invite to visit the school library for the Literary Festival?

Which author would you most like to invite for remote visits?

How will you build teacher buy-in in the library program?

How will you transition a teaching staff in a building that has had the same librarian for many years?

How will you make decisions about what should be changed in the library or program and what should stay the same?

Which clubs or activities would you be interested in sponsoring?

If you became our librarian, what services are you excited about providing to students, staff, and administrators?

Conclusion/Feedback

Why are you interested in our school/district?

If you were responsible for selecting a teacher-librarian, what professional and personal qualities would you look for?

You have had a chance to look around a bit. What do you like about this facility? What changes do you think you would make?

What questions do you have for us?

[It's a good idea to have questions about school culture ready for your interviewers.]

How much risk taking is encouraged?

Are there any major initiatives being planned for this coming school year?

Is the budget site-based or district-funded?

If you have not yet seen it, ask if you might take a peek at the library. Please also refer to:

AASL. School Librarian Interview Question Matrix. https://standards .aasl.org/wp-content/uploads/2020/04/SL-Interview-Matrix.pdf

Appendix C:
List of Student Volunteer Activities

Note: Volunteer activities should be tailored to the ages and interests of your students. Take time to discover your student volunteers' individual preferences and abilities. Create a student advisory committee. Ideally, student contributions should support both the library and the students themselves; volunteering should be a part of their authentic learning, allowing students to share and celebrate their talents while they engage in meaningful community service.

Displays/Creativity

- Plan, post, and replace bulletin boards
- Evaluate and create signage
- Plan and create book displays
- Develop strategies to promote (new) books to be added to the library and placed throughout the school, including bathroom stalls)
- Plan and create book fair decorations and promotional materials
- Create informational bookmarks (perhaps highlighting information literacy tips, for example)
- Create "If you liked ____, try _____" displays
- Design READ-style posters to display around the school to promote their favorite books
- Design murals for glass doors or windows to be created using window markers

Library-Specific Tasks

- Open new books boxes
- Check items against purchase orders
- Process new books
- Identify books to be repaired or weeded, perhaps using a rubric
- Scan resources for inventory, looking for missing books
- Engage in competitive book displays
- Write peer book reviews
- Create book trailers or announcements of great reads
- Produce promotional video announcements for the library: e.g., library news, events, orientation information, videos about returning materials at the end of the semester or year, or videos about information literacy skills
- Weed magazines
- Create lists of recommended books
- Collaborate in planning programs and special events
- Test-drive new applications before they are used in instruction
- Write book reviews for a news show to advertise new or "lonely" books (great books with little or no circulation)
- Design genre labels
- Create topical curations or bibliography lists or pull books from a resource list for a teacher/project
- Check out and deliver books and materials to teachers
- Process new books (cover, barcode, and stamp), and then put the call number labels on once new items are cataloged
- Check books in/out
- Collaborate on creating and maintaining a library website or blog
- Create murals or library graffiti on glass doors with window markers (seasonal themes are good; local news is cool, and so are author quotes)
- Participate in a student-run library advisory panel or library club to discuss programming and improvements that students/volunteers can implement
- Create *book talkers* for placement on shelves (these could be little signs that identify books in a series)
- Make sure the online public access catalog (OPAC) is saved as a favorite on the bookmark bar for all look-up stations in the library
- Re-cover books: remove damaged jackets, run them through a laminator, and replace them on the books
- Help with book fairs or other fundraisers

- Survey fellow students for books and genres they would like to see more of in the library
- Help prepare vendor wish lists
- Distribute the textbooks from the reserve shelf
- Display new periodicals and file older issues
- Decorate for holidays and events
- Cover new hardbacks and paperbacks for circulation
- Shelve an assigned or selected section(s)
- Maintain the makerspace area and brainstorm ideas for it
- Assist students who need help with technology—printing, formatting, etc.
- Put bookends on all the shelves
- Plan and organize reading contests, challenges, games like March Madness
- Assist with genrefying the library
- Create and maintain pathfinders, websites, or LibGuides on curriculum-related topics
- Create passive readers' advisory signage
- Check the collection for books in need of repair
- Make QR codes linking to reviews or trailers to attach to book covers

Assorted Tasks

- Run errands (take mail down to the office, etc.)
- Update the whiteboard calendar with dates, class visits, and activities at end of day or in the morning
- Distribute resources to teachers
- Organize Chromebook or iPad carts
- Help with computer software updates
- Answer the phone and take messages if library staff is busy
- Cut materials for displays
- Maintain the supply box, sharpen pencils, etc.

Educational Ideas

- Support or co-teach Hour of Code/Scratch coding
- Form a social media team to suggest campaign content for promoting resources and services

- Enter contests or register as student ambassadors for institutions or favorite applications or software platforms
- Run the "tech support" area (students might assist in distributing Chromebooks, laptops, and iPads and offer training in software applications)
- Master the applications that are in heavy use in the school and co-teach use of those apps when appropriate
- Become expert in research tools and documentation styles and function as tutors

Appendix D:
Messaging: The Elevator
Speech or Signature Pitch

Template for Preparing an Elevator Speech
by Deb Kachel

An *elevator speech* is a short, highly focused way of sharing your message to persuade a specific stakeholder. The speech should be approximately one to two minutes and less than 200 to 250 words.

Steps	Think About	Articulation
Identify potential stakeholders	• Stakeholders who will care about and can influence decisions about your position/"ask" • Find out what these people are interested in/care about	Example: Technology coordinator
STEP 1 **Introduction/greeting**	• Think of a way to introduce yourself, if the stakeholder does not know you	Example: "I'm the school librarian where your son goes to school."
STEP 2 **Create a "hook"**	• Personalize the conversation • Capture attention • Focus on something that would interest the stakeholder being addressed	Example: "Librarians in our district could help roll out the 1:1 initiative by teaching teachers how to use the licensed databases our district pays for and your department manages."

(Continued)

(Continued)

Steps	Think About	Articulation
STEP 3 **State your position**	• How/why this affects students and student learning • Use compelling words • Do not use jargon • Focus on the stakeholder's concerns and students, not the needs of the librarian or the library • One declarative sentence	Example: "We [the librarian and the technology coordinator] could work together to provide curriculum-aligned e-resources for students and provide cost-effective professional development for teachers."
STEP 4 **Supporting points or proof**	• One or two sentences of research/data to support your position • Can be a supporting talking point • Makes your position credible	Examples: "A search engine finds thousands of 'hits,' but a librarian teaches how to find the right ones." OR "Our district technology survey found that 60% of the teachers feel unprepared to integrate digital resources in their instruction." OR "I learned that our science teachers are unaware of the new STEM e-resources our IT Department just licensed. That suggests that the students don't know we have them either. Those are great resources we could be using."
STEP 5 **The "ask"/ invite**	• Tell a short story about your students/teachers/library that the stakeholder would care about regarding your position • Show that you know and care about the stakeholder's concerns • Restate or include your position if needed • Invite the stakeholder to further discuss the issue • OR make a request (your "ask") • Press for a specific time or follow-up	Example: "When could we meet to discuss how we could develop some afterschool professional development for the high school teachers? Maybe we could customize it by department." OR "I'm sure if the IT Department and the librarians got together, we could figure out ways to facilitate the 1:1 initiative. Could we set up a meeting?"

Text of Your Elevator Speech:

Appendix E:
Journals to Know

This appendix lists journals that school librarians typically subscribe to, consult, or read online. Although some content is available online to non-subscribers, full content is generally available only to subscribers or members. Some journals no longer publish in print, but generally make selected online content available to nonsubscribers. Several of these journals also offer webinars, conferences, and special events.

American Libraries: https://americanlibrariesmagazine.org
> Published six times a year, *American Libraries* is the official magazine of the American Library Association (ALA). Each issue offers news, trends, features, columns, conference information, job listings, and more. American Libraries Online also offers the monthly podcast "Call Number with *American Libraries*" and "The Scoop" blog for breaking news and conference coverage.

Booklist: http://booklistonline.com
> ALA's book-review magazine has been published for more than 100 years. Widely respected as a collection development and readers' advisory tool, *Booklist* offers reliable reviews across media formats to help libraries decide what to buy and help users decide what to read. In addition to two magazines, *Booklist*'s offerings include the *Booklist Online* website (http://booklistonline.com) and database, e-newsletters, and webinars. *Booklist Online* offers free content to nonsubscribers which includes selected reviews. Subscribers can access the full *Booklist Online* database with its thousands of reviews dating back to 1992. *Booklist Blog* and *Booklist Reader* (http://booklistonline.com) are monthly digital publications which extend the magazine's and website's coverage to library users. Published online monthly, *Booklist's Quick Tips for Schools & Libraries* (https://www.booklistonline.com/quick-tips-for-schools-and-libraries) offers tips for integrating children's and young-adult books into the curriculum, thematic bibliographies, and author interviews.

The Bulletin of the Center for Children's Books:
> https://bccb.ischool.illinois.edu
> Established in 1945, *The Bulletin* is one of the leading sources of summaries and critical evaluations of children's books to help school and public librarians make choices for their collections. Published by the University of Illinois School of Information, it partners with the Center for Children's Books on that campus and provides a center for research in children's and youth resources, literature, and librarianship.

Canadian School Libraries Journal:
> https://journal.canadianschoollibraries.ca
> Published by the nonprofit Canadian School Libraries, this journal focuses on school library-related professional research and development, connecting Canadian practitioners and educators with examples of reflective, effective practice.

The Horn Book: https://www.hbook.com
> A classic publication for those who care about and study the world of children's and young adult literature, *Horn Book* presents thoughtful articles and sharp editorials along with its highly respected reviews.

Journal of Research on Libraries and Young Adults:
> https://www.yalsa.ala.org/jrlya
> This open-access, peer-reviewed online research journal, published by ALA's Young Adult Library Services Association (YALSA), is devoted to development of theory, research, and practice relating to young adult services in support of YALSA's National Research Agenda.

Knowledge Quest: https://knowledgequest.aasl.org
> Published bimonthly September through June by ALA's American Association of School Librarians, *Knowledge Quest* is one of the benefits of annual membership. The journal is devoted to school library theory, practice, and services and frequently shares articles on new developments in education. The Knowledge Quest blog offers reflections and advice from leaders, experts, and practitioner and may be browsed by topic.

Publishers Weekly: https://www.publishersweekly.com
> *PW* is a staple for many in the book business, including librarians, publishers, booksellers, and authors. Online and in print, *Publishers Weekly* offers feature articles, news of the book world, bestseller lists, and thousands of prepublication reviews each year.

School Libraries Worldwide:
> https://journals.library.ualberta.ca/slw/index.php/slw/index
> IASL's refereed research journal is now published online only on a rolling basis, offering access to school library research internationally.

School Library Connection: http://schoollibraryconnection.com
> Led by an editorial team of school library leaders and educators, *SLC* offers professional learning experiences, materials to support curricula, and a "Reviews+" section with its own search tool to support collection development.

School Library Journal: https://www.slj.com

Devoted to librarians who serve children and young adults, *SLJ* offers highly relevant features and news relating to technology, literacy, and best practices, as well as profiles of inspiring leaders and reviews of books, media, and digital content.

School Library Research: https://www.ala.org/aasl/pubs/slr

AASL's scholarly, peer-reviewed journal offers research on a wide variety of topics of interest to school librarians and school library educators, including studies on instructional theory, literacies, collaboration, school library preparation, program evaluation, advocacy, and teaching methods.

Appendix F:
Article for the *Los Angeles Times*

"How to Make Your Voice Heard in Washington"
George Miller and John Lawrence

Since the November elections, we've seen unprecedented numbers of Americans speaking out on public policy. Voters want to influence their lawmakers on high-stakes issues from health care to climate change, education to immigration, foreign affairs to trade policy. The question, for many, is how to communicate effectively, especially when Washington sometimes seems impervious to the average citizen. Between us, we've spent eighty years working in Congress and we know something about effective constituent communications. There are a handful of unwritten rules that can amplify your voice in these tempestuous times.

Every year, concerned groups and individuals flock to Washington to make their cases on Capitol Hill. That's worthwhile, but there is an easier way, and one that may give you an even better chance of meeting face to face not with a staffer but with your senator and Congress member themselves.

Check the "full calendar" listings on Web pages for the House and Senate—or use the portal at the Library of Congress website—www .congress.gov—to see when a district or state "work period" is scheduled. . . . That means your representatives will be in their home districts.

Call your representative's local office to find out when and where he or she will be holding office hours, touring schools and businesses, and holding town hall meetings.

Then call the legislator's D.C. office—the operator at (202) 224-3121 can connect you—and request a meeting in the district office. Be respectful but persistent: if your representatives can't see you during the upcoming district or state work period, when can they?

Originally published in the *Los Angeles Times*, Wednesday, February 15, 2017, p. A13. Reprinted with permission from the authors.

341

Make sure to explain that you are a constituent; politicians do not enjoy long careers if they snub their voters. Request a 10-minute meeting. Be clear about the topic and be flexible about when you can meet. If you want to advocate for or against an education matter, include a representative of a teachers group, PTA parents; if health care is your issue, bring along a doctor, a hospital administrator, or a patient advocate.

Know the status of the issue or the bill in question. Is it in committee; is it scheduled for the floor? Again, the Library of Congress website can help. Demonstrating knowledge of the legislative process will make your discussion more effective.

Argue your position clearly and simply, and be very specific about what you expect the legislator to do. Don't issue threats or be confrontational. Keep the small talk brief and the meeting short; former Rep. Morris K. Udall (D-Arizona) used to complain about meetings that go on and on because "everything has been said, but not everyone has said it." Choose your best spokesperson to make the case, take a picture, and say thank you.

If you can't be a part of a face-to-face meeting, emails, texts, tweets, and other communication can be effective. Follow the same rules as above: Be courteous, clear, and brief, and always say what action you support. Despite public skepticism, legislators do pay attention when the calls and messages roll in; and don't forget letters to the editor, again cosigned by a diverse group of constituents.

Consider a media strategy: you may be able to arrange to speak with reporters after a meeting to describe what your group requested and the response. And show up at the legislator's town halls and other public appearances: Sometimes, questions and issues need to be raised in public.

A key rule of politics is to assume nothing. You may think you know how your representative will vote, but it never hurts to weigh in to make sure. If your perspective is not heard and the other side's is, the legislator may feel pressured to cast a vote you would never have anticipated. Besides, politicians like to hear from supporters.

Follow-up is crucial as well; if you are granted a meeting, send a thank-you note immediately that reiterates your request. No matter how cordial the encounter, never presume you have persuaded anyone. The other side has cordial meetings too.

Continue to make calls and send emails as the issue is debated and the vote nears. No matter what happens, send another note: a thank you if you got the result you wanted, or a civil note of deep disappointment. Always maintain open communications and good relations; in politics, today's adversary is the crucial ally you may need on another issue.

You can extend your influence by joining or volunteering with advocacy organizations. Our suggestion: Throw your lot in with groups that have proven records of success rather than newly minted, single-issue start-ups.

You don't need to have been in politics for decades to know that you win some and you lose some. We hope this advice will help you win more often than you lose in this critical period for our country.

George Miller (D-Martinez) represented California in Congress from 1975 to 2015 and John Lawrence teaches at the University of California's Washington Center. He was chief of staff for Miller and House Minority Leader Nancy Pelosi (D-San Francisco) from 1975 through 2013.

Appendix G:
A School Librarian's
Desert Island Toolkit
(a free or low-cost
technology starter kit
for new school librarians)

In addition to using the resources listed in this appendix, we recommend that you also keep up with AASL's annual list of "Best Digital Tools for Teaching & Learning" (https://www.ala.org/aasl/awards/best)

Design, Publishing, Infographics

Adobe Express

Canva

Google Slides

PicMonkey

SlidesCarnival

Slidesmania

Online Newsletter Tools

Adobe Express

BookCreator

Canva

Smore

Remote Instruction/Screencasting

Google Classroom

Google Meet

Loom

Microsoft Teams

Screencastify

Zoom

Documentation

EasyBib

NoodleTools (or NoodleTools Express)

Notetaking/Annotation

Google Docs

Kami

Microsoft 365

Curation

Collections by Destiny

Google Slides

LibGuides

MackinVIA

Padlet

Pearltrees

SlidesCarnival

Slidesmania

Smore

Symbaloo

Thinglink

Wakelet

Places to Celebrate and Keep Track of Reading

Biblionasium

Epic!

Zoobean (Beanstack)

Places to Read Online

DK Findout

DK Learning

EPIC!

KidLitTV

Lit2Go (audio)

Read Alongs with Ryan and Craig

Storyline Online

Storytime in Space

Places to Support Reading

Immersive Reader

Microsoft Reading Coach

Microsoft Reading Progress

Interactivity, Feedback, Brainstorming, and Formative Assessment

AnswerGarden

Blooket

Classroom Screen

EdPuzzle

Gimkit

Jamboard

Kahoot!

Mentimeter

Nearpod

Padlet

Pear Deck

Poll Everywhere

Slido

Digital Storytelling

Adobe Express

Book Creator

Buncee

Canva

Game Creation

Blooket

BreakEDU

Buncee

Class Dojo

ClassTools.net

Flash Card Factory from Pear Deck

Flippity.net

Gimkit

goosechase EDU

Kahoot!

Nearpod

Quizizz

Media Creation/Podcasting

Anchor

Headliner

Loom

MySimpleShow

Powtoon

Screencastify

SoundTrap

Typestudio

WeVideo

Reflection and Student Voice

Flip (formerly Flipgrid)

Portfolio

Book Creator

Class Dojo Student Stories

PebbleGo Create

Seesaw

Spaces

Wakelet

Interactive Images/Video

GoogleSlides/Docs (used as Hyperdocs)

Padlet

Thinglink

Media Literacy/Digital Citizenship

Allsides.com

Be Internet Awesome Google and Pear Deck

Checkology

Civic Online Reasoning Curriculum

CommonSenseMedia.com

News Literacy Project

Newsela Pear Deck Daily Deck

General Online Learning

Achievery

Crash Course

Google Arts and Culture

Khan Academy

Smithsonian Learning Lab

For many more instructional portals, see the Wakelet list available at http://tinyurl.com/instructionalportals

Reproduced with permission from Shannon McClintock Miller and Joyce Valenza.

Appendix H:
Librarian Checklist
of Reminders

Joyce Valenza

https://tinyurl.com/SLMMonthlyChecklist

Awareness Months, Themes, Celebrations:

- ALA's Programming Librarian
  https://programminglibrarian.org/articles/calendar-events-celebrations
- Wikipedia's List of Month-Long Observances
  https://en.wikipedia.org/wiki/List_of_month-long_observances
- Florida State University: Equity and Inclusion: Monthly Observances and Celebrations
  https://diversity.fsu.edu/resources/monthly-observances-and-celebrations
- Shannon Miller's Choice Boards (check for blog posts)
  https://vanmeterlibraryvoice.blogspot.com
- National Day Calendar https://nationaldaycalendar.com

Authors' Birthdays:

Picture Book Planet: Writers' & Illustrators' Birthdays
https://picturebookplanet.com/writers-birthdays

Annual/Monthly:

- ❏ Attend department/grade meetings often.
- ❏ Offer to collaborate with teachers to create online units or curate lists. If you anticipate a need, create a draft solution as a gift. Do not wait to be asked.

❏ Schedule inquiry/research/digital literacy lessons throughout the year with all grades.

❏ Assess teachers' teaching and learning needs and develop professional development in the form of digital tutorials or informal meetings (e.g., Lunch & Learns) to address those needs or introduce exciting trends and tools.

❏ Collaborate with classroom teachers on a curriculum map/schedule noting major research units and projects. (Link this to established and growing lesson plans and resources.)

❏ Solicit student work from teachers for display or posting. What better way to illustrate your contribution to the learning process!

❏ Communicate library news broadly with newsletters, email, and social media. (Find out where your users live online!)

❏ Update your website frequently as you make discoveries that will keep it fresh.

❏ Check the public library schedule of events to promote with students and teachers. Facilitate the process of signing up for library cards.

❏ Contact your public library colleagues with news of mass assignments and reading lists.

❏ Send updates to your administrators and faculty relating to their personal research needs and interests. Give them what they want before they know they need it. (For instance, if your principal is interested in data-driven management, send copies of any related articles as they come in.)

❏ Create frequent, informal "what are you reading" displays and posts schoolwide.

❏ Create or share already-created booktalks and/or trailers for materials you want to promote. Engage students in the process.

❏ Get to know clubs and teams by inviting them in for read-style group posters.

❏ Planning:

    ❏ Curate LibGuides/pathfinders/websites for student projects and to address student/faculty research needs and interests

    ❏ Maintain a consideration file of teacher requests and items that would support curricular and student needs across formats

    ❏ Investigate dates for National History Day, science fair, wax museum biographies, art show, musicals, concerts, etc.

    ❏ Set dates for Book Fair, author visits, and other important library-initiated events.

    ❏ Create digital folders for photographs, videos, images, and notes to build and prepare your annual report.

    ❏ During slower times, read/weed your shelves.

August/September Reminders:

- ❏ Organize your space and sort through boxes.
- ❏ Open boxes and check new arrivals against purchase orders.
- ❏ Return copies of completed purchase orders to the central office.
- ❏ See if all equipment and furniture are in the right place. Retrieve any "borrowed" items.
- ❏ Explore your usual social media search tools (like Pinterest and Instagram) for fresh bulletin board and book display themes for back to school. Enlist student help if possible.
- ❏ Complete and submit fall book order (if appropriate).
- ❏ Schedule grade-level meetings/visits for the returning week.
  - ❏ Share schedule for student orientations with grade levels.
  - ❏ Prepare class sign-up sheets so they are ready for teachers.
  - ❏ Make plans to celebrate Dot Day or other early Fall activities.
- ❏ Enlist library partners for Global Read Aloud to take place in October.
- ❏ Meet with any new faculty members (host them during lunch, free periods, or after school). Discuss services/resources for their programs. Feature them on an interactive bulletin board. (What are they reading?) Suggest future planning meetings.
- ❏ Develop and share this year's library services menu for teachers.
  - ❏ Include updated media and database lists and any forms they will need to get started. Invite collaboration!
  - ❏ This menu could be a blog, online posting, LibGuide, etc.
  - ❏ If your newsletter begins as a print tool, remember to save a copy in document or PDF form to post on your website.
  - ❏ Update your list of professional magazines and other resources available/relevant for faculty use.
  - ❏ Share information on professional/action/academic research with faculty in graduate programs.
- ❏ Prepare or distribute all technology for use.
- ❏ Organize iPad/Chromebook lab or lending cart for opening first.
- ❏ Create signs and forms to solicit new or returning student volunteers. (Make sure your forms allow you to discover volunteers' talents and preferences.)
- ❏ For adult volunteers, advertise on any school mailings and create a digital form for responses. (Make sure your forms allow you to discover volunteers' talents and preferences.)
- ❏ Create or update forms and passes.
- ❏ Prepare, review, and update procedures for circulation, computer use, etc. Inform assistant(s) or volunteers of changes during a beginning-of-the-year meeting.

❏ Regularly update user resource lists/pathfinders/guides/curations to meet demands for digital instruction for any fall lessons.

❏ Catalog and process any new materials (assign this to an assistant if one is available).

❏ Meet with on-site and district administrative staff:

  ❏ Share annual goals with the principal and/or district administrator.

  ❏ Approach the principal (in-person or by memo or email) with initial plans for any major events—book fairs, author visits, etc. (You may have begun this at the end of the last school year.)

  ❏ Volunteer for any building/district committee that seems relevant to your mission.

❏ Solicit new members for the Advisory Committee (parents, students, faculty, administrators).

❏ Design a plan to gently retrieve summer loans and pick up any books left with the public library for summer loan.

Bulletin Board/Display Celebrations (also check themes/links listed earlier):

Hispanic Heritage Month, International Dot Day, Grandparents Day, Labor Day, Jewish New Year (Rosh Hashanah), Constitution Day/Week, National POW/MIA Recognition Day, Banned Books Week, Banned Websites Awareness Day, Study Skills, Library Card Sign-up Month, UNESCO International Literacy Day, National Literacy Month, Grandparents' Day, Google's Birthday, 9/11 Remembrance, Patriot Day, Talk Like a Pirate Day, Deaf Awareness Week, Clean Air Day, Video Games Day, Full Harvest Moon.

Themes:

teachers' or students' favorite summer reads; plan Constitution Day events with social studies teachers; discuss intellectual freedom with classes

Encourage your students to "make their marks" by signing up to participate in International Dot Day (https://www.internationaldotday.org) festivities.

October Reminders:

❏ Drop into the various department or grade-level meetings. (You may want to ask in advance.)

❏ Discover any curricular changes to be addressed with new materials, instruction, and/or technology.

❏ Invite faculty in to examine new resources and discuss upcoming units and assist with weeding the collection in their areas of expertise.

❏ Conduct initial, relevant online surveys relating to reading interests, user satisfaction, and self-efficacy, creating a baseline for comparison later in the year. You can use online polling tools.

❏ Begin preparing the winter book order if appropriate.

❏ Prepare for the Storybook Character Parade or Halloween events.

❏ Attend parent night and PTA meetings. Prepare packets for parents that include introductory brochures, database password lists, your academic integrity policy, and so on. Consider proposing author visits, grants, book fairs, one-book-one-school ideas to parents at these events. Introduce your "Birthday Book" program.

❏ Analyze results of standardized tests, and target areas of need for instruction in such areas as reading, writing, analysis, problem solving, and information processing.

❏ Submit forms to ensure permission and funding to attend state/national professional conferences.

❏ Distribute Mock Caldecott sign-up and packet to teachers.

Bulletin Board/Display Celebrations (also check themes/links listed earlier):

National Book Month, Teen Read Week, Halloween, School Library Month, Computer Learning Month, Columbus Day/Indigenous Peoples' Day, United Nations Day, National Book Month, Country Music Month, National Dental Hygiene Month, Child Health Day, Diversity Awareness Month, Dinosaur Month, Family History Month, Dictionary Day, Breast Cancer Awareness Month, National Coming Out Day, National Reading Group Month, National Character Counts Week, Internet Day, International Open Access Week, Day of the Girl, Diwali, Yom Kippur

Themes:

autumn, harvest, mysteries, bats, monsters, spiders, pumpkins, indigenous peoples

Introduce the concept of open access. Discuss Creative Commons and OER materials.

Launch or engage in a book-character costume parade.

November Reminders

❏ Prep for the Mock Caldecott:

❏ Choose 15–20 books to order.

❏ Send out Mock Caldecott sign-up and packet to teachers (should be done by November 1)!

❏ Complete and send in winter book order, including Caldecott contenders for Mock Caldecott.

❏ Celebrate Picture Book Month (even in the high school!).

❏ Host an activity for Children's Book Week.

❏ Offer to host a faculty meeting and request a few minutes to discuss and display new materials and databases.

Bulletin Board/Display Celebrations (also check themes/links above):

Picture Book Month, Thanksgiving, National Day of Mourning, Native American Heritage Month, Elections, Children's Book Week, Veteran's Day, National Young Readers Week, National Game and Puzzle Week, All Saints Day, Universal Children's Day, Black Friday, National No Bullying Week, National Novel Writing Month (NaNoWriMo), Dia de los Muertos

Themes:

elections, harvest, veterans, immigration
Planning/Lesson Ideas: Host a mock election with the social studies classes.

Invite local veterans to share experiences, perhaps in partnership with history classes.

December Reminders

- ❏ Buy small holiday gifts for volunteers.
- ❏ Consider a holiday reception, breakfast, or luncheon for volunteers.
- ❏ Consider hosting a staff holiday reception and highlight library materials.
- ❏ Distribute reminders about end-of-semester overdues.
- ❏ Prepare for holiday break by turning off all electronic equipment.

Bulletin Board/Display Celebrations (also check themes/links listed earlier):

Christmas, Chanukah, Kwanzaa, New Year's Eve, Universal Human Rights Month, Pearl Harbor Remembrance, Nobel Prize Awards, Bill of Rights, Computer Science Education Week, World AIDS Day

Themes:

winter, snowflakes, holidays, gingerbread houses, gifts
Planning/Lesson Ideas: Partner with your computer science teachers to engage learners in Hour of Code (https://hourofcode.com/us) activities during Computer Science Education Week.

January Reminders

- ❏ Update teachers about new materials.
- ❏ Invite student volunteers to decorate the library with snowflakes.
- ❏ Second-semester curriculum updates—meet with as many teachers as possible, especially new teachers, to discuss changes or refinements in curricular units.
- ❏ Update principal about progress toward meeting annual goals.
- ❏ Consider presenting at a PTA/PTO meeting on such subjects as improving student research, new digital and print resources to support the curriculum, etc.
- ❏ Host a *marking party*. Invite faculty to grade finals in the library. Offer snacks, music, and create a fun and collegial environment.
- ❏ Begin developing a budget for next year, examining categories for expenditure: supplies, databases, print materials, professional dues.

Bulletin Board/Display Celebrations (**also check themes/links listed earlier**):

ALA Youth Media Awards, New Year's Day, Football Bowls, Martin Luther King, Jr. Day, Winter Olympics, National Hobby Month, Catholic Schools Week, Inauguration, National Skating Month, Oatmeal Month, National Trivia Day, World Braille Day, International Holocaust Remembrance Day, Dia de los Reyes

Themes:

resolutions, winter, snowflakes

Planning/Lesson Ideas: Invite students/classes to view the livestream of ALA's Youth Media Awards.

Suggest that students create their own reading resolutions for the coming year.

February Reminders

❑ Analyze focused sections of your collection for upcoming purchasing.

❑ Target teachers you did not collaborate with in the first semester for unit planning.

❑ Celebrate Library Lovers Month.

❑ Order promotional materials for National Library Week.

Bulletin Board/Display Celebrations (**also check themes/links listed earlier**):

African-American History Month, National Freedom Day, Valentine's Day, American Heart Month, Super Bowl, National School Counseling Week, National Bird Feeding Month, Winter Olympics, Groundhog Day, Presidents' Day, Abraham Lincoln's Birthday, George Washington's Birthday, Job Shadow Day, National Children's Dental Health Month, Read Me Week, Ash Wednesday/Lent, Mardi Gras, National Tooth Fairy Day, Children's Authors and Illustrators Week, Digital Learning Day, World Read Aloud Day, Chinese/Lunar/Korean New Year, World Day of Social Justice

Themes:

romance, snow

March Reminders

❑ Check budget, reconcile purchase orders, and plan to spend any remaining funds.

❑ Begin to solicit teacher input for consideration in filing for next year's budget.

❑ Host a Read-Across-America activity.

❑ Check on possible district budget freezes.

Bulletin Board/Display Celebrations (also check themes/links listed earlier):

Read Across America (March 2), Read Me Week, Women's History Month, National Craft Month, National Crayon Day, March Madness (basketball), Pi Day, Freedom of Information Day, American Red Cross Month, Poison Prevention Awareness Month, Youth Art Month, Iditarod Sled Dog Race, Teen Tech Week, National Cheerleading Week, World Folktales and Fables Week, Ides of March, St. Patrick's Day, Music in Our Schools Month, Holi Festival (India), Gender Equity Month, National Developmental Disabilities Month

Themes:

spring, wind, kites, growth, metamorphosis

Planning/Lesson Ideas: Focus across inquiry projects through a women's history lens.

Launch a unit on comparative folktales across the world. Partner with a class or library in another country.

April Reminders

- Consider inventorying a section or two of your collection. Read shelves first. Plan to weed as you go along.

- Alert appropriate administrators about your weeding project. Investigate new homes for usable books and connect with custodian(s) about strategies for removing remaining books.

- Consider appropriate presents (or flowers) for your assistants and other very special administrative assistants in the school or district!

- Begin your major campaign (notices, posters, letters home, etc.) to retrieve problem overdue materials. Remind teachers to return materials they no longer need.

- Prepare your annual report.

- Set and publicize the last date for all loans and the last date for returns—Regular loans? Graduating class? Interlibrary loan? Faculty?

Bulletin Board/Display Celebrations (also check themes/links listed earlier):

Easter, Passover, Ramadan, Earth Day, April Fools Day, National Library Week, School Library Media Month, National Poetry Month, Young People's Poetry Month, Easter, National D.E.A.R. [drop everything and read] Day, Administrative Assistants Day, National Volunteer Week, Mathematics Awareness Month, National Humor Month, Teacher Appreciation Week, TV Turn-off Week, Reading Is Fun Week, National Kite Month, National Dance Week, Tax Day, El Dia de los Niños, El Dia de los Libros, Global Youth Service Day, Day of Silence, Arab American Heritage Month, Autism Acceptance Month, Eid al-Fitr (end of Ramadan)

Themes:

rain, flowers, gardening, humor

Planning/Lesson Ideas: If you are in a high school, create a display where students post their college, job, or service plans following graduation. Encourage card decoration with logos, mascots, and colors.

Develop book/genre brackets *a la* March Madness.

May/Early June Reminders

- Work with the English/Language Arts Department to finalize summer reading lists. Post the new lists on the library website and share with students and the public library.

- Schedule a yearbook signing party for after school or lunch. Invite teachers to pop in. Celebrate with snacks.

- Create an overdue list and run overdue notices.

- Communicate with the office about students who neglect to return materials and develop a plan for retrieving materials when possible.

- Distribute overdue notices to students and send friendly reminders to teachers with outstanding materials. Offer to extend loans to teachers for summer use.

- For elementary and middle schoolers, ask the local public librarian to promote the public library's summer programs.

- Inventory collection or additional portions of collection. Read shelves first; consider weeds as you inventory!

- Collect and inventory outstanding equipment—digital cameras, projectors, etc.

- Inventory supplies and equipment to assess needs for next school year.

- Check vendors' prices for regularly ordered items for next year's budget.

- Schedule summer cleaning projects with custodial staff.

- Examine consideration file and survey faculty by email for final input on materials before preparing purchase orders.

- Decide on renewals of databases, periodicals, and the like.

- Prepare purchase orders and enter orders in the P.O. database.

- Conduct end-of-year surveys relating to reading interests, user satisfaction, and skills self-efficacy. Compare with surveys conducted earlier in the year.

- Run statistical reports.

- Finalize and submit your annual report to the school administrators, other librarians, central office staff, and school board members, ensuring that it highlights achievements and addresses progress toward meeting goals and engaging learners. Personally thank appropriate administrators for their support over the past school year.

- Distribute annual report to building/central-office administrators, board members, and PTA officers.

- Invite a librarian serving the next grade levels to visit with a few "moving up" classes.

- Arrange a Zoom or face-to-face visit with an academic library of a college that many of your students plan to attend for a welcome/ orientation to college libraries and research.

- Purge the graduating class from your OPAC. "Promote" other classes in the database.

- Create "virtual camp" choice boards to keep learners engaged in literacy activities over summer break.

- Write thank-you notes to volunteers.

- Arrange for summer cleaning and repair of equipment.

- Straighten up! Shelve everything left on book trucks, take down bulletin boards and displays, remove materials from shelves/desktops for more effective summer cleaning.

- Enter new students in the OPAC (get file from feeding school if possible).

- Take your staff out to lunch or dinner!

***Bulletin Board/Display Celebrations* (also check themes/links listed earlier):**

May: Mother's Day, National Teacher's Day, May Day, Cinco de Mayo, Physical Fitness Month, Memorial Day, National PTA Teacher Appreciation Week, Older Americans Month, Get Caught Reading Month, Cartoon Art Appreciation Week, National Mental Health Awareness Month, National Pet Week, Nurse's Day, Jewish American Heritage Month, Haitian Heritage Month, Asian Pacific American Heritage Month, National Bike Month, National Oceans Month

June: LGBT Pride Month, Juneteenth, Flag Day, Father's Day, National Oceans Month

Themes:

flowers, graduation, "good-bye" messages

Planning/Lesson Ideas: Host an after-school or lunchtime yearbook signing event for graduating or "moving-up" students.

Appendix I:
Your Library Website:
It's a Destination, Not
a Brochure!

This list is designed to generate brainstorming about your own digital library space as your second front door. It represents you as a professional.

General tips:

- Start small. Your site will grow as you better understand needs and discover your own digital voice.

- Begin by getting the basics out there. Begin by linking to or embedding your catalog and databases and sharing contact information.

- Design for your users. No two libraries are exactly the same. Our community needs and interests vary. Do your research. Observe students and teachers using the existing webspace. Who are your users? What do they need? What are the most grade-relevant elements? What will engage and delight them? Try to gather analytics to determine how many visitors the site attracts, where they go, and when.

- Make sure users can get to the library site with no more than three clicks. Can they find it? If they cannot, connect with whomever works on the building or district site to get a recognizable logo or link upfront!

- Simplify navigation. Navigation must be clear and easy. Remove barriers to access whenever possible. Eliminate the need for lengthy scrolling.

- Make your site accessible. Images should have alt text(alternative text) tags to describe them for screen readers. Colors should be viewable by all users.

- Establish your brand. Be consistent across pages as you select colors and a limited number of fonts and font sizes.

- Make it pretty! Use the power of images to attract attention. Engage your community by inviting them to share images. Model the use of the new tools you promote in your design choices and your embedded resources.

- Avoid library-specific jargon. Speak to the audience you hope to engage!

- Establish brand friendships. For databases, use the buttons and banners provided by the publishers to build familiarity and leverage visual identification.

- Identify yourself. Present the librarian you want your students and community to know. Decide whether to focus on photos or Bitmojis or other avatars that become familiar.

- Be proud of your school. How might you use or include the mascot, school colors, mottoes, themes, and so on?

- Curate platforms creatively! Consider how you might use various curation platforms to take best advantage of their affordances. You might choose to create and/or embed YouTube channels, Pinterest boards, Wakelets, books using Book Creator, Bitmoji scenes using Google Slides, etc. Check out this Curation Petting Zoo hyperdoc to explore some options: https://tinyurl.com/curationsituationshyperdoc

- Invite users in and keep them coming back. Your site should engage and offer students real reasons to visit and return frequently.

- Keep it fresh! Your site is not a "one and done." New content will keep them coming back. Engage users in helping you discover dead links.

The basics! Start with these and gradually build beyond:

- Contact information for library staff: share email, phone, and text contact information at the point of need beyond the contact page

- Link to your OPAC

- Link to your subscription databases, those purchased by your state or region, and any subscriptions you initiate

- Library hours (and note that your virtual space is available 24/7 across devices)

- Information for visitors (perhaps a map of the building or an interactive map of the library)

- Policies and procedures relating to circulation, visits, etc.

- Information about the librarian and library staff. Introduce yourself and any associates as friendly humans! Use fun photographs and avatars.

- Your attractive menu of services (this should look different for students, teachers, administrators, and parents)

- Your social media presence (if you have one)

Supporting search and discovery (students, teachers, parents, administrators):

Note: You will also want to embed some of this content in teachers' learning management systems or websites.

- Search strategies, tips sheets, tutorials
- Your OPAC (or you might embed your website on your OPAC homepage. You get to decide which platform is the *parking lot* and which other platforms are the *cars.*)
- Links to the research sources available at your local public library
- Curated lists or galleries of age-relevant newsrooms presenting print and broadcast/media news from local, national and global sources. Not all news is Western!
- Databases to support research, which you will try to present with as few barriers as possible. Embedded search boxes are ideal. Databases should be organized strategically to meet learners' needs. Use logos provided by the database publishers as buttons to support recognition and add visual interest.
  - Magazines, news sources, journals
  - Ebooks, audiobooks, reference (for research and enjoyment)
  - Reader advisory tools
- Age-relevant free reference sources and portals containing encyclopedias, dictionaries, almanacs, thesauruses, biographical tools, etc.
- Google Programmable Search boxes (https://developers.google.com/custom-search) (customized searches that eliminate noise and point to focused, quality content; for instance, primary source portals, zoo and aquarium sites, etc.)
- Curated lists of primary source portals organized by categories or course or class needs
- Interactive form for support or reference
- If you have a large collection and adequate funding, consider a "discovery search" that allows users to quickly search across all digital assets.
- IMPORTANT: Develop a strategy to ensure that students and faculty have access to any necessary passwords. An updatable, private Google Doc may be a solution. Ask state purchasing representatives about the availability of geolocation access.

Supporting professional learning and growth (teachers, librarians administrators):

- Video tutorials and tip sheets on information literacy skills and processes
- Video tutorials and tip sheets on frequently used digital tools
- Materials to support the research of teachers and administrators; links to professional journals, magazines, and databases

- Free ERIC search box (https://eric.ed.gov) and links or search boxes for other education databases
- Resources to support action research
- Links to sites regularly offering professional development, webinars, certifications, etc.
- Links to instructional portals
- Curated list/gallery of portals presenting OER materials for teachers to search
- Curated list/gallery of instructional portals
- Curated list/gallery of portals featuring conversation protocols and instructional strategies (for instance, gamification templates)
- Curated archive/gallery of previous, hands-on professional development sessions
- Links to standards and frameworks (subject area, ISTE, Future Ready, AASL)

Celebrating a learner-driven culture (students, teachers, parents, administrators):

- Galleries of student work
- Celebrations of student events
- Archived events (for instance, visits with authors and experts)
- Historical archive of the school community
- Galleries of library and school events
- Galleries of student art and projects, perhaps for use as exemplars
- Curated opportunities for students to engage in informal learning opportunities and microcredentials
- Resources to promote design thinking and inspire making

Supporting ethical use and remix of intellectual property and digital citizenship (students, teachers, parents, administrators):

- Documentation style guides and citation generators
- Scaffolds and tools to support activities such as note-taking, essay writing, debate, current events sharing
- Curated galleries of Creative Commons and OER search tools and portals
- Advice on attributing credit across media formats and intellectual property licenses
- Expectations for a culture of academic honesty/integrity and the school or district's academic honesty policy
- Curated materials related to digital citizenship

Supporting collaborative instruction (teachers, administrators):

- Collaborative lessons with their linked resources, scaffolds, assessment descriptions, rubrics, etc., organized by grade level and content areas
- Individual project pages to support those big inquiry units that come around regularly. You'll be refining these go-to resources with your classroom teacher partners.
- Playlists, hyperdocs, choice boards relating to classroom learning and assessments and personal interests
- Curated video playlists (e.g., created or selected YouTube channels) to support learning
- Relevant virtual field trips and AI experiences
- Embedded calendar/schedule open for sign-ups and appointments for planning
- Digital forms to request instructional collaboration
- Digital forms for suggesting new materials
- Current and archived newsletters and handouts shared with faculty

Building a reading culture and literacies (students, teachers, administrators, parents):

- Reading lists or highlighted titles to support curriculum and student interests
- Links to award-winning books and media. Connect lists to reviews sites such as Goodreads, when appropriate.
- Regularly updated lists or galleries of new titles (your OPAC may help with this!)
- Digital booktalks, read-alouds, and trailers (make some and embed others)
- News and archived evidence of literacy events and celebrations
- Book and media reviews and book discovery/readers advisory sites (e.g., YALSA's Teen Book Finder, https://www.ala.org/yalsa/products/teenbookfinder)
- Student reviews

Supporting workflow and creativity (students, teachers, administrators, parents):

- Digital makerspace challenges
- Curated lists of frequently used applications organized by categories or tasks
- Scaffolds for note-taking, outlining, current events, thesis generators, debate and comparison organizers, etc.

- Links to best digital tools lists and app review sites (AASL Best Digital Tools, Common Sense Media, etc.)

Encouraging community engagement, interaction, and feedback (students, teachers, administrators, parents):

- Strong statement which ensures that parents know who you are and that you are there to support their children
- Wish list for parent gifts (Amazon lists are handy!)
- Birthday book program information
- Invitation to get involved
- Volunteer information and descriptions about how parents can help (with clearances information)
- Checkout procedures and loan periods
- Video tutorials and tip sheets on information literacy skills and processes
- Video tutorials and tip sheets on frequently used digital tools
- Links to your own and other relevant and useful school social media feeds (e.g., blogs, Instagram, podcasts, Pinterest boards, Wakelet curations)
- Club resources (e.g., book club or Reading Olympics)
- Materials to support school-wide initiatives such as Science Fair or History Day
- Materials to help parents support learning at home (e.g., Google Classroom and heavily used apps tutorials)
- Translation tools for families whose first language is not English
- Archive of community history and oral history (using images and video)
- Acknowledgements of community support (for book fair, gifts, signage, etc.)
- Links to resources to help parents guide students in digital citizenship

Supporting and documenting your professional efforts (librarian, administrators):

- AASL Position Statements and Toolkits
- Your materials selection policy (make sure it is discoverable)
- Links to portals for discovering booktalking and book trailer ideas and your own archive of these creations
- Links to curations of display, bulletin boards, promotional materials, and social media inspiration
- Archive of the library's annual, quarterly, and/or monthly reports and newsletters

- Links to standards and frameworks (e.g., AASL, ISTE, Future Ready Librarians)
- Your mission, vision, and goal statements
- Your strategic plan, aligned with school and district goals
- Archive of your booktalks and trailers
- Your library manual
- Links to vendor catalogs, book and app reviews to support selection and purchasing
- Professional blogs and podcasts
- Professional journals, magazines, blogs, webinars to support your own research and professional development
- Feeds connecting to your blog and social media content

   Joyce Valenza

Index

Note: Page numbers in *italics* indicate figures.

About the Authors

BLANCHE WOOLLS is a former school librarian, school district supervisor, professor, and LIS director who has served as president of AASL.

JOYCE KASMAN VALENZA is associate teaching professor of library and information science at Rutgers University. She has been a school, public, reference, and special librarian. For 10 years, Valenza was the techlife@ school columnist for the *Philadelphia Inquirer*. She wrote the *NeverEndingSearch* blog for *School Library Journal*, contributes to a variety of edtech journals, and speaks internationally about issues relating to libraries and thoughtful use of technology. Valenza is active in ISTE, ALISE, AASL, ALA, and online communities of practice.

APRIL M. DAWKINS was a practicing high school librarian for 15 years in four different North Carolina school systems before completing her dissertation on the factors that influence selection decisions by school librarians. She has studied and written about intellectual freedom, the role of school librarians in academic achievement, and diversity in young adult literature. She teaches in the areas of school libraries, intellectual freedom, information literacy, and children's and young adult literature at the University of North Carolina at Greensboro.